FORMAL LOGIC

FORMAL LOGIC

BY

A. N. PRIOR

SECOND EDITION

OXFORD
AT THE CLARENDON PRESS

Oxford University Press, Ely House, London W. 1

GLASGOW NEW YORK TORONTO MELBOURNE WELLINGTON
CAPE TOWN IBADAN NAIROBI DAR ES SALAAM LUSAKA ADDIS ABABA
DELHI BOMBAY CALCUTTA MADRAS KARACHI LAHORE DACCA
KUALA LUMPUR SINGAPORE HONG KONG TOKYO

ISBN 0 19 824156 9

First published 1955
Second edition 1962
Reprinted with corrections
1963, 1973

Printed in Great Britain
at the University Press, Oxford
by Vivian Ridler
Printer to the University

PREFACE TO THE FIRST EDITION

This book is designed primarily as a textbook; though like most writers of textbooks I hope it will prove to be of interest to others beside Logic students. Part I covers what I would regard as the 'fundamentals' of the subject—the propositional calculus and the theory of quantification. Part II deals with the traditional formal logic, and with developments which have taken that as their starting-point. I do not regard this as covering different ground from that covered in Part I under quantification theory, but rather as covering the same ground in a different way. Both ways seem to me to have their merits, and to throw light on one another and the subject. I would say the same of the logic of classes and relations in extension, discussed in Part III, Ch. III; but the other chapters of this last Part deal with what I take to be genuine extensions of the subject-matter opened up in Part I, in two different directions—modal logic, and 'non-classical' systems of propositional calculus. Negatively, I have attempted to keep within the range indicated by my title: I have touched hardly at all upon 'scientific method', and have indulged in a minimum of metaphysical reflection (avoiding, for example, such topics as the relations between 'propositions' and sentences).

In the greater part of the book the symbolic notation used is that of Łukasiewicz, with minor modifications. This seems to me unquestionably the best logical symbolism for most purposes, and I should like to have helped to show that it is. In Part III, Ch. III, however, I have used the notation of *Principia Mathematica* (referred to throughout this work as PM); in the particular field there covered, there is no other as fully developed or as deservedly well known. It does students no harm to learn to use two different notations, and to employ the one that is best for whatever they may have in hand at the time.

Other innovations beside the symbolism are these: (i) throughout the book, a fairly frequent setting out of formal proofs (something to which the Polish notation particularly lends itself); (ii), in Part I, the devotion of particular attention to completeness proofs, and to forms of the propositional calculus not yet widely studied, especially to varieties of it which use the 'standard false proposition' o, and variable operators as well as propositional variables; (iii), in Part II, considerable use of scholastic material and of material from the writings of de Morgan. I have included these items from a sense of their importance rather than of their novelty, and have placed them where their appearance seems to me most rational and economical; but if any teacher wishes to use this book for a more orthodox type of logic course, there are various ways in which he may do so. If, for example, he wishes to introduce the traditional logic at an early stage, he could pass to Part II immediately from Part I, Ch. I, Ch. II, § 1, and Ch. IV, §§ 1 and 2. (This procedure would have in any case the advantage of giving the student an interval of rest from pure symbolism before passing to the more interesting but more difficult aspects of the propositional calculus.) If he wishes to give the more usual sort of 'modern' course, he could pass immediately on from the same portions of Part I to Part III, Ch. I, § 2 and Ch. III.

There are innumerable people to whom I should like to express my thanks for help of one kind and another. It is inevitable that many should be left out, but I should like to mention in particular the following: my wife, and my students, out of discussions with whom many things in this book have arisen; some of my colleagues in New Zealand and Australia, who have given the same kind of help, and some of whom have read through a great deal of an earlier draft (especially Mr. J. L. Mackie of Sydney, who read the whole, and made a number of valuable suggestions); Misses Hanna and Roche, who coped with the none-too-easy task of typing my manuscript; and above all Mr. Jonathan Bennett, who read the proofs and suggested, among much else, the Appendixes.

I dedicate this book, with gratitude and affection, to the memory of Ivan Sutherland, Professor in this College from 1937 to 1952.

A. N. P.

CANTERBURY COLLEGE
CHRISTCHURCH
May 1953

PREFACE TO THE SECOND EDITION

APART from one or two very small corrections, I have in this edition left the body of the work just as it was, but have completely revised the two original appendixes and placed a wholly new appendix (the present Appendix II) between them. These alterations and additions will, I hope, make the appendixes much more valuable both for general reference and for pedagogical use. In the latter connexion I would particularly recommend that what I have said in the body of the book on quantification theory—which has met with some just criticisms—be read in conjunction with § 4 of Appendix I. There is also abundant material for exercises in simply verifying some of the relations asserted to hold between postulate-sets in this Appendix, using to this end the techniques sketched in the one that follows it. For some, however, 'cribs' may be located by Appendix III.

In the revision of Appendix I, the postulate sets have been rearranged, some rather peripheral material deleted, and much also added. Of the added sets, a remarkable number represent discoveries made since the first edition was written, and some of them (2.13; 2.14(*d*)–(*h*); 2.2; 8.5 and 6; the axiom of 9.22; 10.23; 11.24, 711 and 73; 12.7 and 71) have not been published before. Both for this new material and for information about earlier postulate-sets, I am especially indebted to Dr. C. Lejewski, Mr. E. J. Lemmon, Mr. C. A. Meredith, and Father Ivo Thomas, O.P. In the new Appendix II, I am indebted to Father Thomas, Dr. B. Sobociński, and Dr. J. A. Faris for details incorporated in §§ 1, 2, and 3 respectively. And in the whole revision I am much indebted to the services of Miss P. Horne in typing this mass of difficult material; also to Mr. E. E. Dawson for correcting the proofs.

A. N. P.

MANCHESTER UNIVERSITY
April 1960

CONTENTS

PART I

THE CLASSICAL PROPOSITIONAL AND FUNCTIONAL CALCULI

PART II

THE TRADITIONAL LOGIC OF TERMS

PART III

MODAL, THREE-VALUED, AND EXTENSIONAL SYSTEMS

PART I
THE CLASSICAL PROPOSITIONAL AND FUNCTIONAL CALCULI

I

Truth-functions and Tautologies

§ 1. *The Subject-matter of Logic*

THE best way to discover what logic is about is simply by doing logic. I shall therefore dispense with a full introductory discussion of the nature of the subject, but will say just enough about it now to lead us rapidly to the particular topic within the subject with which our 'doing logic' will begin.

Logic is commonly thought of as having something to do with argument, in fact as being the systematic discrimination of good arguments from bad; and, as a first approximation, this will do. It should be noted, however, that the 'goodness' of an argument from a logical point of view ('validity' is the technical term) does not lie in its conclusion's being true. An argument may have a true conclusion, and true premisses too, and be a poor argument for all that. Conversely, a false conclusion may be drawn by flawless logic from a false premiss. Indeed, it is often by observing the falsehood of consequences fairly drawn that we come to see the falsehood of the proposition from which we draw them. There is, nevertheless, a certain connexion between logical validity and truth; for an argument can only be counted valid if no argument of the same form will ever lead us from true premisses to a false conclusion.

The term 'form', as it occurs in the last sentence, is not easy to define, but it is easy enough to illustrate. Consider, for example, the argument

Every equilateral triangle is equiangular,
∴ Every equiangular triangle is equilateral.

Here both premiss and conclusion happen to be true, but the premiss all the same does not really establish the conclusion. For if it did, we could equally well argue as follows:

Every horned animal is four-footed,
∴ Every four-footed animal is horned.

These two arguments, though different in their subject-matter, are of the same form; in both we proceed from a proposition of the form 'Every *XY* is *Z*' to the corresponding proposition of the form 'Every *ZY* is *X*'; the second example shows that, even if we can sometimes get away with it, this procedure is not a safe one. On the other hand, we will never be led astray by proceeding from a proposition of the form 'No *XY* is *Z*' to the corresponding proposition of the form 'No *ZY* is *X*', though we may of course have been already astray in affirming our 'No *XY* is *Z*' to begin with. In other words, 'No *XY* is *Z*, ∴ No *ZY* is *X*' is a 'valid inferential form'.

The simplest way of exhibiting the 'form' of a proposition or inference is that exemplified above—the replacement of those elements which do not contribute to this 'form' by simple letters. We owe this device to Aristotle, the first systematic writer on our subject. Aristotle's main interest was in inferences involving propositions of the forms 'Every *X* is a *Y*', 'No *X* is a *Y*', 'Some *X* is a *Y*' and 'Some *X* is not a *Y*', and especially in inferences of the sort he called syllogisms, such as

Every animal is a living thing,
And every man is an animal,
Therefore every man is a living thing.

The 'form' of this argument is plainly 'Every *Y* is a *Z*, and every *X* is a *Y*, therefore every *X* is a *Z*'. This abstract scheme contains all the features of the argument on which its force depends; that it happens to be about men, animals, and living things is irrelevant to the question of its logical worth.

The letters in Aristotle's abstract schemata stand for those parts of propositions which he called 'terms'. The forms of inference in which he was chiefly interested depended for their force upon the functioning of sets of words like 'Every . . . is a . . .', by means of which propositions were constructed out of 'terms' like 'man' and 'animal'; *what* terms were thus built into the propositions concerned was not of logical importance. There are other forms of inference which depend for their force, not upon the functioning of sets of words by which we construct propositions out of terms, but upon the functioning of sets of words, like 'Either . . . or . . .' and 'It is not the case that . . .', by which we construct propositions out of other entire propositions. For example, this:

> Either every man is a living thing or there are animals that are not living things,
> But it is not the case that there are animals that are not living things,
> Therefore every man is a living thing.

The 'form' of this inference is plainly 'Either *P* or *Q*, but not *Q*, therefore *P*', where '*P*' and '*Q*' take the place, not of terms merely, but of entire propositions; for the force of the given argument will remain unaltered not only when the propositions 'Every man is a living thing' and 'There are animals that are not living things' are replaced by propositions with other terms but even when they are replaced by propositions with a totally different internal structure. Aristotle had very little to say about inferences of this sort; his pupil Theophrastus had more; but they were systematically studied by the Stoics about a century after Aristotle's time; again by some of the logicians of the later Middle Ages; and then again, and much more thoroughly, by the logicians of the present century and a little before it. In most contemporary logical treatises, and in some medieval ones, this 'logic of propositions' (sometimes called the 'propositional calculus', sometimes the 'theory of deduction'; in the Middle Ages, the theory of *consequentiae* or implications) is treated as basic, and the rest of logic built upon it. This procedure will be adopted here.

The classical twentieth-century treatment of the propositional calculus is that in A. N. Whitehead and B. A. W. Russell's *Principia Mathematica*, vol. i (1910), Part I, Section A. To this work we shall have frequent occasion to refer,[1] and also to the later *Principles of Mathematical Logic* of D. Hilbert and W. Ackermann (1928; 1st English edition, 1950); though the symbolism which we shall for the most part be employing will

[1] Henceforward the initials PM will be used for the title of this book.

not be that of either of these works, but a more recent and convenient notation due to the Polish logician J. Łukasiewicz. Frequent reference will also be made, and that not only in the present Part but also later, to the nineteenth-century American logician Charles Sanders Peirce, whose writings are relatively unsystematic and often extremely difficult, but who perhaps had a keener eye for essentials than any other logician before or since.

§ 2. *Truth-functions*

A word or set of words by means of which we construct one proposition out of another proposition or propositions may be called a 'propositional operator'. For example, 'I believe that . . .' and 'It is not the case that . . .' are propositional operators. But between these two examples there is an important difference. The truth or falsehood of a proposition of the form 'I believe that *p*' does not depend solely on the truth or falsehood of the proposition '*p*' out of which it is constructed. Given that '*p*' is true, 'I believe that *p*' might also be true or might not, and similarly when '*p*' is false. But given the 'truth-value' (i.e. truth or falsehood) of '*p*', the truth-value of 'It is not the case that *p*' immediately follows. If '*p*' is a true proposition (say '2+2 = 4'), 'It is not the case that *p*' will be a false one, and if '*p*' is a false proposition, 'It is not the case that *p*' will be a true one. We may express this peculiarity of the propositional operator 'It is not the case that . . .' by calling it a 'truth-operator' or 'truth-functor', and by calling the propositions formed by it 'truth-functions' of the propositions to which it is attached. Thus 'It is not the case that grass is green' is a truth-function of 'Grass is green.' 'Grass is green' may in turn be called the 'argument' of this truth-function, or of the operator by means of which the truth-function is formed from it. There are, as we shall see, many other truth-functions beside those formed by means of the operator 'It is not the case that . . .'; and this particular one is called the 'negation' of the proposition occurring as its argument. ('It is not the case that grass is green' is the negation of 'Grass is green.')

In studying truth-functions, it is convenient to use certain symbolic abbreviations for the operators by which they are formed. We might, for example, represent the negation of a proposition by putting a bar over it. Thus 'It is not the case that *p*' might be abbreviated to '$\bar{p}$', as in Hilbert and Ackermann. In the symbolism of Russell and Whitehead's PM, adapted from that of the Italian mathematician Peano, 'It is not the case that ...' is symbolized by the *tilde* or 'curl', '∼'. Thus 'It is not the case that *p*' is abbreviated in this symbolism to '∼*p*'. In the symbolism of Łukasiewicz, the curl is replaced by the capital letter *N*, 'It is not the case that *p*' being written '*Np*'. Where we are dealing, not with specific propositions such as 'Grass is green' but with symbols like '*p*' which may stand indifferently for any proposition at all, the negation-sign may be read simply as 'Not', e.g. '*Np*' as 'Not *p*'. In some cases it would be possible to express the negation of a concrete proposition in this way too, e.g. the negation of 'Every animal is a living thing' is 'Not every animal is a living thing', but in many other cases this would not be idiomatic (the negation of 'Grass is green', for example, would be expressed as 'Grass is not green' rather than as 'Not grass is green'), and the more long-winded 'It is not the case that ...' is the only device which covers all cases in ordinary speech. If we use the symbol '1' to stand indifferently for any true proposition, and '0' for any false one, the special features of negation may be summed up by the following equations

$$N1 = 0$$

$$N0 = 1$$

(the negation of a true proposition is a false one, and of a false one, a true), or by the following table or 'matrix':

N	
1	0
0	1

'It is not the case that ...' is a truth-operator which takes a single argument; there are others which take more. For example, the compound 'Grass is green and the sky is blue' is a truth-function, formed by means of the operator 'and', of the two arguments 'Grass is green' and 'The sky is blue'. For, given the truth-value of the parts, the truth-value of the whole is immediately fixed. If 'Grass is green' and 'The sky is blue' are both true, then the compound 'Grass is green and the sky is blue' will be true also, but if either or both of the component propositions be false, then the compound will be false. Medieval logicians described compounds of the form '*p* and *q*' as 'copulative' propositions; they are now generally called 'conjunctive' propositions or 'conjunctions'.

In some modern symbolisms, notably that of Hilbert and Ackermann, the abbreviation used for 'and' is the ordinary ampersand, '&'; in PM it is a dot, placed like a full stop. Thus '*p* and *q*' is represented by Hilbert and Ackermann as '*p* & *q*' and by Russell and Whitehead as '*p* . *q*'. In some writers simple juxtaposition is used ('*pq*' for '*p* and *q*'). Łukasiewicz has the letter '*K*', placed not between but before the two arguments ('*Kpq*'). This placing of the operator obviates the necessity of using brackets (or, as in PM, further dots) in complicated cases. 'Not (*p* and *q*)', for example, must be distinguished in some way from '(Not *p*) and *q*', and where the symbol for 'and' is placed between the arguments, this can only be done by some form of bracketing; but in Łukasiewicz's symbolism the first compound is represented unambiguously by '*NKpq*' and the second by '*KNpq*'. We might read off '*NKpq*' as 'Not both *p* and *q*' and '*KNpq*' as 'Both not *p* and *q*', though this use of 'Both' before pairs of whole sentences would generally be not quite idiomatic. The main advantage of this elimination of brackets is that no special rules about bracketing and rebracketing need to be included among the rules for proving one formula from another. We shall frequently use them with this notation, all the same, as aids to the eye (though not in proofs unless the eye's need of assistance is considerable).

Using '1' and '0' as before, the equations for '*K*' are plainly $K11 = 1$, $K10 = 0$, $K01 = 0$ and $K00 = 0$, and its 'matrix' is

K	1	0
1	1	0
0	0	0

where the figures down the side represent the possible truth-values of the first component and the figures along the top those of the second, the truth-values of the four possible combinations being given in the body of the table. It will be observed that these tables are the same as those for multiplication, when '1' and '0' are given their ordinary arithmetical meaning

($1 \times 1 = 1$, $1 \times 0 = 0$, $0 \times 1 = 0$, $0 \times 0 = 0$), and the conjunction of two propositions is often called their 'logical product'. We may also have a conjunction or logical product of more than two propositions, the analogy with arithmetical multiplication still holding. ('*p* and *q* and *r* and *s* . . .' is true if all its components are true, and false otherwise, just as '$x \times y \times z \times w$ . . .' has the value 1 if all its factors have that value, and the value 0 if any factor is 0.) In the symbolism of Hilbert and Ackermann, '*p* and *q* and *r* and *s* . . .' is abbreviated to '*p* & *q* & *r* & *s* . . .', and in that of PM to '*p*.*q*.*r*.*s* . . .'. Łukasiewicz's method of avoiding the use of brackets makes it necessary for each operator to have a fixed number of arguments, and as for '*K*' this is two, we cannot have such forms as '*Kpqrs* . . .'. '*p* and *q* and *r*' must therefore be changed to 'Both both-*p*-and-*q* and *r*', and written '*KKpqr*' (where the second '*K*' forms the proposition '*Kpq*' out of '*p*' and '*q*', and the first '*K*' combines this '*Kpq*' with '*r*'); '*p* and *q* and *r* and *s*' similarly becomes '*KKKpqrs*', and so on.

We may also form a truth-function of two arguments by means of the word 'or', or the set of words 'Either . . . or . . .'. A proposition of the form 'Either *p* or *q*', e.g. 'Either every man is a living thing or there are animals which are not living things', is plainly false if both '*p*' and '*q*' are false propositions, for it would then be false that we have only the two alternatives mentioned. It is equally plainly true if '*p*' is a true proposition and '*q*' a false one, or vice versa. But in ordinary speech there is often some doubt as to whether the truth of both alternatives is or is not meant to be excluded. Łukasiewicz uses '*Apq*' for 'Either *p* or *q*' in the 'non-exclusive' sense (i.e. the sense in which the truth of both '*p*' and '*q*' would verify it), and '*Jpq*' for the 'exclusive' sense (i.e. the sense in which the truth of both would falsify it). The equations for these two functors are plainly

$A11 = 1$		$J11 = 0$
$A10 = 1$	and	$J10 = 1$
$A01 = 1$		$J01 = 1$
$A00 = 0$		$J00 = 0$

and their matrices

A	1	0
1	1	1
0	1	0

and

J	1	0
1	0	1
0	1	0

We shall have very little occasion to use the functor '*J*', and the words 'Either . . . or . . .' will be understood hereafter (unless the contrary is explicitly stated) as having the meaning of '*A*', i.e. as meaning not 'Either but not both', but 'Either or both.' '*p* or *q*' in this sense is represented in the Peano–Russellian symbolism as '$p \vee q$' (there is no Peano–Russellian symbol corresponding to Łukasiewicz's '*J*'). Hilbert and Ackermann use the simple '*pq*'. Russell and Whitehead call '*p* or *q*' the 'disjunction' of '*p*' and '*q*', but in many writers this term is used only for '*p* or *q*' in the exclusive sense (*Jpq*), and some, e.g. Johnson, use it for mutual exclusion pure and simple, i.e. for the truth-function which excludes the joint truth of its arguments but excludes nothing else. Łukasiewicz uses '*Dpq*' for this: we might read it as 'Not-both *p* and *q*'. Its equations are $D11 = 0$, $D10 = 1$, $D01 = 1$, $D00 = 1$, and its matrix

D	1	0
1	0	1
0	1	1

Writers who use 'disjunction' in this way generally call the non-exclusive 'Either *p* or *q*', the 'alternative' function or 'alternation' of its arguments (hence Łukasiewicz's letter '*A*'). The alternation of two propositions is also often called their logical sum, the table for the functor '*A*' being like that for addition, apart from its first item. (We have not $1+1 = 1$, but we have $1+0 = 1$, $0+1 = 1$, and $0+0 = 0$, corresponding to $A10 = 1$, $A01 = 1$ and $A00 = 0$.)

From a logical point of view, however, the most important truth-function is not any of those yet considered, but the one constructed out of a pair of arguments by means of the operator 'If . . . then . . .'. In PM this operator is written as a 'hook' between the two arguments, 'If *p* then *q*' appearing in that work as '$p \supset q$', often read as '*p* implies *q*'. Hilbert and Ackermann use '$p \rightarrow q$' in the same way. In the notation of Łukasiewicz, 'If *p* then *q*' is '*Cpq*'. This function is called the 'implication' by *p* of *q*, also a 'hypothetical' or 'conditional' proposition, and the implying proposition is called the 'antecedent' or 'protasis', and the implied proposition the 'consequent' or 'apodosis'. In ordinary speech the use of 'If' is often not truth-functional at all (it is a propositional operator of quite a different sort, like 'I believe that . . .'), but we may construct the matrix for '*C*' by considering one of the everyday cases in which the use of 'If' *is* truth-functional. A man might say, for instance, 'If I did not plant peas in that row, I planted beans there.' Suppose it turned out that he had in fact not planted peas there, but had planted beans—i.e. suppose the arguments 'I did not plant peas there' and 'I planted beans there' to be both true. We would in this case say that the man has spoken truly; that is, $C11 = 1$. Suppose it turned out that he had not planted peas there and had not planted beans there either; i.e. suppose the antecedent 'I did not plant peas there' to be true and 'I did plant beans' false. We would then say that his 'If I did not plant peas I planted beans' was false; that is, $C10 = 0$. Suppose that he had planted peas there, and beans as well, i.e. suppose the argument 'I did not plant peas' to be false and 'I planted beans' true. We would then say that his conditional was true; i.e. $C01 = 1$. Finally, suppose that he had planted peas there, but not beans, i.e. suppose 'I did not plant peas' and 'I planted beans' both false. We would in this case again allow that the man had made no mistake; i.e. $C00 = 1$. Summing up, we have for 'If' in the truth functional sense the equations $C11 = 1$, $C10 = 0$, $C01 = 1$, and $C00 = 1$, and the matrix

C	1	0
1	1	0
0	1	1

The only case in which the truth-functional 'If *p* then *q*' is false is that in which *p* is true but *q* is not.

§ 3. *Evaluation of Truth-functional Forms, and the Inter-definability of Truth-functions*

The equations for the truth-functions so far considered are worth tabulating together for future use. They are

$N1 = 0$	$K11 = 1$	$A11 = 1$	$J11 = 0$	$D11 = 0$	$C11 = 1$
$N0 = 1$	$K10 = 0$	$A10 = 1$	$J10 = 1$	$D10 = 1$	$C10 = 0$
	$K01 = 0$	$A01 = 1$	$J01 = 1$	$D01 = 1$	$C01 = 1$
	$K00 = 0$	$A00 = 0$	$J00 = 0$	$D00 = 1$	$C00 = 1$.

By means of these tables it is easy to calculate the truth-values, for the different possible cases, of truth-functions of a more complicated order. Consider, for example, the complex propositional form 'Both if p then q and if q then p', $KCpqCqp$. The possible truth-values of this may be calculated as follows:

$$\text{For } p = 1, q = 1, KCpqCqp = KC11C11 = K11 = 1$$
$$\text{For } p = 1, q = 0, KCpqCqp = KC10C01 = K01 = 0$$
$$\text{For } p = 0, q = 1, KCpqCqp = KC01C10 = K10 = 0$$
$$\text{For } p = 0, q = 0, KCpqCqp = KC00C00 = K11 = 1.$$

The steps in these calculations should be sufficiently obvious; in the second line, for instance, we pass from $KC10C01$ to $K01$ by using the facts, given in the table for C, that $C10 = 0$ and $C01 = 1$, and then from $K01$ to 0 by using the equation $K01 = 0$ in the table for K. The net result is that a compound of the form 'If p then q and if q then p', or more briefly 'If and only if p then q', is true if both its components are true or if they are both false, and false otherwise. Hence if we were told that the form 'Epq' may be used as an abbreviation for '$KCpqCqp$', we could learn from the above calculation that the equations for the operator 'E' (read 'If and only if . . . then . . .') are $E11 = 1$, $E10 = 0$, $E01 = 0$, and $E00 = 1$, and its matrix is

E	1	0
1	1	0
0	0	1

In PM, the corresponding operator is '$\equiv$', '$p \equiv q$' being read as 'p if and only if q' or 'p is equivalent to q' ('equivalent' in the sense of having the same truth-value). Hilbert and Ackermann use '$p \sim q$' similarly.

This manner of introducing new operators by relating them to others already given is what is understood in the systematic and quasi-mathematical presentation of logic by 'definition'. Another operator which we might introduce in this way is 'X', read 'Neither . . . nor . . .' and defined by the statement that 'Xpq' is to be used as an abbreviation for '$NApq$' (we might in this case say more briefly that 'X' is to be used as an abbreviation for 'NA'). Its equations and matrix may be derived by the following calculation:

$$\text{For } p = 1, q = 1, NApq = NA11 = N1 = 0$$
$$\text{For } p = 1, q = 0, NApq = NA10 = N1 = 0$$

For $p = 0, q = 1$, $NApq = NA01 = N1 = 0$
For $p = 0, q = 0$, $NApq = NA00 = N0 = 1$.

That is, 'Neither p nor q' is true if both its arguments are false, and false otherwise—$X11 = X10 = X01 = 0$, and $X00 = 1$. The matrix is

X	1	0
1	0	0
0	0	1

Some of the operators listed in the last section might also have been introduced in this way, e.g. 'D' as an abbreviation for 'NK' (for we have $NK11 = N1 = 0$, $NK10 = N0 = 1$, $NK01 = N0 = 1$, and $NK00 = N0 = 1$, giving the same table as that for 'D' above); and indeed the reading of 'D' as 'Not both' suggests its introduction in this manner. There are, moreover, a variety of ways in which the same truth-operator may be 'defined'. We might, for example, introduce 'Neither p nor q' as an abbreviation of 'Both not p and not q' ($KNpNq$) rather than of 'Not either p or q', and the same matrix and set of equations will result. Again, the senses of 'and' and 'not' being understood, we might take the non-exclusive sense of 'or' as already known and 'define' the exclusive sense by introducing 'Jpq' as an abbreviation for '$KApqNKpq$' ('Both either-p-or-q and not-both-p-and-q'); or we might take the exclusive sense as already known and define the non-exclusive by introducing 'Apq' as an abbreviation for '$JJpqKpq$' ('Either either-p-or-q or both-p-and-q', 'either' being here understood exclusively).[1]

An exercise which has occupied many modern logicians is that of starting with as few undefined truth-operators as possible, and introducing all the rest in the above manner as abbreviations. Confining ourselves for the moment to operators taking one and two arguments, it is easy to show that there are four ways in which the truth-values of truth-functions of one argument, and sixteen ways in which those of truth-functions of two arguments, may be determined by the truth-values of the argument or arguments. Suppose we write $(x, y)p$ for a truth-function of p which has the value x when $p = 1$ and y when

[1] Cf. J. N. Keynes, *Studies and Exercises in Formal Logic*, 4th ed. (1906), p. 278.

$p = 0$, then the possible truth-functions of p are $(1, 1)p$, $(1, 0)p$, $(0, 1)p$, and $(0, 0)p$.[1] $(1, 1)p$ is that function of p which is true when p is true and also when it is false ('It either is or is not the case that p' would have these properties), $(1, 0)p$ that function which is true when p is true and false when p is false ('It is the case that p', or p itself, considered as a truth-function of itself), and so on with the others. And suppose we write $(x, y, z, t)pq$ for a truth-function of p and q which has the value x for $p = 1$ and $q = 1$, y for $p = 1$ and $q = 0$, z for $p = 0$ and $q = 1$, and t for $p = 0$ and $q = 0$. The sixteen possible truth-functions of this sort are

$(1, 1, 1, 1)pq$, $(1, 1, 1, 0)pq$, $(1, 1, 0, 1)pq$, $(1, 1, 0, 0)pq$,
$(1, 0, 1, 1)pq$, $(1, 0, 1, 0)pq$, $(1, 0, 0, 1)pq$, $(1, 0, 0, 0)pq$,
$(0, 1, 1, 1)pq$, $(0, 1, 1, 0)pq$, $(0, 1, 0, 1)pq$, $(0, 1, 0, 0)pq$,
$(0, 0, 1, 1)pq$, $(0, 0, 1, 0)pq$, $(0, 0, 0, 1)pq$, $(0, 0, 0, 0)pq$.

Some of these we have already encountered. For example, the second, $(1, 1, 1, 0)pq$—the function which is true when p and q are both true, when p is true but q false, and when p is false but q true, but false when both are false—is Apq; $(1, 0, 1, 1)pq$ is Cpq; $(1, 0, 0, 1)pq$ is Epq; $(1, 0, 0, 0)pq$ is Kpq; $(0, 1, 1, 1)pq$ is Dpq; $(0, 1, 1, 0)pq$ is Jpq; and $(0, 0, 0, 1)pq$ is Xpq. It is an easy matter to construct compounds of these which will answer to the remaining descriptions, and which can therefore be used to 'define' the remaining possible truth-operators. The following, for example, would do:

$$
\begin{aligned}
(1, 1, 1, 1)pq &= Vpq &&= K(ApNp)(AqNq) \\
(1, 1, 0, 1)pq &= Bpq &&= Cqp, \text{ or } CNpNq \\
(1, 1, 0, 0)pq &= Ipq &&= A(Kpq)(KpNq) \\
(1, 0, 1, 0)pq &= Hpq &&= A(Kpq)(KNpq) \\
(0, 1, 0, 1)pq &= Gpq &&= A(KpNq)(KNpNq) \\
(0, 1, 0, 0)pq &= Lpq &&= KpNq \\
(0, 0, 1, 1)pq &= Fpq &&= A(KNpq)(KNpNq) \\
(0, 0, 1, 0)pq &= Mpq &&= KNpq \\
(0, 0, 0, 0)pq &= Opq &&= A(KpNp)(KqNq).
\end{aligned}
$$

[1] Cf. C. S. Peirce, *Collected Papers*, 4.261.

(The second column contains the Łukasiewicz symbols for these operators, but they are not often used.)[1] The reader may easily verify by calculation that these will give the required results. Also, given '*Np*' for '(0, 1)*p*', the remaining truth-functors of one argument can be defined in terms of '*N*', '*K*', and '*A*' as follows: (1, 1)*p* = *ApNp*; (1, 0)*p* = *NNp*; (0, 0)*p* = *KpNp*. We have already seen, moreover, that '*E*' may be defined in terms of '*K*' and '*C*' (*Epq* = *KCpqCqp*), '*D*' in terms of '*N*' and '*K*' (*Dpq* = *NKpq*) and '*J*' in terms of '*K*', '*A*', and '*N*' (*Jpq* = *KApqNKpq*). This leaves us with '*N*', '*K*', '*A*', and '*C*' as the only undefined truth-operators. Can we go further than this?

The answer is that we certainly can, and that in several ways. In the system of PM the operators corresponding to '*A*' and '*N*' are taken as 'primitive' or undefined, and 'Both *p* and *q*' introduced as an abbreviation for 'Not either not *p* or not *q*', and 'If *p* then *q*' as an abbreviation for 'Either not *p* or *q*'. In the earlier system of W. E. Johnson's 'Logical Calculus',[2] operators corresponding to '*K*' and '*N*' are undefined, and 'Either *p* or *q*' introduced as an abbreviation for 'Not both not *p* and not *q*', and 'If *p* then *q*' as one for 'Not both *p* and not *q*'. In the still earlier system of Gottlob Frege's *Begriffschrift* (1879) operators corresponding to '*C*' and '*N*' are undefined, and 'Either *p* or *q*' introduced as an abbreviation for 'If not *p* then *q*', 'Not-both *p* and *q*' as an abbreviation for 'If *p* then not *q*', and 'Both *p* and *q*' as an abbreviation for 'Not not-both *p* and *q*', i.e. for 'Not if-*p*-then-not-*q*'. We can, moreover, go even further than this. C. S. Peirce showed in papers (then unpublished) of about 1880 and 1902,[3] and H. M. Sheffer discovered independently in 1913, that all the others might be derived from '*X*' or '*D*' alone. For both 'Neither *p* nor *p*' and 'Not both *p* and *p*' have the force of 'Not *p*' (they are false when *p* is true and true when *p* is false), so that we may define '*Np*' as an abbreviation either for '*Xpp*' or for '*Dpp*', and then introduce '*Kpq*' as an abbreviation for '*XNpNq*' ('Neither not *p* nor not *q*') or for '*NDpq*' ('Not

[1] These functions are tabulated systematically in I. M. Bocheński's *Précis de logique mathématique* (1949), 3.32, and an interesting use is made of the tabulation by I. Thomas in *Dominican Studies*, vol. iv (1951), pp. 72–77.

[2] *Mind*, 1892. A calculus in '*K*' and '*N*' was developed in a more modern manner by B. Sobociński in 1939. (See Sobociński's *An Investigation of Protothetic*, Brussels, 1949, pp. 10–11.)

[3] Peirce, *Collected Papers*, 4.12–20, 264–5.

not-both *p* and *q*'), or '*Apq*' as an abbreviation for '*NXpq*' ('Not neither *p* nor *q*') or for '*DNpNq*' ('Not-both not *p* and not *q*'), and thereafter proceed as in Johnson's system or in Russell and Whitehead's.[1]

Some of the equivalences employed in these procedures have been known to logicians for a very long time. In particular, some of the later medieval logicians were aware that the negation of a conjunction always has the same truth-value as the alternation of the negations of its conjuncts ($NKpq = ANpNq$), and the negation of an alternation always has the same truth-value as the conjunction of the negations of its alternants ($NApq = KNpNq$). They expressed this by saying that 'the contradictory of a copulative proposition is equipollent to the disjunction of the contradictories of the members of the copulative', and 'the contradictory of a disjunction is equipollent to the copulative proposition having as its members the contradictories of the members of the disjunction'.[2] Nowadays these two equivalences are generally called 'de Morgan's Laws', though what the nineteenth-century logician Augustus de Morgan in fact laid down were not these laws but certain analogous ones in the logic of 'terms'.

Any truth-function of more than two arguments can easily be defined in terms of *A*, *K*, and *N*. Suppose, for example, we wish to define a truth-function of three arguments *p*, *q*, and *r* which is true when *p* is true but *q* and *r* are false, when *q* is true but *p* and *r* are false, and when *r* is true but *p* and *q* are false, and false otherwise. Such a function would plainly be given by $A(KpKNqNr)A(KqKNpNr)(KrKNpNq)$, i.e. 'Either both *p* and both not *q* and not *r*, or either both *q* and both not *p* and not *r*, or both *r* and both not *p* and not *q*', or more briefly '*p* and not *q* and not *r*, or *q* and not *p* and not *r*, or *r* and not *p* and not *q*'. Similarly with others. All truth-functional formulae can therefore be expressed either by means of the operators we have so far considered or by means of operators definable in terms of them.

[1] It was shown by E. Żyliński in the 1920's that *X* and *D* are the only truth-functions of two arguments that can be thus used (Sobociński, op. cit., p. 37).

[2] See, e.g. W. Burleigh, *De Puritate Artis Logicae* (ed. Boehner, 1951), p. 10, ll. 25 ff. For the history of these laws see P. Boehner, 'Bemerkungen zur Geschichte der De Morgansche Gesetze in der Scholastik', *Archiv für Philosophie*, vol. iv (1951), pp. 113–46, and A. Church's review of this in the *Journal of Symbolic Logic*, vol. xvii (1952), p. 123.

§ 4. *Tautologous Formulae, and Rules of Inference*

Let us return for a moment to the two forms 'Not *p*-and-*q*' and 'Not-*p* and *q*'. Their truth-values for the different possible cases work out as follows:

$$NK11 = N1 = 0$$
$$NK10 = N0 = 1$$
$$NK01 = N0 = 1$$
$$NK00 = N0 = 1,$$

and

$$KN11 = K01 = 0$$
$$KN10 = K00 = 0$$
$$KN01 = K11 = 1$$
$$KN00 = K10 = 0.$$

Comparing these two results, it may be seen that the only case in which a proposition of the form 'Both not *p* and *q*' is true (the case in which *p* is a false proposition and *q* a true one) is a case in which the corresponding proposition of the form 'Not both *p* and *q*' is true also, though the converse is not the case. 'Both not *p* and *q*', in other words, is never true except when 'Not both *p* and *q*' is true too, though 'Not both *p* and *q*' is sometimes true when 'Both not *p* and *q*' is false (this happens in the two cases in which *q* is a false proposition). We can therefore never be led astray if we pass from 'Both not *p* and *q*' to 'Not both *p* and *q*', though we may be if we pass from 'Not both *p* and *q*' to 'Both not *p* and *q*'. 'Both not *p* and *q*, therefore not both *p* and *q*' is thus a safe or valid form of inference, while 'Not both *p* and *q*, therefore both not *p* and *q*' is not.

This illustrates one method of distinguishing valid from invalid forms of inference in cases in which (1) we draw a conclusion from a single premiss, (2) both premiss and conclusion are truth-functions, and (3) it is solely on their truth-functional character that the force of the inference depends or purports to depend. A truth-functional inference is valid if no combination of truth-values in the propositions involved as arguments makes the premiss true without making the conclusion true also.[1] This method may be easily extended to inferences with more premisses than one by first combining

[1] Cf. L. Wittgenstein, *Tractatus Logico-Philosophicus*, 5.12.

these into a single premiss by means of 'and'. But there is another method of reaching the same end. Suppose we consider, instead of the two propositional forms 'Both not p and q' and 'Not both p and q', the single form 'If both not p and q, then not both p and q', $C(KNpq)(NKpq)$. The possible truth-values of this work out as follows:

$$CKN11NK11 = CK01N1 = C00 = 1$$
$$CKN10NK10 = CK00N0 = C01 = 1$$
$$CKN01NK01 = CK11N0 = C11 = 1$$
$$CKN00NK00 = CK10N0 = C01 = 1.$$

It will be seen that this complex implication holds as true no matter what the truth-values of its unanalysed arguments 'p' and 'q' may be. And since an implication is false if its antecedent is true and its consequent not, this means that there is no case in which an implication of this particular form has a true antecedent and a false consequent. Hence it is always a safe procedure to pass from a proposition which could form the antecedent of such an implication to the proposition which would then form its consequent. So quite generally, the inferential form 'A, therefore B' will be valid if all propositions of the form 'If A then B' are true, where the contained forms 'A' and 'B' are the same as in the inferential form.

Truth-functional forms which result in true propositions no matter what may be the truth-value of the propositions substituted for their unanalysed arguments (i.e. for the simple p's, q's, etc. appearing in them) are called 'tautologous' or 'tautological', and propositions which exemplify them are called 'tautologies'. The detection of tautologies, and especially of tautologous implications, is clearly an important part of the branch of logic with which we are now concerned. The first to see this was perhaps Peirce, but in the present century the writer who did most to make clear, at least to English logicians, the importance of looking for tautologies was Ludwig Wittgenstein, in his *Tractatus Logico-Philosophicus* (1922).

The most obvious method of detecting tautologies is the process of calculation illustrated above (which in substance we owe to Peirce, though its details come from Łukasiewicz), but there are means of abbreviating this in cases where large numbers of 'propositional variables', i.e. letters standing indifferently for any propositions at all, are involved. The point may be illustrated by considering the propositional form *C*(*CApqKrs*)(*CKpqArs*), 'If either-*p*-or-*q* implies both-*r*-and-*s*, then both-*p*-and-*q* implies either-*r*-or-*s*.' To work out the possible truth-values of this by calculation of the sort so far given, we must consider the sixteen different possible combinations of truth-values for its four arguments '*p*', '*q*', '*r*', and '*s*' ($p = 1$, $q = 1, r = 1, s = 1; p = 1, q = 1, r = 1, s = 0; p = 1, q = 1,$ $r = 0, s = 1$; and so on). We would need, that is, sixteen lines of calculation like this:

$$CCA11K11CK11A11 = CC11C11 = C11 = 1$$
$$CCA11K10CK11A10 = CC10C11 = C01 = 1$$
$$CCA11K01CK11A01 = CC10C11 = C01 = 1.$$

In such cases as this, much time may be saved by proceeding as follows[1] (the numbers indicate the order of the steps):

CCApqKrsCKpqArs

(i) *CCA1qKrsCK1qArs*
(ii) *CC1KrsCqArs*
(iii) *CKrsCqArs*
(iv) *CK1sCqA1s*
(v) *CsCq1*
(vi) *Cs1*
(vii) 1
(viii) *CKosCqAos*
(ix) *CoCqs*
(x) 1
(xi) *CCAoqKrsCKoqArs*
(xii) *CCqKrsCoArs*
(xiii) *CCqKrs1*
(xiv) 1.

Here we arrive at (i) by considering the case in which $p = 1$, leaving the other variables in the meantime untouched. In passing to (ii), we replace *A1q* by 1 on the ground that an alternation is true whenever one of its members is, and *K1q* by *q* on the ground that whether a conjunction with one true member is true depends on the truth-value of the other member (*K1q* will be true if *q* is true, and false if it is false, i.e. its truth-value is that of *q* simply). In passing to (iii), we replace *C1Krs* by *Krs* on the ground that whether an implication with a true antecedent is true depends on the truth-value of the consequent ($C11 = 1$ and $C10 = 0$). We then consider in succession the

[1] The method here given is an adaptation to Łukasiewicz's symbolism of that in W. V. Quine's *Methods of Logic* (1950), § 5.

sub-possibilities in which $r = 1$ and $r = 0$ (r rather than q because at this stage r appears more often, and so more variables are eliminated at one stroke). The step from (iv) to (v) is like that from (i) to (ii). That from (v) to (vi), in which $Cq1$ is replaced by 1, and that from (vi) to (vii) in which $Cs1$ is replaced by 1, depend on the fact that a conditional is always true if its consequent is true ($C11 = 1$ and $C01 = 1$). With (vii) we are 'out', as far as the possibility '$p = 1, r = 1$' is concerned, and we turn in (viii) to the sub-possibility in which $r = 0$. The step to (ix), in which $K0s$ is replaced by 0 and $A0s$ by s, uses the facts that a conjunction with a false member is always false and that an alternation with one false member has the truth-value of the remaining member ($A01 = 1$, $A00 = 0$). The step from (ix) to (x), where $C0Cqs$ is replaced by 1, depends on the fact that a conditional with a false antecedent is always true ($C01 = 1$ and $C00 = 1$). We are now 'out' so far as the possibility '$p = 1$' is concerned, and turn in (xi) to the case in which $p = 0$; the grounds of the steps taken after this should now be obvious.

The equations which are most useful in abbreviated evaluations of this sort are the following (not all are used in the above example):

(1) $K1p = Kp1 = p$
(2) $K0p = Kp0 = 0$
(3) $A1p = Ap1 = 1$
(4) $A0p = Ap0 = p$
(5) $C0p = Cp1 = 1$
(6) $C1p = p, Cp0 = Np$
(7) $E1p = Ep1 = p$
(8) $E0p = Ep0 = Np$
(9) $NNp = p$.

These follow simply enough from the basic equations for K, A, C, E, and N, but (5) is worth looking at a little more closely, as the equations $C0p = 1$ and $Cp1 = 1$ bring out particularly clearly the difference between the truth-functional use of 'if' and some of its more ordinary uses. '$C0p = 1$' in effect asserts (we have in fact expressed its sense in this way already) that a conditional with a false antecedent is always true, and '$Cp1 = 1$'

asserts the same of conditionals with true consequents. And this, when we reflect on it, seems a little strange. Its strangeness becomes still more obvious when we use the term 'implication', and say that an implication *by* a false proposition, and an implication *of* a true one, are always true. The strangeness lies primarily in the fact that we often say 'If *p* then *q*' or '*p* implies *q*' to mean that *q* is *deducible* from *p*, i.e. that the inference of *q* from *p* is a valid one,[1] and of course the mere circumstance that *p* is a false proposition, or that *q* is a true one, is not sufficient to guarantee this. 'President Lincoln is alive today' is a false proposition, but we cannot in consequence of that validly infer from it either that walnuts grow on banana trees or that walnuts do not grow on banana trees. And 'Walnuts do not grow on banana trees' is a true proposition, but we cannot in consequence of that validly infer it either from 'President Lincoln is alive today' or from 'President Lincoln is not alive today.' Yet the three implications

(*a*) If President Lincoln is alive today, then walnuts grow on banana trees,
(*b*) If President Lincoln is alive today, then walnuts do not grow on banana trees,
(*c*) If President Lincoln is not alive today, then walnuts do not grow on banana trees,

are all of them true, if 'If' is understood as translating the truth-functional '*C*'. For in all of these cases, for one reason or another, the antecedent is not true without the consequent being true—in (*a*) and (*b*) because the antecedent just is not true at all, and in (*b*) and (*c*) because the consequent is true

[1] It is a not uncommon error to suppose that this is the *only* ordinary use of 'if' and 'implies'. This is an error because, if this were so, the first premiss would always be either false or superfluous in an inference of the form 'If *p* then *q*, and *p*, therefore *q*' (the *ponendo ponens*; see Ch. III § 1). If 'If *p* then *q*' here means '*q* follows from *p*', then if this be true, '*p*, therefore *q*' alone would be a valid inference. This fact was used by the ancient sceptical writer Sextus Empiricus as a criticism of all inferences of the '*Cpq*, and *p*, ∴ *q*' form. (See his *Outlines of Pyrrhonism*, ii. 159. His argument is repeated in J. Anderson's 'Hypotheticals', *Australasian Journal of Philosophy* for May 1952, pp. 9–10.) In Lewis Carroll's fable 'What the Tortoise said to Achilles' (*Mind*, April 1895), bringing out the same fact in another way, the moral intended seems to be that 'If *p* then *q*' does not always mean '*q* is deducible from *p*'; for the piece appeared shortly after A. Sidgwick had asserted, in a discussion of an earlier puzzle of Carroll's, that it does always mean this (*Mind*, Jan. 1895, p. 143).

whether the antecedent is true or not—and this suffices to verify a conditional of the merely truth-functional sort.

This merely truth-functional sort of conditional is sometimes called a 'material' conditional or (as by Russell and Whitehead) a 'material implication'. The connexion between a material conditional and the sort which asserts deducibility has been indicated earlier in the present section—the conditional which asserts deducibility is true when it does not merely happen that the given antecedent is not true without the consequent being true, but antecedents of the form of the given one are *never* true without consequents formally related to them as the given consequent is to the given antecedent, being true too. Or to use our other way of putting the matter, the conditional which asserts deducibility is true when the corresponding 'material' conditional is not merely true but a tautology, i.e. has a form which none but true propositions possess.

Not all tautologies, it may be observed, are conditionals. 'Either *p* or not *p*', for example, is true whether its argument *p* be a true proposition or a false one, and so is 'Not both *p* and not *p*.' The former is sometimes called the Law of Excluded Middle (it excludes any third possibility beyond those of the truth of *p* and the truth of not-*p*), and the latter the Law of Contradiction (it forbids the joint affirmation of a proposition and its negation or contradictory). Both go back in one form or another to the very beginnings of logical reflection, but they are a little difficult to fit into our preliminary rough definition of logic as the attempt to discriminate systematically between valid and invalid inference. Tautologous implications have a direct bearing on this task which has already been indicated, but can the same be said of tautologies and tautologous propositional forms quite generally?

In answer to this, it may be pointed out that it has seldom if ever proved profitable to draw the boundaries of a science too tightly. At bottom the proper business of any sort of scientist is not to study a 'subject' but to study actual problems, and problems have a habit of gathering other problems about them in a somewhat unpredictable way.[1] In the case under consideration, the *systematic* study of tautologous implications is quite

[1] Cf. K. R. Popper, 'The Nature of Philosophical Problems and their Roots in Science,' *British Journal for the Philosophy of Science*, Aug. 1952, pp. 124–5.

impossible apart from the study of tautologies generally, whether this study be called 'logic' or not. For tautological forms are all subtly interconnected, in a way which is best made clear by setting them out in a 'deductive' system rather like Euclid's geometry—taking some tautological formulae as 'axioms' and deriving others from them as 'theorems' by a few fixed rules of transformation or inference. And in at least a large number of such systems tautologous alternations, conjunctions, etc., are indispensable deductive links between one tautologous implication and another, so that even if our primary interest continues to be in the implications, we are bound to consider the others too.

It should be said at the same time that there is another possible answer to this query, but it cannot be given until we have studied deductive systems of propositional logic in some detail.

II

Axiomatizations of the Propositional Calculus

§ 1. *The System of* Principia Mathematica

As has just been indicated, the laws which arise in the logic of truth-functions can be set out as a series of theorems derived from a small set of axioms, and we shall now illustrate how this might be done.

It is plain that when we thus set out to deduce logical laws by logical processes from other logical laws, we must tread carefully if we are to avoid circularity. Not only must the axioms from which our deduction proceeds be clearly listed at the outset, but we must also lay down clearly the rules by which we are going to proceed from one formula to another. And to give the whole a quite mechanical accuracy, a rigorously fixed symbolism is employed, not only for expressing the laws laid down and established, but also for representing the processes of proof.

The formulae occurring in the system, or rather fragment of a system, which we shall here set out, are all constructed by means of the 'propositional variables' '*p*', '*q*', '*r*', '*s*', etc., and the operators '*A*', '*N*', and '*C*'. Certain of these symbols, and certain sequences of them, will be called 'propositional formulae', and of these some will be called 'theses' or laws of the system. As to the first point, (1) the propositional variables will count as propositional formulae, (2) the complex consisting of '*N*' followed by any propositional formula will count as a propositional formula, and (3) the complex consisting of '*A*' or '*C*' followed by any two propositional formulae will count as a propositional formula. For example, *CCpNqNACNpqCNqp* is a propositional formula. For by (1), '*p*' and '*q*' are propositional formulae; applying (2) to this result, '*Np*' and '*Nq*, are propositional formulae; applying (3) to the results achieved so far, '*CpNq*', '*CNpq*', and '*CNqp*' are propositional formulae; by (3) again, since '*CNpq*' and '*CNqp*' are propositional formulae, '*ACNpqCNqp*' is a propositional formula; applying (2) to this, '*NACNpqCNqp*' is a propositional formula; and finally, again by (3), since '*CpNq*' and '*NACNpqCNqp*' are propositional formulae, '*CCpNqNACNpqCNqp*' is a propositional formula. It is not, however, a thesis.

The following formulae are theses: *CAppp*, *CqApq*, *CApqAqp*, *CApAqrAqApr*, *CCqrCApqApr*; and any formula derived from any thesis by certain permitted transformations, to be listed later, is also a thesis. So any formula thus derived from one of the five listed formulae is a thesis; any formula thus derived from any of these immediately derived formulae is a thesis, and so on. For convenience in the setting out of proofs, our theses will be numbered. Of the five listed formulae—the 'axioms'—the first, *CAppp*, may be read 'If either *p* or *p*, then *p*.' To say 'Either grass is green or grass is green' really leaves no alternative to 'Grass is green'; if it is true, the proposition which does not even give the appearance of offering an alternative is true too. The second listed formula, *CqApq*, reads 'If *q* then either *p* or *q*.' Expressing this as a rule of inference, it tells us that if any proposition is true, then so is any alternation in which it is the second alternant. For example, since 'Walnuts do not grow on banana trees' is a true proposition, 'Either President Lincoln is now alive or walnuts do not grow on banana trees' is a true proposition. We do not generally bother to state alternatives of this sort in ordinary life, but the rule of inference just given is one which we do make use of occasionally. For example, if a not very intelligent History student, when asked the name of the last Queen Regnant of England, replied that it was either 'Veronica' or 'Victoria', we would have to admit that what he said was in fact true, because it is true that her name was 'Victoria', though we would no doubt mark him down for being insufficiently specific. It is also true, we may note, that if any proposition is true, then so is any alternation in which it is the *first* alternant; that is, we have *CqAqp* as well as *CqApq*. But the former is not an axiom in our system, it is something we must prove. In proving it we make use, in a fairly obvious fashion, of *CqApq* together with the third of our listed formulae *CApqAqp*. Translated into a rule of inference, this tells us that from any alternation we may infer the alternation of the same components in the reverse order. This law, or rather the conjunction of laws *CApqAqp* and *CAqpApq*, is an analogue of the arithmetical law $x+y=y+x$. Logical 'addition', like arithmetical, is commutative. It is also associative. Just as $x+(y+z) = y+(x+z)$, so '*p* or (*q* or *r*)' is equivalent to '*q* or (*p* or *r*)'. This law is partly given in our fourth listed formula, *CApAqrAqApr* (the rest of it is *CAqAprApAqr*). Our fifth listed formula, *CCqrCApqApr*, may be read 'If *q* implies *r*, then either-*p*-or-*q* implies either-*p*-or-*r*.' Its main use is in the derivation of the theorem *CCqrCCpqCpr*, 'If *q* implies *r*, then if *p* implies *q*, *p* implies *r*.' This is one form of the 'principle of pure hypothetical syllogism', i.e. of inferences very like the syllogistic inferences of Aristotle, but having implications for both their premisses and for their conclusion. In the Middle Ages, it was stated in the rule: *Quod antecedit ad antecedens, antecedit ad consequens*, 'What implies the antecedent (of a true implication), implies its consequent.' (Thus if 'If *q* then *r*' is a true implication, then if *p* implies its antecedent *q*, *p* also implies its consequent *r*.) Allied to this is the rule *Quod sequitur ad consequens, sequitur ad antecedens*, 'What follows from the consequent (of a true implication) follows from the antecedent.' In our symbols this would be *CCpqCCqrCpr*. Both this and the preceding are now often simply called the 'principle of syllogism'.

Of the three operators '*A*', '*N*', and '*C*', the first two are given in our system as undefined, and '*C*' is introduced as a permissible abbreviation for '*AN*'. Hence we may replace '*AN*' by '*C*', or '*C*' by '*AN*', wherever we please. We may do this, moreover, in any part of a formula without doing it in another—a point which distinguishes this mere abbreviation and expansion from another kind of substitution to be mentioned shortly. The definition '$C = AN$' has the number 1.01 in our system, and the transformation of a formula by means of it is expressed in our proofs by the operation '$\times$ 1.01'. For example,

$$1.6\ p/Np \times 1.01 = 2.05$$ [1]

means that if we replace *p* by *Np* throughout in the formula 1.6, and then apply the definition 1.01, we will obtain the formula 2.05. The formula 1.6 is in fact the axiom *CCqrCApqApr*. If we perform upon this the substitution *p*/*Np*, we obtain

[1] This way of writing 'derivational lines' is the modification of Łukasiewicz's that is used in the writings of I. M. Bocheński, and explained in his article 'On the Categorical Syllogism', *Dominican Studies*, vol. i (1948), pp. 40–41. Łukasiewicz himself, e.g. in his *Aristotle's Syllogistic*, has '$\times$' where we have '=', and expresses the application of definitions differently.

CCqrCANpqANpr. And if we here abbreviate '*AN*' to '*C*', we obtain the principle of syllogism *CCqrCCpqCpr*, which is the formula numbered 2.05.

We come now to the rules which we may use in deriving theorems from other theorems and from the axioms. The first, which has already been illustrated, is the 'rule of substitution', to the effect that in any thesis of the system we may replace any simple propositional variable by any propositional formula whatsoever, and affirm the resulting new formula as a thesis, provided only that the same substitution is made wherever the propositional variable in question appears in the original thesis. The rationale of this rule is simple enough. The formula *CCqrCApqApr*, for example, laid down as a logical law, states that given any implication, the alternation of *any proposition whatever* with the antecedent implies the alternation of that same proposition with the consequent. Hence the alternation of any *negation* with the antecedent implies the alternation of that negation with the consequent; and this is in effect what we pass to when we perform in 1.6 the substitution *p*/*Np*, i.e. replace *p* by *Np* wherever it occurs in the formula.

The second rule of inference, the 'rule of detachment', is that if any formula α is a thesis, and the implication $C\alpha\beta$ is also a thesis, then the consequent β may be detached from the implication as a further thesis. To illustrate the symbolic representation of proofs of this kind, we may take the proof of the theorem *CpApq*:

1.3. *CqApq*
1.4. *CApqAqp*
2.06. *CCpqCCqrCpr*
  1.3 *p*/*q*, *q*/*p* = I
I. *CpAqp*
  1.4 *p*/*q*, *q*/*p* = II
II. *CAqpApq*
  2.06 *q*/*Aqp*, *r*/*Apq* = III
III. *CCpAqpCCAqpApqCpApq*
  III = *C*I—IV
IV. *CCAqpApqCpApq*
  IV = *C*II—2.2
2.2. *CpApq*.

Here the line leading to thesis IV informs us that thesis III is an implication in which the antecedent is the thesis I, so that its consequent may be detached as a new thesis, to which we give the number IV, and which we proceed immediately to lay down. The proof leading to the final conclusion 2.2 is similar. Our proof may, however, be considerably abbreviated. In the first place, instead of writing out the thesis obtained by performing the substitutions *q*/*Aqp*, *r*/*Apq* in 2.06 and labelling it III, we may simply say immediately that the result of this substitution is the implication *C*I—IV, thus:

2.06 *q*/*Aqp*, *r*/*Apq* = *C*I—IV

IV. *CCAqpApqCpApq*

(though of course we would then number our conclusion not 'IV' but 'III'). Further, instead of separately asserting that 2.06 *q*/*Aqp*, *r*/*Apq* is *C*I—IV, and then that IV is *C*II—2.2, we express this double detachment by asserting immediately that

2.06 *q*/*Aqp*, *r*/*Apq* = *C*I—*C*II—2.2.

And finally, instead of writing down, as the separate theses I and II, what we obtain by performing the substitutions *p*/*q* and *q*/*p* in 1.3 and 1.4, we may put '*C*1.3 *p*/*q*, *q*/*p*—*C*1.4 *p*/*q*, *q*/*p*—2.2' instead of '*C*I—II—2.2', and compress our entire proof into the single line

2.06 *q*/*Aqp*, *r*/*Apq* = *C*1.3 *p*/*q*, *q*/*p*—*C*1.4 *p*/*q*, *q*/*p*—2.2.

These two processes of substitution and detachment, together with abbreviation and expansion by definition, are the only forms of inference employed in our proofs, with which we may therefore immediately proceed.

Undefined Operators: *A*, *N*.

Definition: 1.01. *C* = *AN*.

Axioms:

1.2. *CAppp*

1.3. *CqApq*

1.4. *CApqAqp*

1.5. *CApAqrAqApr*

1.6. *CCqrCApqApr*.

Theorems:

$1.2\ p/Np \times 1.01 = 2.01$

2.01. $CCpNpNp$

$1.3\ p/Np \times 1.01 = 2.02$

2.02. $CqCpq$

$1.4\ p/Np,\ q/Nq \times 1.01 = 2.03$

2.03. $CCpNqCqNp$

$1.5\ p/Np,\ q/Nq \times 1.01 = 2.04$

2.04. $CCpCqrCqCpr$

$1.6\ p/Np \times 1.01 = 2.05$

2.05. $CCqrCCpqCpr$

$2.04\ p/Cqr,\ q/Cpq,\ r/Cpr = C2.05—2.06$

2.06. $CCpqCCqrCpr$

$1.3\ q/p = 2.07.$

2.07. $CpApp$

$2.05\ q/App,\ r/p = C1.2—C2.07—2.08$

2.08. Cpp

$2.08 \times 1.01 = 2.1$

2.1. $ANpp$

$1.4\ p/Np,\ q/p = C2.1—2.11$

2.11. $ApNp$

$2.11\ p/Np \times 1.01 = 2.12$

2.12. $CpNNp$

$1.6\ q/Np,\ r/NNNp = C2.12\ p/Np—C2.11—2.13$

2.13. $ApNNNp$

$1.4\ q/NNNp \times 1.01 = C2.13—2.14$

2.14. $CNNpp$

$2.05\ p/Np,\ r/NNq = C2.12\ p/q—2.141$

2.141. $CCNpqCNpNNq$

$2.05\ p/Nq,\ q/NNp,\ r/p = C2.14—2.142$

2.142. $CCNqNNpCNqp$

$2.05\ p/CNpq,\ q/CNpNNq,\ r/CNqNNp$

$= C2.03\ p/Np,\ q/Nq—C2.141—2.143$

2.143. *CCNpqCNqNNp*

2.05 *p/CNpq, q/CNqNNp, r/CNqp*
= *C*2.142—*C*2.143—2.15

2.15. *CCNpqCNqp*

2.05 *r/NNq* = *C*2.12 *p/q*—2.151

2.151. *CCpqCpNNq*

2.06 *p/Cpq, q/CpNNq, r/CNqNp*
= *C*2.151—*C*2.03 *q/Nq*—2.16

2.16. *CCpqCNqNp*

2.05 *q/NNq, r/q* = *C*2.14 *p/q*—2.161

2.161. *CCpNNqCpq*

2.06 *p/CNqNp, q/CpNNq, r/Cpq*
= *C*2.03 *p/Nq, q/p*—*C*2.161—2.17

2.17. *CCNqNpCpq*

2.06 *p/CNpp, q/CNpNNp, r/NNp*
= *C*2.141 *q/p*—C2.01 *p/Np*—2.171

2.171. *CCNppNNp*

2.06 *p/CNpp, q/NNp, r/p* = *C*2.171—*C*2.14—2.18

2.18. *CCNppp*

2.06 *q/Aqp, r/Apq* = *C*1.3 *p/q, q/p*—*C*1.4 *p/q, q/p*—2.2

2.2. *CpApq*

2.2 *p/Np* × 1.01 = 2.21

2.21. *CNpCpq*

2.04 *p/Np, q/p, r/q* = *C*2.21—2.24

2.24. *CpCNpq.*

We shall not take this process of deduction any further, but will now indicate just what we have been doing. The theorems proved above are in fact the first group of theorems proved in Russell and Whitehead's PM, and the proofs are drawn from there also, but set out differently. The numbers are as in PM, except that 2.141–143 are in that work unnumbered steps in the proof of 2.15; 2.161 is an unnumbered step in the proof of 2.17; and 2.171 an unnumbered step in the proof of 2.18. In PM, moreover, the numbers have an asterisk before them, and after them a 'sign of assertion'; both of these have been dispensed with here. In later sections of the *Principia*, further symbols corresponding to '*K*' and '*E*' are introduced by definition, and theses involving them are proved; but we may for the present ignore these.

Theorem 2.01, *CCpNpNp* ('If *p* implies not *p*, then not *p*') expresses one form of the principle of *reductio ad absurdum*—if a proposition implies its own falsehood, then it *is* false. The ancients applied this principle to the statement 'Everything is false'. Since this implies, among other things, that 'Everything is false' is false, i.e. that not everything is false, it cannot be true.[1] An allied principle is expressed by 2.18, *CCNppp* ('If not *p* implies *p*, then *p*'). This asserts that if a proposition is implied even by its own denial, it must be true. Some of the early Jesuits called this the *consequentia mirabilis*; Łukasiewicz calls it, after one of them, the 'law of Clavius'.[2] Theorem 2.02, *CqCpq* ('If *q* then if *p* then *q*'), is one way of saying that an implication with a true consequent is always true, and theorems 2.21, *CNpCpq* ('If not *p* then if *p* then *q*'), and 2.24, *CpCNpq* ('If *p* then if not *p* then *q*'), are ways of saying that an implication with a false antecedent is always true. The proof of 2.21 is instructive. It starts from the law—surely quite unobjectionable—that if any proposition *p* is true then the alternation 'Either *p* or *q*' is true too, whatever the newly introduced alternative *q* may be. Hence if any negation 'Not-*p*' is true, so is the alternation 'Either not *p* or *q*'. But 'Either not *p* or *q*' is precisely what 'If *p* then *q*', as it occurs in this system, is defined as meaning. Hence the truth of 'Not *p*', i.e. the falsehood of *p*, implies the truth of the 'material' implication 'If *p* then *q*.'[3]

Theorem 2.08, *Cpp* ('If *p* then *p*'), forms part of the 'Law of Identity' (in full the Law of Identity is 'If and only if *p* then *p*'), which is one of the three traditional 'Laws of Thought', the others being the Law of Excluded Middle (*ApNp*) and the Law of Contradiction (*NKpNp*). Theorems 2.12, *CpNNp*, and 2.14, *CNNpp*, between them express the 'law of double negation', 'Not not *p* = *p*'. Theorems 2.03 (*CCpNqCqNp*), 2.15 (*CCNpqCNqp*), 2.16 (*CCpqCNqNp*), and 2.17 (*CCNqNpCpq*)

[1] Cf. Aristotle, *Metaphysics*, 1012^b 15–16.
[2] J. Łukasiewicz, *Aristotle's Syllogistic*, p. 80. See also pp. 50–51.
[3] Cf. W. E. Johnson, *Logic*, Part I, pp. 39–40.

express various forms of the 'principle of transposition', that from any implication we may infer another in which the antecedent and consequent of the first are transposed and their 'signs' reversed, so to speak, i.e. α replaced by $N\alpha$ or $N\alpha$ by α. It should be noted that for this type of inference to be valid, we must perform *both* the transposition of the members *and* the reversal of their signs, neither *CCpqCqp* nor *CCpqCNpNq* (in which one of the changes only is made) being laws of the propositional calculus.

If John comes to the party I shall be miserable

does not entail

If I am miserable John will have come to the party,

nor does it entail

If John does not come to the party I shall not be miserable,

though it does entail (and is entailed by)

If I am not miserable John will not have come to the party;

and

If I am miserable John will have come to the party

and

If John does not come to the party I will not be miserable

do entail one another. (Letting p = 'John will come to the party' and q = 'I will be miserable', the student might well, as an exercise, consider which of the four Russellian theses would express each of these entailments.)

§ 2. *Single-axiom Systems and Systems without Axioms*

Since PM appeared, a number of writers have shown that more economical foundations for the propositional calculus are possible. Hilbert and Ackermann, for example, have shown that the fourth of Russell and Whitehead's axioms (*CApAqrAqApr*) is in fact provable from the rest, and Łukasiewicz, that the number of axioms may be further reduced if, instead of taking *A* and *N* as undefined and introducing *C* by definition, we follow the earlier procedure of Frege and take *C* and *N* as undefined, introducing *A* as an abbreviation for *CN*. Frege's own '*C–N*' system, indeed, had six axioms—*CpCqp*, *CCpCqrCCpqCpr*, *CCpCqrCqCpr*, *CCpqCNqNp*, *CNNpp*, and *CpNNp*. But Łukasiewicz has shown that the three axioms *CCpqCCqrCpr*, *CCNppp*, and *CpCNpq* will suffice. But even before these abridgements were suggested, a still more striking economy was shown to be possible by Jean Nicod in 1918.

Nicod made use of Sheffer's demonstration that all truth-operators are definable in terms of 'Not-both' (considered, of course, not as a combination of 'Not' and 'Both' but as a single operator). What Nicod further showed was that, using this operator, all the axioms of PM are derivable from a single one which, using Łukasiewicz's '*D*' for 'Not-both', we may express by the formula

$$D(DpDqr)D(DtDtt)(DDsqDDpsDps).$$

Given the definitions of *Np* as *Dpp* and of *Cpq* as *DpNq*, i.e. as *DpDqq*, we may abbreviate this axiom to

$$D(DpDqr)D(Ctt)(CDsqDps).$$

And given the further definition of *K* as *ND*, and the fact (provable from the axiom) that *Dqp* is equivalent to *CpNq*, we may see that this is equivalent to

$$C(CpNDqr)ND(Ctt)(CCsNqCpNs)$$

and so to $$C(CpKqr)K(Ctt)(CCsNqCpNs),$$

i.e. to 'If *p* implies both *q* and *r*, then both *t* implies *t* and if *s* implies not *q*, *p* implies not *s*.' Very little reflection is required to see that this is true; for if *p* implies both *q* and *r*, then *p* implies *q*, and this implies that if *s* implies not *q*, *p* implies not *s*; while '*t* implies *t*', being true anyway, can be added to the consequent of any implication whatever without making it false. These considerations do not, of course, constitute a formal proof of the formula; at least they cannot do so in Nicod's system, where on the contrary the laws which they presuppose are proved from it; but they will serve to make the truth of the axiom clear to the mind.

In his deductions, Nicod uses the ordinary rule of substitution, but not quite the ordinary rule of detachment. His rule of detachment is that if α is a thesis and $D\alpha D\gamma\beta$ is also a thesis, then β may be detached as a new thesis. The ordinary rule of detachment with $C\alpha\beta$ is a special case of this one, since $C\alpha\beta$ is in this system an abbreviation for $D\alpha D\beta\beta$. The validity of Nicod's wider rule will be clear if we remember that Dpq is equivalent to $CpNq$, so that $D\alpha D\gamma\beta$ is equivalent to $C\alpha ND\gamma\beta$, i.e. $C\alpha K\gamma\beta$ (if α, then both γ and β) from which, given α, β can certainly be inferred. The details of his proofs are given in Jørgensen's *Treatise of Formal Logic*,[1] an important correction to the first part of Jørgensen's exposition being made by Quine in *Mind*, 1932.[2] Nicod's first step is to prove $DtDtt$, i.e. the law of identity Ctt. In the representation of the proof which follows (adapted from Quine), the following abbreviations will save space:

'π' for '$DtDtt$'
'ρ' for '$DDstDDtsDts$'
'α' for '$DD\rho\pi\pi$'
'β' for '$D(Dst)D(DD\rho\pi s)(DD\rho\pi s)$'
'τ' for '$D\pi D\pi\rho$'.

This is the proof:

1. $D(DpDqr)D(DtDtt)(DDsqDDpsDps)$
 $1\ p/\pi,\ q/\pi,\ r/\rho = D1\ p/t,\ q/t,\ r/t—D(\pi)—2$
2. $DDs\pi DD\pi sD\pi s$
 $1\ p/Ds\pi,\ q/D\pi s,\ r/D\pi s,\ s/u = D2—D(\pi)—3$
3. $D(DuD\pi s)D(DDs\pi u)(DDs\pi u)$
 $3\ u/\alpha,\ s/\beta = D1\ p/D\rho\pi,\ q/t,\ r/Dtt—D(4)—4$
4. $DD\beta\pi\alpha$
 $1\ p/\tau,\ q/\alpha,\ r/\alpha,\ s/D\beta\pi = D3\ u/\pi,\ s/\rho—D(\pi)—D4—D(D\tau D\beta\pi)—D1\ p/t,\ q/t,\ r/t—D(\beta)—5$
5. π (i.e. $DtDtt$).

The following are among the simpler deductions of PM axioms from what we now have (we shall at this stage put down our definitions formally):

Df. 1. $Np = Dpp$
Df. 2. $Cpq = DpNq = DpDqq$
Df. 3. $Apq = DNpNq = DDppDqq$
 $1\ p/t,\ q/t,\ r/t = D5—D(5)—6$

[1] Vol. ii, pp. 150 ff.
[2] pp. 345 ff.

6. *DDstDDtsDts*

   6 *s*/*Np*, *t*/*DNpNp* = *D*5 *t*/*Np*—*D*(7)—7

7. *DDNpNpNp*

   7 × Dff. 2, 3 = 8

8. *CAppp* (PM 1.2)

   6 *s*/*Np*, *t*/*Nq* × Dff. 2, 3 = 9

9. *CApqAqp* (PM 1.4).

The above definition of *C*, it should be noted, is not identical with the PM one, since in Nicod's system *ANpq* = *DNNpNq* = *DDDppDppDqq*. However, the equivalence of *DpDqq* to this can be proved in Nicod's system as a theorem.

Other workers, particularly in Poland, have improved upon this result in various ways. Nicod's axiom was shown by one Polish worker, Wajsberg, to be deducible from

D(*DpDqr*)*D*(*DDsrDDpsDps*)(*DpDpq*),

and Łukasiewicz proved this equivalent to

D(*DpDqr*)*D*(*DpDrp*)(*DDsqDDpsDps*).

These axioms have fewer variables than Nicod's, though they are of the same length (23 letters).[1] It will be found that the few derivations given above follow from Łukasiewicz's axiom in exactly the same way as they do from Nicod's. Single axioms have also been found for *C*–*N* and *A*–*N* systems, such as the following 21-letter one for the former

CCCCCpqCNrNsrtCCtpCsp

and the following for the latter

CCCpqArAstCCspArAtp,

or writing it out in full ('*C*' being in this system an abbreviation for '*AN*')

ANANANpqArAstANANspArAtp

(24 letters).[2] Although these systems have two undefined constants instead of Nicod's one, it is not necessary in them

[1] See Z. Jordan, *The Development of Mathematical Logic and of Logical Positivism in Poland between the Two Wars* (1945), Note 10 *b*.

[2] C. A. Meredith, *Journal of Computing Systems*, July, 1953, Paper 10.

to use Nicod's strengthened rule of detachment, the ordinary one being sufficient.

Only one further diminution in the number of axioms is possible, and there are some systems which achieve it, though only by a complication of the other side of their basis, the inferential rules. To show how it is possible to have a system of propositional calculus without any axioms at all, we may begin by observing that although to any thesis of the form $C\alpha\beta$ there corresponds a rule 'From a proposition of the form α we may infer the corresponding proposition of the form β', there may be rules used in the development of deductive systems which have no implicative thesis corresponding to them. For example, from any thesis $Cp\alpha$, where the variable p does not occur in the consequent α, we may infer the thesis $CNp\alpha$. For we may infer it by performing in $Cp\alpha$ the substitution p/Np. (This will not alter α if p does not occur in α.) But we have no such thesis in the propositional calculus as *CCpqCNpq* (this is false for $p = 0$ and $q = 0$, for $CC00CN00 = C1C10 = C10 = 0$).[1] Cases like this arise, of course, because in developing deductive systems we can use rules (like the rule of substitution) which only apply when the premisses are theses. The rules which correspond to implicative theses, on the other hand, may be used not only for deriving one logical thesis from another but also for passing from one proposition to another when neither has the form of a logical thesis at all. For example, the rule that from any proposition we may infer any alternation in which that proposition occurs—i.e. the rule corresponding to *CpApq*—enables us not only to infer, say, *ACppq* from *Cpp* but also to infer 'Either Socrates is dead or Plato is dead' from 'Socrates is dead.'[2] It may be noted that the rule of detachment, unlike the rule of substitution, is capable of this extended use. We may use it not only to infer, say, *C*(*CAppp*)(*Cpp*) when given *C*(*CpApp*)*C*(*CAppp*)(*Cpp*) and *CpApp*, or *Cpp* when given *C*(*CAppp*)(*Cpp*) and *CAppp* but also to infer, say, 'I planted beans here' when given 'If I did not plant peas here I planted beans'

[1] For another example see Łukasiewicz, *Aristotle's Syllogistic*, pp. 108, 110.

[2] The direct study of 'rules of inference' in this wider sense (the traditional subject-matter of logic), instead of approaching them via the tautologous forms of a calculus, was given particular attention in the 1930's by G. Gentzen and S. Jaśkowski. (See W. V. Quine's *Methods of Logic* (1950), §§ 27 ff. Also R. Feys, *Revue Philosophique de Louvain*, 1946, pp. 370 ff. and 1947, pp. 60 ff.)

and 'I did not plant peas here'. Another such rule involving two premisses is the rule of adjunction, 'Given any proposition *p*, and given also any proposition *q*, we may infer the conjunctive proposition *Kpq*'.

Suppose we start with a set of rules of this kind, in which neither the premiss (or no one of the premisses) nor the conclusion need have the form of a logical thesis, the inference being possible because of some definite logical relation between what is inferred and what it is inferred from (e.g. because of the conclusion's being an alternation with the premiss as an alternant). We may then find (if the rules are suitably chosen) that propositions which do have the form of some logical thesis are deducible by these rules from any proposition whatever. For example, we might start with the three rules which we may write as

(1) $p \rightarrow AKpqKpNq$
(2) $AKpqKpr \rightarrow KpAqr$
(3) $Kpq \rightarrow q$.

By (1) we can pass from, say, 'Socrates is dead' to 'Either Socrates and Plato are both dead, or Socrates is dead and Plato is not'. By (2) we can pass from, say, 'Either Socrates and Plato are both dead, or Socrates is dead and Plato is not' to 'Socrates is dead, and either Plato is dead or he is not'. By (3) we can pass from 'Socrates is dead, and either Plato is dead or he is not' to 'Either Plato is dead or he is not'. So by using these three rules in succession we may pass from 'Socrates is dead' to 'Either Plato is dead or he is not'. That is, using these three rules, we may pass from any proposition at all, say *p*, to any alternation of any proposition with its contradictory, say *AqNq*. Suppose now we call a proposition 'demonstrable' if our rules would thus enable us to derive it from any proposition whatever.[1] A system without any axioms at all will be as strong as, say, the system of PM if we can show that in it (1) all the axioms of PM are 'demonstrable' (derivable by the rules from any proposition

[1] That such 'demonstrability' is equivalent to deducibility without any premisses may be shown by putting 0 for *n* in the rule that a proposition follows from a set of *n* premisses if and only if, when we add another premiss, it will follow from the resulting set of $n+1$ premisses no matter what the added premiss may be. The properties of 'following from a set of 0 premisses' were studied in the 'formalized metalogic' of Tarski. (See Z. Jordan, *Polish Science and Learning, No. 6*, p. 19.)

at all), and (2) the rules of substitution and detachment are applicable to all 'demonstrable' propositions. It would equally do, of course, to show the 'demonstrability' of any axiom or set of axioms from which those of PM are derivable.

In 1948 R. Suszko showed that, given seven rules of inference (none of them already asserting that some tautologous form follows from any proposition at all), any proposition of any of the forms *CCpqCCqrCpr*, *CCNppp*, and *CpCNpq*, i.e. any proposition of the form of one of Łukasiewicz's three *C–N* axioms, is derivable from any proposition whatever.[1] We may illustrate the procedure by a short proof of demonstrability (though not of one of the Łukasiewicz axioms) using four of Suszko's rules, namely

(1) $q \to Cpq$
(2) $Cpq \to CCrpCCqsCrs$
(3) $CpCqr \to CCpqCpr$
(4) $CCpqr \to CNpr$.[2]

By successively applying rules (1) and (2), it is plain that we may pass from any proposition *q* to a proposition of the form *CCrpCCqsCrs*, where *q* is the proposition from which we start, and *p*, *r*, and *s* are any propositions at all. That is,

By (1) and (2), $q \to CCrpCCqsCrs$.

Now *CCrpCCqsCrs* is a proposition of the form *CpCqr*, so by (3) we may derive from it the corresponding proposition of the form *CCpqCpr*, which is *C*(*CCrpCqs*)(*CCrpCrs*). That is,

By (3), $CCrpCCqsCrs \to CCCrpCqsCCrpCrs$.

But *CC*(*Crp*)(*Cqs*)(*CCrpCrs*) is a proposition of the form *CCpqr*, so by (4) we may derive from it the corresponding proposition of the form *CNpr*, which is *CNCrpCCrpCrs*. That is,

By (4), $CCCrpCqsCCrpCrs \to CNCrpCCrpCrs$.

So by the successive application of (1), (2), (3), and (4) we may pass from any proposition *q* to any proposition at all of the form *CNCrpCCrpCrs*. For *p*, *r*, and *s* here may be any propositions at all, and *q*—which would, of course, if present, have had to be

[1] Suszko's paper is briefly reviewed by A. Mostowski in the *Journal of Symbolic Logic*, vol. xv (1950), p. 66.

[2] In a system like PM's, the implicative thesis corresponding to this would be proved from *CNpCpq* and *CCpqCCqrCpr* by substitution (*p*/*Np*, *q*/*Cpq* in the longer formula) and detachment.

the proposition with which we began—does not occur in this formula. (If we wish to verify independently that *CNCrpCCrpCrs* is a thesis of the propositional calculus, we may either work out its possible truth-values or observe that it follows by the substitution *p*/*Crp*, *q*/*Crs* from the more familiar thesis *CNpCpq*.)

Axiomless systems which are more familiar to logicians in English-speaking countries are the earlier and more complicated ones due to K. R. Popper.[1] Popper divides the rules from which he starts into (*a*) 'general' ones which contain no reference to the logical forms of the propositions involved, e.g.

$$p \rightarrow p$$
$$\text{If } p \rightarrow r, \text{ then } p, q \rightarrow r$$

(where '$p, q \rightarrow r$' means '*r* may be inferred when we are given *p* and are also given *q*'), and (*b*) 'special' ones referring to propositions of specific logical forms (conjunctions, etc.), e.g.

$$Kpq \rightarrow p$$
$$Kpq \rightarrow q$$
$$p, q \rightarrow Kpq.$$

He makes it his aim to have the smallest possible number of underived rules of type (*a*), and derives his rules of type (*b*) from what he calls 'inferential definitions' of the truth-operators involved, e.g. 'To say that *Kpq* is deducible from *r* and vice versa, is to say that *p* is deducible from *r*, *q* is deducible from *r*, and *r* is deducible when we are given *p* and are also given *q*'.[2]

§ 3. *Normal Forms and the Proof of Completeness*

Are there any tautologous formulae in the logic of truth-functions which cannot be proved from Russell and Whitehead's five axioms by means of substitution and detachment (together with abbreviative definition)? If there are none, a similar 'completeness' may naturally be claimed for any alternative set of axioms from which, and rules by means of which, the *Principia* basis is itself deducible. But how do we set about establishing such 'completeness' for a set of axioms and rules?

[1] See, in particular, his paper 'New Foundations for Logic' in *Mind*, 1947. Our use above of the term 'demonstrable' is taken over from Popper.

[2] Cf. Peirce, *Collected Papers*, 3.199.

We shall sketch one method of doing so, that of Hilbert and Ackermann,[1] in the present section, and in the next chapter will consider others, for forms of the propositional calculus which we have not yet encountered.

Hilbert and Ackermann's method rests on the fact that any formula of the propositional calculus is equivalent to one of a certain standard or 'normal' form, formulae in such a form being capable of proof or disproof by a standard method. There are in fact a number of 'normal forms' which could be used for this purpose. For example, there is what von Wright[2] calls the 'perfect disjunctive normal form', which is rather like an alternation of the truth-value combinations of its elements for which the given formula is true, '$p = 1$' being replaced by 'p' and '$p = 0$' by 'Np'. Thus $CpCpq$ is true when $p = 1$ and $q = 1$, when $p = 0$ and $q = 1$, and when $p = 0$ and $q = 0$, and otherwise false; so is equivalent to 'Either both p and q, or both not p and q, or both not p and not q', i.e. $AA(Kpq)(KNpq)(KNpNq)$. A formula of this sort is tautologous if and only if it contains alternants corresponding to all possible truth-value combinations—two if it has one variable, four if it has two, eight if it has three, and so on. The normal forms used in Hilbert and Ackermann's completeness proof are a little different. They are not alternations of conjunctions, but, in a rather broad sense, conjunctions of alternations. What they show is that any formula of the propositional calculus is equivalent either (i) to a single propositional variable or the negation of one, or (ii) to an alternation of which all the members are either propositional variables or their negations, or alternations (or alternations of alternations, etc.) of such, or (iii) to a conjunction of which all the members are of the forms listed under (i) and (ii), or conjunctions (or conjunctions of conjunctions, etc.) of such. We may describe all these forms as 'conjunctions of alternations of propositional-variables-or-their-negations', if (*a*) we call a form like '$KKpqr$' a 'conjunction of p, q, and r' instead of calling it a 'conjunction of the-conjunction-of-p-and-q and r', and similarly with alternations, and (*b*) we regard a single propositional variable (or negation of one) as an alternation with a single alternant (it is as it were a limiting

[1] Set out in their *Principles of Mathematical Logic*, Ch. i, §§ 1–4, 10 and 11.

[2] For example, in *Form and Content in Logic* (1944), p. 34, and in *An Essay in Modal Logic* (1951), pp. 12 ff.

case of alternation; in any case such a variable is equivalent to the alternation of itself with itself—*EpApp*), and (*c*) we also regard a single propositional variable (or negation of one) as a conjunction with a single conjunct, and a single alternation as a conjunction-of-alternations with a single conjunct. The forms which would be 'conjunctions of alternations of propositional variables or their negations' would include such examples as

(i) *p* and *Np* (conjunctions-with-one-member of alternations-with-one-member).

(ii) *ApNq* (a conjunction-with-one-member of an alternation with two members).

(iii) *AApNqNp* (a conjunction-with-one-member of an alternation with three members).

(iv) *KpApq* (a conjunction of an alternation-with-one-member and an alternation with two members).

(v) *KApqApNq* (a conjunction of two alternations-with-two-members).

(vi) *KApAqrKApqApAst* (a conjunction-with-three-members of an alternation-with-three-members, an alternation-with-two-members, and another alternation-with-three-members.

That every truth-functional formula can be 'put into normal form', i.e. shown to be equivalent to (i.e. to imply and be implied by) a formula of the above sort, can be shown if it can be shown that we can always eliminate from a formula, without altering its logical force, (1) operators other than *A*, *N*, and *K* (e.g. *C* or *E*), (2) negations of negations, alternations, and conjunctions, and (3) alternations of conjunctions (i.e. of conjunctions other than 'one-membered' quasi-conjunctions). (1) is easily settled, in an '*A*–*N*' system such as that of PM, by replacing formulae containing symbols other than *A*, *N*, and *K* by the formulae to which they are equivalent by definition. (2) requires, for negations of negations, the laws of double negation, *CNNpp* and *CpNNp*, and for negations of alternations and conjunctions, de Morgan's laws (by means of which we can transform any negation of a conjunction into an alternation of negations, and any negation of an alternation into a conjunction of negations). (3) requires the pair of implications

C(*ApKqr*)(*KApqApr*) and *C*(*KApqApr*)(*ApKqr*). These jointly equate 'Either *p* or both *q* and *r*' with 'Both either *p* or *q* and either *p* or *r*'. (It is plain that 'Either *p* or both-*q*-and-*r*' implies both 'Either *p* or *q*' and 'Either *p* or *r*', and so implies 'Both either *p* or *q* and either *p* or *r*'; and the converse implication will be seen to be true if we restate 'Either *p* or *q*' as 'If not *p* then *q*'—'Both if not *p* then *q* and if not *p* then *r*' implies 'If not *p* then both *q* and *r*'.)

This set of laws, however, is not by itself sufficient to show that all propositional formulae can be put into normal form. Certainly if we have a formula of the form $NN\alpha$, the law *CNNpp* will enable us, by performing the substitution p/α and then detaching the consequent, to replace this by α, and *CpNNp* will show that we can equally perform the converse replacement, i.e. that our formulae $NN\alpha$ and α are strictly equivalent (or have the same logical force, so that anything deducible from either is deducible from the other). But suppose that the formula before us is not itself of the form $NN\alpha$, i.e. is not preceded by a double negation, but has a double negation somewhere within it. Simple substitution in *CNNpp* and *CpNNp* will not then enable us to establish the equivalence we require. Similarly, if a formula is itself of the form $NA\alpha\beta$, substitution in de Morgan's laws *C*(*NApq*)(*KNpNq*) and *C*(*KNpNq*)(*NApq*) will enable us to equate it with $KN\alpha N\beta$. But this will not help us with a negation-of-an-alternation occurring *within* a formula.

What we really require is a new rule of inference, namely that if any pair of formulae are mutually deducible, i.e. if we have both $C\alpha\beta$ and $C\beta\alpha$, then either may be substituted for the other in any formula in which it occurs. (This would enable us, given *CNNpp* and *CpNNp*, to equate *CApqANNqp*, for example, with *CApqAqp*.) Can we justify substitution of this sort without simply laying down its permissibility at the outset as a *datum*? Hilbert and Ackermann justify it, for *A*–*N* systems, by the following considerations: In such systems, all formulae from which defined symbols have been eliminated by means of their definitions are constructed by negation and alternation. Now (i) given the law of transposition *C*(*Cpq*)(*CNqNp*), it can easily be shown that if any two formulae are equivalent, their negations are equivalent. For if we have $C\alpha\beta$ and $C\beta\alpha$ we can derive $CN\alpha N\beta$ and $CN\beta N\alpha$—$CN\beta N\alpha$ from $C\alpha\beta$ and $CN\alpha N\beta$

from $C\beta\alpha$, both by substitution in $C(Cpq)(CNqNp)$ and subsequent detachment. Also, (ii) given the law $C(Cpq)(CArpArq)$, it can be shown that if any two formulae are equivalent the alternation of any formula with the first is equivalent to the alternation of the same formula with the second. For if we have $C\alpha\beta$ and $C\beta\alpha$ we can use this law to infer $CA\gamma\alpha A\gamma\beta$ and $CA\gamma\beta A\gamma\alpha$. And (iii) from these we can infer $CA\alpha\gamma A\beta\gamma$ and $CA\beta\gamma A\alpha\gamma$ if we have the law $C(Apq)(Aqp)$ and the principle of syllogism. So we can prove the equivalence of, let us say, $A(Apq)(NANNqp)$ with $A(Apq)(NAqp)$, (i.e. we can prove the legitimacy of erasing the double N *within* this formula) by arguing as follows: Since q and NNq are deductively equivalent (i.e. mutually deducible), Apq and $ApNNq$ are equivalent also, by (ii) above; and hence, by (iii), Aqp and $ANNqp$ are too. And since these are equivalent, $NAqp$ and $NANNqp$ are equivalent, by (i). And since $NAqp$ and $NANNqp$ are equivalent, so, by (ii), are $A(Apq)(NAqp)$ and $A(Apq)(NANNqp)$. We simply start with the symbols immediately adjacent to those on which we wish to perform the 'substitution of equivalents', and work outwards, using the new equivalences arrived at by the earlier steps, until we have equated the entire formulae. If we wished to set out our procedure as a formal deduction, it would appear thus:

1. $CNNpp$
2. $CpNNp$
3. $CCpqCNqNp$
4. $CCpqCArpArq$
5. $CApqAqp$
6. $CCqrCCpqCpr$

   4 $p/NNq,\ r/p = C1\ p/q$—7

7. $CApNNqApq$

   4 $p/q,\ q/NNq,\ r/p = C2\ p/q$—8

8. $CApqApNNq$

   6 $p/ApNNq,\ q/Apq,\ r/Aqp = C5$—$C7$—9

9. $CApNNqAqp$

   6 $p/ANNqp,\ q/ApNNq,\ r/Aqp = C9$—$C5\ p/NNq,\ q/p$—10

10. $CANNqpAqp$

   6 $p/Aqp,\ q/Apq,\ r/ApNNq = C8$—$C5\ p/q,\ q/p$—11

11. *CAqpApNNq*
   6 *p/Aqp, q/ApNNq, r/ANNqp* = *C*5 *q/NNq*—*C*11—12
12. *CAqpANNqp*
   3 *p/ANNqp, q/Aqp* = *C*10—13
13. *CNAqpNANNqp*
   3 *p/Aqp, q/ANNqp* = *C*12—14
14. *CNANNqpNAqp*
   4 *p/NAqp, q/NANNqp, r/Apq* = *C*13—15
15. *C(AApqNAqp)(AApqNANNqp)*
   4 *p/NANNqp, q/NAqp, r/Apq* = *C*14—16
16. *C(AApqNANNqp)(AApqNAqp)*.

Here 15 and 16 jointly express the equivalence of *AApqNANNqp* and *AApqNAqp*, which is thus proved from the equivalence of *NNq* and *q* by substitution and detachment, without employing any special rule of substitutability of equivalents. We may proceed similarly in other cases.

We can now list the theses we need in order to deduce from any formula of an *A–N* system an equivalent formula in normal form, and also to perform the reverse deduction. (Actually, as we shall see shortly, the latter process is more important than the former, when a proof of completeness is in question.) For eliminating (or, in the reverse procedure, inserting) negations of negations, alternations, and conjunctions, we need

(1) *CNNpp*
(2) *CpNNp*
(3) *C(NApq)(KNpNq)*
(4) *C(KNpNq)(NApq)*
(5) *C(NKpq)(ANpNq)*
(6) *C(ANpNq)(NKpq)*.

For eliminating (or inserting) alternations of conjunctions, we need

(7) *C(ApKqr)(KApqApr)*
(8) *C(KApqApr)(ApKqr)*.

And for the substitution of equivalents, we need

(9) $C(Cpq)(CNqNp)$
(10) $C(Cpq)(CArpArq)$
(11) $C(Apq)(Aqp)$
(12) $CCqrCCpqCpr$.

Take, for example, the formula $A(Apq)(NANNqp)$. By double negation we may equate this with $A(Apq)(NAqp)$, i.e. we may infer either of these formulae from the other. (The establishment of their mutual implication as a pair of theses from (1), (2), and (9)–(12) has been set out in the last paragraph.) $A(Apq)(NAqp)$ may be equated in turn, using (3), (4), and (10), with $A(Apq)(KNqNp)$. Formally, the proof of the former from the latter would work out as

1. $CKNpNqNApq$
2. $CCpqCArpArq$
3. $AApqKNqNp$
   $2\ p/KNqNp,\ q/NAqp,\ r/Apq = C1\ p/q,\ q/p\text{—}C3\text{—}4$
4. $AApqNAqp$,

the proof of 3 from 4 making a similar use of $C(NApq)(KNpNq)$. $A(Apq)(KNqNp)$ is an alternation of Apq with a conjunction. This may be equated by means of (7) and (8) with the conjunction of alternations

$$K(AApqNq)(AApqNp).$$

And this is in normal form.

When a formula is in this conjunctive normal form, whether it is tautologous or not can be decided very simply. If each of its component alternations contains a propositional variable together with its negation, the formula is tautologous; if any of its component alternations does not contain a propositional variable together with its negation, it is not. For example, in the formula just above, the component $AApqNq$ contains both q and Nq, and the component $AApqNp$ contains both p and Np, and there are no other conjuncts; the formula is therefore tautologous. The reason for this is as follows: Taking $AApqNq$ first, this is equivalent to $ApAqNq$, for quite generally 'Either

either-*p*-or-*q* or *r*' is equivalent to 'Either *p* or either-*q*-or-*r*' (*CAApqrApAqr* and *CApAqrAApqr*). Now *AqNq* is quite obviously tautologous (by the Law of Excluded Middle), and since the component *AqNq* in *ApAqNq* is true no matter what *q* may be, *ApAqNq* will have at least one true component no matter what the other component *p* may be, and so will be a true alternation no matter what *p* and *q* may be. This reasoning can be turned into a formal proof from *CqApq* and *ApNp* thus:

1. *CqApq*
2. *ApNp*

   1 *q*/*AqNq* = *C*2 *p*/*q*—3

3. *ApAqNq*.

Turning now to the conjunct *AApqNp*, this may be equated, again by *C*(*AApqr*)(*ApAqr*) and its converse, with *ApAqNp*. And this in turn may be equated, by *C*(*ApAqr*)(*AqApr*), with *AqApNp*, which is tautologous for the same reason as the other. (Sometimes this shuffling will give us *ANpp* rather than *ApNp* as a component, but this is just as plainly tautologous.) Turning finally to the whole formula, since a conjunction is true if all its components are, a conjunctive propositional form will be true in all possible exemplifications if all its components are true in all possible exemplifications, i.e. a conjunction of tautologies is a tautology. In the given case, this reasoning can be turned into a formal proof if we have the theses *CpCqKpq* (If *p* then if *q*, both *p* and *q*), thus:

1. *CpCqKpq*
2. *AApqNq*
3. *AApqNp*

   1 *p*/*AApqNq*, *q*/*AApqNp* = *C*2—*C*3—4

4. *KAApqNqAApqNp*.

If our conjunction has the form $K\alpha K\beta\gamma$, we would prove $K\beta\gamma$ from β and γ as above, and then $K\alpha K\beta\gamma$ from α and $K\beta\gamma$ similarly. Where it has the form $KK\alpha\beta\gamma$, we would equate this with $K\alpha K\beta\gamma$ by means of the theses *C*(*KKpqr*)(*KpKqr*) and *C*(*KpKqr*)(*KKpqr*), and then proceed as before. For proving theses which are in normal form and with components of the type indicated, we thus need the following laws:

(13) *ApNp*
(14) *ANpp*
(15) *CqApq*; or *CpApq*, with (11)
(16) *C(AApqr)(ApAqr)*
(17) *C(ApAqr)(AApqr)*
(18) *C(ApAqr)(AqApr)*
(19) *CpCqKpq*
(20) *C(KKpqr)(KpKqr)*
(21) *C(KpKqr)(KKpqr)*.

It remains to be shown that the *only* formulae in normal form which are tautologous are those in which all the conjuncts are alternations containing a propositional variable together with its negation. Any conjunct (of a formula in normal form) which is not of this kind will either be a simple variable such as *p*, to which in some possible cases the value 0 will be assigned, or a negation of one, which will be false when $p = 1$, or an alternation which will be false in the case in which all the non-negated variables have the value 0 and all the negated ones the value 1 (so that their negations, and so all the alternants, have the value 0). Only the presence of a variable together with its negation could prevent the latter case arising (for we must give the same variable the same value throughout a formula—we cannot substitute 0 for *p* where it is not negated and 1 where it is). Hence any conjunctive form with such a component will have exemplifications in which this component is false, and so the whole conjunction false.

We can therefore now say that, in an *A–N* system, if from our axioms, and by our rules, we can deduce theses (13)–(21) above, we can prove any tautologous formula which is in normal form. And if we can also deduce (1)–(12), we can by their means deduce any tautologous formula whatever from its 'normal' equivalent. The axioms and rules of PM, for example, are 'complete' if they suffice to establish (1)–(21), and in fact they do. Three items from (1)–(21), namely (10), (11), and (15), are indeed among the axioms themselves. Hilbert and

Ackermann give the proofs of those items in (1)–(21) which they do not already assume as axioms, from the four axioms *CAppp*, *CpApq*, *CApqAqp*, and *CCpqCArpArq*.[1] These are all theses of PM, and conversely the only axioms of PM which are not also axioms of Hilbert and Ackermann (*CqApq* and *CApAqrAqApr*) are among their theorems.

It is also shown by Hilbert and Ackermann that their axioms are 'complete' in a stronger sense, sufficing not only to prove all tautologous formulae in the propositional calculus, but also to disprove all non-tautologous ones, by showing that if we treat them as theses the result is an absurd one. More precisely, what is shown is that if any non-tautologous formula is combined with the axioms as if it were a thesis, we may deduce as a thesis the simple variable '*p*', from which any formula at all, including the negations of the axioms, could be obtained as a thesis by substitution. For by means of the axioms and rules we may deduce from any formula at all an equivalent formula in normal form, and if the given formula is not tautologous this equivalent formula will be either (i) itself a simple variable, or (ii) the negation of one, say *Np*, in which case the substitution *p*/*Np* will give us *NNp*, from which *p* will follow by *CNNpp*, or (iii) an alternation in which we may substitute *p* for all non-negated variables and *Np* for all negated ones, the whole then becoming by the law of double negation an alternation of *p*'s, from which the simple *p* will follow by *CAppp*, or (iv) a conjunction containing forms of the preceding kinds, which forms may be deduced from the whole by the laws *CKpqp* and *CKpqq*, which are deducible from the axioms.

For *C–N* systems an analogous method has been devised by Łukasiewicz.[2] In his proof of 'strong' completeness, instead of showing that from the axioms and any non-tautologous formula we could prove as a thesis the simple variable *p*, Łukasiewicz shows that if the simple variable *p* is axiomatically rejected as a thesis, the axioms will lead to the consequent rejection of any non-tautologous formula. To indicate the rejection of a formula as a thesis, he places an asterisk before its number, and for deriving one rejection from another he uses the two

[1] A representation of the first several of Hilbert and Ackermann's proofs in the Polish symbolism is given in Bocheński's *Précis de logique mathématique*, § 8.

[2] *Aristotle's Syllogistic*, pp. 106–18.

rules (*a*) if a formula *F* could be derived by substitution from a formula *G*, and *F* is not a thesis, then *G* is not a thesis, and (*b*) if $C\alpha\beta$ is a thesis, but β is not one, then neither is α. The following will sufficiently illustrate his procedure:

1. *CCNppp*

*2. *p*

1 = *C**3—*2

*3. *CNpp*

*3 = *4 *q*/*Np*

*4. *Cqp*.

Here 1 is one of the three formulae axiomatically affirmed as theses in Łukasiewicz's *C–N* system, and *2 is the one formula axiomatically rejected as a thesis.

III

Systems with Propositional Constants and Functorial Variables

§ 1. *The Implicational Calculus, and Wajsberg's System in* C *and* o

IF we are to build up a propositional calculus with a single undefined operator, it seems a pity that it should be such an out-of-the-way one as 'Neither' or 'Not-both', and Peirce[1] gave expression in the nineteenth century to the feeling, shared since by many logicians, that the ideal would be to develop everything else, if that were possible, in terms of *implication*. To the question 'Why should the logician, whose primary interest is in inference, study other tautologous formulae beside those which are implications?', it would be very satisfying to be able to answer that all tautologous formulae in fact *are* either implications or definitional abbreviations for them. We shall consider in this chapter a group of systems which realize this ideal of Peirce's more fully than any we have so far discussed, and which also have other features of uncommon interest.

We may note, to begin with, that there is a large segment of the propositional calculus which requires for its formulation, beside propositional variables, only the operator *C*. Obvious examples of tautologous forms within this field are the principles of syllogism *CCpqCCqrCpr* and *CCqrCCpqCpr*, and the law of commutation *CCpCqrCqCpr* by which either of these may be proved from the other. Then we have the law of identity *Cpp* and the paradoxical law *CpCqp* ('a true proposition is implied by any proposition at all'). We have also the law *CpCCpqq*, 'If *p*, then if *p* implies *q*, then *q*', expressing the principle that from the antecedent of a true implication we may infer its consequent. The inferential form '*p*, and if *p* then *q*, therefore *q*', was studied by the Stoics, and is sometimes described as an inference in the *modus ponens* or 'affirming mood'. Contrasted with it is the 'denying mood' or *modus tollens*, 'Not *q*, but if *p* then *q*, therefore not *p*', by which from the denial of the con-

[1] See especially his *Collected Papers*, 3.182–97, also 2.356.

sequent of an implication we infer the denial of its antecedent. The principle of this would be *CNqCCpqNp*; this is not, of course, one of the formulae expressible solely by means of *C* and propositional variables. We can, however, express in this way all formulae involving only *C* and *A*, for instead of defining *A* as *CN*, we could define *Apq* as *CCpqq*. This gives the required table—*CC*111 = *C*11 = 1; *CC*100 = *C*00 = 1; *CC*011 = *C*11 = 1; and *CC*000 = *C*10 = 0. And we can see that 'If *p* implies *q*, then *q*', has the force of 'Either *p* or *q*' by reflecting that the only ways in which '*p* implies *q*' could imply *q* would be (*a*) by *p* being true (in which case *q* would follow by the *modus ponens*) and (*b*) by *q* being true (in which case the whole implication would have a true consequent and so be true). Using this definition, we could regard the thesis *CApqAqp* as an abbreviation for the purely implicational thesis *C*(*CCpqq*)(*CCqpp*), and similarly with other theses involving *C* and *A* alone. *CpApq*, we may note, becomes when thus conceived a symbolic abbreviation of the principle of the *modus ponens*, *CpCCpqq*.

It was shown in the 1920's by Tarski and Bernays that all tautologous formulae in this restricted field are provable from the three axioms *CCpqCCqrCpr*, *CCCpqpp*, and *CpCqp*. The second of these laws,

If *p*'s implying *q* implies *p*, then *p*'

was known to Peirce.[1] Its truth is not evident at a glance, but we might look at it this way: It means

If *p* does not imply *q* without being true, then it *is* true.

That is, it means

Either *p* implies *q* without being true, or it is true.

If *p* is true, the second of these alternatives holds. And if *p* is false, then it does imply *q* (for *Coq* = 1, whatever *q* may be) and of course does so without being true, so in this case the first alternative holds. Like the PM axioms for the larger calculus, these three of Tarski and Bernays have since been reduced to one, and that in a number of ways. Łukasiewicz has shown that a single axiom for the 'implicational calculus' must contain at

[1] *Collected Papers*, 3.384.

least 13 letters, and has himself deduced the Tarski–Bernays axioms from the 13-letter formula *CCCpqrCCrpCsp*,

If *p*'s implying *q* implies *r*, then if *r* implies *p*, *s* implies *p*.[1]

We may work out the truth of this informally by saying that if *p*'s implying *q* implies *r*, and *r* implies *p*, then *p*'s implying *q* implies *p* (by the principle of syllogism) and so *p* is true (by 'Peirce's law'), and so is implied by any proposition *s* (by *CpCqp*).

Given this basis for the 'implicational' calculus, we may ask what needs to be added to it in order to obtain a basis for the full calculus of propositions. It has been shown by Wajsberg that what is required is surprisingly little. We must in the first place obtain an equivalent of '*N*', and although it is not possible to define '*N*' in terms of '*C*' in a context which includes propositional variables alone, we can do if it we introduce the symbol '0' as a propositional *constant*, to stand, not indifferently for any proposition at all, but for some arbitrarily chosen proposition which must, however, be a false one. For the truth-values of *Cp*0 for the two values of *p* are precisely those of *Np*—*C*10 = 0 and *C*00 = 1. Peirce saw the possibility of defining 'not' in terms of 'if' in this way, and even found a certain colloquial justification for it. Instead of saying 'Not every man is mortal' we sometimes say 'If every man is mortal then I am very much mistaken', the consequent of this being something which the speaker cannot but regard as false; it is a kind of 'standard false proposition' like Wajsberg's '0'.[2] When '*N*' is given in this way, we can define other operators as in the *C*–*N* systems of Frege and Łukasiewicz.

If '*Np*' is thus defined as '*Cp*0', many of the characteristic formulae of the full propositional calculus are derivable from its implicational segment simply by substituting 0 for a variable. For example, performing the substitution *r*/0 in the law of syllogism *CCpqCCqrCpr*, we obtain *CCpqCCq*0*Cp*0, which the definition of '*N*' turns into the law of transposition *CCpqCNqNp*. The same substitution in the other syllogistic law *CCqrCCpqCpr* gives us the principle of the *modus tollens*, *CNqCCpqNp*; and from

[1] J. Łukasiewicz, 'The Shortest Axiom of the Implicational Calculus of Propositions', *Proceedings of the Royal Irish Academy*, 52 A 3 (1948).

[2] See Peirce's article on 'Syllogism' in the *Century Dictionary*.

the law of commutation *CCpCqrCqCpr* we similarly derive another law of transposition, *CCpNqCqNp*. The substitution *q*/0 in Peirce's law, *CCCpqpp*, gives us the *consequentia mirabilis CCNppp*; and in the principle of the *modus ponens*, *CpCCpqq*, this substitution gives us the law of double negation

CpNNp (*CpCCp*00 = *CpCNp*0 = *CpNNp*).

Most of these results were known to Peirce,[1] and it is indeed remarkable how many of the properties of negation can be immediately accounted for when it is treated as a species of implication. Not all of them, however. For example, we cannot thus derive the other part of the law of double negation, *CNNpp*. Expanded by the definition *Np* = *Cp*0, this becomes *CCCp*00*p*, but we cannot derive this simply by substitution in the formula *CCCpqqp*, as the latter formula is not a logical law. (Remembering that *Apq* = *CCpqq*, *CCCpqqp* amounts to 'If either *p* or *q* then *p*', and this is false for *p*/0 and *q*/1.) To obtain the full propositional calculus from its implicational segment, we need not only a new symbol but a new axiom, enabling us to derive those properties of negation which depend not merely on its being a kind of implication but on the peculiarities of the proposition 0 that is implied. Wajsberg discovered that the only axiom we need for this purpose is *C*0*p*. We can then derive, for example, the law *CNNpp* as follows:

Df. *N*: *Np* = *Cp*0.

1. *CCqpCCCpqqp*

2. *C*0*p*

 1 *q*/0 = *C*2—3

3. *CCCp*00*p*

 3 × Df. *N* = 4

4. *CNNpp*.

Here thesis 1 is a law of the implicational calculus which can easily be seen to hold if we restate it (by means of the definition *Apq* = *CCpqq*) as *CCqpCApqp* 'If *q* implies *p*, then if either *p* or *q* then *p*.' (For we have 'If *q* then *p*' by hypothesis, and 'If *p* then *p*' in any case.) Another law which *C*0*p* enables us to derive is

[1] See his *Collected Papers*, 3.381–4.

CpCNpq, which is obtainable thus (the first two premisses being theses of the implicational calculus):

1. *CCqrCCpqCpr*
2. *CCpCqrCqCpr*
3. *Cop*

    1 *q*/o, *r*/*q* = *C*3 *p*/*q*—4

4. *CCpoCpq*

    2 *p*/*Cp*o, *q*/*p*, *r*/*q* = *C*4—5

5. *CpCCpoq*

    5 × Df. *N* = 6

6. *CpCNpq*.

This conclusion is one of the three theses which Łukasiewicz has shown to be sufficient for the full *C–N* calculus; another, *CCNppp*, was derived in the last paragraph from one of the Tarski–Bernays axioms; and the third, *CCpqCCqrCpr*, is itself one of the Tarski–Bernays axioms. The Tarski–Bernays axioms, with *Cop*, are therefore a sufficient basis for the full calculus. Another sufficient basis would be *Cop* and Łukasiewicz's single axiom *CCCpqrCCrpCsp*; and yet another, the single 19-letter axiom

CCCCCpqCrostCCtpCrp.[1]

Beside showing the completeness of the set of axioms *CCpqCCqrCpr*, *CCCpqpp*, *CpCqp*, and *Cop* by proving from them another set which has been already shown to be complete, we might establish their completeness directly. One method of doing this, due to the contemporary American logician W. V. Quine,[2] is worth studying in some detail, as the standard forms of proof which it shows to be available for all tautologous formulae simply translate into formal deductions the informal method of verifying such formulae by truth-value calculations.

§ 2. *Quine's Completeness Proof for the Full Calculus*

This proof is an adaptation of one given by Wajsberg for the purely implicational calculus (without o and its derivatives)

[1] C. A. Meredith, *Journal of Computing Systems*, July 1953, Paper 10.

[2] W. V. Quine, 'Completeness of the Propositional Calculus', *Journal of Symbolic Logic*, vol. iii (1938), pp. 37–40. Quine uses the PM notation.

using the three Tarski–Bernays axioms.[1] Wajsberg's proof also is worth sketching, but it will be simpler to consider Quine's first, because of its more direct relation to the calculating procedures with which we are familiar.[2]

Let us suppose, to begin with, that we are proving by calculation that *CpCqCpq* is a logical law. Our calculation could be set out as follows:

$$CpCqCpq = \begin{cases} C1CqC1q = \begin{cases} C1C1C11 = C1C11 = C11 = 1 \\ C1C0C10 = C1C00 = C11 = 1 \end{cases} \\ C0CqC0q = \begin{cases} C0C1C01 = C0C11 = C01 = 1 \\ C0C0C00 = C0C01 = C01 = 1. \end{cases} \end{cases}$$

If this is to be turned into a deduction, the main steps of the deduction may be indicated by reversing it, thus:

$$\left.\begin{array}{l} \left.\begin{array}{l} 1 \to C11 \to C1C11 \to C1C1C11 \\ 1 \to C11 \to C1C00 \to C1C0C10 \end{array}\right\} \to C1CqC1q \\ \left.\begin{array}{l} 1 \to C01 \to C0C11 \to C0C1C01 \\ 1 \to C01 \to C0C01 \to C0C0C00 \end{array}\right\} \to C0CqC0q \end{array}\right\} \to CpCqCpq$$

In order to make this type of deduction possible we clearly require

(1) Some 'standard true proposition', provable from the axioms, to be symbolized by '1'. (This will be the first premiss in each proof of the standard form.)

(2) For the next few steps, the substitutability of equivalents must be established, and equivalences must be proved which correspond to the equations $C11 = 1$, $C10 = 0$, $C01 = 1$ and $C00 = 1$.

(3) For the final steps, it must be shown that if a formula holds when one of its variables is replaced by 0, and also when the same variable is replaced by 1, then it holds as it stands.

To meet requirement (1), Quine takes as his standard true proposition, to be expressed by the symbol '1' where desirable,

[1] M. Wajsberg, 'Metalogische Beiträge', *Wiadomości Matematyczne*, vol. xliii (1937); reviewed by C. H. Langford in the *Journal of Symbolic Logic*, vol. ii (1937), pp. 93–94.

[2] I shall, moreover, alter some of the less important details of both Quine's method and Wajsberg's in order to bring out more clearly their relation to such informal verifications.

the proposition *Coo*, which follows from Wajsberg's fourth axiom, *Cop*, by the substitution *p*/o. This definition automatically gives us the equivalence *Coo* = 1 required under (2). The proofs of the remaining equations for *C* from the axioms are simple enough, and could be set out as follows:

1. *CpCqp*
2. *CCCpqpp*
3. *Cop*
   1 *p*/*Coo*, *q*/*CoCoo* = *C*3 *p*/o—4
4. *C*(*CoCoo*)(*Coo*)
   1 *p*/*CoCoo*, *q*/*Coo* = *C*3 *p*/*Coo*—5.
5. *C*(*Coo*)(*CoCoo*)
   2 *p*/o, *q*/o = 6
6. *C*(*CCooo*)(o)
   3 *q*/*CCooo* = 7
7. *C*(o)(*CCooo*)
   1 *p*/*Coo*, *q*/*CCooCoo* = *C*3 *p*/o—8
8. *C*(*CCooCoo*)(*Coo*)
   1 *p*/*Coo*, *q*/*Coo* = 9
9. *C*(*Coo*)(*CCooCoo*).

Here 4 and 5 equate *C*o1 and 1, 6 and 7 equate *C*1o and o, and 8 and 9 equate *C*11 and 1.

In proving the substitutability of equivalents, Quine first shows that, where *G* is the result of substituting β for α in *F*,[1] we have both

(*a*) $C(C\alpha\beta)C(C\beta\alpha)(CFG)$

and

(*b*) $C(C\alpha\beta)C(C\beta\alpha)(CGF)$

when *F* contains no occurrences of *C*. He then shows that if (*a*) and (*b*) hold for formulae with *m* occurrences of *C* (where *m* is any number from o upwards), they will hold also for formulae

[1] That is, *G* differs from *F*, if at all, only in β's being substituted at some place or places for α. The laws established hold also for the limiting case in which *G* is simply *F* left as it is.

with $m+1$ occurrences of *C*. This means that since they hold when $m = 0$, they hold when $m = 1$, and since they hold when $m = 1$, they hold when $m = 2$, and so on for any number of occurrences of *C* at all. A formula *F* with no occurrences of *C*, in a *C*–0 system, must be either a simple propositional variable or the constant proposition 0. (It is assumed, of course, that all defined symbols, such as '1', have been expanded by their definitions.) If the single symbol which makes up *F* is identical with α, then *G* (the result of substituting β for α in *F*) will be β, and (*a*) and (*b*) will become respectively *C*(*C*αβ)*C*(*C*βα)(*C*αβ), which is provable by substitution in the axiom *CpCqp*, and *C*(*C*αβ)*C*(*C*βα)(*C*βα), which is provable from the axioms as follows:

1. *CCpqCCqrCpr*
2. *CCCpqpp*
3. *CpCqp*

   1 *q*/*CCpqp*, *r*/*p* = C3 *q*/*Cpq*—C2—4
4. *Cpp*

   3 *p*/*C*(*C*βα)(*C*βα), *q*/*C*αβ = C4 *p*/*C*βα—5
5. *C*(*C*αβ)*C*(*C*βα)(*C*βα).

If the one letter which makes up *F* is identical with β, or with neither α nor β, the substitution of β for α will leave *F* unchanged, so that in this case our (*a*) and (*b*) will both become *C*(*C*αβ)*C*(*C*βα)(*CFF*), provable from 3 and 4 above as follows:

   3 *p*/*CFF*, *q*/*C*βα = C4 *p*/*F*—6.
6. *C*(*C*βα)(*CFF*).

   3 *p*/*C*(*C*βα)(*CFF*), *q*/*C*αβ = C6—7
7. *C*(*C*αβ)*C*(*C*βα)(*CFF*).

So much for the simplest case. For the others: in a system with no truth-operator but '*C*', any formula which consists of more than one letter will be an implication in which the number of *C*'s in each component is less than the number in the whole formula. Using symbols, we may say that if *F* has $m+1$ occurrences of *C* it will be of the form *CF′F″*, where neither *F′* nor *F″* has more than *m* occurrences of *C*. *G*, the result of substituting

β for α in F, will also be an implication, which we may write as $CG'G''$,[1] so that (*a*) and (*b*) will become

(*a*) $C(C\alpha\beta)C(C\beta\alpha)C(CF'F'')(CG'G'')$

(*b*) $C(C\alpha\beta)C(C\beta\alpha)C(CG'G'')(CF'F'')$

On the hypothesis that (*a*) and (*b*) hold for formulae with no more than *m* occurrences of *C*, we will have, for F' and F'',

(*a'*) $C(C\alpha\beta)C(C\beta\alpha)(CF'G')$

(*b'*) $C(C\alpha\beta)C(C\beta\alpha)(CG'F')$

(*a''*) $C(C\alpha\beta)C(C\beta\alpha)(CF''G'')$

(*b''*) $C(C\alpha\beta)C(C\beta\alpha)(CG''F'')$

And Quine shows from the axioms that (*b'*) implies that (*a''*) implies (*a*), and that (*a'*) implies that (*b''*) implies (*b*), so that if we have (*a'*), (*b'*), (*a''*) and (*b''*) we can infer (*a*) and (*b*). The proof of (*a*) amounts to this (the proof of (*b*) being similar); (*b'*) asserts that under certain conditions we have $CG'F'$, and (*a''*) that under the same conditions we have $CF''G''$. Hence if, under the same conditions, we have $CF'F''$, we will have the chain of antecedents $CG'F'$, $CF'F''$, and $CF''G''$, from which we may infer $CG'G''$ by what the Schoolmen called the *consequentia a primo ad ultimum*. That is, if we have $CG'F'$ and $CF''G''$, we have $C(CF'F'')(CG'G'')$. The actual thesis that must be proved here, to turn this reasoning into simple substitution in a formula, is

$$C(CpCqCrs)C(CpCqCtu)(CpCqCCstCru),$$

i.e. if *Crs* holds under the conditions *p*, *q*, and *Ctu* holds under the same conditions, then we will have, again under the same conditions, *CCstCru* (since the chain *Crs*, *Cst*, *Ctu* leads to *Cru*). This is a formula of the purely implicational calculus, provable from its three axioms as follows:

1. *CCpqCCqrCpr*
2. *CCCpqpp*
3. *CpCqp*

1 $p/CpCpq$, $q/CCCpqqCpq$, r/Cpq
$= C1\ q/Cpq,\ r/q — C2\ p/Cpq — 4$

[1] Where G' could be F' unaltered, and G'' could be F'' unaltered.

4. *CCpCpqCpq*

1 *p*/*CCpqp*, *q*/*CCpqCCpqq*, *r*/*CCpqq*
= *C*1 *p*/*Cpq*, *q*/*p*, *r*/*q*—*C*4 *p*/*Cpq*—5

5. *CCCpqpCCpqq*

1 *q*/*CCpqp*, *r*/*CCpqq* = *C*3 *q*/*Cpq*—*C*5—6

6. *CpCCpqq*

1 *q*/*CCpqq* = *C*6—7

7. *CCCCpqqrCpr*

1 *p*/*CpCqr*, *q*/*CCCqrrCpr*, *r*/*CqCpr*
= *C*1 *q*/*Cqr*—*C*7 *p*/*q*, *q*/*r*, *r*/*Cpr*—8

8. *CCpCqrCqCpr*

8 *p*/*Cpq*, *q*/*Cqr*, *r*/*Cpr* = *C*1—9

9. *CCqrCCpqCpr*

1 *p*/8, *q*/*CCCpsCpCqrCCpsCqCpr*,
r/*CCCsCqrCCpsCpCqrCCsCqrCCpsCqCpr*
= *C*9 *p*/*Cps*, *q*/*CpCqr*, *r*/*CqCpr*—*C*9 *p*/*CsCqr*,
q/*CCpsCpCqr*, *r*/*CCpsCqCpr*—*C*8—*C*9 *q*/*s*, *r*/*Cqr*—10

10. *CCsCqrCCpsCqCpr*

10 *p*/*s*, *q*/*Cpq*, *r*/*Cpr*, *s*/*Cqr* = *C*9—11

11. *CCsCqrCCpqCsCpr*

10 *p*/*s*, *q*/*Cqr*, *r*/*Cpr*, *s*/*Cpq* = *C*1—12

12. *CCsCpqCCqrCsCpr*

12 *p*/*Cpq*, *q*/*CpCpr*, *r*/*Cpr*, *s*/*CpCqr* = *C*11 *s*/*p*—*C*4 *q*/*r*—13

13. *CCpCqrCCpqCpr*

12 *p*/*Cqr*, *q*/*Cpr*, *r*/*CCrsCps*, *s*/*Cpq* = *C*1—*C*1 *q*/*r*, *r*/*s*—14

14. *CCpqCCqrCCrsCps*

12 *p*/*Cps*, *q*/*CpCqr*, *r*/*CCpqCpr*, *s*/*CsCqr*
= *C*9 *q*/*s*, *r*/*Cqr*—*C*13—15

15. *CCsCqrCCpsCCpqCpr*

1 *p*/*Crs*, *q*/*CCstCCtuCru*, *r*/*CCtuCCstCru*
= *C*14 *p*/*r*, *q*/*s*, *r*/*t*, *s*/*u*—*C*8 *p*/*Cst*, *q*/*Ctu*, *r*/*Cru*—16

16. *CCrsCCtuCCstCru*

15 *p*/*q*, *q*/*Ctu*, *r*/*CCstCru*, *s*/*Crs* = *C*16—17

17. *CCqCrsCCqCtuCqCCstCru*

15 *q*/*CqCtu*, *r*/*CqCCstCru*, *s*/*CqCrs* = *C*17—18

18. *CCpCqCrsCCpCqCtuCpCqCCstCru*.

This proof formalizes our intuitive movement from 1 to 14, from 14 *p*/*r*, *q*/*s*, *r*/*t*, *s*/*u* to 16 by means of 8, and from 16 to 18.[1]

For requirement (3), Quine has to show that if *H* is the formula obtained by substituting 1 (i.e. *C*oo) for α in *F*, and *J* the formula obtained by substituting o for α in *F*, then if both *H* and *J* hold, *F* itself must hold. He does this in three steps. First he shows that if *H* is the formula obtained by substituting *C*oo for α in *F*, we have

(*c*) $C\alpha CFH$, and

(*d*) $C\alpha CHF$.

In substance, his proof amounts to this: If α is true, then it is implied by *C*oo (we have $C\alpha CCoo\alpha$ by substitution in *CpCqp*), while it implies *C*oo in any case (since *C*oo is true), so that if α is true it is equivalent to *C*oo, and α and *C*oo are mutually substitutable in any formula. The proof of (*d*) might be set out formally thus:

1. *CCpqCCqrCpr*

2. *CpCqp*

3. *Cop*

4. $CC\alpha CooCCCoo\alpha CHF$

1 *p*/*C*oo, *q*/$C\alpha Coo$, *r*/$CCCoo\alpha CHF$ = *C*2 *p*/*C*oo, *q*/α—*C*4—*C*3 *p*/o—5

5. $CCCoo\alpha CHF$

1 *p*/α, *q*/$CCoo\alpha$, *r*/*CHF* = *C*2 *p*/α, *q*/*C*oo—*C*5—(*d*)

(*d*) $C\alpha CHF$.

Here 1–3 are from the axioms, and 4 is what (*b*) becomes when β is *C*oo.

[1] 14 is the scholastic *consequentia a primo ad ultimum*. Burleigh (*De Puritate Artis Logicae*, Boehner's edition, p. 2) gives this as a corollary of the rule *quidquid sequitur ad consequens sequitur ad antecedens*, i.e. our 1.

With some of the steps on the way, it is an instructive exercise to see what we obtain by replacing some consequent-variable (e.g. *q* in 4, 5, and 7, or *r* in 13) by o, and applying the definition *Np* = *Cp*o.

Secondly, Quine shows that if any proposition α is *not* true, i.e. if we have $C\alpha o$, then α is interchangeable with the standard false proposition o in any formula F. That is, if $\mathcal{J}$ is formed by replacing α by o in F, we will have

(*e*) $CC\alpha oCF\mathcal{J}$, and

(*f*) $CC\alpha oC\mathcal{J}F$.

In substance, the proof is that since $Co\alpha$ is true in any case (by the axiom Cop), when we have $C\alpha o$ our α will both imply and be implied by o, so that the substitutability of equivalents will apply to this pair. We might formalize the proof of (*f*) thus:

1. Cop
2. $CCpCqrCqCpr$
3. $CC\alpha oCCo\alpha C\mathcal{J}F$

    $2\ p/C\alpha o,\ q/Co\alpha,\ r/C\mathcal{J}F = C3\text{—}C1\ p/\alpha\text{—}(f)$

(*f*) $CC\alpha oC\mathcal{J}F$.

Here 3 is what (*b*) becomes when β is o.

From (*d*) and (*f*) Quine proves what we require, namely

(*g*) $C\mathcal{J}CHF$,

as follows:

1. $CCpqCCqrCpr$
2. $CCCpqpp$
3. $CCpCqrCqCpr$
4. $CCsCqrCCpsCqCpr$
5. $CCsCpqCCqrCsCpr$

(*d*) $C\alpha CHF$

(*f*) $CC\alpha oC\mathcal{J}F$

    $5\ p/Cps,\ q/CqCpr,\ r/CCtqCpCtr,\ s/CsCqr = C4\text{—}C4\ p/t,\ q/p,$
    $s/q\text{—}6$

6. $CCsCqrCCpsCCtqCpCtr$

    $5\ p/Crp,\ q/CCpqp,\ r/p,\ s/CCpqr = C1\ p/Cpq,\ q/r,\ r/p\text{—}C2\text{—}7$

7. $CCCpqrCCrpp$

    $1\ p/CCpqr,\ q/CCrpp,\ r/CCprr = C7\text{—}C7\ p/r,\ q/p,\ r/p\text{—}8$

8. $CCCpqrCCprr$

    $6\ p/s,\ q/Cpr,\ s/CCpqr = C8\text{—}9$

9. *CCsCCpqrCCtCprCsCtr*
   6 *p*/*CCpqCsr*, *q*/*CtCpr*, *r*/*CsCtr*, *s*/*CsCCpqr*, *t*/*CpCtr*
   = *C*9—*C*3 *p*/*Cpq*, *q*/*s*—*C*3 *q*/*t*—10
10. *CCCpqCsrCCpCtrCsCtr*
   10 *p*/α, *q*/0, *r*/*F*, *s*/*J*, *t*/*H* = *C*(*f*)—*C*(*d*)—(*g*)

(*g*) *CJCHF*.

Here 1 and 2 are axioms, and 4 and 5 were proved earlier (they are 10 and 12 in the long proof given under 'substitutability of equivalents').

This is all we require to prove any tautologous formula from the axioms. The axioms also suffice to prove the simple propositional variable *p* from any formula which is not tautologous. For ordinary calculation, with such a formula, will give us at least one line which finishes with 0; thus *CpCpq* gives us, for *p*/1 and *q*/0,

$$C1C10 = C10 = 0.$$

And the proof '*CpCpq* → *C*1*C*10 → *C*10 → 0 → *p*' can be formalized in this system, as *CpCpq* yields *C*1*C*10 by substitution, 0 follows from *C*1*C*10 by the substitutability of equivalents and the equivalences corresponding to *C*10 = 0, and *p* follows from 0 by the axiom *C*0*p*. Similarly in other cases.

Quine points out that other versions of the propositional calculus can be proved complete by this method if the symbol '0' is introduced into them by definition. It can be an abbreviation for the contradictory of any thesis which the axioms of a system suffice to prove, e.g. for *NCqq*. Given this, we need simply to prove Wajsberg's four axioms in the system, and then proceed as above. Taking the system of PM as an example, the proofs of *CCpqCCqrCpr* and *CpCqp* (or of the equivalent *CqCpq*) from its axioms have already been given in the last chapter; those of the other two might be as follows:

1. *CCpqCCqrCpr* (PM 2.06)
2. *CNpCpq* (PM 2.21)
3. *CCNppp* (PM 2.18)
4. *Cpp* (PM 2.08)
5. *CqCpq* (PM 2.02)

6. *CCNpqCNqp* (PM 2.15)
   1 *p*/*Np*, *q*/*Cpq*, *r*/*p* = *C*2—7
7. *CCCpqpCNpp*
   1 *p*/*CCpqp*, *q*/*CNpp*, *r*/*p* = *C*7—C3—8
8. *CCCpqpp* (Peirce's Law)
   5 *q*/*Cqq*, *p*/*Np* = *C*4 *p*/*q*—9
9. *CNpCqq*
   6 *q*/*Cqq* = *C*9—10
10. *CNCqqp* (i.e. *Cop* when o = *NCqq*).

§ 3. *Wajsberg's Completeness Proof for the Restricted Calculus*

We may now turn to the other completeness proof from which Quine's took its origin, Wajsberg's establishment of the sufficiency of the three Tarski–Bernays axioms for the purely implicational calculus, without the propositional constant o or the operators definable by means of it.

In the ordinary method of calculating the possible truth-values of a purely implicative formula containing two different propositional variables, say *p* and *q*, we consider four collectively exhaustive and mutually exclusive alternative cases—$p = 1$, $q = 1$; $p = 1$, $q = 0$; $p = 0$, $q = 1$; and $p = 0$, $q = 0$. We might instead, however, take the three alternative cases $p = 1$, $q = 1$, and $p = q$. These alternatives are not mutually exclusive (when *p* and *q* are both true, we have all three of them at once —*p* true, *q* true, and *p* of the same truth-value as *q*). They are, however, collectively exhaustive; that is, if any two of them do not hold, the third one does. (If neither *p* is true nor *q* is true, *p* and *q* will have the same truth-value, namely 0; if *p* is not true and *p* and *q* do not have the same truth-value, *q* will be true; and so on.) If we 'evaluate' the formula *CpCqCpq* in this way we obtain

For *p*/1, *CpCqCpq* = *C*1*CqC*1*q*
For *q*/1, *CpCqCpq* = *CpC*1*Cp*1
For *p*/*q*, *CpCqCpq* = *CqCqCqq*.

The formulae arising in the three cases do not, as in the ordinary method, have all their variables replaced by constants; but the number of different variables used is brought down to one. And in evaluating formulae of this sort we do not use the equations $C11 = C01 = C00 = 1$ and $C10 = 0$, but we may use $Cpp = Cp1 = C11 = 1$ and $C1p = p$, thus:

$$C1CqC1q = C1Cqq = C11 = 1$$
$$CpC1Cp1 = CpC11 = Cp1 = 1$$
$$CqCqCqq = CqCq1 = Cq1 = 1.$$

Where the given formula is not tautologous, at least one of the final results will be not 1 but a variable, thus:

$$\text{For } p/1,\ CpCpq = C1C1q = C1q = q.$$

If the formula has three variables, say p, q, and r, we may begin by considering the cases $r/1$, $q/1$, and r/q, obtaining three formulae in which the only variables are p and q, which may each be dealt with as above. Similarly where the number of variables is larger still.

Wajsberg's completeness proof may be most simply understood as a formalization of the procedure just outlined. If the above informal proof of $CpCqCpq$ were turned into a formal deduction, its main steps would have to be

$$\left.\begin{array}{l} 1 \to C11 \to C1Cq1 \to C1CqC1q \\ 1 \to Cp1 \to CpC11 \to CpC1Cp1 \\ 1 \to Cq1 \to CqCq1 \to CqCqCqq \end{array}\right\rangle \to CpCqCpq.$$

We plainly require here

(1) A provable formula of the system to be identified with 1.

(2) Equivalences corresponding to the equations

$$Cpp = Cp1 = C11 = 1 \text{ and } C1p = p,$$

and the substitutability of equivalents.

(3) A way of proving a formula when given the formulae resulting from that to be proved by the substitutions $p/1$, $q/1$, and p/q.

The proof of the substitutability of equivalents from the three Tarski–Bernays axioms has been given in the preceding section. '1' cannot now be a propositional constant, as the restricted system contains no propositional constants in terms of which it may be defined. (There are, as we shall see in the next chapter, operators by means of which a proposition with a fixed meaning may be constructed from formulae containing variables, but such operators are not among the symbols of the calculus now being considered.) However, in that segment of the implicational calculus in which only one propositional variable is used, we may identify '1' with the implication of this variable by itself. If the one variable we are using be p, 1 will be Cpp. This has already been proved from the Tarski–Bernays axioms, and the definition automatically gives us the equation $Cpp = 1$. The equivalences corresponding to our other equations $Cp1 = 1$, etc., may be proved as follows:

1. $CCCpqpp$
2. $CpCqp$
3. Cpp

   2 $p/Cpp,\ q/CpCpp = C3$—4
4. $C(CpCpp)(Cpp)$

   2 $p/Cpp,\ q/p = 5$
5. $C(Cpp)(CpCpp)$

   2 $p/Cpp,\ q/CCppCpp = C3$—6
6. $C(CCppCpp)(Cpp)$

   2 $p/Cpp,\ q/Cpp = 7$
7. $C(Cpp)(CCppCpp)$

   1 $q/p = 8$
8. $C(CCppp)(p)$

   2 $q/Cpp = 9$
9. $C(p)(CCppp)$.

Here 4 and 5 correspond to $Cp1 = 1$, 6 and 7 to $C11 = 1$, and 8 and 9 to $C1p = $ p.

By these equivalences and the substitutability of equivalents, we may, with any formula using only the one propositional variable p, either prove the formula from Cpp, or prove p from it. And to justify the last step in our calculation, we need to show that if any formula using both p and q holds (i) when p is replaced by Cqq, (ii) when q is replaced by Cpp, and (iii) when p is replaced by q, it holds as it stands. (Each of these three substitutions will replace our formula by one using one variable only. And repetition of the procedure will give us the same result when the given formula contains more than two different variables.) If *G* be the result of substituting *q* for *p* in *F*, *H* the result of substituting *Cqq* for *p*, and *J* the result of substituting *Cpp* for *q*, what we need is a standard method of proof for formulae of the form

CHCJCGF,

'If *F*-with-*p*-replaced-by-*Cqq*, then if *F*-with-*q*-replaced-by-*Cpp*, then if *F*-with *p*-replaced-by-*q*, then *F*.' Now *F*-with-*p*-replaced-by-*Cqq* (*H*) implies *F* when *p* is true (for then *p* and *Cqq* are equivalent), and *F*-with-*q*-replaced-by-*Cpp* (*J*) implies *F* when *q* is true, i.e. we have

CpCHF, and
CqCJF.

These are both provable in the same way as Quine's (*d*), using *Cpp* and *Cqq* instead of *Coo*. And *F*-with-*p*-replaced-by-*q* (*G*) implies *F* when *p* and *q* are co-implicant, i.e. we have

CCpqCCqpCGF

(proved as for substitutability of equivalents). And from these three we may obtain *CHCJCGF* by substitution (*r*/*H*, *s*/*J*, *t*/*G*, *u*/*F*) and detachment from the formula

C(*CpCru*)*C*(*CqCsu*)*C*(*CCpqCCqpCtu*)(*CrCsCtu*),

which is provable from the Tarski–Bernays axioms.

§ 4. *Logic, Metalogic, and Functorial Variables*

It is important to observe that a proof of the completeness of a deductive system is not itself a deduction within the system, though the fact that certain deductions, and certain kinds of deduction, are possible within the system, will be an important part of it. The proof of completeness is a proof of something *about* the system; it involves viewing the system, as it were, from outside. And if we describe the deduction of tautologous formulae from other tautologous formulae as 'logic', the consideration of these deductions from outside may be called 'metalogic', and that is in fact the name now commonly applied to it.

To illustrate this distinction, let us look again at one of the formulae appearing in Quine's completeness proof, namely his (*a*),

$$C(C\alpha\beta)C(C\beta\alpha)(CFG).$$

This, though it may look a little like it, is not itself a formula of the *C*–o system which Quine is discussing. 'α', 'β', '*F*', and '*G*' are not propositional variables for which we can substitute in the ordinary way, as if (*a*) were just *CCpqCCqpCst* with different letters, and this were a thesis of the system. The case is rather that (*a*), accompanied by a verbal explanation of the relations that are understood to hold between '*F*', '*G*', 'α' and 'β' (that *G* is *F* with α replaced by β), is just a schematic indication of a *kind* of formula which is provable in the system. It is a way of referring to any such formula as

C(*CNNpp*)*C*(*CpNNp*)*C*(*Crp*)(*CrNNp*)

or *C*(o*C*10)*C*(*CC*100)*C*(o*C*11)(*CC*10*C*11).

It represents all such formulae; but not in such a way that we can, within the system, obtain the latter by performing the substitutions α/o, β/*C*10, *F*/o*C*11, *G*/*CC*10*C*11 in (*a*). We obtain it, rather, by the appropriate proof of the sort which Quine shows is always possible for this sort of formula.

'Metalogical' demonstrations ought of course to be themselves 'logical' in the sense of being cogent, and although in the examples which we have been studying they have been set out verbally and somewhat informally, it is possible also to set out the principles drawn upon in an appropriate symbolism, and to derive them in a rigorous manner from metalogical axioms. Such a 'formalized metalogic' would of course be capable of being reviewed in a 'meta-metalogic', and so on *ad infinitum*. What can also be done, in the interests of rigour, is to transfer much of our 'metalogical' material into an enlarged version of the original 'logical' system. We can, in particular, add to the propositional calculus a new type of variable, standing not for propositions but for operators on propositions. Let δ, for example, be such a variable, being so used that, where α is any propositional formula, $\delta\alpha$ stands indifferently for any truth-function into which α enters as an argument. δp, for example, stands indifferently for any such function of *p* as *Np*, *Cpq*, *Cpp*, *CpNq*, *CCpqCCqrCpr*, and so on. It can also stand for *p* itself. In a system thus enlarged we could have such formulae as

CCpqCCqpC$\delta p \delta q$

from which we *could* derive, say,

$$C(CoC1o)C(CC1oo)C(CoC11)(CC1oC11)$$

by simple substitution, in this case by the substitution p/o, $q/C1o$ and $\delta/C'C11$. The apostrophe in the last substitution-instruction stands for the place where the argument of the operator δ is to go. Thus the substitution $\delta/C'C11$ in δp gives us $CpC11$; in δo it gives us $CoC11$; in $\delta C1o$ it gives $C(C1o)C11$. The substitution-instruction $\delta/'$ gives us simply the argument itself, i.e. in δp it gives us p; in δo, o; and so on. The substitution-instruction δ/C'' gives us, in δp, Cpp; in δo, Coo; in $\delta C1o$, $CC1oC1o$; and so on. These will do as examples.

The first writer to study propositional calculi enlarged in this way was the Polish logician Leśniewski, who gave the name 'protothetic' to this form of the theory of deduction. Given the definition of 1 as Coo, the following theses in protothetic will serve to turn any verification by truth-value calculation into a formal deduction:

1. 1
2. $C\delta 1\delta C11$
3. $C\delta o\delta C1o$
4. $C\delta 1\delta Co1$
5. $C\delta 1C\delta o\delta p$.

Take, e.g., the calculation for $CCpqCpp$:

$$CC11C11 = C11 = 1$$
$$CC1oC11 = Co1 = 1$$
$$CCo1Coo = C11 = 1$$
$$CCooCoo = C11 = 1.$$

If we only make one substitution at a time, this enlarges to

$$CC11C11 = C11 = 1$$
$$CC1oC11 = CoC11 = Co1 = 1$$
$$CCo1Coo = C1Coo = C11 = 1$$
$$CCooCoo = C11 = 1.$$

Using the above five theses, we may turn this into a deduction as follows (working back from the right in each line):

2 δ/' = *C*1—6

6. *C*11

2 δ/*C*'' = *C*6—7

7. *CC*11*C*11

4 δ/' = *C*1—8

8. *C*01

3 δ/*C*'1 = *C*8—9

9. *CC*101

2 δ/*CC*10' = *C*9—10

10. *CC*10*C*11

6×Df. 1 = 11

11. *C*1*C*00

4 δ/*C*'*C*00 = *C*11—12

12. *CC*01*C*00

6×Df. 1 = 13

13. *CC*00*C*00

5 *p*/*q*, δ/*CC*1'*C*11 = *C*7—*C*10—14

14. *CC*1*qC*11

5 *p*/*q*, δ/*CC*0'*C*00 = *C*12—*C*13—15

15. *CC*0*qC*00

5 δ/*CC*'*qC*'' = *C*14—*C*15—16

16. *CCpqCpp*.

Other cases may be dealt with similarly.

Łukasiewicz has recently shown that, of the above theses 1–5, the first four are deducible from the fifth, *C*δ1*C*δ0δ*p*, or, in its full form, *C*δ*C*00*C*δ0δ*p*.[1] He has also shown that if any non-tautologous formula were laid down as a thesis, this same thesis *C*δ1*C*δ0δ*p* would enable us to deduce from it as a thesis the simple variable *p*. He shows this by proving from *C*δ1*C*δ0δ*p* the thesis *C*0*p*, together with the converses of 2, 3, and 4 above, i.e. *C*δ*C*11δ1, *C*δ*C*10δ0 and *C*δ*C*01δ1. The use of these theses may

[1] J. Łukasiewicz, 'On Variable Functors of Propositional Arguments', *Proceedings of the Royal Irish Academy*, 54 A 2 (1951), §§ 4 and 5.

be illustrated by the result of putting beside them the non-tautologous thesis *CCppCpq* (which, for *p*/1, *q*/0, becomes *CC*11*C*10, i.e. *C*1*C*10, i.e. *C*10, i.e. 0):

1. *C*0*p*
2. *C*δ*C*11δ1
3. *C*δ*C*10δ0
4. *CCppCpq*
   4 *p*/1, *q*/0 = 5
5. *CC*11*C*10
   2 δ/*C*'*C*10 = *C*5—6
6. *C*1*C*10
   3 δ/*C*1' = *C*6—7
7. *C*10
   3 δ/' = *C*7—8
8. 0
   1 = *C*8—9
9. *p*.

This means that we have a complete basis for the ordinary propositional calculus in the single axiom *C*δ*C*00*C*δ0δ*p*. This contains only 10 letters, and so is considerably shorter than single axioms of the usual type; it is, moreover, vastly more obvious than these others. It corresponds to Quine's metalogical principle (*g*), and directly reflects the fact that 1 and 0 are the only truth-values that any proposition can take, so that a truth-function which holds both when its argument is true and when it is false will hold with any argument at all.

Short as it is, *C*δ*C*00*C*δ0δ*p* is not the shortest single axiom from which all ordinary tautologous forms are deducible. C. A. Meredith has discovered that the same purpose may be served by the still shorter axiom *C*δδ0δ*p*. This formula is far from self-evident, and indeed it is difficult to put its sense into words. We might read it, roughly, as 'If any truth-function of that truth-function of a false proposition, then that truth-function of any proposition at all'. We can establish its truth mechanically by making use of the fact that there are only four ways in which the truth-value of a truth-function of one argument can be determined by the truth-value of that argument. Either $\delta 1 = 1$ and $\delta 0 = 1$, or $\delta 1 = 1$ and $\delta 0 = 0$, or $\delta 1 = 0$ and $\delta 0 = 1$, or $\delta 1 = 0$ and $\delta 0 = 0$. In other words, the four possible 'values' of δ are (1, 1), (1, 0), (0, 1), and (0, 0). If δ appears in a formula as, say, $C'q$, which of these four it is will depend on the truth-value of q, but for any assigned value of the other propositional variables thus involved, the 'value' of δ is fixed as one of the four mentioned. Thus if $q = 1$, $C'q$ is (1, 1), since $C11 = 1$ and $C01 = 1$, while if $q = 0$ it is (0, 1), since $C10 = 0$ and $C00 = 1$. Now if δ is any other operator than (1, 1), $\delta\delta 0$ has the value 0; for the operator (1, 0), however often applied, simply preserves, in the function it forms, the value of its argument; (0, 1) reverses it, but a double reversal will bring us back where we were; and (0, 0) gives a function of value 0 with any argument at all, however often it is applied. Hence unless δ is (1, 1), the antecedent of $C\delta\delta 0\delta p$ will have the value 0, and the whole be true; while if δ is (1, 1), the consequent will have the value 1, and so the whole be true again.

Of this peculiar axiom, Meredith has shown not only that it suffices to prove all tautologous formulae that we can construct by means of C, 0 and propositional variables, but that it suffices to prove also all tautologous formulae involving beside these the 'functorial' variable δ; i.e. not only all formulae like $CCpqCpp$, $C0p$, and so on, but also all formulae like $CCpqCCqpC\delta q\delta p$, corresponding to Quine's (*b*); $CpC\delta C00\delta p$, corresponding to Quine's (*d*); $CCp0C\delta 0\delta p$, corresponding to Quine's (*f*); and Łukasiewicz's $C\delta C00C\delta 0\delta p$.[1] The one axiom $C\delta\delta 0\delta p$, together with the rules of substitution and detachment (and such definitions as we care to introduce), thus serves as a complete basis not only for what we have hitherto called (by contrast with the implicational calculus) the 'full' propositional calculus, but also for the extended calculus that is made possible by introducing the new type of variable. Meredith shows this by proving from his axiom (*a*) the standard true proposition $C00$, and (*b*) all the theses required to turn into formal proofs (i) the 'evaluation' of the system's formulae (i.e. the removal from them of all propositional and functorial variables) and (ii) the 'reduction' of all the evaluants of tautologous formulae to

[1] C. A. Meredith, 'On an Extended System of the Propositional Calculus', *Proceedings of the Royal Irish Academy*, 54 A 3 (1951), §§ 1 and 2.

*C*oo. *C*oo follows by the substitution *p*/o in *Cop*, which follows immediately from *C*δδoδ*p* by the substitution δ/'.

It should be observed that even where a system of propositional calculus contains functorial as well as propositional variables, there is still a distinction to be made between what can be said *in* the system and what can be said about it. It is not possible, for example, to express in the symbols of protothetic itself the rules by which the other theses are derived from the axioms; for there are no symbols in protothetic for nouns, such as 'variable' (and we could not state, for example, the rule of substitution without a symbol for this). Systems with symbols for nouns and verbs will be considered in the next chapter, but we may note here that it *is* possible to construct a calculus rich enough in its symbolism for the direct statement within itself of its own rules of procedure. To speak technically, there are symbolic languages rich enough for their own 'syntax' to be stated within them, i.e. that part of their 'metalogic' in which we talk about symbols without mentioning their relation to what they signify.[1] This covers rules of inference, so far as these can be expressed as permissions to replace one formula by another. What a rigorously formulated system cannot include within itself is its own 'semantics', i.e. that part of its 'metalogic' which does refer to relations between its symbols and what they signify. It cannot be said within any system, for example, that that system is 'complete', i.e. that its unproved theses and rules suffice to prove all theses within it which are true for all interpretations of their variables (or which, if the theses contain no variables, are true *simpliciter*). But as it happens—this can be shown from outside the system—no set of axioms and rules for a system containing its own syntax ever *is* 'complete', at least not if the system is free from inconsistency. For in any such system, we will have the materials for constructing a formula *G* with the following meaning:

We cannot prove the statement which results
from replacing the variable in the statement-form
'*We cannot prove the statement which results*
from replacing the variable in the statement-form
y *by the name of the statement-form in question*'
by the name of the statement-form in question.

[1] For such languages see R. Carnap in *The Logical Syntax of Language* (1937).

If we construct the statement which *G* says that we cannot prove by replacing '*y*' in the statement-form in quotation marks by the 'name' of that statement-form itself, i.e. by the same statement-form in quotation marks,[1] the statement we shall obtain is *G* itself. That is, *G* asserts its own unprovability. Now if in fact *G* is a thesis of the system, it is false (since it then *is* provable, and it asserts that it is not); and moreover, if *G* is a thesis of the system, it will be asserted in a 'complete' system that it is, so that the system will assert both *G* and its denial. If, however, *G* is not a thesis of the system, i.e. is not provable, then it will be true, so that there will be at least one true formula, namely *G*, which can be constructed in the system, but which the rules and axioms of the system will not suffice to prove. (This proof is in its substance due to K. Gödel; in the form in which it is here presented, to J. N. Findlay.)[2]

[1] The phrase 'name of the statement-form' must of course here be defined, not semantically as 'name naming the statement-form', but syntactically as 'expression consisting of the statement-form in quotation marks'.

[2] 'Goedelian sentences: a non-numerical approach', *Mind*, 1942, pp. 259–65.

IV

The Theory of Quantification

§ 1. *Predicates and Quantifiers*

The only 'operators' which we have so far considered are those by which we construct propositions out of other propositions, and even of these we have considered only those which form truth-functions. Propositional operators other than truth-operators we must set aside for later treatment; what will concern us now will be operators which form propositions, not out of other propositions, but out of names. Ordinary speech is full of these, and we commonly call them 'verbs'. Thus we might say that '... is sitting down' is an operator by which we construct the proposition 'Theaetetus is sitting down' out of the name 'Theaetetus'. Or we might call 'Theaetetus' the 'subject' of the proposition and '... is sitting down' the 'predicate', the subject being definable as 'what the proposition is about', or as the name of that, and the predicate as 'what is said about it'.

'Theaetetus sits' was given by Plato as an example of the simplest form of proposition, his argument being that a proposition, in the sense of a form of speech capable of truth and falsity, must be at least complex enough to contain a noun and a verb.[1] 'Theaetetus is sitting down' is true if he is in fact doing so, and false if he is not, while 'Theaetetus is not sitting down' is false if he is, true if he is not. Plato's concern was to distinguish the notion of falsehood from that of unreality—a false belief cannot be simply an unreal belief, i.e. no belief at all; it involves a mental putting together of real elements which are in fact apart, or a mental putting apart of real elements which are in fact together.

This analysis of propositions into nouns and verbs, or subjects and predicates, is of course easy enough to represent symbolically. Given the symbols 'x', 'y', 'z' as name-symbols, and 'ϕ', 'ψ', 'θ', etc. as predicate-symbols, and treating predicates as operators which form propositions out of names, we

[1] *Sophist*, 262–3.

have 'ϕx', 'ϕy', 'ψx', 'ψy', as propositional formulae of a new sort. We may also form truth-functions of these by means of the usual operators, giving us such formulae as $N\phi x$, $C\phi x\psi x$, $C\phi x\phi y$, and so on (or in the symbolism of PM, $\sim \phi x$, $\phi x \supset \psi x$, $\phi x \supset \phi y$, etc.). A question which then arises is whether we may also speak of a subject and a predicate of these more complex forms. Putting aside for a while those cases in which there is more than one name-variable, we may say that the predicate of $N\phi x$ is $N\phi$; of $C\phi x\psi x$, $C\phi$'ψ', and so on. Thus in a concrete case, we might say that in 'Theaetetus is not sitting down', 'Theaetetus' is the subject, naming what the proposition is about, and '. . . is not sitting down' the predicate—what is said of him is that he is not sitting down. And in 'If Caesar was a tyrant, Caesar deserved death', we might say that 'Caesar' is the subject, and 'If . . . was a tyrant then . . . deserved death' the predicate, what is said of Caesar being that if he was a tyrant he deserved death. Truth-operators, we may say, not only construct propositions out of other propositions, but also construct predicates out of other predicates.

Just as a proposition constructed out of another proposition by a truth-operator may be called a function of the latter, and the latter the argument of the function or of the operator, so a proposition constructed from a name by a predicate may be called a function of its subject, its subject being the argument of the function or of the predicate. Thus ϕx is a function of x, and x is the argument of ϕx or of ϕ, just as Np is a function of p, p being the argument of Np or of N. We might call ϕx, following Johnson,[1] a 'predicational' function.

When these new types of propositional formulae are introduced, we can of course add them to the formulae which may be substituted for propositional variables in theses of the propositional calculus. Thus we may have such substitutions as $p/\phi x$ in Cpp, giving us $C\phi x\phi x$. Such an extension of the propositional calculus is, however, in itself quite trivial. The calculus of predicational functions (often simply called the functional calculus, or the predicate calculus) only begins to be interesting when certain further symbols are introduced into it, namely a pair of operators called 'quantifiers' by means of which propositions are constructed out of predicates. Consider, for

[1] *Logic*, Part II, Ch. iii, § 7.

example, the proposition 'Something burns'. This does not say of an object called 'Something' that it burns, in the way that 'Theaetetus sits' says of an object called 'Theaetetus' that it sits. If it did, we would deny it by saying 'Something does not burn', as we deny 'Theaetetus sits' by saying 'Theaetetus does not sit', but there is no opposition between 'Something burns' and 'Something does not burn'—both are, as it happens, true. 'Something burns' is denied, rather, by 'Nothing burns', or by 'Everything does-not-burn', and is a proposition of a more complicated sort than 'Theaetetus sits'. We might bring out its force by restating it as 'There is at least one x such that x burns', or more briefly, 'For some x, x burns', which we can write, given that 'ϕ' means 'burns', as '$\Sigma x\phi x$'. Here 'Σx', meaning 'For some x', is a quantifier. 'Something does not burn' would become in a similar way 'For some x, it is not the case that x burns', $\Sigma xN\phi x$, the true denial of $\Sigma x\phi x$ being not this but rather $N\Sigma x\phi x$, 'It is not the case that for some x, x burns.' The other quantifier is 'Πx', 'For all x'; thus $\Pi xN\phi x$ would mean (with the same sense assigned to 'ϕ') 'For all x, it is not the case that x burns', or 'Everything does-not-burn'. In the notation of PM '(x)' is used for 'Πx' and '$(\exists x)$' for 'Σx', being prefixed to the predicational function in the same way. 'For all x' is generally called the 'universal' quantifier and 'For some x' the existential quantifier.

A certain difference should be observed between the functioning of the name-variable 'x' in '$\Pi x\phi x$' and '$\Sigma x\phi x$' and its functioning in formulae like '$C\phi x\phi x$'. '$C\phi x\phi x$' is not, strictly speaking, a proposition, but is rather the form of a proposition, and it remains something less than a proposition even when a definite meaning is assigned to 'ϕ'. Thus if 'ϕ' be 'burns', '$C\phi x\phi x$' is 'If x burns then x burns', which makes no actual assertion until a meaning is assigned to x (though since the formula is tautologous we know beforehand that any actual assertion of this form will be true). Russell and Whitehead express this fact a little confusingly by saying that 'If x burns then x burns' is not a proposition but a 'propositional function'. But once a meaning has been assigned to 'ϕ', '$\Pi x\phi x$' and '$\Sigma x\phi x$' make definite assertions—given that 'ϕ' = 'burns', the one says that everything burns, the other that something does. We do not need to replace the 'x' by a name in order to obtain a proposition; and indeed if we do so we obtain something rather less like a proposition than the original. ('For all Theaetetus, Theaetetus burns' is of doubtful significance, though I suppose a man might choose this way of expressing the proposition that Theaetetus is burning all over and all through.) This difference is expressed by describing the variable '*x*' as being 'free' in such formulae as $C\phi x\phi x$ and as 'bound' by the quantifier in such formulae as $\Pi x\phi x$ (or by saying that in the former case it is a 'real' variable and in the latter an 'apparent' one). And once quantifiers are introduced into a system, all rules of substitution for variables must be qualified by the proviso that they apply only to 'free' occurrences of variables. At 'bound' occurrences, substitution is not permissible. But of course entire formulae containing bound variables, such as $\Pi x\phi x$ or $\Pi xC\phi x\psi x$, count as propositional formulae and may be substituted in theses for free propositional variables.

As with the calculus of propositions, there are different ways in which the calculus of predicates may be systematized. One way of dealing with what is called the 'lower' functional calculus, i.e. that part of the predicate calculus in which we have name-variables bound by quantifiers (as in Πx) but not predicate-variables (as in $\Pi\phi$), is by dovetailing it into the propositional calculus, without further axioms, but with two new rules. The first of these two rules, which are used in this way by Łukasiewicz, is that, given any thesis that has the form of an implication, we may bind any free variable in the antecedent by the universal quantifier. That is, if we have a thesis of the form $C\phi x\beta$, 'If *x* ϕ's then β', we may pass to the corresponding thesis of the form $C(\Pi x\phi x)\beta$, 'If everything ϕ's then β'. The validity of this rule is evident enough; for clearly if β is implied by the assertion that *x* ϕ's it will be implied by the stronger assertion that everything ϕ's. The second rule for Π is that, given any implicative thesis, we may bind by a universal quantifier any variable in the consequent that is not free in the antecedent. That is, if we have a thesis of the form $C\alpha\phi x$, 'If α then *x* ϕ's', where *x* is not free in α, we may pass to the corresponding formula $C\alpha\Pi x\phi x$, 'If α then everything ϕ's'. This rule is only applicable where our initial 'If α then *x* ϕ's' is a thesis, i.e. yields a true proposition no matter what '*x*' stands for. The thesis to which we pass by it, 'If α then everything ϕ's', may be thought of as a reflection within the system of the fact that where 'If α then x ϕ's' is a thesis, any name-variable whatever may be substituted for the 'x' in it. But if 'x' occurs freely in the antecedent as well as the consequent, i.e. if our initial $C\alpha\phi x$ is of the form $C\psi x\phi x$, 'If x ψ's then x ϕ's', even when this is a thesis, we cannot substitute without restriction for the 'x' in the consequent—we can only substitute whatever we have already substituted for it in the antecedent. The quantified thesis which we can derive in this case is not $C\psi x\Pi x\phi x$, 'If x ψ's then everything ϕ's', but rather (as we shall see more fully later) $\Pi xC\psi x\phi x$, 'Everything ϕ's-if-it-ψ's'. Summing up, then, we have for Π the two rules

1. $C\phi x\beta \rightarrow C\Pi x\phi x\beta$
2. $C\alpha\phi x \rightarrow C\alpha\Pi x\phi x$, for x not free in α.

In proofs, the application of these rules will be signalized by writing '$\times\Pi 1$' or '$\times\Pi 2$' after the formula to which the rule is applied. And when later we are regarding more than one variable as available for binding, the one to be bound by the introduced quantifier will be indicated by writing it after the '$\Pi 1$' or '$\Pi 2$', thus: '$\times\Pi 1y$', '$\times\Pi 2x$'.

Alternatively, we might work from a pair of rules for Σ, but it is not necessary to have both, as either pair is derivable from the other. We do not, in fact, need both Π and Σ as independent operators; for $\Sigma x\phi x$ has the same force as $N\Pi xN\phi x$ ('Something ϕ's' = 'Not everything does not ϕ'), and $\Pi x\phi x$ has the same force as $N\Sigma xN\phi x$ ('Everything ϕ's' = 'Not anything does not ϕ', i.e. 'It is not the case that there is an x such that x does not ϕ'). Using either equivalence as a definition, the other is derivable as a thesis. We shall here take Π as fundamental, and use the definition

Df. Σ: $\Sigma x = N\Pi xN$.

The consequent equivalence of Πx and $N\Sigma xN$ may be proved as follows:

1. $CCpqCCqrCpr$
2. $CpNNp$

    $2\ p/\phi x = 3$

3. $C\phi xNN\phi x$

    $3\times\Pi 1 = 4$

4. $C\Pi x\phi xNN\phi x$

$4\times\Pi 2 = 5$

5. $C\Pi x\phi x\Pi xNN\phi x$

$1\ p/\Pi x\phi x,\ q/\Pi xNN\phi x,\ r/NN\Pi xNN\phi x$

$= C5\text{—}C2\ p/\Pi xNN\phi x\text{—}6$

6. $C\Pi x\phi xNN\Pi xNN\phi x$

$6\times\text{Df. }\Sigma = 7$

7. $C\Pi x\phi xN\Sigma xN\phi x$.

The converse implication $C(N\Sigma xN\phi x)(\Pi x\phi x)$ may be proved similarly from *CNNpp*. It should be noted that the application of $\Pi 2$ to 4 in the proof of 5 is legitimate, as x is bound in 4 by the quantifier Πx. Other theses of the same general sort which are easily provable are $C(\Sigma xN\phi x)(N\Pi x\phi x)$ (from 7 and *CCpNqCqNp*, $p/\Pi x\phi x$, $q/\Sigma xN\phi x$) and its converse, and $C(\Pi xN\phi x)(N\Sigma x\phi x)$ and its converse. We may abbreviate these results to $\Sigma xN = N\Pi x$ and $\Pi xN = N\Sigma x$ ('Some not' = 'Not all', and 'All not' = 'Not any'). These theses correspond to certain medieval rules about what was called 'equipollence', i.e. the equivalence of certain propositions obtained from one another by inserting 'not' in appropriate places.

Corresponding in a similar way to one of the traditional rules of what was called 'subalternation' is another thesis of the logic of quantifiers, $C(\Pi x\phi x)(\Sigma x\phi x)$, 'If everything ϕ's then something ϕ's', which may be proved as follows:

1. *CCpqCCqrCpr*

2. *Cpp*

3. *CCpNqCqNp*

$2\ p/\phi x\times\Pi 1 = 4$

4. $C\Pi x\phi x\phi x$

$2\ p/N\phi x\times\Pi 1 = 5$

5. $C\Pi xN\phi xN\phi x$

$3\ p/\Pi xN\phi x,\ q/\phi x = C5\text{—}6$

6. $C\phi xN\Pi xN\phi x$

$6\times\text{Df. }\Sigma = 7$

7. $C\phi x\Sigma x\phi x$

    1 $p/\Pi x\phi x$, $q/\phi x$, $r/\Sigma x\phi x$ = $C4$—$C7$—8

8. $C\Pi x\phi x\Sigma x\phi x$.

Here thesis 4 could be read 'If everything ϕ's then any given thing ϕ's', and thesis 7, 'If any given thing ϕ's then something ϕ's', from which 8 follows by syllogism. The proposition 4 x/y is used by Hilbert and Ackermann as a special axiom (the only one) for the lower functional calculus.

If we combine the results of the last two paragraphs, and remember that $CpNq$ is equivalent to Dpq and $CNpq$ to Apq, we have a set of theses which may be represented by the following diagram, which in the traditional logic would be called a 'square of opposition':

$$\Pi x\phi x \qquad\qquad \Pi x N\phi x$$
$$(= N\Sigma x N\phi x) \xleftarrow{\quad D\quad} \qquad (= N\Sigma x\phi x)$$

$$\Sigma x\phi x \qquad\qquad \Sigma x N\phi x$$
$$(= N\Pi x N\phi x) \xleftarrow{\quad A\quad} (= N\Pi x\phi x)$$

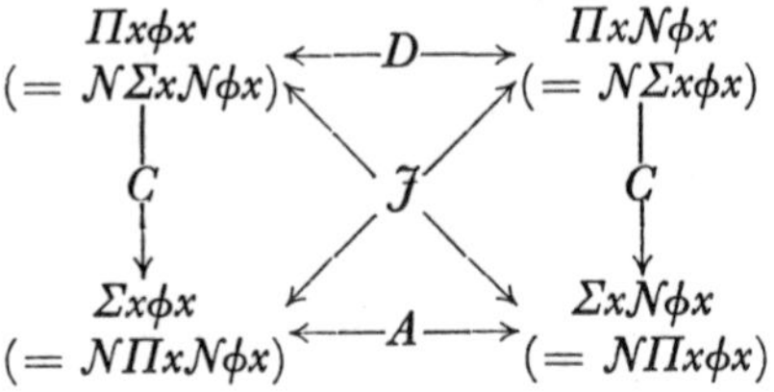

It was noted in the Middle Ages that there is a close resemblance between the laws of equipollence mentioned in the last paragraph and the principles now known as de Morgan's Laws, and the similarity may be brought out by arranging the propositions involved in de Morgan's Laws into a parallel square,[1] thus:

$$Kpq \qquad\qquad KNpNq$$
$$(= NANpNq) \xleftarrow{\quad D\quad} \quad (= NApq)$$
$$\quad C \qquad\qquad J \qquad\qquad C$$
$$Apq \qquad\qquad ANpNq$$
$$(= NKNpNq) \xleftarrow{\quad A\quad} (= NKpq)$$

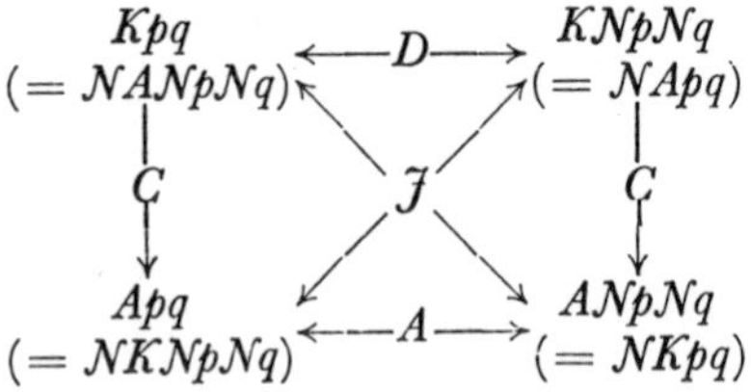

There are many other points at which the same analogy between universal quantification and conjunction, and existential quantification and alternation, may be drawn, and some writers have attempted to account for it by saying that universally quantified propositions in fact *are* conjunctions, and

---

[1] Cf. Bocheński, *Précis de logique mathématique*, 3.92.

existentially quantified ones alternations.[1] For suppose we use the letters '*a*', '*b*', '*c*', etc., not as name-variables but as actual names, so that when 'ϕ' is assigned a meaning, 'ϕa', 'ϕb', etc., will be not mere forms of propositions but actual propositions. Then, it is argued, the proposition 'Everything ϕ's' is equivalent to the conjunction of all such propositions as '*a* ϕ's', '*b* ϕ's', '*c* ϕ's', etc., i.e. '$\Pi x\phi x$' = 'ϕa and ϕb and ϕc, etc.'; and '$\Sigma x\phi x$' is similarly equivalent to 'ϕa or ϕb or ϕc, etc.' This argument will not, I think, bear examination, for we cannot deduce 'Everything ϕ's' from 'ϕa and ϕb and ϕc, etc.', without the added premiss that *a*, *b*, *c*, etc., are all the things there are. It remains true, however, that there is a close connexion between these two propositions (the universally quantified one and the conjunction), and we shall find that there are certain branches of logic into which quantifiers may be introduced in which the required additional premiss is a logical law.

Another group of theses in connexion with which the same analogy is evident, is the group relating to what is called the 'movement' of quantifiers. Not only '$\mathcal{N}$' but operators such as '*A*' and '*K*', may be introduced into quantified formulae in two ways—before the quantifier and after it. Thus we can distinguish such forms as $\Pi xA\phi x\psi x$ ('Everything either ϕ's or ψ's') and $A\Pi x\phi x\Pi x\psi x$ ('Either everything ϕ's or everything ψ's). Of forms related in this way, some are equivalent and some are not, though where they are not equivalent there will be a one-way implication. 'Either everything ϕ's or everything ψ's' for example, implies 'Everything either ϕ's or ψ's', though not vice versa. That the converse implication does not hold becomes plain if we let $\psi x = \mathcal{N}\phi x$. 'Everything either ϕ's, or does not ϕ' ($\Pi xA\phi x\mathcal{N}\phi x$) is a logical law, true no matter what ϕ may be (we shall prove it later); but 'Either everything ϕ's or everything does-not-ϕ' i.e. 'Either everything ϕ's or nothing ϕ's', is in many cases not true at all. That the original implication, on the other hand, does hold, is plain from the consideration that (1) 'Everything ϕ's' implies 'Everything either ϕ's or ψ's', and so does 'Everything ψ's' and (2) where *p* implies *r* and

[1] So, e.g., W. E. Johnson, in 'The Logical Calculus' (*Mind*, 1892); Wittgenstein, *Tractatus Logico-Philosophicus*, 5.501, 502, 52; F. P. Ramsey, *The Foundations of Mathematics*, pp. 8–9. For an instructive criticism of this point of view see G. H. von Wright's *Form and Content in Logic* (1949), pp. 16–21.

q also implies r, 'Either p or q' implies r. The implications and equivalences arising with forms of this sort may be exhibited in the first of the following hexagons, the analogous implications and equivalences involving conjunctions and alternations being given in the second:

$$\begin{array}{ccc} & \Pi xK\phi x\psi x & \\ & (= K\Pi x\phi x\Pi x\psi x) & \\ \swarrow & & \searrow \\ \Sigma xK\phi x\psi x & & A\Pi x\phi x\Pi x\psi x \\ \downarrow & (1) & \downarrow \\ K\Sigma x\phi x\Sigma x\psi x & & \Pi xA\phi x\psi x \\ \searrow & & \swarrow \\ & \Sigma xA\phi x\psi x & \\ & (= A\Sigma x\phi x\Sigma x\psi x) & \end{array} \qquad \begin{array}{ccc} & KK\phi a\psi aK\phi b\psi b & \\ & (= KK\phi a\phi bK\psi a\psi b) & \\ \swarrow & & \searrow \\ AK\phi a\psi aK\phi b\psi b & & AK\phi a\phi bK\psi a\psi b \\ \downarrow & (2) & \downarrow \\ KA\phi a\phi bA\psi a\psi b & & KA\phi a\psi aA\phi b\psi b \\ \searrow & & \swarrow \\ & AA\phi a\psi aA\phi b\psi b & \\ & (= AA\phi a\phi bA\psi a\psi b) & \end{array}$$

(The relations between the corresponding propositions in the two hexagons will become very clear if in both hexagons we let 'ϕ' = 'smokes' and 'ψ' = 'drinks', in the second let 'a' = 'Socrates' and 'b' = 'Plato', and in the first say 'Everyone' and 'Someone' instead of 'Everything' and 'Something').[1]

The universally quantified implicative form $\Pi xC\phi x\psi x$, 'For all x, if x ϕ's then x ψ's', or as we might say 'If anything ϕ's it ψ's', is of sufficient importance to have been given a special name, though the name for it to which Russell and Whitehead have given currency is in some ways unfortunate. They call it the 'formal implication' of ψx by ϕx, thereby distinguishing it from the 'material' implication of q by p, Cpq. This name suggests that when implications of this sort hold the consequent follows from the antecedent in virtue of its form, but this is by no means always the case. Let 'ϕ' be 'is a dinosaur' and 'ψ' be 'is dead'; then so far as we know, 'For all x, if x is a dinosaur then x is dead' is true, but it is not a logical law, and propositions of the form 'x is dead' do not follow from the corresponding propositions of the form 'x is a dinosaur' in virtue of what is purely logical in their form, but (if we can speak of such 'following' at all) in virtue of a fact of nature. So-called formal implications are in fact very close in their meaning to the 'Every X is Y' of the Aristotelian logic, and it is easy to establish laws involving them which sound very like laws of

[1] Cf. W. E. Johnson, in *Mind*, 1892, pp. 239–41.

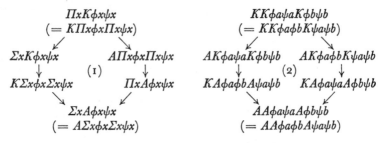

Aristotelian syllogism. For example, the law which appears at the end of the following deduction:

1. $CCpqCCqrCpr$
2. $CCpCqrCqCpr$
3. $CCpCqrCKpqr$

   $1\ p/\phi x,\ q/\psi x,\ r/\theta x = 4$

4. $C(C\phi x\psi x)C(C\psi x\theta x)(C\phi x\theta x)$

   $4 \times \Pi 1 = 5$

5. $C(\Pi xC\phi x\psi x)C(C\psi x\theta x)(C\phi x\theta x)$

   $2\ p/\Pi xC\phi x\psi x,\ q/C\psi x\theta x,\ r/C\phi x\theta x = C5\text{—}6$

6. $C(C\psi x\theta x)C(\Pi xC\phi x\psi x)(C\phi x\theta x)$

   $6 \times \Pi 1 = 7$

7. $C(\Pi xC\psi x\theta x)C(\Pi xC\phi x\psi x)(C\phi x\theta x)$

   $3\ p/\Pi xC\psi x\theta x,\ q/\Pi xC\phi x\psi x,\ r/C\phi x\theta x = C7\text{—}8$

8. $CK(\Pi xC\psi x\theta x)(\Pi xC\phi x\psi x)(C\phi x\theta x)$

   $8 \times \Pi 2 = 9$

9. $CK(\Pi xC\psi x\theta x)(\Pi xC\phi x\psi x)(\Pi xC\phi x\theta x)$.

Here 3 is a thesis from the calculus of propositions called the 'law of importation', to the effect that if p implies that q implies r, then 'Both p and q' implies r. The converse also holds, and we have already assumed this equivalence without mentioning the fact in our informal comments on various implications which we have had to consider. The conclusion, thesis 9, reads

If both if-anything-ψ's-it-θ's, and if-anything-ϕ's-it-ψ's, then if-anything-ϕ's-it-θ's.

The resemblance of this to the Aristotelian principle

If every *Y* is a *Z* and every *X* is a *Y*, then every *X* is a *Z*,

is obvious.

There are, however, other features of the Russellian 'formal implication' which make it questionable whether we should identify it with the Aristotelian 'Every *X* is a *Y*' without more ado. In particular, it is easy to deduce from the 'paradoxical' law for material implication, $CNpCpq$, an analogous law for formal, namely $C(\Pi xN\phi x)(\Pi xC\phi x\psi x)$, 'If nothing at all ϕ's, then if anything ϕ's it ψ's', whatever ψ-ing may be. Thus from the fact that there are no mermaids, we could infer that, in the sense in which 'if' is here used, if anything is a mermaid it wears spectacles. But would we automatically count 'Every mermaid is a spectacle-wearer' true on the ground that there are no mermaids? It is at least doubtful.

Before passing on to the next section, a little should be said on the 'metalogic' of this branch of logic. There are, in particular, a number of subsidiary rules which are derivable from $\Pi 1$ and $\Pi 2$. The most important of these are the two for Σ, mentioned earlier.[1] These are:

Σ 1. $C\phi x\beta \rightarrow C\Sigma x\phi x\beta$, for x not free in β.

Σ 2. $C\alpha\phi x \rightarrow C\alpha\Sigma x\phi x$, unrestrictedly.

The derivation of $\Sigma 2$ is as follows: By $\Pi 1$, $C\phi x\beta \rightarrow C\Pi x\phi x\beta$. Let β be a negative formula $N\alpha$, and ϕ a negative predicate $N\phi$. Then we have $CN\phi xN\alpha \rightarrow C\Pi xN\phi xN\alpha$. But by substitution in $CCpqCNqNp$ we can always obtain $CN\phi xN\alpha$ from $C\alpha\phi x$; and by substitution in $CCpNqCqNp$ we can always obtain $C\alpha N\Pi xN\phi x$, i.e. $C\alpha\Sigma x\phi x$, from $C\Pi xN\phi xN\alpha$. So we have

$$C\alpha\phi x \rightarrow CN\phi xN\alpha \rightarrow C\Pi xN\phi xN\alpha \rightarrow C\alpha N\Pi xN\phi x = C\alpha\Sigma x\phi x,$$

and so, by syllogism, $C\alpha\phi x \rightarrow C\alpha\Sigma x\phi x$. $\Sigma 1$ follows from $\Pi 2$ similarly.

Another derivative rule is that if any thesis is of the form ϕx, with x free, then Πx may be prefixed to the whole. Thus, since we have $ApNp$ as a thesis of the propositional calculus, we have $A\phi xN\phi x$ by the substitution $p/\phi x$, and from this we may pass to $\Pi xA\phi xN\phi x$, 'Everything either ϕ's or does not ϕ.' The other 'laws of thought' $NKpNp$ and Epp have the similar analogues $\Pi xNK\phi xN\phi x$ and $\Pi xE\phi x\phi x$. The general proof of this rule is as follows: Given any thesis of the form ϕx, we may substitute ϕx for p, and any thesis α in which x is not free for q, in $CpCqp$; giving us $C\phi xC\alpha\phi x$. Since ϕx is a thesis, we may detach $C\alpha\phi x$ from this, and since x is not free in α, we may obtain $C\alpha\Pi x\phi x$ by $\Pi 2$. Finally, since α is a thesis, we may detach $\Pi x\phi x$. For example, we may prove $\Pi xE\phi x\phi x$ from $E\phi x\phi x$ as follows:

1. $E\phi x\phi x$
2. $CpCqp$

$$2\ p/E\phi x\phi x,\ q/CpCqp = C1\text{—}3$$

[1] See Łukasiewicz, *Aristotle's Syllogistic*, pp. 61–66, 84–85.

3. $C(CpCqp)(E\phi x\phi x)$

$3 \times \Pi 2 = C2—4$

4. $\Pi x E\phi x\phi x$[1]

(Here our ϕx is $E\phi x\phi x$, and our α, $CpCqp$.)

It should be noted also, on the metalogical side, that when quantifiers are introduced it is necessary to modify slightly the rule that any predicational function may be substituted for any propositional variable in a thesis. To see what the restriction on this rule must be, we may consider a particular case. Among the theses which arise in the logic of quantification are ones in which a quantifier is prefixed to a compound predicational function which contains both a simple predicational function and a simple propositional variable; for example, the thesis at the end of the following proof:

1. Cpp
2. $CCKpqrCpCqr$
3. $CCpCqrCKpqr$

$2\ p/\phi x,\ q/p,\ r/K\phi xp = C1\ p/K\phi xp—4$

4. $C\phi xCpK\phi xp$

$4 \times \Pi 1 = 5$

5. $C\Pi x\phi xCpK\phi xp$

$3\ p/\Pi x\phi x,\ q/p,\ r/K\phi xp = C5—6$

6. $CK\Pi x\phi xpK\phi xp$

$6 \times \Pi 2 = 7$

7. $CK\Pi x\phi xp\Pi xK\phi xp$.

Here we might read 7 as 'If it is true both that everything ϕ's and that p, then it is true of everything that both it ϕ's and p'; for example, if it is true both that everything either-smokes-or-does-not-smoke and that $2+2 = 4$, then we can truly say of everything 'It either-smokes-or-does-not-smoke, and $2+2 = 4$.' This is a genuine logical law. But if for the propositional variable p we substitute ψx, we obtain

$$C(K\Pi x\phi x\psi x)(\Pi xK\phi x\psi x),$$

'If it is true both that everything ϕ's and that a certain given

[1] For another example see Łukasiewicz, op. cit., pp. 86–87.

thing ψ's, then it is true of everything that it both ϕ's and ψ's', which is not a logical law at all. The restriction we require to prevent the derivation of such results is that where a free variable occurs in a thesis as part of a predicational function in which some other variable is bound by a quantifier outside the function, then the variable thus bound cannot be substituted for the free one, nor can any function in which it occurs freely. In the above example, the free variable p occurs in the latter part of thesis 7 as part of the predicational function $K\phi xp$, in which the variable x is bound by the quantifier Πx outside the function; hence we cannot here subtitute for p the function ψx in which x occurs freely. Similarly in the thesis

$$C(K\Pi x\phi x\psi y)(\Pi xK\phi x\psi y),$$

which is a result of legitimate substitution in 7, and in the latter part of which the free variable y occurs as part of the predicational function $K\phi x\psi y$, in which the variable x is bound by the quantifier Πx outside the function, we cannot substitute x for y. (If we could we would again obtain $CK\Pi x\phi x\psi x\Pi xK\phi x\psi x$.)

The rules $\Pi 1$ and $\Pi 2$, with the qualified substitutability of predicational functions for propositional variables, superimposed on the rules and axioms of the propositional calculus, will provide a complete basis for the lower functional calculus. They will do so, at least, in the sense that by these means we may derive as theses all formulae constructible in this calculus which yield true propositions no matter what objects and predicates we let the name-variables and predicate-variables stand for. We can, that is, prove all logical laws in this field in this way. But in the stronger sense of 'complete', in which the addition to our basis of any formula not provable from it would make the system inconsistent, this calculus is not completable. Consider, for example, the formula $C\phi x\Pi x\phi x$, 'If x ϕ's then everything ϕ's.' This is not provable by means of $\Pi 1$, $\Pi 2$, etc., and it is as well that it is not, for it is certainly not true regardless of what 'x' and 'ϕ' may stand for. (Its assertion as a thesis would amount to the assertion that there is only one object.) If, however, we add it to our basis (or to any basis from which the lower predicate calculus may be 'completed' in the weaker sense), the resulting system will not be inconsistent, but will merely be one in which quantification is pointless, since

Πxφx, *Σxφx*, and the simple *φx* will all be equivalent, and substitutable for one another in all formulae. The system will, in fact, collapse into the propositional calculus with some superfluous symbols; but the propositional calculus is not inconsistent.

§ 2. *Predications of a Plurality of Subjects, and Multiple Quantification*

A proposition often concerns more than one subject at once. We have already remarked that it is not easy to identify 'the' subject in forms with more than one name-variable, e.g. *Cφxφy*. We might exemplify this form by the proposition 'If Caesar was a tyrant then Brutus acted rightly in killing him'. Is 'Brutus' or 'Caesar' the subject of this? (Is the proposition 'about' Brutus or 'about' Caesar?) We can, moreover, raise this question even about the simple 'Brutus killed Caesar'. No doubt grammarians would have no hesitation in identifying the subject of this as 'Brutus', dismissing 'Caesar' as merely the 'object'; and it is certainly true that the proposition is about Brutus, and that what it says of him is that he killed Caesar. But it is equally true that the proposition is about Caesar, saying of him that Brutus killed him. 'Brutus' and 'Caesar' are *both* of them 'subjects' in the logical sense, and the predicate is the 'dyadic' predicate '... killed ....' We could in the same way describe *C*, *A*, and *K* as 'dyadic' truth-operators, and *N* a 'monadic' one, as '... sits' is a monadic predicate or operator upon subjects. We owe this distinction to Peirce,[1] who observed that there are also predicates of still higher 'adinity', such as '... gives ... to ...', which would be 'triadic'. Given a dyadic predicate, we can of course construct an artificial monadic one out of it by filling in one of its blanks, e.g. '... killed Caesar', and we may similarly construct monadic and dyadic predicates out of triadic ones, e.g. '... gave ... to Joan' and 'Richard gave ... to Joan.'[2] But the fact remains that these predicates of higher 'adinity' exist, and associated with them are distinct forms of inference which the logician cannot ignore.

To symbolize dyadic predicational functions, we can use

[1] *Collected Papers*, 3.465.

[2] Conversely, we may regard predicates as propositions with so many holes punched in them. From this point of view a proposition is a predicate with an adinity of zero—a 'medadic' predicate, as Peirce called it.

such forms as 'ϕxy'. These, like monadic predicational functions, may have quantifiers prefixed to them, and such quantifiers may, moreover, bind either or both of their variables. Thus we may have the forms '$\Pi x\phi xy$', 'For all x, x ϕ's y' or 'Everything ϕ's y'; '$\Pi y\phi xy$', 'For all y, x ϕ's y' or 'x ϕ's everything', and '$\Pi x\Pi y\phi xy$', 'For all x, and for all y, x ϕ's y', or 'Everything ϕ's everything'. We may have, too, the form '$\Pi x\phi xx$', 'For all x, x ϕ's x', or 'Everything ϕ's itself', which is another way of constructing an artificial monadic predicate out of a dyadic one. The form '$\Pi xC\phi x\psi x$' could be regarded as a special case of this. If we wished to bring this out verbally, we could say that 'If anything ϕ's it ψ's' amounts to 'Everything ψ's if ϕ-ing is done by it', so that the predicate which links each thing with itself is '. . . ψ's if ϕ-ing is done by . . .'.

Double quantification may be the same or different for different variables, and where it is different, the order in which the quantifiers are placed makes a difference to the force of the proposition. For example, $\Pi x(\Sigma y\phi xy)$, 'For every x, there is some y such that x ϕ's y', or 'Everything ϕ's something', is a weaker form than $\Sigma y(\Pi x\phi xy)$, 'For some y, it is true of every x that x ϕ's y', or 'Something has everything ϕ-ing it'. For in the former case, the things ϕ'd by each thing might be different. At this point the analogy with conjunction and alternation is again helpful. 'Everything ϕ's something' behaves like 'Everything either ϕ's a or ϕ's b or ϕ's c, etc.', while 'Something has everything ϕ-ing it' behaves like 'Either everything ϕ's a or everything ϕ's b or everything ϕ's c, etc.'[1] The relations of equivalence and implication between doubly quantified forms may be exhibited by a hexagon like that for $\Pi xK\phi x\psi x$, etc., and the analogous forms placed in a hexagon beside it, thus:

$$\begin{array}{ccc} & \Pi x\Pi y\phi xy & \\ & (=\Pi y\Pi x\phi xy) & \\ \swarrow & & \searrow \\ \Sigma x\Pi y\phi xy & & \Sigma y\Pi x\phi xy \\ \downarrow & (1) & \downarrow \\ \Pi y\Sigma x\phi xy & & \Pi x\Sigma y\phi xy \\ \searrow & & \swarrow \\ & \Sigma x\Sigma y\phi xy & \\ & (=\Sigma y\Sigma x\phi xy) & \end{array} \qquad \begin{array}{ccc} & \Pi xK\phi xa\phi xb & \\ & (=K\Pi x\phi xa\Pi x\phi xb) & \\ \swarrow & & \searrow \\ \Sigma xK\phi xa\phi xb & & A\Pi x\phi xa\Pi x\phi xb \\ \downarrow & (2) & \downarrow \\ K\Sigma x\phi xa\Sigma x\phi xb & & \Pi xA\phi xa\phi xb \\ \searrow & & \swarrow \\ & \Sigma xA\phi xa\phi xb & \\ & (=A\Sigma x\phi xa\Sigma x\phi xb) & \end{array}$$

[1] Cf. W. E. Johnson, in *Mind*, 1892, pp. 244–6.

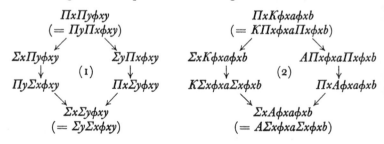

(To see the analogies, let 'ϕ' be 'influences' in both hexagons, and in the second let 'a' be 'Mars' and 'b' be 'Jupiter'.) Like the laws relating to $A\Pi x$ and ΠxA, etc., these laws are called 'laws of movement' of the quantifiers. To illustrate their proof by means of Łukasiewicz's rules, we may take the following derivation of $C(\Sigma x\Pi y\phi xy)(\Pi y\Sigma x\phi xy)$:

1. Cpp

   $1\ p/\phi xy \times \Pi 1y = 2$
2. $C\Pi y\phi xy\phi xy$

   $2 \times \Sigma 2x = 3$
3. $C\Pi y\phi xy\Sigma x\phi xy$

   $3 \times \Sigma 1x = 4$
4. $C\Sigma x\Pi y\phi xy\Sigma x\phi xy$

   $4 \times \Pi 2y = 5$
5. $C\Sigma x\Pi y\phi xy\Pi y\Sigma x\phi xy$.

Where the two quantifiers are of the same sort, we may abbreviate '$\Pi x\Pi y$' to 'Πxy' and '$\Sigma x\Sigma y$' to 'Σxy'; the formula '$\Pi xy\phi xy$' may be read 'For all pairs x, y, x ϕ's y', and '$\Sigma xy\phi xy$' may be read 'There is at least one pair x, y, such that x ϕ's y'.

'Triadic' predicational functions may be dealt with similarly. Where there are three variables to quantify, there are not six but twenty-six non-equivalent quantified forms. To illustrate the distinctions arising, we may take the four possible cases in which the first variable is universally quantified and the second and third existentially—(i) $\Pi x\Sigma yz\phi xyz$; (ii) $\Sigma y\Pi x\Sigma z\phi xyz$; (iii) $\Sigma z\Pi x\Sigma y\phi xyz$; (iv) $\Sigma yz\Pi x\phi xyz$. Restricting our x's and z's to persons, we might illustrate (i) by 'Everyone gives something to someone'; (ii) then becomes 'There is something which everyone gives to someone'; (iii) 'There is someone to whom everyone gives something'; and (iv) 'There is at least one thing and at least one person such that everyone gives the first to the second'. Here (iv) implies both (ii) and (iii), and each of the latter implies (i). These implications follow easily enough from those occurring with two quantifications. Thus we might derive $\Pi x\Sigma y\Sigma z\phi xyz$ from $\Sigma y\Pi x\Sigma z\phi xyz$ by $C(\Sigma y\Pi x\phi xy)(\Pi x\Sigma y\phi xy)$, by arguing that $\Sigma z\phi xyz$ is a predicational function of x and y, and so may be substituted for ϕxy in any thesis. In setting out such a proof formally, we might lay down a special rule of substitution for predicate-variables, to the effect that a predicate-variable followed by name-variables may be replaced in a thesis by any predicational function containing those name-variables in argument-places, it being understood that (*a*) a predicate variable followed by name-variables (one or more) is a predicational function, (*b*) truth-functions of predicational functions are predicational functions, and (*c*) predicational functions with variables (one or more) bound by quantifiers are predicational functions. Alternatively, we might do without such a rule, and work out each case by appropriate substitutions in theses of the propositional calculus, and applications of the rules for quantifiers. Thus for the above case we would have

1. Cpp

   $1\ p/\Sigma z\phi xyz \times \Pi 1x = 2$

2. $C\Pi x\Sigma z\phi xyz\Sigma z\phi xyz$

   $2 \times \Sigma 2y = 3$

3. $C\Pi x\Sigma z\phi xyz\Sigma y\Sigma z\phi xyz$

   $3 \times \Sigma 1y = 4$

4. $C\Sigma y\Pi x\Sigma z\phi xyz\Sigma y\Sigma z\phi xyz$

   $4 \times \Pi 2x = 5$

5. $C\Sigma y\Pi x\Sigma z\phi xyz\Pi x\Sigma y\Sigma z\phi xyz$.

The alternative proof, with direct substitution for predicational functions, would be

1. $C\Sigma y\Pi x\phi xy\Pi x\Sigma y\phi xy$

   $1\ \phi xy/\Sigma z\phi xyz = 2.$

2. $C\Sigma y\Pi x\Sigma z\phi xyz\Pi x\Sigma y\Sigma z\phi xyz$,

1 being proved from *Cpp* at an earlier point in the system.

It should be noted that substitution for predicate-variables in quantified formulae, as in the proof last given, does not break the rule that substitutions cannot be made for variables that are bound, unless of course we are dealing with formulae containing quantifiers like '$\Pi\phi$' and '$\Sigma\phi$', as we are not in the above case. And we may let this point be a reminder to us that the multiplication of name-variables and quantifiers, which can of course be continued indefinitely, does not in itself take us beyond what we called the 'lower' functional calculus. We have noted that for this calculus, in the form in which we have presented it, and in a variety of other forms (e.g. with different unproved rules and the axiom $C\Pi x\phi x\phi x$, or—what amounts to the same thing—$C\Pi x\phi x\phi y$), at least 'weak' completeness may be proved.[1] With the 'higher' functional calculus, however, in which such bindings as '$\Pi\phi$' and '$\Sigma\phi$' do occur, the matter is vastly more complicated.

If predicates, i.e. operators on names, are to be thus bound, in formulae like $\Pi\phi Cf\phi g\phi$, there is no reason why operators on predicates should not be bound by quantifiers also, giving us such formulae as $\Pi fCFfGf$, where f stands indifferently for any proposition-forming operator on predicates, e.g. $\Pi x'x$. As an example of a thesis of the form $\Pi fCFfGf$, we may take this: 'If f is any quantifier, then either $f\phi$ implies $NfN\phi$, whatever ϕ may be, or $NfN\phi$ implies $f\phi$, whatever ϕ may be', the predicate-of-predicates-of-predicates '. . . is a quantifier' being so defined that it will be true only of $\Pi x'x$, $\Sigma x'x$, $\Pi xN'x$, $\Sigma xN'x$, and operators equivalent to one or the other of these, e.g. $NN\Pi x'x$, $\Sigma xNN'x$, and so on. $\Pi x'x$ is an example of an f such that $f\phi$ always implies $NfN\phi$ (for we have $\Pi\phi C\Pi x\phi xN\Pi xN\phi x$), while $\Sigma x'x$ is an example of an f such that $NfN\phi$ always implies $f\phi$ (for we have $\Pi\phi CN\Sigma xN\phi x\Sigma x\phi x$); and our thesis states that all quantifiers (defined as indicated) are of one or the other of these two sorts. Written out entirely in symbols (with F for '. . . is a quantifier'), the thesis is

$$\Pi fC(Ff)A(\Pi\phi Cf\phi NfN\phi)(\Pi\phi CNfN\phi f\phi).$$

This is of the form $\Pi fCFfGf$, G here being the (monadic) predicate-of-predicates-of-predicates

$$A(\Pi\phi C'\phi N'N\phi)(\Pi\phi CN'N\phi'\phi).$$

From this thesis we may easily derive another like it, namely

$$\Pi fC(Ff)A(\Pi\phi CfN\phi Nf\phi)(\Pi\phi CNf\phi fN\phi),$$

i.e. if f is any quantifier then either $fN\phi$ always implies $Nf\phi$ (as $\Pi xN\phi x$, for example, implies $N\Pi x\phi x$) or $Nf\phi$ always implies

[1] See Hilbert and Ackermann, *Principles of Mathematical Logic*, Ch. ii, § 10.

fNφ (as *NΣxφx*, for example, implies *ΣxNφx*). In deriving the second thesis from the first we would make use of the laws of transposition *CCpNqCqNp* and *CCNqpCNpq*, with the substitutions *p/fφ*, *q/fNφ* and vice versa.[1]

We can clearly carry this process still further, binding variables of higher and higher types; and what is usually understood by the 'higher functional calculus' of 'higher predicate calculus' is the calculus 'of order ω', i.e. with no limit to the types of variables that may be bound by quantifiers. And for the higher functional calculus in this sense, a 'complete' basis is not possible; for it has been shown to be the kind of system in which we can construct formulae which are true if and only if they are not provable within the system.[2] For various limited segments of the higher functional calculus, however, even 'strongly' complete bases can be found, and we shall now consider something which in a way falls under this head, namely the direct use of quantifiers in the calculus of propositions to bind both propositional and functorial variables. (Of the higher functional calculus with predicational functions at its base, more will be said in II. iii. 4 and especially in III. iii.)

§ 3. *Quantification within the Propositional Calculus*

What might be called the standard modern approach to logic proceeds somewhat as follows: We begin by considering the use of truth-operators to form propositions out of other propositions, and are supplied with symbols for the various truth-operators, and for propositional variables. When we have seen what can be done with this material, we are introduced

[1] C. S. Peirce noted (*Collected Papers*, 4.83) that, in 'second-intentional logic', 'the forms of logisteria [i.e. quantifiers] themselves become subjects of study, and certain general propositions with regard to them are expressed as if they were shops or trees', and 'we find that we have to resort to logisteria of logisteria, and to their logisteria again, and so on indefinitely'. 'Operator on predicates' or 'operator on operators' might perhaps be a more accurate translation of Peirce's 'logisterium', for he remarks in the same place that 'among the forms of logisteria which require attentive study and which are found to possess interesting properties are particularly those which are infinite series,' and that 'the distinctive characters of different such infinite series of logisteria have to be discriminated.' Some such series of operators would be 'quantifiers' as described above, and some not, e.g. the series 'Precisely one thing ——s', 'Precisely two things ——', etc. (see III. iii. 2).

[2] Cf. what was said in the last chapter of systems in which we can formulate the systems' own 'syntax'.

to the operators ('predicates') which form propositions, not out of other propositions, but out of names, and so we have two new kinds of variable. We learn how to construct complex predicational functions out of simpler ones by means of the already familiar truth-operators; and finally, we are introduced to the use of quantifiers to bind name-variables, and so the lower functional calculus is built on to the calculus of propositions. This is the normal procedure; but here it has been varied a little. The constant proposition o has been introduced; and before proceeding to the functional calculus at all, variables for operators have been introduced, though for truth-operators upon propositions rather than for 'predicational operators' upon names. And we might easily have departed from the standard practice still more radically, by introducing not only operator-variables but also quantifiers while still in the realm of propositions unanalysed into predicates and names. This was in fact the procedure in the original 'protothetic' of Leśniewski.

Given a 'protothetic' thus enriched, we may define the symbol 'o' within it as an abbreviation for '*Πpp*', 'For all *p*, *p*'. It is doubtful whether the precise sense of this proposition can be expressed without using variables, but it is near enough to 'Everything is true', which is quite an interesting candidate for the position of Standard False Proposition. Meredith[1] has shown that if we thus add *Π*, with its two rules, to a *C*–δ system, the formula equivalent by Df.o to *C*δδoδ*p*, i.e. the formula *C*δδ*Πpp*δ*p*, is the only axiom we need to deduce all tautologous formulae which our new symbolic apparatus will enable us to construct. All tautologous formulae in which '*Π*' occurs only as part of the proposition '*Πpp*', i.e. 'o', can be proved by rewriting the axiom (as permitted by the definition) as *C*δδoδ*p*, and proceeding as before (or by writing '*Πpp*' for 'o' throughout the previous procedure). But beside these, there are tautologous formulae in which '*Π*' is used in other ways, e.g. the thesis *CΠp*δ*p*δ*p*, and theses in which the quantifier is used to bind functorial variables, e.g. *CΠ*δδ*p*δ*p*. 'Completeness' is established for Meredith's axiom and rules by showing that there are standard ways of proving all tautologous formulae of the latter type from those of the former type, using only certain theses derivable from the axiom.

[1] Op. cit., §§ 3 and 4.

Where the quantifier is used to bind propositional variables only, the standard form of proof is simple. The theses required for it are

(1) *CζK*δ0δ1*ζΠq*δ*q*

(2) *CζΠq*δ*qζK*δ0δ1,

where 'ζ' is a variable of the same sort as 'δ'. Between them, these theses assert that any truth-function of *K*δ0δ1 ('1' being defined as '*C*00', and '*Kpq*' as '*NCpNq*', i.e. as '*CCpCq*00') is equivalent to the same truth-function of *Πq*δ*q*. For example, the thesis *CΠqCpqCp*0 implies and is implied by *CKCp*0*Cp*1*Cp*0 (the first being *ζΠq*δ*q* with the substitutions δ/*Cp*' and ζ/*C*'*Cp*0, and the second being *ζK*δ0δ1 with the same substitutions). Hence, given thesis (1) above, substitution and detachment will enable us to prove *CΠqCpqCp*0 from *CKCp*0*Cp*1*Cp*0, the latter being a thesis of the sort earlier shown to be provable from *C*δδ0δ*p*. Meredith does not actually prove thesis (1) from his axiom, but he proves thesis (2), and for the other relies on a metalogical theorem established by Łukasiewicz, that from theses of the form *C*δ*P*δ*Q* (or *CζPζQ*) we can always derive the corresponding thesis of the form *C*δ*Q*δ*P* (or *CζQζP*). (We shall return to this metalogical theorem later.) Intuitively, theses (1) and (2) are obvious enough, if it be remembered that it is truth-functions with which we are dealing. For if the truth-function δ*q* holds both when $q = 0$ and when $q = 1$, i.e. if we have *K*δ0δ1, it will hold for any proposition *q* at all, i.e. we will have *Πq*δ*q*; and vice versa. And since *K*δ0δ1 and *Πq*δ*q* thus always have the same truth-value, any truth-function of either will have the same truth-value as that truth-function of the other, i.e. we will have both *CζK*δ0δ1*ζΠq*δ*q* and *CζΠq*δ*qζK*δ0δ1. Meredith's proof employs the formulae corresponding to these intuitive principles, i.e. *CK*δ0δ1δ*p* for the first part of the proof, and *CCpqCCqpCζpζq* for the second.

Just as the binding of propositional variables is eliminated by drawing upon the consideration that what holds for 0 and 1 holds for all propositions, so the binding of functorial variables is eliminated by the consideration that (within the limits of truth-functional logic) what holds for all of the functors (1, 1), (1, 0), (0, 1), and (0, 0) holds for all functors whatever. A pair of theses asserting this equivalence in a given case will have the form

(i) $C\zeta KKK\Phi(0, 0)\Phi(1, 0)\Phi(0, 1)\Phi(1, 1)\zeta\Pi\delta\Phi\delta$

(ii) $C\zeta\Pi\delta\Phi\delta\zeta KKK\Phi(0, 0)\Phi(1, 0)\Phi(0, 1)\Phi(1, 1)$,

'$\Phi\delta$' being some sub-formula containing 'δ', and '$\Phi(0, 0)$', etc., being the same sub-formulae with 'δ' replaced by (0, 0), etc. (i) and (ii) as written above are not, of course, themselves formulae of the system, since the system does not contain any such symbol as 'Φ' standing indifferently for any 'functor of functors'. (It does contain formulae like '$\delta\delta 0$', but here the first 'δ' does not stand for a functor with the second functor 'δ' as argument, but for a functor with the proposition '$\delta 0$' as argument. '$\delta\delta 0$' in its entirety is a function of 'δ', and is the sort of thing that '$\Phi\delta$' could stand for if the system did include such formulae.) (i) and (ii) are simply metalogical aids to the eye; and what Meredith shows is that a standard type of proof may be found for any pair of genuine formulae of this general shape, e.g. for

(*a*) $C\{\zeta KKK[C(0, 0)p(0, 0)p][C(1, 0)p(1, 0)p][C(0, 1)p(0, 1)p]$—
—$[C(1, 1)p(1, 1)p]\}\{\zeta\Pi\delta C\delta p\delta p\}$

(*b*) $C\{\zeta\Pi\delta C\delta p\delta p\}\{\zeta KKK[C(0, 0)p(0, 0)p][C(1, 0)p(1, 0)p]$—
—$[C(0, 1)p(0, 1)p][C(1, 1)p(1, 1)p]\}$

(where our functor-of-functors Φ is $C'p'p$), so that by substitution (for 'ζ') and detachment we can prove any formula with a '$\Pi\delta$' in it from one without.

'(0, 0)', etc., it may be noted, *are* symbols of the system, or rather certain others with the same meaning which Meredith uses are; his four 'constant functors' being defined by means of the system's primitive symbols as follows:

$(1, 0)p = p$

$(0, 1)p = Cp0$, i.e. Np

$(1, 1)p = C0p$ (this is always true, being a thesis)

$(0, 0)p = CC0p0$, i.e. $NC0p$

Thus (*a*) above turns by definition into

$(a')C\zeta KKK(CNC0pNC0p)(Cpp)(CNpNp)(CC0pC0p)\zeta\Pi\delta C\delta p\delta p$, which can in its turn be given its full form (something quite enormous) by referring to the definitions of 'o', '*N*', and '*K*'.

It is even possible, given the two rules for the introduction of *Π*, to prove all tautologous formulae in this field from a single axiom which does not itself contain *Π*. Meredith mentions three 8-letter axioms of this sort, any one of which would do—*CδpCqδδq*, *CpCδqδδp*, and *CδpδδCqq*. To establish their sufficiency, given the rules for introducing *Π*, one would need simply to prove *CδδΠppδp* from each of them. Without the rules for introducing *Π*, any one of these formulae would serve as a single axiom for the more restricted calculus formed by adding functorial variables to the 'implicational' calculus.[1]

§ 4. *Quantification and Equivalential Calculi: Definition Re-examined*

Leśniewski himself, and some of his earliest collaborators, were particularly interested in the extension, by the use of quantifiers and functorial variables, of versions of the propositional calculus in which the only undefined truth-functor is *E*, 'If and only if'.

Just as there is a restricted segment of the propositional calculus in which no symbols are needed but propositional variables and the operator '*C*', so there is another restricted segment in which no symbols are needed but propositional variables and the operator '*E*'. We may call this the 'equivalential' calculus. Among the more obvious theses occurring in it would be *Epp*, *EEpqEqp*, and *EEpqEEqrEpr*, or in the Peano–Russellian symbolism, $p \equiv p$, $p \equiv q . \equiv . q \equiv p$, and $p \equiv q : \equiv : q \equiv r . \equiv . p \equiv r$. Leśniewski and Łukasiewicz have shown that any formula thus constructed by equating equivalences is a thesis if every propositional variable in it occurs an even number of times,[2] and Łukasiewicz has shown that any one of the formulae *EEpqEErqEpr*, *EEpqEEprErq* and *EEpqEErpEqr* will serve as a sole axiom for the system.[3] These are much simpler axioms than Łukasiewicz's *CCCpqrCCrpCsp* for the 'implicational' calculus; but of course the theses which they suffice to prove are of a much more jejune and less varied kind, though they may be very long. But if quantifiers and functorial variables are introduced, we may obtain just as rich a system of 'protothetic' as if we start with '*C*'.

[1] Meredith, op. cit., § 1.
[2] Jordan, op. cit., p. 24.
[3] Sobociński, op. cit., p. 10.

In the first place, given 'Π', we may, as before, define '0' as 'Πpp', and 'Np' may then be defined either as '$Ep0$' or as '$E0p$'. Given 'E' and 'N', we may define 'Jpq' as '$NEpq$'; for Epq is true if and only if p and q have the same truth-value, while Jpq ('Either p or q but not both', or 'Either p but not q or q but not p') is true if and only if they have *not* the same truth-value, so that Jpq is true if and only if Epq is false.[1] There is a quite interesting segment of the propositional calculus in which the only truth-operators employed are E and J;[2] but with this we are still far from the full propositional calculus. In particular, 'C', 'K', and 'A' cannot be defined by means of the operators so far obtained. However, if we can obtain 'K' we can obtain the others; for $Cpq = EpKpq$ and $A = CN$. (We can show the former by truth-value calculation; or, thinking in terms of a calculus with implication as fundamental, we may reflect that 'If-and-only-if p then both p and q' asserts both 'If both p and q then p' and 'If p then both p and q'. The former holds in any case, and the latter holds if and only if p implies q. So we have *both* 'If both p and q then p' and 'If p then both p and q', i.e. we have $EpKpq$, if and only if we have Cpq.)

One of Leśniewski's collaborators, A. Tarski, showed that the problem of defining 'K' in terms of 'E' and 'Π' can be solved if we introduce functorial variables and bind them; and it can then be solved in more ways than one. A comparatively simple definition offered by Tarski is

$$Kpq = \Pi\delta EpE\delta p\delta q.$$

We may easily show that this gives the usual equations $K11 = 1$ and $K10 = K01 = K00 = 0$ by examining each case in turn. For $p = 1$ and $q = 1$ the defining formula becomes

$$\Pi\delta E1E\delta 1\delta 1.$$

Now we do have $E\delta 1\delta 1$ no matter what operator δ may be (by substitution in Epp), i.e. $E\delta 1\delta 1$ has the value of a true proposition no matter what δ may be, i.e. $\Pi\delta E1E1\delta 1\delta 1$. So with this

[1] 'Jpq' could also be defined as $EpNq$ ('If and only if p then not q') or as $ENpq$ ('If and only if not p then q'). For Jpq means that each of its arguments, being of the opposite truth-value to the other, is equivalent to the other's negation.

[2] A considerable amount of work has been done on this in Rumania. See reviews in the *Journal of Symbolic Logic*, vol. ii, p. 173; vol. iii, p. 55; vol. xv, p. 139. Examples of theses in this field would be $J(Epq)(Jpq)$ and $E(Jpq)(Jqp)$, from which pair we could infer $J(Jpq)(Epq)$.

definition of K, $K11 = 1$. For $p = 1$ and $q = 0$ the defining formula becomes

$$\Pi\delta E1E\delta1\delta0.$$

Suppose δ is the truth-operator (1, 0), so that $\delta1 = 1$ and $\delta0 = 0$. $E\delta1\delta0$ will then become $E10$, which has the value not of a true but of a false proposition; i.e. for this δ we have not $E1E\delta1\delta0$ but $E0E\delta1\delta0$. So the assertion that for any δ we have $E1E\delta1\delta0$ is false, i.e. $K10 = 0$. For $p = 0$ and $q = 1$ the defining formula becomes

$$\Pi\delta E0E\delta0\delta1.$$

Suppose δ is the truth-operator (1, 1), so that $\delta1 = 1$ and $\delta0 = 1$. $E\delta1\delta0$ will then become $E11$, which has the value not of a false but of a true proposition; i.e. for this δ we have not $E0E\delta0\delta1$ but $E1E\delta0\delta1$. So the assertion that for any δ we have $E0E\delta0\delta1$ is false, i.e. $K01 = 0$. Finally, for $p = 0$ and $q = 0$ the defining formula becomes

$$\Pi\delta E0E\delta0\delta0.$$

But whatever δ may be, by the law of identity $E\delta0\delta0$ has the value not of a false but of a true proposition; i.e. we have not $\Pi\delta E0E\delta0\delta0$ but rather $\Pi\delta E1E\delta0\delta0$. So with this definition, $K00 = 0$.

Leśniewski's special interest in a protothetic with an 'equivalential' basis arose from a theory he held respecting the nature of definition in formal systems. In his view, the simplicity achieved by Sheffer and Nicod in defining all truth-operators in terms of '*D*' was to some extent spurious, for '*D*' is not really the only undefined symbol employed—there is also the '=' used in the natural process of definition. Moreover, the rules of inference employed in such a system as Nicod's include not only the rule of substitution and the rule of detachment associated with '*D*' but also the rule of mutual substitutability of defined and defining formulae associated with '='. If we had to begin with no truth-operator but '*E*', with the rule of substitutability of equivalents proved or derivable, the simplicity achieved would not be spurious but genuine, for we could use '*E*' (or in the other symbolism, '≡') instead of '=' for definitions. Consequently in Leśniewski's writings, and in those who follow him at this point (e.g. Tarski and Sobociński), definitions are always written, not with a special symbol, but as equivalences. For example, Tarski's definition of '*Kpq*' is written

$$EKpq\Pi\delta EpE\delta p\delta q,$$

or in the Peano–Russellian symbolism

$$p.q.:\equiv:.(\delta):p.\equiv.\delta p\equiv\delta q.$$

Łukasiewicz, accepting the view that it is desirable to dispense with a special symbol for definitions, and a special associated rule, has shown that this can be done in an 'implicational' as well as in an 'equivalential' protothetic. For it can be shown that if we have any thesis of the form $C\delta P\delta Q$, P and Q will be interchangeable in any formulae in which they occur. It is plain that $C\delta P\delta Q$ will enable us, by substitution for δ and then detachment, to pass from any formula containing P to the same formula with P replaced by Q. (For example, given $C\delta p\delta NNp$, we can pass from Cpp to $CNNpp$ by performing the substitution $\delta/C'p$ in $C\delta p\delta NNp$.) But we can equally pass from a formula containing Q to the same formula with Q replaced by P; for from a thesis of the form $C\delta P\delta Q$ we can always deduce the corresponding thesis of the form $C\delta Q\delta P$ as follows:

1. $C\delta P\delta Q$
   1 $\delta/CC\delta P\delta' C\delta Q\delta P = C1\ \delta/C\delta'\delta P$—$C1$—2
2. $C\delta Q\delta P$.

Hence Łukasiewicz sometimes expresses definitions in this way (expressing, e.g., the definition of 'Np' as '$C\delta Np\delta Cp0$', and of '1' as '$C\delta 1\delta C00$'), and the same procedure is adopted by Meredith.

I have outlined this account of definitions as assertions of equivalence partly because the logicians who have espoused it—including Leśniewski, Tarski, Sobociński, and with modifications Łukasiewicz and Meredith—are about as distinguished a group as any theory could muster, and partly because it has had such fruitful by-products (the definition of '*K*' in terms of '*E*' and '*Π*', and the metalogical theorem reproduced in the last paragraph, are solid achievements). But I shall not conceal my own belief that it is wrong-headed. A grave objection to it is that it makes it difficult to distinguish between the definitions of a system and additional axioms; and the use of '=' can be defended against the charge of being a surreptitious introduction of a new primitive symbol. The authors of PM, for example, argue that definitions are not genuine parts of the deductive systems to which they are attached, but simply indicate alternative ways of symbolizing the same thing within the system. On this view—and this consequence of it is made very explicit by Whitehead and Russell—all defined symbols are in principle superfluous; the entire system could be set forth without them, only it would then be insufferably cumbrous. For example, if '*C*' be defined as '*AN*', the thesis '*CCpqANpq*', 'If if-*p*-then-*q*, then either-not-*p*-or-*q*, really tells us no more than '*CANpqANpq*', 'If either-not-*p*-or-*q* then either-not-*p*-or-*q*', and both of them say the same thing as '*ANANpqANpq*', 'Either not either-not-*p*-or-*q*, or either-not-*p*-or-*q*.' These three theses are in fact no more than three ways of writing a single thesis. And the 'rule' that we may pass from any one of them to either of the others (and also, of course, to '*CANpqCpq*' and '*CCpqCpq*') is not a rule of inference at all, but simply a rule of translation. No doubt, where $\alpha = \beta$ by definition, the thesis $E\alpha\beta$ will in general hold; but it holds simply because it is a way of writing $E\alpha\alpha$ (or $E\beta\beta$), which is a result of substitution in the law of identity.

The importance of the law of identity in the transformation of definitions into equivalences may be vividly brought out by considering systems in which that law is not provable. This would be the case, for example, with the system which has as its sole axiom

1. *E*(*EsEpp*)[*E*(*EsEpp*)(*EEpqEErqEpr*)],

and as its rules the usual rule of substitution for variables, and the rule of detachment in the form '$\alpha, E\alpha\beta \rightarrow \beta$'. It can be shown that nothing is provable in this system except what follows from the one axiom by substitution alone. For to apply the rule of detachment we must find substitutions for '*s*' and '*p*' which will turn the antecedent *EsEpp* into something which is also a substitution in the entire axiom; and very little trying will make clear the impossibility of this. Nor would the situation be substantially altered if we introduced the symbol '*V*' by the definition '*Vp* = *Epp*'. If, however, we introduce the equivalence

2. *EVpEpp*,

which is the Leśniewskian form of this definition, we may at once proceed as follows:

1 $s/Vp = E2—E2—3$

3. *EEpqEErqEpr*.

And from this last, Łukasiewicz has shown that all purely equivalential laws are derivable.[1] The very great difference that here appears between the definition '*Vp* = *Epp*' and the corresponding asserted equivalence may be put down to the impossibility of proving the law of identity in the initial system. The same difference would in fact be made if we introduced the law of identity itself as our second axiom. For we could then proceed as follows:

1. *EEsEppEEsEppEEpqEErqEpr*
2. *Epp*

1 $s/Epp = E2\ p/Epp—E2\ p/Epp—3$

3. *EEpqEErqEpr*.

The Russellian account of the matter no doubt needs to be modified a little in the light of the fact that logical laws may be systematized in different ways, so that what is an undefined symbol in one system is introduced by definition in another, with consequential changes in the proofs, and even, in a manner, in what is provable. Thus in a *C–N* system, with '*Kpq*' introduced as an abbreviation of '*NCpNq*', *C*(*Kpq*)(*NCpNq*) is a way of writing a result of substitution in *Cpp* (namely *CNCpNqNCpNq*), whereas *C*(*Cpq*)(*NKpNq*) is short for *C*(*Cpq*)(*NNCpNNq*) and requires a more elaborate proof. On the other hand, in a *K–N* system, with '*Cpq*' introduced as an abbreviation for '*NKpNq*', it is *C*(*Cpq*)(*NKpNq*) which expresses a result of substitution in *Cpp* (i.e. in *NKpNp*), whereas *C*(*Kpq*)(*NCpNq*) is short for *C*(*Kpq*)(*NNKpNNq*), i.e. for *NK*(*Kpq*)*N*(*NNKpNNq*), and requires the more elaborate proof. Moreover, although the three axioms *CCpqCCqrCpr*, *CCNppp*, and *CpCNpq* suffice for the proof of all laws in *C*, *N*, and *K*, including *CKpqNCpNq*, if '*Kpq*' is introduced by definition as '*NCpNq*', they will not suffice for

[1] The whole example is due to Łukasiewicz, as reported by H. Scholz in *Zentralblatt für Mathematik und ihre Grenzgebiete*, 1940. (I owe this reference to Professor A. Church.)

the proof of all laws in *C*, *N*, and *K* if it is '*N*' and '*K*' which are undefined and '*Cpq*' is introduced as short for '*NKpNq*'. In this second system the three axioms will themselves be short for

NK(*NKpNq*)*N*[*NK*(*NKqNr*)*N*(*NKpNr*)],
NK(*NKNpNp*)*Np*, and
NKpN(*NKNpNq*)

respectively; and among the theses not provable from these by substitution and detachment (i.e. detachment by the rule 'α, $NK\alpha N\beta \rightarrow \beta$') is the law just mentioned, *CKpqNCpNq*, i.e. *NK*(*Kpq*)*N*(*NNKpNNq*).[1] For a complete *K–N* system we need a different set of axioms, e.g. the four due to Sobociński

1. *NKNKNprKNKNqrKNKpqr*
2. *NKNpKpq*
3. *NKNqKpKrq*
4. *NKNKpqNNKpNNq* (i.e. *CNKpqCpNq*).

Confronted with these alternative approaches, we cannot refrain from asking ourselves, 'But which is *really* the operator whose function we understand without explanation, and which is *really* complex, though it may be given a simple symbol to save trouble?' And it is important to understand why the answer to this question does not matter, as far as the systematization is concerned. We might put it this way: the elaborator of, let us say, an *A–N* system in effect says to us, 'You understand, do you not, the use of "not" and of the non-exclusive "or"? Above all, you understand that "Not *p*" is true when "*p*" is false and false when "*p*" is true, and that "Either *p* or *q*" is true so long as "*p*" and "*q*" are not both false? Now you may, when you think of "or", say, be thinking of a relation between propositions which defies analysis, or you may be conscious that it is something complex—you may, e.g., think of "and" as something simple, and think of "Either *p* or *q*" as meaning "Not both not *p* and not *q*". Well, never mind about this—however you think of them, we shall use "*A*" for "Either" and "*N*" for "Not". And we shall use "*Kpq*" as an abbreviation for "*NANpNq*", and read it "Both *p* and *q*". If when you think of "and" you normally think of something simple, then we are

[1] The underivability of this from these axioms is shown in III. ii. 1.

not now using "*K*" for that, though we are using it for something which happens to be true and false under the same conditions.' The elaborator of a *K–N* system says much the same to us, but with 'and' and 'or' interchanged. And the elaborator of a system starting from '*D*' may say something like this: 'You understand the meaning of "Not both". You almost certainly understand something complex by this, but with that I am not concerned. Whether what you understand by it be simple or complex, we are going to use the symbol "*D*" for it. And we shall use "*Np*" as short for "*Dpp*" and read it "Not *p*". That is almost certainly not what you generally understand by "Not", but with that, again, I am not concerned; "*Np*" in the sense of "*Dpp*" will in any case be true and false under the same conditions as your "Not *p*". Your usual "Not *p*" will not in fact be symbolized in this system at all, but every thesis in which my "*Np*" occurs will hold for your "Not *p*" also, though the ones for your "Not *p*" will not always be provable in the way I prove mine for "*Np*".'

The same symbols, in short, do not have the same meanings in the different systems, and in any system what they mean to one person may not be precisely what they mean to another; but if any formula in any system expresses a logical law, then the formula composed of the same symbols in any other system will also express a logical law. In framing our definitions we take care (perhaps by doing truth-value calculations) that this shall be so.

The 'inferential definitions' which appear in Popper's system without axioms do not quite fit either Russell's or Leśniewski's pattern. What must be remembered about such systems as Popper's is that in them we move entirely on the 'metalogical' plane. The real reason why they need no axioms is that, strictly speaking, they contain no theses. They contain only rules of inference, and derived rules of inference, though among the latter are rules to the effect that certain forms of proposition (the forms which in other systems would be theses) will follow from any proposition whatever, or, if we care to put it this way, that they just 'follow'. In a system of this sort we do not really need to define any of the truth-operators in isolation; we need only to explain the meaning of, say, '*r* follows from *Cpq*' and '*Cpq* follows from *r*' (and similarly with other operators);

and this is what Popper's 'inferential definitions' do. We might, for example, say that 'It may be inferred from *r* that *p* implies *q*' is a way of saying 'Given *r*, and given *p*, we may infer *q*', i.e.

$$r \rightarrow Cpq = r, p \rightarrow q.$$

'If-*p*-then-*p* follows from *r*' will then mean 'Given *r*, and given *p*, we may infer *p*', i.e.

$$r \rightarrow Cpp = r, p \rightarrow p.$$

Given (either directly or derivately) the two rules

(1) $p \rightarrow p$

(2) If $p \rightarrow q$, then $r, p \rightarrow q$,

it will be an easy matter to prove $r \rightarrow Cpp$ in the sense indicated, i.e. to prove that a proposition of the form *Cpp* may be inferred from any proposition at all.

PART II
THE TRADITIONAL LOGIC OF TERMS

I
The Aristotelian Syllogistic

§ 1. *The Aristotelian Propositional Forms, and their Logical Relations*

In the logic of Aristotle, and in its development at the hands of medieval and earlier commentators, numerous theses were developed which closely resemble theses of the modern functional calculus. There is, in fact, much to be said for regarding them as simply the same theses differently formulated, but they are organized in a different way from the modern way, and this different approach to them, whether or not it be anything more than that, is worth studying on its own account. In the study of it which follows, we shall be drawing principally upon (*a*) Aristotle's own *Prior Analytics* (in which he studies syllogisms) and *De Interpretatione* (in which his main problem is that of arranging propositions of various forms into pairs of 'contradictories'), (*b*) a medieval handbook, the *Summulae Logicales* of Peter of Spain, and (*c*) Whately's *Elements of Logic*, a work which did much to revive the study of the subject in England in the earlier part of the nineteenth century.

Propositions which are not compounded of other propositions are called, in the traditional logic, 'categorical'. In a categorical proposition, there is always something, the 'predicate', which is either affirmed or denied of something else, the 'subject'. The subject and the predicate are the 'terms' of the proposition; and where the predicate is affirmed of the subject, as in 'Socrates is a sage', the proposition is an 'affirmative' one; where it is denied of the subject, as in 'Socrates is not a sage', the proposition is 'negative'. The 'quality' of a proposition is its being affirmative or negative (affirmations and denials 'differ in quality'). The 'predicate', as that term is here used, is not a verb, and is best expressed by a common noun, attached to the subject by '— is a —' or '— is not a —', these two signs being called 'copulae'. The quality of a proposition is generally indicated by its copula, but there is an exception which we shall shortly notice.

Of the terms of propositions, some are 'singular' (*termini singulares*), some 'general' (*termini communes*). Singular terms are those, like 'Socrates', which are (when used unambiguously) appropriated to a single individual; general terms are those, like 'man', which *could* apply to any of a number of individuals, though there may in fact be only one answering to them (as in the case of 'sun', at least by medieval astronomical notions). Propositions with singular subjects are called singular propositions; in the meantime we shall have little further to do with them. In a proposition with a general term as subject, definiteness of meaning requires that the subject be introduced by a 'sign of quantity', normally 'Every', 'No' or 'Some'. Propositions introduced by 'Every' or 'No', e.g. 'Every man is a rogue', are said to be 'universal' propositions; introduced by 'Some', 'particular'; this universality or particularity being the 'quantity' of the proposition. A proposition introduced by 'Every' is called a 'universal affirmative', and one introduced by 'No', a 'universal negative'. (This is the case in which the quality of the proposition is not indicated by the copula. 'No *X* is a *Y*' is a universal negative proposition, although its copula is not '— is not a —'. Its negativeness is part of what is conveyed by the introductory sign 'No'.) 'Some *X* is a *Y*' is a 'particular affirmative' form, 'Some *X* is not a *Y*' a 'particular negative'. There are alternative ways of expressing these forms, e.g. 'All *X*'s are *Y*'s' for the universal affirmative, 'Some *X*'s are *Y*'s' for the particular; here, however, we shall generally use the forms first given, which are, I think, the most accurate English renderings of the medieval forms *omnis a est b*, *nullus a est b*, *quidam a est b*, *quidam a non est b*. It is important to note that 'Some' as here used means 'At least one'; it neither excludes nor implies more than one, and neither excludes nor implies all.

In the Middle Ages, the universal affirmative form 'Every *X* is a *Y*' was called the '*A*' form (from the first vowel in *affirmo*), the particular affirmative form 'Some *X* is a *Y*' the '*I*' form (from the second vowel in *affirmo*), the universal negative 'No *X* is a *Y*' the '*E*' form (from the first vowel in *nego*) and the particular negative 'Some *X* is not a *Y*' the '*O*' form (from the second vowel in *nego*). We shall here, following Łukasiewicz, use the small letters '*a*', '*b*', etc., for term-variables, and the traditional letters '*A*', '*E*', '*I*', and '*O*' to indicate the four main operators by which propositions are formed from these. We shall thus have

'*Aba*' for 'Every *B* is an *A*',
'*Iba*' for 'Some *B* is an *A*',
'*Eba*' for 'No *B* is an *A*',
'*Oba*' for 'Some *B* is not an *A*'.

We may now consider pairs of propositions with the same terms in the same order, of these four forms. Such pairs in which the members differ in both quantity and quality are called pairs of 'contradictories'; thus *Aba* and *Oba* are contradictories, and so are *Eba* and *Iba*. Universals differing in quality, i.e. *Aba* and *Eba*, are called 'contraries', and particulars differing in quality, i.e. *Iba* and *Oba*, 'sub-contraries'. Propositions of the same quality but opposed in quantity, e.g. *Aba* and *Iba*, or *Eba* and *Oba*, are called 'subalterns', the universal being 'subalternant' to the corresponding particular, and the particular 'subalternate' to the universal. In medieval logic books this terminology is often summarized by a diagram of this general appearance, called a 'square of opposition':

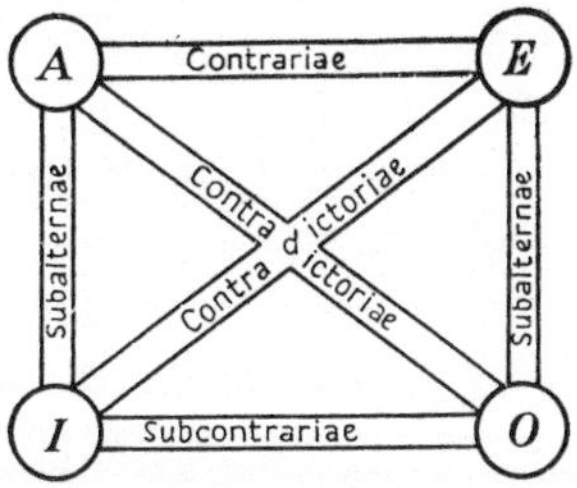

Given any pair of terms *b* and *a*, it must either be the case (i) that every *B* is an *A*, or (ii) that no *B* is an *A*, or (iii) that at

least one *B* is an *A* and at least one is not. In case (i), the two affirmatives are both true, and the two negatives both false. In case (ii) the two negatives are both true and the two affirmatives both false. In case (iii), the two particulars are both true and the two universals both false. We may tabulate these facts as follows:

	Aba	*Eba*	*Iba*	*Oba*
Case (i)	1	0	1	0
Case (ii)	0	1	0	1
Case (iii)	0	0	1	1

The results which may be read off from this table[1] include the following:

1. Comparing the columns for the contraries *Aba* and *Eba*, we find that if either of these is true the other is false (i.e. we have as theses *CAbaNEba* and *CEbaNAba*), but from the falsehood of either we can infer nothing about the truth or falsehood of the other (for the two cases in which *Aba* is false include one in which *Eba* is true and one in which it is false; similarly with *Aba* in the two cases in which *Eba* is false). Or to put it another way, *Aba* and *Eba* are in one case both false, but in no case are they both true.

2. Comparing the columns for the subcontraries *Iba* and *Oba*, we find that if either of these is false the other is true (we have as theses *CNIbaOba* and *CNObaIba*), but from the truth of either nothing can be inferred about the falsehood of the other. Or to put it in another way, *Iba* and *Oba* are in one case both true, but in no case both false.

3. Comparing the columns for the contradictories *Aba* and *Oba*, we find that if either of these is true the other is false (we have *CAbaNOba* and *CObaNAba*), and if either is false the other is true (we have *CNAbaOba* and *CNObaAba*). Or putting it the other way, *Aba* and *Oba* are in no case both true, and in no case both false. The other contradictories *Eba* and *Iba* are related similarly.

[1] For this method of verifying the rules of opposition see Whately's *Elements*, II. ii. 3. Whately takes it from Aldrich's *Artis Logicae Rudimenta*, and there is something not unlike it in Peter of Spain's *Summulae* (Bocheński's edition, Turin 1947) 1.15–1.17. For a Platonic use of the same division of the possibilities see I. Thomas in *Dominican Studies*, vol. iv (1951), pp. 69–70.

4. Comparing the columns for the subalterns *Aba* and *Iba*, we find that if the universal is true the particular is (*CAbaIba*), and if the particular is false the universal is (*CNIbaNAba*), but nothing can be inferred from the falsehood of the universal or the truth of the particular. The other subalterns *Eba* and *Oba* are related similarly.[1]

We may summarize these results (in the first three cases in their second form of expression) in the following modification of the square of opposition:

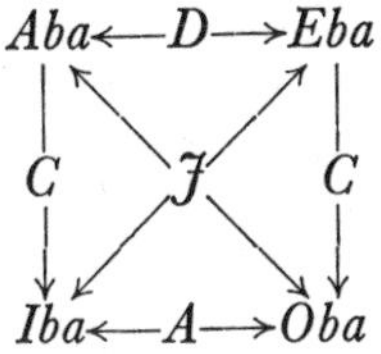

The term 'contradictories', it may be noted, is often extended to *any* pair of forms α and β such that $J\alpha\beta$ (i.e. $E\alpha N\beta$) is a thesis, and the term 'contraries' to any pair of forms α and β such that $D\alpha\beta$ (i.e. $NK\alpha\beta$) is a thesis. Thus *Kpq* and *ANpNq* may be called contradictory forms, and *Kpq* and *KNpNq* contraries.

We may now turn to pairs of propositions which are alike in quality, and which have the same terms, but in reversed order —i.e. the pairs (*Aba*, *Aab*), (*Aba*, *Iab*), (*Iba*, *Aab*), (*Iba*, *Iab*), (*Eba*, *Eab*), (*Eba*, *Oab*), (*Oba*, *Eab*), and (*Oba*, *Oab*). In order to determine where implications hold between the members of such pairs, and where they do not, it is necessary to subdivide the three possibilities so far considered. The possibility (i) that every *B* is an *A* includes both cases in which it is also true that every *A* is a *B*, so that the *A*'s and the *B*'s are coextensive, and

[1] If we think of an implicative thesis like 'If every *B* is an *A* then some *B* is an A' as being verified in the above manner, it is natural to equate this thesis with the universal proposition 'Every case in which every *B* is an *A* is a case in which some *B* is an *A*'. It is, I suspect, the consideration of examples of this kind which has led some writers to imagine that the logic of propositions can be incorporated in the Aristotelian syllogistic by 'reducing' the form 'If *P* then *Q*' to 'Every case of *P* is a case of *Q*'. This theory was propounded by John Wallis in the latter part of the seventeenth century, and had considerable popularity in the nineteenth, being adopted by Whately (*Elements*, II. iv. 6), de Morgan, Boole, Jevons, Peirce, and Keynes; though Keynes, after employing it in the first edition of his *Formal Logic*, abandoned it in the later editions, and in the later writings of Boole and Peirce also it is somewhat modified. It is in fact only plausible where what is being 'reduced' is not a genuine implicative *proposition* but an implicative *form* taken as expressing a logical law.

cases in which this is not so. We might represent these two cases by the following diagrams:

(α) 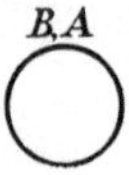

(β) 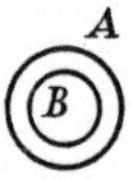

Then the possibility (iii) that at least one *B* is an *A* and at least one is not includes both the case in which, although not every *B* is an *A*, every *A* is a *B*, and the case in which this is not so. The following diagrams represent these:

(γ) 

(δ) 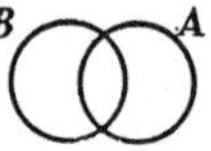

Finally we have possibility (ii), which we shall not subdivide, and which may be represented thus:

(ε) 

A glance at the diagrams will verify the following 'truth-tables':

	Aba	*Eba*	*Iba*	*Oba*	*Aab*	*Eab*	*Iab*	*Oab*
(α)	1	0	1	0	1	0	1	0
(β)	1	0	1	0	0	0	1	1
(γ)	0	0	1	1	1	0	1	0
(δ)	0	0	1	1	0	0	1	1
(ε)	0	1	0	1	0	1	0	1

Comparing the columns for *Eba* and *Eab*, we notice that they are the same, and likewise *Iba* and *Iab*. So we have both *CEbaEab* and *CEabEba* as theses, and likewise both *CIbaIab* and *CIabIba*. In technical parlance, both *E* and *I* propositions are capable of 'simple conversion', *Eba* and *Eab* being 'converses' of one another, and likewise *Iba* and *Iab*. But from *Aba* we cannot infer *Aab*, for of the two cases in which *Aba* is true, one is a case in which *Aab* is true and one a case in which it is not; and similarly from *Aab* we cannot infer *Aba*. However, the two cases in which *Aba* is true are both of them cases in which *Iab* is true, so we have *CAbaIab*, and also *CAabIba*; though we have not *CIabAba* or *CIbaAab*. The universal affirmative form is said to be capable of 'conversion *per accidens*', and *Iab* is called the 'converse *per accidens*' of *Aba* (and *Iba* of *Aab*). We also have *CEbaOab* and *CEabOba*, though in neither case vice versa. *Oba* and *Oab* do not convert either *per accidens* or simply, though if negative terms such as 'non-*A*' and 'non-*B*' are introduced we may pass from 'Some *B* is not an *A*' to 'Some non-*A* is not a non-*B*', and back, and from 'Some *A* is not a *B*' to 'Some non-*B* is not a non-*A*', and back. We may also pass from 'Every *B* is an *A*' to 'Every non-*A* is a non-*B*', and back, and from 'Every *A* is a *B*' to 'Every non-*B* is a non-*A*', and back. We shall consider negative terms more fully in the next chapter; in the meantime we may note that this combined transformation and negation of the terms of *A* and *O* propositions is called 'conversion by contraposition' or simply 'contraposition', and the forms thus equivalent are called 'contrapositives' of one another. The Schoolmen summed up the sorts of conversion of which the different forms are capable in the jingle

Simpliciter feci convertitur, eva per acci,
Asto per contra, sic fit conversio tota.[1]

The vowels of the word *feci* indicate the forms capable of conversion *simpliciter*; the vowels of *eva* indicate the forms capable of conversion *per accidens*, and the vowels of *asto* indicate the forms capable of conversion *per contrapositionem*.

The five diagrams used above are generally associated with the name of the eighteenth-century mathematician Euler, but the method of ascertaining logical laws by considering these five mutually exclusive and collectively exhaustive types of case goes back at least to Boethius. Boethius selected concrete terms answering to each type of case (e.g. 'man' and 'animal' for the case in which every *B* is an *A* but not vice versa) and compared the truth-values of propositional forms when exemplified by each type of subject-predicate pair. In Boethius, however, as we shall see in the next chapter, this technique was misapplied.

One method of distinguishing valid from invalid conversions is to apply what is called the 'rule of distribution'. The Schoolmen described a term *T* occurring in a proposition as being

[1] *Summulae Logicales* (Bocheński's edition), 1.21.

'distributed', or as having 'distributive supposition', if we could pass from the given proposition to the same proposition with '*T*' (or '*T*' with its quantifier) replaced by 'This *T*'.[1] For example, from 'Every man is an animal' we may infer 'This man is an animal' but not 'Every man is this animal'; 'man' is therefore distributed in this proposition, and 'animal' not. Again, from 'No man is a horse' we may infer both 'This man is not a horse' and 'No man is this horse'; hence both terms of this proposition are distributed. From 'Some man is an albino' we may pass neither to 'This man is an albino' nor to 'Some man is this albino' ('this' albino might be a mouse); so neither term is distributed here. From 'Some man is not a rogue' we may infer 'Some man is not this rogue' but not 'This man is not a rogue'; here, therefore, the predicate is distributed but not the subject. Summing up, we may say that the subjects of universal propositions and the predicates of negatives are distributed, while the subjects of particulars and predicates of affirmatives are not. And the 'rule of distribution' is simply that it is never legitimate to pass from a proposition in which a term is not distributed to one in which it is (though the converse inference is not forbidden). '*Aba*, ∴ *Aab*' is invalid because the term *A*, which is not distributed in the premiss (being there the predicate of an affirmative), is distributed in the conclusion (where it is the subject of a universal). '*Oba*, ∴ *Oab*' suffers from a similar 'illicit process' in respect of the term *B* (which in the premiss is subject of a particular, and so undistributed, but in the conclusion the predicate of a negative, and so distributed).

§ 2. *The Aristotelian Syllogistic Forms and their Logical Relations*

To bring out what is meant by a 'categorical syllogism', we may begin from the example

Every animal is a living thing,
And every man is an animal,
Therefore every man is a living thing.

This is an inference involving three categorical propositions—two as premisses and one as conclusion—and with three terms ('man', 'animal', and 'living thing'), distributed as follows: the predicate of the conclusion, called the 'major term', appears

[1] *Summulae Logicales* (Bocheński's edition), 6.11, 12.26.

in one of the premisses, called in consequence the 'major premiss' (here stated first—this is usual, but not essential); the subject of the conclusion, called the 'minor term', appears in the other premiss, called in consequence the 'minor premiss'; and the third term, called the 'middle term', appears in both premisses, but is not in the conclusion at all. These characteristics suffice to define 'categorical syllogism'.

Syllogisms are classified according to 'mood' and according to 'figure'. The 'mood' of a syllogism is determined by the quantity and quality of its premisses and conclusion. Thus our example above, consisting of three universal affirmative propositions, is in the mood *AAA*. The 'figure' of a syllogism is determined by the way the middle term functions in the premisses. In the first figure, of which the syllogism above is an example, the middle term is subject of the major premiss and predicate of the minor; in the second, predicate of both; in the third, subject of both; and in the fourth, predicate of the major and subject of the minor. Using '*P*' for the major term, '*S*' for the minor, and '*M*' for the middle, we may exhibit these various dispositions by the following schemata:

Fig. 1	*Fig. 2*	*Fig. 3*	*Fig. 4*
M–P	*P–M*	*M–P*	*P–M*
S–M	*S–M*	*M–S*	*M–S*

(If a line is drawn joining the various occurrences of the letter *M*, moving as far as possible from left to right, we will have something like a sprawled-out '*W*'; this fact may aid the memory.[1]) In most of the ancient and medieval logicians, the valid moods of the fourth figure are counted as being merely 'indirect' moods of the first. The first three figures are in any case much more important than the fourth.

Figure 1, as Kant observed, is the figure in which we take some *rule*, note that something is a *case* to which the rule applies, and deduce the *result* which the rule indicates. For example,

Everything real is created by God,
And some evils are real
Therefore some evils are created by God.

The principle of such reasoning is that if all (or no) members of

[1] This hint is given in L. S. Stebbing's *Modern Elementary Logic*, p. 58 n.

a certain class possess a certain property (there is our 'rule'), and if certain objects are members of that class (i.e. cases to which the rule applies), then those objects possess (or, if the rule is negative, do not possess) that property. This is sometimes called the *dictum de omni et nullo*, or 'principle about all and none'. The major premiss in this figure, being the statement of a rule, must be universal; and the minor, stating that certain objects *are* of the sort which the rule concerns, must be affirmative. Peirce saw that reasoning in the second and third figures could be handled in a similar way. In Figure 2, we again start from a rule, but instead of observing next that something is a case to which the rule applies, we observe that something does *not* exhibit the property that the rule mentions, and so conclude that this something is *not* a case to which the rule applies. That is, instead of 'Rule—Case—Result', we have 'Rule—Denial of Result—Denial of Case'. For example,

Everything real is created by God,
But nothing evil is created by God,
Therefore nothing evil is real.

The principle of such reasoning, sometimes called the *dictum de diverso*, is that if all (or no) members of a certain class possess a certain property, and certain objects have not (or if the rule is negative, have) that property, then those objects are not members of that class. The major premiss, again asserting a rule, must be universal, as in Figure 1, and the conclusion is always negative. In Figure 3, we begin by observing that something does not exhibit the property mentioned in a supposed rule, but observe that nevertheless this something *is* a case to which the rule would apply if true, and conclude that the rule is not true. For example,

Nothing evil is created by God,
But some evils are real,
Therefore not every real thing is created by God.

The scheme here is 'Denial of Result—Case—Denial of Rule', and the principle is that if certain objects possess (or lack) a certain property, and these objects are members of a certain class, then some members of that class possess (or lack) that property (i.e. the rule that all lack it, or in the other case that all possess it, is false). In its affirmative form (i.e. leading to the conclusion 'Some possess . . .') this principle is sometimes called the *dictum de exemplo*, and in its negative form the *dictum de excepto*. The minor premiss must be affirmative ('the thing *is* a case to which the rule would apply'), and the conclusion must be particular (denying a universal rule).[1] The principles of all three figures are deducible from the single rule that it cannot be simultaneously true that (*a*) certain objects lack (or possess) a certain property, that (*b*) these objects are members of a certain class, and that (*c*) all members of this class possess (or lack) the property—e.g. that

(*a*) Evils are not created by God,
(*b*) Evils are real, and
(*c*) Everything real is created by God.

(Calling this *NKKpqr*, we obtain one syllogism from it by *CNKKpqrCKpqNr*, another by *CNKKpqrCKrpNq*, and a third by *CNKKpqrCKrqNp*.) A statement of inconsistency of this kind is called an 'antilogism'.[2]

Beside the above-mentioned rules for the three figures (minor affirmative and conclusion particular in Figure 3, and so on), there are general rules covering syllogisms in all figures, the most important being (i) the rules of distribution—that the middle term must be distributed at least once, and that (as with conversions) a term cannot be distributed in the conclusion if it is not distributed in its premiss; (ii) the rules of quality—that at least one premiss must be affirmative, that if either premiss is negative the conclusion must be negative, and that if both are affirmative so must the conclusion be; and (iii) the rules of quantity—that at least one premiss must be universal, and if either premiss is particular the conclusion must be

[1] Peirce's development of this approach to the three figures is in his *Collected Papers*, 2. 479–83, 794–5. It was taken over from Peirce by Keynes (*Formal Logic*, 4th ed., §§ 268–71).

[2] We owe this word to Mrs. C. Ladd-Franklin (see *Mind*, 1928, pp. 532–4), but the thing itself was not unknown to the ancients. In the *De Sophisticis Elenchis*, 182^b 40–183^a 7, Aristotle refers to the practice of 'perplexing' disputants by showing that at least one of three 'probable' propositions must be false because any two of them will prove (syllogistically) the contradictory of the third.

particular. The special rules for the figures are deducible from these; and the general rules themselves are not independent of one another.[1]

The valid moods of the different figures have been given special names, most of them being listed in the following jingle:

Barbara, Celarent, Darii, Ferio-que prioris
Cesare, Camestres, Festino, Baroco secundae
Tertia *Darapti, Disamis, Datisi, Felapton*
Bocardo, Ferison habet. Quarta insuper addit
Bramantip, Camenes, Dimaris, Fesapo, Fresison.

These are medieval verses, as altered by post-Renaissance scholars to fit in with the view which separates off a fourth figure.[2] The moods are indicated by the vowels in the names. Thus in Figure 1 we have *AAA* (Barbara), *EAE* (Celarent), *AII* (Darii), and *EIO* (Ferio). Most of the consonants have a meaning also, in all lines but the first; but we shall attend to this shortly. Not all the valid moods are given here; there are a few trivial ones missed out, called the five 'subaltern' moods, in which, although the premisses warrant the drawing of a universal conclusion, we content ourselves with drawing a particular. Thus in Figure 1, since it is legitimate to draw *Aca* from *Aba* and *Acb*, it would also be legitimate to draw *Ica*, as the universal implies the subalternate particular. Similarly from *Eba* and *Acb* we might draw *Oca* instead of *Eca*. These moods may be called 'Barbari' and 'Celaront'. In Figure 2, similarly, we have 'Cesaro' and 'Camestrop', and in Figure 4, 'Camenop'.

The consonants in the mood-names are connected with what is called the 'reduction' of the other figures to the first, i.e. the *de*duction of the validity of second-, third-, and fourth-figure syllogisms when only the validity of the first-figure moods is initially assumed. Take, for example, Cesare. The '*s*' after the first '*e*' here indicates that if we convert the major premiss *simpliciter*, we shall have a syllogism in Figure 1, and the initial '*C*' indicates that the mood of Figure 1 in which our new

[1] On this point see Keynes, *Formal Logic*, 4th ed., §§ 199–204 and 244; Johnson's *Logic*, II. iv. 11; and a note on the latter by I. Thomas, *Dominican Studies*, vol. iv (1951), pp. 71–72.

[2] For the older form see Peter of Spain's *Summulae* (Bocheński's edition), 4.17.

syllogism will be is Celarent. That is, a syllogism of the form

No *A* is a *B*,
But every *C* is a *B*,
Therefore no *C* is an *A*

can be restated as a two-step inference of the form

No *A* is a *B*,
Therefore no *B* is an *A* (by *conversio simplex*),
And every *C* is a *B*
Therefore no *C* is an *A* (by first-figure syllogism).

Or, more briefly, we break up

Eab, *Acb*—(by Cesare) → *Eca*

into

Eab, *Acb*—(*s*) → *Eba*, *Acb*
—(by Celarent) → *Eca*.

Where we encounter the letter '*p*' in a mood-name, as in Darapti, Felapton, and Fesapo, the instruction is to convert, not *simpliciter*, but *per accidens*. Thus we break up

Aba, *Abc*—(by Darapti) → *Ica*

into

Aba, *Abc*—(*p*) → *Aba*, *Icb*
—(by Darii) → *Ica*.

The letter '*m*', as in Camestres, indicates a further complication. Camestres is

Aab, *Ecb* → *Eca*.

Conversion of the minor turns the premisses here into *Aab*, *Ebc*, but to derive *Eca* from this would be to reason not in Figure 1 but in Figure 4. If, however, we transpose the premisses before performing this conversion (the consonant '*m*' means that we must do this), the result of both changes is *Ebc*, *Aab*, from which we can derive *Eac* in Figure 1, and *Eca* from this by conversion. That is, we break up Camestres into

Aab, *Ecb*—(*m*) → *Ecb*, *Aab*
—(*s*) → *Ebc*, *Aab*
—(by Celarent) → *Eac*
—(*s*) → *Eca*.

The letter '*c*' in Baroco and Bocardo (sometimes written 'Baroko' and 'Bokardo', the letter '*k*' having the same significance as '*c*') indicates that here we must proceed 'indirectly', as the conversion of the *O* premiss is impossible, and the conversion *per accidens* of the *A* premiss to *I* would land us with two particulars. The 'indirect' method is to argue that if you combine the *A* premiss with the denial of the conclusion you can infer (in Figure 1, in Barbara) the denial of the other premiss, so if you wish to affirm *both* premisses you cannot deny the conclusion; *ergo*, the passage from the given premisses to their conclusion is warranted. Thus

$$Aab,\ Ocb\text{—(by Baroco)} \rightarrow Oca$$

is broken up into

$$\begin{aligned} Aab,\ NOca\text{—}(c) &\rightarrow Aab,\ Aca \\ &\text{—(by Barbara)} \rightarrow Acb \\ &\text{—}(c) \rightarrow NOcb \end{aligned}$$

$\therefore$ *Aab*, *Ocb*, *NOca* is an impossible combination.

$\therefore$ *Aab*, *Ocb* $\rightarrow$ *Oca*.

If we wish to set out these transformations as formal proofs in the modern style, we must first of all restate our inferences as implications. This is in fact how Aristotle himself regularly asserts the validity of a syllogistic inference. He does not say 'Given a premiss of the form "Every *B* is an *A*", and another of the form "Every *C* is a *B*", it is legitimate to infer the corresponding proposition of the form "Every *C* is an *A*."' He says, rather, 'If *A* is predicable of all *B*, and *B* of all *C*, then *A* is predicable of all *C*.' Łukasiewicz[1] goes so far as to say that an implicative formula of this sort, rather than an inference, is what Aristotle meant by a 'syllogism', but his evidence for this is flimsy. The implicative forms which Aristotle uses are a perfectly natural way of talking *about* syllogisms (asserting their validity), but a statement *about* a syllogism is not itself a syllogism; and on the few occasions when Aristotle gives actual examples which he calls syllogisms, they are not implications but inferences. Moreover, although Aristotle does thus constantly talk in conditionals, the implications we need for

[1] *Aristotle's Syllogistic*, §§ 1 and 8.

formalizing his proofs are not quite the ones he uses, which are actual propositions about inferences; we need not propositions but implicative propositional forms, corresponding to the inferential forms, which are true in all their exemplifications—not 'If *A* is predicable of all *B*, etc.', which talks obliquely *about* the propositional form 'Every *B* is an *A*', but 'If every *B* is an *A*, and every *C* is a *B*, then every *C* is an *A*', which *contains* 'Every *B* is an *A*', and the others, and like its components is a propositional form rather than a proposition. In symbols, we need such formulae as

CKAbaAcbAca.

Thus for proving Cesare from Celarent, we need

1. *CKEbaAcbEca.*

We need also the principle of conversion

2. *CEabEba.*

And to derive *CKEabAcbEca* (Cesare) from these by substitution and detachment alone, we need the thesis of propositional logic

3. *CCpqCCKqrsCKprs.*

The proof then becomes

3 *p/Eab*, *q/Eba*, *r/Acb*, *s/Eca* = *C*2—*C*1—4

4. *CKEabAcbEca.*

Thesis 3 above is among the implicational theses or *consequentiae* laid down by the medieval logician Walter Burleigh. Burleigh was fully conscious, as Aristotle was not, of the propositional logic presupposed by the syllogistic; and, quite in the modern style, elaborated his propositional calculus at the beginning of his work, before touching on the typically Aristotelian topics at all.[1] He states thesis 3 as *Quicquid sequitur ad consequens cum aliquo addito, sequitur ad antecedens cum eodem addito*, 'What follows from the consequent (of a true implication) with anything added, follows from the antecedent with the

[1] On the development of this way of doing things there is much valuable material in P. Boehner's *Medieval Logic*, Part III. On Burleigh in particular see my 'On Some *Consequentiae* in Walter Burleigh', *The New Scholasticism*, Oct. 1953.

same thing added', i.e. if *p* implies *q*, then if anything, say *s*, is implied by *q* together with anything, say *r*, then *s* is implied by *p* together with the same thing *r*. And Burleigh deduces this from two other principles—the syllogistic principle that 'what follows from the consequent follows from the antecedent', and the principle *Antecedens cum aliquo addito infert consequens cum eodem addito*, 'The antecedent (of a true implication) with anything added, implies the consequent with the same thing added', i.e. if *p* implies *q*, then *p* together with anything else, say *r*, implies *q* together with *r*, *CCpqCKprKqr*. We may formalize his proof thus:[1]

1. *CCpqCCqrCpr*
2. *CCpqCKprKqr*

   1 *p/Cpq*, *q/CKprKqr*, *r/CCKqrsCKprs*
   = *C*2—*C*1*p/Kpr*, *q/Kqr*, *r/s*—3

3. *CCpqCCKqrsCKprs*.

(Thesis 2 here is PM 3.45.)

For the deduction of moods with '*s*' after '*i*' we require the law of conversion *CIbaIab*, and for that of moods with a '*p*', *CAbaIab*; and where it is the minor premiss that is converted we require, instead of *CCpqCCKqrsCKprs*, *CCqrCCKprsCKpqs*. For moods with an '*m*', coupled with a conversion-instruction at the end, we require *CCKpqrCKqpr* for the transposition of the premisses, and *CCpqCCqrCpr* for the argument that since the conclusion of a syllogism we obtain implies (by conversion) the conclusion we require, its premisses imply the conclusion we require. For the 'indirect' reductions we require the laws of opposition *CAbaNOba* and *CNObaAba*, and the propositional theses

C(*CKpqr*)(*CKpNrNq*); for Baroco.

C(*CKpqr*)(*CKNrqNp*); for Bocardo.

The similar law *C*(*CKpqr*)(*CKNrpNq*) was known to the Stoics, and proved by them from simpler laws.[2] For the deduction of the 'subaltern moods', not mentioned in the verses, we need only the principles of subalternation (*CAbaIba* and *CEbaOba*) and the

[1] For the original see Burleigh's *De Puritate Artis Logicae* (Boehner's edition, 1951), p. 5, ll. 8–13.

[2] For this proof see Łukasiewicz, *Aristotle's Syllogistic*, pp. 58–59, and Bocheński, *Ancient Formal Logic* (Amsterdam, 1951), p. 99.

principle of (hypothetical) syllogism *CCpqCCqrCpr*. Barbari, for instance, is provable from Barbara thus:

1. *CKAbaAcbAca*
2. *CAbaIba*
3. *CCpqCCqrCpr*
   3 *p*/*KAbaAcb*, *q*/*Aca*, *r*/*Ica* = *C*1—*C*2 *b*/*c*—4
4. *CKAbaAcbIca*.

The proofs indicated in the medieval mnemonic are all of them employed by Aristotle, who must therefore be credited with having constructed something approaching an 'axiomatized' system in the modern sense. The mnemonic lines, moreover, do not give the whole story. Aristotle showed that some of the laws of conversion follow from others together with the rules of opposition,[1] and that of the rules of opposition some are deducible from others,[2] thereby narrowing down his axiomatic basis; and at the other end, he showed that more may be inferred from this basis than valid moods of ordinary syllogism. For syllogistic inferences with more than two premisses (the so-called 'sorites'), e.g. '*Aba*, *Acb*, *Adc*, ∴ *Ada*' may be 'reduced' to ones with two (in the given case, '*Aba*, *Acb*, ∴ *Aca*; and *Adc*, ∴ *Ada*').[3] Further, he was aware that there are different ways in which the axiomatization of syllogistic logic is possible, and that the system sketched above can be improved upon in point of economy. He gives alternative proofs for some of his theses;[4] notes that the conversions by which he derives second- and third-figure syllogisms from first-figure ones may also be used to derive first-figure syllogisms from the others, and second- and third-figure syllogisms from one another;[5] and notes also that the 'indirect' method may be used for the deduction of all the second- and third-figure moods and not only for Baroco and Bocardo,[6] and that if we thus extend the use of the indirect method we need not assume all four moods of Figure 1, but may prove Darii and Ferio from

[1] *Anal. Pr.* 25ᵃ 17–22. Cf. Bocheński, *Ancient Formal Logic*, p. 51.

[2] *Anal. Pr.* 52ᵃ 39–52ᵇ 13.

[3] *Anal. Pr.*, Bk. I, ch. 25.

[4] *Anal. Pr.* 27ᵃ 15; 28ᵃ 22–26, 29–30; 28ᵇ 13–15, 20–22.

[5] *Anal. Pr.*, Bk. I, ch. 45.

[6] *Anal. Pr.*, Bk. II, chs. 11–13.

Celarent. (Camestres from Celarent in the ordinary way, and Darii from this 'indirectly'; Festino from Celarent 'indirectly', and Ferio from this by conversion.)[1]

Considerably later, Leibniz worked out a more ingenious economy. He proved all second- and third-figure moods 'indirectly', then used these to prove the laws of conversion, and finally used conversion to prove the moods of Figure 4. (The indirect method cannot be used for these, for if we combine one premiss of a fourth-figure syllogism with the contradictory of its conclusion to obtain the contradictory of the other premiss, our new syllogism will be in Figure 4 also. Thus Camenes, *CKAabEbcEca*, yields by this method *CKIcaAabIbc*, which is Dimaris, and *CKEbcIcaOab*, which is Fresison.) In his proofs of the various conversions, Leibniz assumes, beside syllogism, the law of identity in the form *Aaa*. For the conversion of *E*, we have *CKEbaAcaEcb* (Cesare), which by the substitution *c*/*a* gives *CKEbaAaaEab*, so that since we have *Aaa* we have *CEbaEab*. Or formalizing,

1. *CKEbaAcaEcb*
2. *Aaa*
3. *CCKpqrCqCpr*
   3 *p*/*Eba*, *q*/*Aaa*, *r*/*Eab* = *C*1 *c*/*a*—*C*2—4
4. *CEbaEab*.

For the conversion of *I*, we have *CKAabIacIcb* (Datisi), which by the substitution *b*/*a* gives *CKAaaIacIca*, from which with *Aaa* we obtain *CIacIca*; and for the conversion *per accidens* of *A*, we have *CKAabAacIcb* (Darapti), which by the substitution *b*/*a* gives *CKAaaAacIca*, and so (with *Aaa*) *CAacIca*. A slight difficulty arising with this procedure is that the mood of Figure 1 from which Darapti is derived by the indirect method is not one of the main four, but the subaltern mood Celaront, but the law of subalternation *CEbaOba* (involved in deriving this from Celarent) may be proved in the ordinary first-figure mood Ferio if we assume beside *Aaa* the weaker law of identity *Iaa*. (The substitution *c*/*b* in *CKEcaIbcOba* gives *CKEbaIbbOba*, from

[1] *Anal. Pr.* 29^{b} 1–19. Cf. Bocheński, *Ancient Formal Logic*, p. 54.

which, with *Ibb*, *CEbaOba* follows. Darii similarly gives us the other law of subalternation *CAbaIba*.)[1]

Combination of the Aristotelian and Leibnizian methods of economizing has enabled modern workers such as Łukasiewicz and Bocheński to base the whole syllogistic logic on four axioms, apart from borrowings from the propositional calculus. Either *Aaa*, *Iaa*, Barbara and Ferio,[2] or the same with Ferio replaced by Datisi,[3] will do; provided that (to take care of some of the rules of opposition) *Oba* is made equivalent by definition to *NAba*, and *Eba* to *NIba*. It may be noted that if, in this system, we regard the terms '*a*', '*b*', etc., as abbreviations for the predicational functions 'ϕx', 'ψx', etc., '*A*' as an abbreviation for 'ΠxC', and '*I*' as an abbreviation for 'ΣxK', the theses *Aaa* *Iaa*, *CKAbaAcbAca* (Barbara), *CKEbaIcbOca* (Ferio) and *CKAbaIbcIca* (Datisi) respectively become

$$\Pi xC\phi x\phi x,$$
$$\Sigma xK\phi x\phi x,$$
$$CK(\Pi xC\psi x\theta x)(\Pi xC\phi x\psi x)(\Pi xC\phi x\theta x),$$
$$CK(N\Sigma xK\psi x\theta x)(\Sigma xK\phi x\psi x)(N\Pi xC\phi x\theta x), \text{ and}$$
$$CK(\Pi xC\psi x\theta x)(\Sigma xK\psi x\phi x)(\Sigma xK\phi x\theta x),$$

and all of these are theses of the modern functional calculus except the second. The significance of this one difference will become apparent later.

§ 3. *Propositions κατὰ πρόσληψιν*

Aristotle does not content himself, in the *Prior Analytics*, with the simple exposition of his system, but discusses a large number of derivative and connected topics and problems. By way of

[1] For details of Leibniz's system see Couturat's *La Logique de Leibniz*, ch. i, §§ 5, 6. Some medieval anticipations of his use of *Aaa* are mentioned by I. Thomas in *Dominican Studies*, vol. iv (1951), pp. 70–71. An indirect use of *Aaa* by Alexander of Aphrodisias to prove *CEbaEab* from Ferio is outlined in Keynes's *Formal Logic*, 4th ed., § 110, and in Łukasiewicz's *Aristotle's Syllogistic*, p. 10.

[2] Bocheński, 'On the Categorical Syllogism', *Dominican Studies*, vol. i (1948), pp. 35 ff., and *Précis de Logique Mathématique*, § 10.

[3] Łukasiewicz, *Aristotle's Syllogistic*, chs. iv and v. Łukasiewicz also gives an expression which is axiomatically *rejected* as a thesis, and a special rule of rejection (due to J. Słupecki), and shows that given these, any formula of the syllogistic which the asserted axioms do not prove must be rejected. A more mechanical 'decision procedure' for this system is elaborated by I. Thomas in *Mind*, for Oct. 1952, and in a slightly different form in *Dominican Studies*, vol. v (1952), pp. 210–11.

illustration, we shall take a topic which is often passed over by expounders of the Aristotelian type of logic, and to which modern logical methods may bring a new clarity.

The assertion that *A* is predicable of all of *B*, Aristotle says in one of these subsidiary discussions,[1] must be distinguished from the assertion that *A* is predicable of all of that, all of which is *B*. Introducing the term '*C*' for the indefinite 'that' which appears in the second formula, we might say that the two forms which Aristotle is here distinguishing are 'Every *B* is an *A*' ('*A* is predicable of all of *B*') and 'If every *C* is a *B*, then every *C* is an *A*' ('*A* is predicable of all of that, all of which is *B*'), or in symbols, *Aba* and *CAcbAca*. The second of these is, of course, implied by the first; in fact *CAbaCAcbAca* follows from the principle of Barbara, *CKAbaAcbAca*, by 'exportation'. But the converse implication, *C*(*CAcbAca*)(*Aba*) does not hold. Aristotle proves this, in effect, by the argument that from 'Every *B* is an *A*' together with 'Some *C* is a *B*' we can infer 'Some *C* is an *A*', but we cannot infer 'Some *C* is an *A*' from 'Some *C* is a *B*' and 'If every *C* is a *B*, every *C* is an *A*.' To exemplify these forms, we might take the propositions 'If every man habitually lies, then every man will be at a loss to know what to believe and what not' (for our *CAcbAca*) and 'Whoever habitually lies is at a loss to know what to believe and what not' (*Aba*). It is plain that the first of these could be true without the second being true, though if the second be true the first is bound to be.

Aristotle's pupil and successor Theophrastus described propositions of the more elaborate sort above as 'propositions κατὰ πρόσληψιν'. But Theophrastus differed from Aristotle about the relation of such propositions to the ordinary *A* form—he held that it *is* the same thing to say that *A* is predicable of all of *B*, and to say that *A* is predicable of all of that, all of which is *B*. Bocheński,[2] commenting on this passage, says that although Theophrastus is undoubtedly muddled here, he was perhaps feeling after the modern analysis of *A* propositions as formal implications. For the latter, i.e. the representation of 'Every *B* is an *A*' as 'For all *x*, if *x* is a *B* then *x* is an *A*', amounts to representing '*A* is predicable of all of *B*' as '*A* is predicable of all of that of which *B* is predicable', and the form '*A* is predicable of

[1] *Anal. Pr.*, Bk. I, ch. 41.

[2] In *La Logique de Théophraste* (Fribourg, 1947), pp. 50–51.

all of that, all of which is *B*' is not unlike this. But it is possible to put up a better defence of Theophrastus than this.

In the form '*A* is predicable of all of that, all of which is *B*', the force of the word 'that' is a little indefinite. Aristotle may mean that we have in mind some definite term *C*, of which we say that if all of it is *B* then all of it is *A*. In this case, his argument against the equivalence of the two forms holds. But he may mean by the form the assertion that *A* is predicable of all of *anything* all of which is *B*, i.e. 'For *any C*, if every *C* is a *B* then every *C* is an *A*', or in symbols, *ΠcCAcbAca*. And this is not only implied by 'Every *B* is an *A*', but implies it.[1] For if *CAcbAca* holds no matter what term occupies the place of '*c*' in the formula, it will hold when the term which does so is *b*, so that we shall have *CAbbAba*, and from this, *Abb* being true by the law of identity, *Aba* follows. In other words, if *every* sub-class of the *B*'s consists wholly of *A*'s, this will be true of the entire class of *B*'s, considered as a kind of maximum sub-class of itself. Setting the proof out formally, we have

1. *Cpp*
2. *CCpCqrCqCpr*
3. *Aaa*

   1 *p*/*CAcbAca* × *Π*1*c* = 4

4. *CΠcCAcbAcaCAcbAca*

   2 *p*/*ΠcCAcbAca*, *q*/*Abb*, *r*/*Aba* = C4 *c*/*b*—C3 *a*/*b*—5

5. *CΠcCAcbAcaAba*.

(Note that in performing the substitution *c*/*b* in 4, we do not substitute for the *c*'s bound by *Π* in the antecedent, but only for the free *c*'s in the consequent *CAcbAca*.) The converse implication is provable as follows:

1. *CAbaCAcbAca*

   1 × *Π*2*c* = 2

2. *CAbaΠcCAcbAca*.

(If the symbols '*A*', '*a*', '*b*', and '*c*' be given the interpretations mentioned at the end of the last section, the equivalence now

[1] This was first pointed out to me by Mr. John Mackie, of the University of Sydney.

proved will become a thesis of the higher functional calculus, namely

$$E(\Pi\phi C\Pi xC\phi x\psi x\Pi xC\phi x\theta x)(\Pi xC\psi x\theta x),$$

which is provable in the same way.)

The question to be determined in adjudicating between Aristotle and Theophrastus thus becomes the question as to what Aristotle means by the 'that' in his *κατὰ πρόσληψιν* form. And some light is thrown on this by the way in which he uses similar forms in a later chapter. This is in Book II of the *Prior Analytics*,[1] in a discussion of the construction of circular arguments, i.e. arguments in which the conclusion is used to prove itself. The following would be an argument of this sort:

Every *C* is an *A*
And every *A* is a *B*
Therefore every *C* is a *B*;
But every *B* is an *A*
Therefore every *C* is an *A*.

The three premisses of this, taking it as a whole, are 'Every *C* is an *A*', 'Every *A* is a *B*' and 'Every *B* is an *A*' (we could treat the inference as a single 'sorites' with these premisses). Of these, the first is identical with the conclusion, and the second and third state between them that the terms *A* and *B* are coextensive, or as Aristotle would say, 'convertible'. It is with such 'convertible' terms, Aristotle says, that circularity is especially liable to arise.[2] But suppose we have an argument beginning

Every *C* is an *A*
And no *A* is a *B*
Therefore no *C* is a *B*.

What is the premiss we must combine with this conclusion, 'No *C* is a *B*', in order to reach our original premiss 'Every *C* is an *A*'? The converse of the other premiss, 'No *B* is an *A*', will not do; 'No *B* is an *A*' is not 'complementary' to 'No *A* is a *B*', in the way that 'Every *B* is an *A*' is complementary to 'Every *A* is a *B*', but is simply equivalent to it; and anyway 'No *B* is an *A*' would give us two negative premisses. Indeed, can *any* premiss combine with the negative 'No *C* is a *B*' to yield the affirmative conclusion 'Every *C* is an *A*'? Not of the ordinary form; but Aristotle

[1] Chs. 5–7. [2] Ibid., ch. 16.

gives us '*A* is predicable of all of that, none of which is *B*'. With 'No *C* is a *B*', this does give us 'Every *C* is an *A*'; at least it does so if the proposition *κατὰ πρόσληψιν* is taken to mean '*Any* kind of thing, such that nothing of that kind is a *B*, is such that everything of the kind is an *A*', i.e. if it means *ΠcCEcbAca*. In this instance at least, the universal quantifier is clearly understood.

So understood, moreover, the proposition *κατὰ πρόσληψιν* can be proved equivalent to the *A* proposition 'Every non-*B* is an *A*.' For if we take 'No *C* is a *B*' to have the force of 'Every *C* is a non-*B*', the form *κατὰ πρόσληψιν* becomes *ΠcCAcnbAca* (where '*nb*' is the negative term 'non-*B*'), and we obtain *Anba* from this in the same way as we obtained *Aba* from *ΠcCAcbAca*. If, moreover, we substitute *Anba* for the form *κατὰ πρόσληψιν* in the Aristotelian pair of syllogisms, and replace negative propositions throughout by their affirmative equivalents, we obtain

Every *C* is an *A*
And every *A* is a non-*B*
Therefore every *C* is a non-*B*;
But every non-*B* is an *A*
Therefore every *C* is an *A*,

which is just like the pair of syllogisms without negations ('Every *A* is a non-*B*' and 'Every non-*B* is an *A*' jointly asserting the 'convertibility' of the terms '*A*' and 'non-*B*').

From much of this last reasoning, however, Aristotle would have dissented. For Aristotle did not recognize the equivalence of 'No *A* is a *B*' and 'Every *A* is a non-*B*'—he argued that we may infer from the fact that something *is* non-*B* that it *is not* *B*, but that we cannot infer from the fact that it *is not* *B* that it *is* non-*B*—every affirmation implies a denial, but not vice versa.[1] He seems here to have confused the bare 'non-*B*' with some positive opposite of *B*, e.g. 'non-happy' with 'unhappy' (we can infer 'No one is happy' from 'Everyone is unhappy', but not vice versa). But however Aristotle reached this opinion, it prevented him from developing a field of logic which later workers showed to be a large and interesting one.

[1] *Anal. Pr.*, Bk. I, ch. 46.

II

Categorical Forms with Negative, Complex, and Quantified Terms

§ 1. *Negative Terms in Boethius and de Morgan*

JUST as modern logicians have built up an elaborate body of thought by introducing one complication after another into the elementary propositional calculus, so logicians of the older type built up an elaborate body of thought by introducing one complication after another into the elementary theory of categorical syllogism as summarized in the last chapter. In studying some of these complications, we shall find that their history has, to a remarkable degree, a common pattern. In practically every case, what happened was that certain possibilities of extending the system were seen and explored by medieval writers—in one case early medieval (Boethius), but generally later medieval—and then, after a long break, they were carried vastly further in the nineteenth century by a single man, Augustus de Morgan. Peirce[1] once called him 'the greatest formal logician that ever lived'; he certainly did more than anyone else has done with the kind of logic that takes the Aristotelian syllogistic as its starting-point.

The first way of enlarging our stock of propositional forms that we shall consider is the admission of not only the negative copula but negative terms, such as 'non-*A*' and 'non-*B*'. Aristotle was aware of this possibility, and listed some of the new propositional forms, and also some of the new forms of inference, to which it gives rise. He notes, for example, the convertibility by contraposition of *A* and *O*,[2] and notes also that from 'Every *B* is a non-*A*' we may infer 'No *B* is an *A*', and that from the denial of the latter, 'Some *B* is an *A*', we may infer the denial of the former 'Not every *B* is a non-*A*.'[3] The inference from a

[1] *Collected Papers*, 2. 533.
[2] *Topics*, 113^b 15–27. Cf. Bocheński, *Ancient Formal Logic*, p. 64.
[3] *De Interpretatione*, 20^a 20–23. Cf. Bocheński, op. cit., p. 50.

given proposition of one in which the quality of the original proposition is changed, and at the same time the 'sign' of its predicate reversed, is nowadays generally called 'obversion' (a term we owe to Bain). Aristotle, as we have already noted, did not admit the obversion of negatives to affirmatives.

There is a much more thoroughgoing and systematic study of inferences involving negative terms (with the Aristotelian limitation implicitly removed) in the fifth-century (A.D.) logician and philosopher Boethius.[1] Boethius uses the term *nomen infinitum* (a mistranslation of the 'indefinite noun' in Aristotle's *De Interpretatione*) for negative terms, and systematically pairs off propositions of the four forms with others in which the form of the proposition as a whole is retained but a negative sign is introduced into one or both terms, and does the same with the cases in which the terms are at the same time transposed. With each sort of pairing he does the thing with five different pairs of terms, exemplifying the five relations between terms that were later illustrated by Euler's diagrams. Then, examining their truth-values, he works out the relations of logical compatibility, etc., between the members of his various pairs of forms. We shall follow his general procedure here, but will omit the cases in which the terms are transposed, will alter his order a little, and will not use quite the same pairs of terms, as his assignment of truth-values might be queried in some cases by a modern reader. For the case in which subject and predicate are coextensive (Euler's first diagram), we shall use the example 'Man, man'. For that in which the subject-class is included in the predicate-class, but not vice versa, we shall use 'Man, animal' (Boethius also uses this sometimes). For the case in which the subject-class *includes* the predicate-class, but not vice versa, we shall use 'Man, Frenchman.' For the case in which they overlap, we shall use 'Man, albino.' And for the case in which they are mutually exclusive, we shall use 'Man, stone' (Boethius's example).

Beginning with pairs of forms in which the first member has

[1] In his *Introductio ad Syllogismos Categoricos*. For a more detailed account of his technique here see A. N. Prior, 'The Logic of Negative Terms in Boethius', in *Franciscan Studies*, March 1953. For Boethius's work on the introduction of negation into hypothetical propositions see K. Dürr, *The Propositional Logic of Boethius* (1951), and Bocheński, op. cit., pp. 106–9.

no negative terms and the second member a negative predicate, we have the following table:

	Aba	*Abna*	*Eba*	*Ebna*	*Iba*	*Ibna*	*Oba*	*Obna*
(α) Man, man	1	0	0	1	1	0	0	1
(β) Man, animal	1	0	0	1	1	0	0	1
(γ) Man, Frenchman	0	0	0	0	1	1	1	1
(δ) Man, albino	0	0	0	0	1	1	1	1
(ε) Man, stone	0	1	1	0	0	1	1	0

From this table it is clear that universals of the same quality but with contradictory predicates are never true together but sometimes false together, while particulars similarly related are never false together but sometimes true together. This, of course, follows immediately from the fact that universals thus related are equivalent to a pair of contraries, *Abna* being equivalent to *Eba* and *Ebna* to *Aba*, and the particulars to a pair of subcontraries. (And these equivalences too are plain from the table.)

Secondly, let us take pairs of forms in which the second member has not the predicate but the subject negated. The table is:

	Aba	*Anba*	*Eba*	*Enba*	*Iba*	*Inba*	*Oba*	*Onba*
(α) Man, man	1	0	0	1	1	0	0	1
(β) Man, animal	1	0	0	0	1	1	0	1
(γ) Man, Frenchman	0	0	0	1	1	0	1	1
(δ) Man, albino	0	0	0	0	1	1	1	1
(ε) Man, stone	0	0	1	0	0	1	1	1

The results which this table yields are similar. Universals of the same quality but with contradictory subjects are never true together but sometimes false together, and particulars similarly related are never false together but sometimes true together. In the case of *E* and *I*, these results may be accounted for by the convertibility of these operators. Thus *Enba* is equivalent by conversion to *Eanb*, and our first table shows that this would be equivalent to *Aab*, the contrary of *Eab*, and so of the equivalent *Eba*. But the similar results for *A* and *O* are a little surprising. Is it really impossible for 'Every *B* is an *A*' and 'Every non-*B* is an *A*' to be true together? Do they not simply assert between them that *everything whatever* is an *A*?

These results have, however, an innocent explanation, and if a certain assumption be made, they must be accepted. That assumption is that terms which have nothing answering to them must not be regarded as substitutable for the '*a*'s' and '*b*'s' of an Aristotelian system. This assumption is involved in the results for negative predicates as well as in those for negative subjects. For if 'empty' terms be admitted, 'No *B* is an *A*' and 'No *B* is a non-*A*' would not be incompatible; they would simply prove between them that there are no *B*'s at all. (Duns Scotus, or another medieval writer using his name, puts an inference of this sort into Camestres, thus: 'Every real thing is either an *A* or a non-*A*, but no *B* is either an *A* or a non-*A*, therefore no *B* is a real thing.')[1] In the results for the *A* propositions in the second table, the same assumption is involved a little obliquely. If all terms are assumed to have something answering to them, then in a system employing negative terms no term may cover everything whatever, for then the corresponding negative term would cover nothing. On the assumption then, that all terms, even negative ones such as 'non-*A*', have instances, 'Every *B* is an *A*' and 'Every non-*B* is an *A*' cannot be true together.[2] It will probably be felt, all the same, that the assumption is one about which one cannot be so happy when negative terms are brought under it as when only positive terms are being considered. We may be willing to treat logical laws as irrelevant to talk which turns out to be about nothing; but it is harder to regard it as irrelevant also to talk that is about everything.

We turn, finally, to pairs of forms in which the second member has both terms negative. The Boethian table for these pairs is as follows:

	Aba	*Anbna*	*Eba*	*Enbna*	*Iba*	*Inbna*	*Oba*	*Onbna*
(α) Man, man . .	1	1	0	0	1	1	0	0
(β) Man, animal . .	1	0	0	0	1	1	0	1
(γ) Man, Frenchman .	0	1	0	0	1	1	1	0
(δ) Man, albino . .	0	0	0	0	1	1	1	1
(ε) Man, stone . .	0	0	1	0	0	1	1	1

[1] *Quaestiones Doctoris Subtilis Ioannis Scoti super lib. Priorum Analyticorum Arist.* xxi. The authenticity of this work is doubtful.

[2] Cf. J. N. Keynes's discussion of this pair of forms in his *Formal Logic*, 4th ed., § 165.

The result here is that with *Aba* and *Anbna* all possible combinations of truth-values are realized (both true, both false, first true and second false, first false and second true), so that these forms are logically independent; similarly with *Oba* and *Onbna*. But *Eba* and *Enbna*, though in several cases both false, are never both true; while *Iba* and *Inbna*, though in several cases both true, are never both false. And this result is very queer indeed, and easily refuted by examples. Take the pair 'man' and 'non-man'. Neither of these is empty, and neither has an empty contradictory. Yet it is true both that no man is a non-man (*Eba*) and that no non-man is a non-non-man (*Enbna*), i.e. that no non-man is a man. And it is false both that some man is a non-man (*Iba*) and that some non-man is a non-non-man (*Inbna*).

The simple fact is that the group of possibilities distinguished by Euler's five diagrams, and by Boethius's way of selecting his terms, is insufficient to determine the truth and falsehood of the forms *Enbna* and *Inbna*. What the form 'No non-*B* is a non-*A*' really asserts is that the terms *B* and *A* between them exhaust the universe—there is nothing that is outside both of them. And *Inbna* asserts the contradictory of this. No doubt if *B* and *A* are coextensive, and empty terms are not admitted as possible substitutions for them, this suffices to falsify the assertion that they cover the universe between them, for if coextensive terms did this, they would each cover the universe singly, and their contradictories would be empty. And if one of the terms is wholly included in the other, again they cannot exhaust the universe between them, as the wider term would then exhaust it singly, and its contradictory be empty. In the three cases α, β, and γ, therefore, *Enbna* is false and *Inbna* true. But the remaining two cases are compatible with either, so that δ (*B* and *A* overlapping) subdivides into the case in which the terms do not exhaust the universe and the case in which they do, and ϵ (mutual exclusion) similarly. Using a square for the universe, we may represent this subdivision of possibilities δ and ϵ as follows:

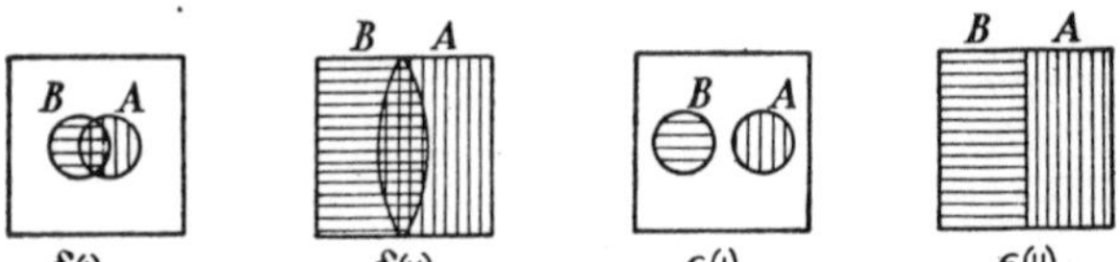

δ(i) δ(ii) ϵ(i) ϵ(ii)

A subject-predicate pair illustrating δ(ii) would be 'man, non-Frenchman', and one illustrating ϵ(ii) would be 'man, non-man'. The trouble with the Boethian examples is that they include only cases of δ(i) and ϵ(i), and this is clear enough from the fact that the column for *Inbna* (and in the earlier table the column for its obverse *Onba*) has '1' all the way down, as if this form were tautological,[1] while the column for *Enbna* (and in the earlier table that for its obverse *Anba*) has '0' all the way down.

So far as I know, the first writer thus to subdivide the Eulerian cases was de Morgan,[2] who arrived at his seven cases by considering the possible ways of combining propositions drawn from the eightfold group: *Aba*, *Anbna*, *Eba*, *Enbna*, *Iba*, *Inbna*, *Oba*, *Onbna*. (When negative terms are introduced, the Aristotelian four non-equivalent forms enlarge to these eight, but no more. The forms with one negative term are equivalent to these by obversion—*Abna* to *Eba*, *Anba* to *Enbna*, *Ebna* to *Aba*, *Enba* to *Anbna*, etc.—and forms with transposed terms to the others by conversion or contraposition—*Aab* to *Anbna*, *Ananb* to *Aba*, *Eab* to *Eba*, *Enanb* to *Enbna*, and so on.) The seven possible combinations are: α, *KAbaAnbna*; β, *KAbaOnbna*; γ, *KObaAnbna*; δ(i), *KIbaKObaKOnbnaInbna*; δ(ii), *KIbaKObaEnbna*; ϵ(i), *KEbaInbna*; ϵ(ii), *KEbaEnbna*. The Eulerian five might be similarly derived by considering possible combinations of propositions drawn from the sixfold group: *Aba*, *Aab*, *Eba*, *Iba*, *Oba*, *Oab*. (When transposed terms are introduced, without negative terms, the Aristotelian non-equivalent forms enlarge to these six, but no more. For *Eab* and *Iab* are equivalent by conversion to *Eba* and *Iba*. *Aab*, we may note, is equivalent to de Morgan's *Anbna*, and *Oab* to his *Onbna*, but *Enbna* and *Inbna* cannot be expressed with Aristotelian operators without negative terms.) The five possibilities are: α, *KAbaAab*; β, *KAbaOab*; γ, *KObaAab*; δ, *KIbaKObaOab*; ϵ, *Eba*. (*E* combines only with the *O*'s, which need not be mentioned as it implies them.)

Syllogistic logic with negative terms introduced has recently

[1] On the same point in connexion with Euler's diagrams see Lewis Carroll's *Symbolic Logic*, p. 171, fourth paragraph.

[2] In his *Formal Logic* (1847), pp. 66–67. The addition to Euler's diagrams of an outer circle representing the universe, in order to distinguish the two new possibilities, is due to Keynes (*Formal Logic*, 3rd ed., 1894, § 93; 4th ed., § 130); it was changed to a square by Johnson (*Logic*, I. ix. 7).

been axiomatized by I. Thomas.[1] The use of negative terms makes it possible to bring down the number of undefined terms from two to one, the form *Iba* being presented as an abbreviation for *NAbna*. ('Some *B* is an *A*' = 'Not every *B* is a non-*A*'.) Moreover, the principle of Barbara may be removed from the axioms; for Celarent, *CKEbaAcbEca*, is provable from the other axioms; this gives by obversion *CKAbnaAcbAcna*; this by the substitution *a*/*na* gives *CKAbnnaAcbAcnna*, and this gives Barbara by the rule that *nna* = *a*. This rule, however, must either be added to the ordinary rules (Thomas's procedure), or an axiom or axioms must be added from which, with the other axioms and rules, this rule is metalogically derivable. (The two axioms *CAbaAbnna* and *CAbnnaAba* would do). Another feature of this modification of the Aristotelian system, on which Thomas does not comment but which was noted by some medieval writers, is that we may produce what appear to be syllogisms violating the ordinary rules. Thus from the two negative premisses 'No non-*B* is an *A*' and 'No *C* is a *B*' we may infer 'No *C* is an *A*' (e.g. from 'No non-animal is a man' and 'No stone is an animal' it follows that no stone is a man). This is not strictly speaking a syllogism, as a syllogism by definition involves only three terms, and this has four—*A*, *C*, non-*B*, and *B*. But the medieval solution was not quite this; they expressed the matter by saying that there were three terms but that *B* was *infinite sumptus*, 'taken infinitely', in one premiss and *finite sumptus* in the other. And of course they were in a manner right —*B* and non-*B* are not totally distinct term-variables as *B* and *D* would be, and we only have to obvert the minor to regularize the syllogism. (We then obtain 'No non-*B* is an *A*, and every *C* is a non-*B*, therefore no *C* is an *A*', which has neither a fourth term nor two negative premisses.)

We may also construct what appear to be irregular syllogisms if we introduce the new operators A', E', I', and O', defined as follows:

$$A'ba = Anbna,$$
$$E'ba = Enbna,$$
$$I'ba = Inbna,$$
$$O'ba = Onbna.$$

[1] '*CS*(*n*): An extension of *CS*', *Dominican Studies*, vol. ii (1949), pp. 145–60.

A'ba may be read 'Only *B*'s are *A*'s', or 'None but *B*'s are *A*'s' ('Every non-*B* is a non-*A*' being equivalent to this); *E'ba* as 'There are only *B*'s and *A*'s', or 'All but *B*'s are *A*'s', or 'Everything is either a *B* or an *A*' (the equivalent of 'No non-*B* is a non-*A*'); *I'ba* as 'There are things beside the *B*'s and the *A*'s', or 'Something is neither a *B* nor an *A*' (the equivalent of 'Some non-*B* is a non-*A*'); and *O'ba* as 'Not only *B*'s are *A*'s' (the equivalent of 'Some non-*B* is not a non-*A*', or 'Some non-*B* is an *A*'). We may then have such a syllogism as 'There are only *B*'s and *A*'s, and no *C* is a *B*, therefore every *C* is an *A*', or 'There are only *B*'s and *A*'s, and some *C* is not a *B*, therefore some *C* is an *A*', which have affirmative conclusions despite, in each case, a negative premiss. But here again the irregularity is more apparent than real; the rule violated applies to 'syllogisms' defined as involving only the usual four operators. In fact both the forms of inference just mentioned were used by Aristotle,[1] though he makes no attempt to fit them into his system. Syllogisms in the enlarged system to which they belong were studied exhaustively by de Morgan. He used the following symbolism for his eight forms:[2]

'*X*))*Y*' for 'Every *X* is a *Y*' (*A*),
'*X*(·(*Y*' for 'Not every *X* is a *Y*' (*O*),
'*X*((*Y*' for 'Only *X*'s are *Y*'s' (*A'*)
'*X*)·)*Y*' for 'Not only *X*'s are *Y*'s' (*O'*),
'*X*)·(*Y*' for 'No *X* is a *Y*' (*E*),
'*X*()*Y*' for 'Some *X* is a *Y*' (*I*),
'*X*(·)*Y*' for 'There are only *X*'s and *Y*'s' (*E'*),
'*X*)(*Y*' for 'There are things beside *X*'s and *Y*'s' (*I'*).

In this notation, distributed terms always appear on the inner side of a bracket, undistributed on the outer. Thus from *X*((*Y*, 'Only *X*'s are *Y*'s', where the predicate appears on the inner side of a bracket and the subject on the outer, we may infer 'Only an *X* is this *Y*', but not 'Only this *X* is a *Y*'. (The Schoolmen noted this distribution of the predicate and non-distribution of the subject in *A'* propositions, which they called 'exclusives'. They derived this result from the equivalence of 'Only

[1] *Anal. Pr.* 52^b 4–9.

[2] 'On the Syllogism', second paper, *Transactions of the Cambridge Philosophical Society*, vol. ix, Part I, p. 91.

X's are *Y*'s' and 'Every *Y* is an *X*'.)[1] For syllogisms, we write down first the brackets (and dot, if any) expressing the relation between *X* and *Y* (in that order), and then those expressing the relation between *Y* and *Z*. Thus in the pair of premisses 'Every *Y* is a *Z*' and 'Every *Y* is an *X*', the relation expressed between *X* and *Y* is that only *X*'s are *Y*'s, and that between *Y* and *Z*, that every *Y* is a *Z*, so we write '(())'. When this is done, any pair of universals (*A'* and *E'* being counted as such), and any universal and particular in which the middle brackets curve in the same direction, will yield a conclusion respecting *X* and *Z*; and the conclusion they yield will be found by removing the two inner brackets (and leaving single dots but removing double ones. The forms with a dot may be considered negative).[2] Thus from '(())', removing the two inner brackets, we obtain '()', i.e. 'Some *X* is a *Z*'. Similarly from ')·()·(', 'No *X* is a *Y*, and no *Y* is a *Z*', we obtain ')(', 'There are not only *X*'s and *Z*'s'. (This could be put into Aristotelian as 'No *Y* is a *Z*, and every *Y* is a non-*X*, therefore some non-*X* is not a *Z*'.)

§ 2. *The Rules of Equipollence*

In the construction of the Aristotelian propositional forms, negation may be involved in three ways—(i) the proposition may be an *E* or an *O* proposition, (ii) one or both terms may be negative, and (iii) the sign of propositional denial, 'Not' in the sense of 'It is not the case that', may be prefixed to a proposition as a whole. With this third sort of negation, as an element in the construction of categorical forms, we have not as yet concerned ourselves, though we have sometimes dropped (as Aristotle sometimes dropped) into saying 'Not every *B* is an *A*' instead of 'Some *B* is not an *A*'.

Propositional negation was dealt with by medieval logicians in connexion with what they called the theory of *aequipollentia*, 'equipollence', i.e. the theory of equivalences between propositions differing only in the ways in which signs of quantity are combined with variously placed signs of negation. In the *Summulae Logicales*,[3] this subject is systematized in three ways—

[1] See, e.g. Burleigh, *De Puritate Artis Logicae* (ed. Boehner, 1951), pp. 27–28.

[2] 'On the Syllogism, No. III', *Transactions of the Cambridge Philosophical Society*, vol. x, p. 219. See also de Morgan's article 'Logic' in the *English Cyclopædia, Arts and Sciences*, vol. v, p. 350.

[3] Bocheński's edition, 1.24–1.27.

in three rules, in a set of mnemonic lines, and in a diagram of opposition. The first Rule of Equipollence is that if 'not' is placed *before* the sign of quantity, the result is equivalent to the contradictory of the original (*si . . . praeponatur negatio, aequipollet suo contradictorio*). Thus 'Not every *B* is an *A*' = 'Some *B* is not an *A*', 'Not (no *B* is an *A*)' = 'Some *B* is an *A*', 'Not (some *B* is an *A*)' = 'No *B* is an A'. In English, 'Not no' and 'Not some' are not quite idiomatic, and the force of 'Not some' we generally express by 'Not any'. (We would say, 'Not any *B* is an *A*' = 'No *B* is an *A*'.) The second rule is that if 'not' is placed *after* a sign of universality, the result is equivalent to the contrary of the original (*si . . . postponatur negatio, aequipollet suo contrario*). Thus 'Every *B* is not an *A*' = 'No *B* is an *A*', and 'No *B* is not an *A*' = 'Every *B* is an *A*'. (In ordinary speech the first of these equivalences is not always observed—we often use 'Every *B* is not an *A*' to mean 'Not every *B* is an *A*'.) The third rule is that if 'not' is placed both before and after the sign of quantity, the result is equivalent to the *subaltern* of the original (*si . . . praeponatur et postponatur negatio, aequipollet suo subalterno*). Thus, 'Not every *B* is not an *A*' = 'Some *B* is an *A*', the subaltern of 'Every *B* is an *A*'; 'Not (no *B* is not an *A*)' = 'Some *B* is not an *A*', the subaltern of 'No *B* is an *A*'; 'Not (some *B* is not an *A*)' ('Not any *B* is not an *A*') = 'Every *B* is an *A*', the subaltern of 'Some *B* is an *A*'.

The mnemonic lines are

'Non omnis' 'quidam non', 'omnis non' quasi 'nullus';
'Non nullus' 'quidam', sed 'nullus non' valet 'omnis';
'Non aliquis' 'nullus', 'non quidam non' valet 'omnis';
'Non alter' 'neuter', 'neuter non' praestat 'uterque'.
Prae contradicit contraria post tibi mansit
Eritque subalternae si postponatur et ante.

A free translation would be

Not all = some not, all not = none;
Not none = some, but none not = all;
Not any = none, not any not = all;
Not either = neither, neither not = both.
Before, it (i.e. 'not') gives the contradictory,
and after, the contrary,

While both before and after, it gives the subaltern.[1]

The introduction of 'Either', 'Neither', and 'Both' here suggests the view that universal and particular quantification amount to prolonged conjunction and alternation, but what Peter has in mind is rather the converse identification. 'Both', he says elsewhere in the *Summulae*,[2] amounts to a sign of universal quantity attached to a pair, i.e. 'Both *B*1 and *B*2 are *A*'s' amounts to 'Every member of the pair *B*1, *B*2, is an *A*'. Similarly 'Neither *B*1 nor *B*2 . . .' amounts to 'No member of the pair *B*1, *B*2, . . .' and 'Either *B*1 or *B*2 . . .' to 'Some member of the pair *B*1, *B*2 . . .'. And the third line of the mnemonic states that 'Not either *B*1 or *B*2 is an *A*' = 'Neither *B*1 nor *B*2 is an *A*', just as 'Not any *B* is an *A*' = 'No *B* is an *A*'; and 'Neither *B*1 nor *B*2 is not an *A*' = 'Both *B*1 and *B*2 are *A*'s', just as 'No *B* is not an *A*' = 'Every *B* is an *A*'.

Finally, the square of opposition may be enlarged by inserting equipollent forms into the corners, thus:

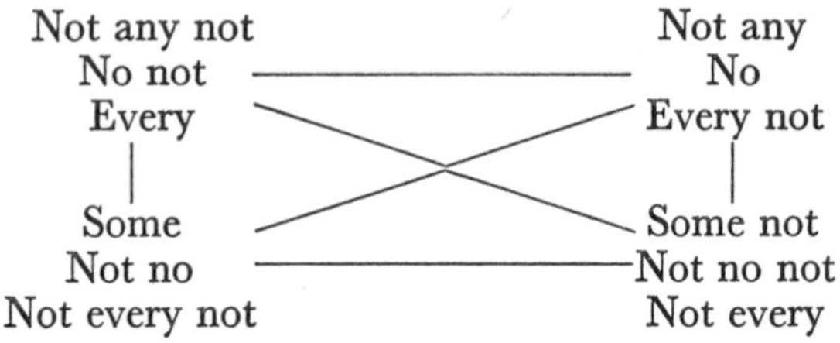

I have slightly rearranged Peter's order, so that the top line in each corner contains 'Some' (or 'any' after 'not') throughout, the second line contains 'no' and the third line contains 'every'. By focusing his attention on the same line in each corner, the reader will find sets of forms equivalent to the traditional four, but each set using only one of the three signs 'some', 'no', and 'every'. With each sign *S*, it will be found that (i) the forms in diagonally opposite corners, being equipollent to ordinary pairs of contradictories, are the pairs '*S*' and 'Not *S*', and '*S* not' and 'Not *S* not'; that (ii) the forms standing side by side,

[1] The last line of this may be regarded as a way of briefly stating the thesis

$$\Pi fC(Ff)A(\Pi\phi Cf\phi NfN\phi)(\Pi\phi CNfN\phi f\phi)$$

given at the end of I. iv. 2, with '*Ff*' meaning '*f* is a quantifier'.

[2] Bocheński's edition, 12.34.

being equipollent to ordinary pairs of contraries or subcontraries, are the pairs '*S*' and '*S* not', and 'Not *S*' and 'Not *S* not'; and that (iii) the forms standing one above the other, being equipollent to ordinary pairs of subalterns, are the pairs '*S*' and 'Not *S* not' on one side, and '*S* not' and 'Not *S*' on the other. These alternative squares indicate how any two of the three signs may be defined in terms of the remaining one. (Cf. Thomas's definition of '*Iba*' as '*NAbna*', and in the modern functional calculus, the definition of 'Σx' as '$N\Pi xN$'.)

It is also possible to tabulate 'equipollences' involving de Morgan's eight propositional forms, with positive and with negative terms. The equipollences between the universal forms may be arranged either as follows:

$$\begin{aligned} &Aba &&= A'nbna &&= Ebna &&= E'nba,\\ &A'ba &&= Anbna &&= E'bna &&= Enba,\\ &Eba &&= E'nbna &&= Abna &&= A'nba,\\ &E'ba &&= Enbna &&= A'bna &&= Anba \end{aligned}$$

or as follows:

$$\begin{aligned} &Aba &&= A'nbna &&= Ebna &&= E'nba,\\ &Anbna &&= A'ba &&= Enba &&= E'bna,\\ &Abna &&= A'nba &&= Eba &&= E'nbna,\\ &Anba &&= A'bna &&= Enbna &&= E'ba. \end{aligned}$$

The first table corresponds very broadly to the old verses giving the equivalents, without signs of negation, of propositions into which such signs have been introduced at various points. (The first column gives us the equivalents, without negative terms, of the forms with two such terms in column 2, with negative predicates in column 3, and with negative subjects in column 4.) The second table[1] corresponds very broadly with the modified square of opposition indicating how to replace a proposition containing one of the signs 'Every', 'No', and 'Some', by one containing one of the remaining two instead, with such introductions or omissions of 'not' as might be required to secure equivalence. (The first column gives the propositions beginning 'Every . . .' which are equivalent to those in column 2 beginning

[1] A modification of one in Keynes's *Formal Logic* (4th ed., § 108), which in turn is derived from one of Mrs. C. Ladd-Franklin's (in *Mind*, 1890, p. 79).

'Only . . .', to those in column 3 beginning 'No . . .', and to those in column 4 beginning 'There are only . . .'.) Using '*B*'—Łukasiewicz's symbol for the truth-operator (1, 1, 0, 1)—for 'Only if', we may rewrite the first line of either table (it is the same in both) in the notation of the modern functional calculus as follows:

$$\Pi xC\phi x\psi x = \Pi xBN\phi xN\psi x = \Pi xD\phi xN\psi x = \Pi xAN\phi x\psi x.$$

These equivalences may be deduced, by the substitutions $p/\phi x$, $q/\psi x$ and the application of Łukasiewicz's rules, from the first line of the following set of equivalences from the propositional calculus:

$$\begin{aligned} Cpq &= BNpNq = DpNq = ANpq, \\ Bpq &= CNpNq = ApNq = DNpq, \\ Dpq &= ANpNq = CpNq = BNpq, \\ Apq &= DNpNq = BpNq = CNpq. \end{aligned}$$

This table corresponds to the first table for the de Morgan operators,[1] some of the equivalences recorded in it being used as definitions in the systems of propositional calculus considered in Part I.

§ 3. *Syllogistic with Conjunctive and Alternative Terms*

The terms of a categorical proposition may be complicated not only by adding a 'not', but also by joining other terms to them by means of 'and' or 'or'. The expression of such complex terms in ordinary speech is a matter attended with many pitfalls. For example, the term 'Frenchman and violinist' must be understood as a way of describing whatever is at once a Frenchman and a violinist; and it would ordinarily be so understood if we said 'Every person here is a Frenchman and violinist.' It would not be so understood, however, in 'Every Frenchman and violinist is excitable'. For we would take this to mean, not 'Whatever is at once a Frenchman and a violinist is excitable', but rather 'Every Frenchman and every violinist is excitable', i.e. 'Whatever is either a Frenchman *or* a violinist

[1] For one similarly corresponding to the second table see Johnson's *Logic*, I. iii. 5. A variant of the one above is given by I. Thomas in *Dominican Studies*, vol. iv (1951), p. 79.

is excitable'.[1] For what corresponds to the conjunctive term 'Frenchman and violinist' we might also use 'French violinist'; but not all juxtapositions of an adjective and a noun thus express conjunction. Plato[2] refers to an old Greek sophism in which, from 'This dog is yours' and 'This dog is a father', we infer 'This dog is your father'. If 'your father' in fact meant 'yours and a father', this conclusion would be fairly drawn, but of course it does not, and the inference is fallacious. There are many other examples of a similar sort, e.g. 'An elephant is an animal, therefore a small elephant is a small animal'. Once again the conclusion would be fairly drawn if it meant 'What is at once small and an elephant is at once small and an animal'; but what it normally means is not this, but something more like 'An elephant that is smaller than most elephants is an animal that is smaller than most animals'.[3]

Genuine conjunctive terms expressed as such do not seem to have been much dealt with by ancient and medieval logicians, but they make various points which become much clearer when it is seen that it is with conjunctive terms that they are in fact dealing. Just as they often preferred to speak of 'non-*B*' not as an 'infinite term' but as the term *B* 'taken infinitely', so instead of calling 'white man' a compound term they spoke of the term 'man' as having its 'supposition' (i.e. what it may stand for, *pro quo supponit*) 'restricted' by the adjectival addition, and noted such facts as that in an *A* proposition the subject term implicitly 'restricts' the predicate but not vice versa. 'Every man is white' is equivalent to 'Every man is a white man', but not to 'Every white man is white' (for the last is true —a truism even—whereas 'Every man is white' is false).[4] Sometimes they dealt, but again only implicitly, with conjunctions of a 'finite' and an 'infinite' term, such as the subject of the 'exceptive' proposition 'Every animal but man is irrational'.

[1] Cf. de Morgan, *Formal Logic*, p. 119.

[2] *Euthydemus* 298*e*. This dog reappears in Aristotle's *De Sophisticis Elenchis* 179ᵃ 35, and Peter's *Summulae* (Bocheński's edition), 7.43, to mention nowhere else.

[3] Cf. C. H. Langford, in *The Philosophy of G. E. Moore* (ed. Schilpp, 1942), pp. 335–6.

[4] A truism of the form 'Every *XY* is *X*' or 'Every *XY* is *Y*' is what Kant appears to have meant by the term 'analytic proposition'. 'Analytic' and 'synthetic' are now often used as synonyms for 'tautologous' and 'non-tautologous' respectively. In this sense the form 'Every *Y* is *XY*' is *not* analytic, though no doubt it has a certain redundancy.

They noted that this does not imply 'Every animal but this man is irrational', but their explanations of this error were tortuous, and might have been simpler had it been clearer to them that they were really dealing with the proposition 'Everything that is at once an animal and a non-man is irrational', which does not imply 'Everything that is at once an animal and not-this-man is irrational', though it *does* imply 'This thing-that-is-at-once-an-animal-and-a-non-man is irrational'. We have another disguised dealing with conjunctive terms when Scotus (or 'Pseudo-Scotus'), giving a list of apparent exceptions to the rule that no conclusion can be drawn from two particular premisses, considers the example 'Something white is Socrates, and that same white thing is running, therefore Socrates is running'.[1] It is obvious that the second premiss here is not a genuine particular; but what is it? Strictly speaking it is not a proposition at all, for it has no definite meaning apart from the other premiss, to which we must refer in order to see what 'that same' means. If we replace the singular term 'Socrates' (which introduces complications best left till later) by, say, 'a man', the inference turns into 'Something white is a man, and that same white thing is running, therefore some man is running', the form of which is really 'Some X is both Y and Z, therefore some Y is Z'. The logical importance of the inference is that it makes clear the difference between the conjunctive-termed 'Something white is at once a man and running', and the conjunction of propositions 'Something white is a man and something white is running', from which 'Some man is running' could not be rightly drawn, as in this case the white man and the white runner might be different. The distinction is substantially that made in the modern functional calculus between the forms $\Sigma xK\phi x\psi x$ and $K\Sigma x\phi x\Sigma x\psi x$. With alternative (or as they called them disjunctive) terms the Schoolmen were more familiar, and they made quite clearly a distinction analogous to that between $\Pi xA\phi x\psi x$ and $A\Pi x\phi x\Pi x\psi x$. Thus Peter of Spain, discussing what was called the 'fallacy of division', says that it is illegitimate to pass from 'Every animal is either rational or irrational' *in sensu composito*, 'in the composite sense', i.e. as meaning that the disjunctive term 'either rational or irrational' is predicable of every animal, to the same sentence *in sensu*

[1] *Quaestiones*, etc., earlier cited, q.xx.

diviso, 'in the divided sense', i.e. as meaning the disjunction of propositions 'Either every animal is rational or every animal is irrational'.[1]

In this branch of the subject we again owe much to de Morgan. De Morgan represented the conjunction of terms by simple juxtaposition, and their alternation by the interposition of a comma; e.g. '*XY*' for 'at once *X* and *Y*', and '*X*, *Y*' for 'either *X* or *Y*'. Negative terms he represented by small letters; and he noted that the term contradictory to '*XY*' is '*x*, *y*', and that contradictory to '*X*, *Y*', '*xy*'.[2] These are 'de Morgan's Laws' in the context in which he gave them. Their importance, in that context, is in connexion with such processes as contraposition and obversion. Thus the obverse of 'Every *XY* is either a *P* or a *Q*' is 'No *XY* is at once a non-*P* and a non-*Q*', and its contrapositive, 'Everything that is at once a non-*P* and a non-*Q* is either a non-*X* or a non-*Y*'. Other laws which de Morgan gives include the following:[3] (1) Any alternant may be dropped from a distributed term, and any conjunct from an undistributed, e.g. from 'No *X* is either a *Y* or a *Z*' we may infer 'No *X* is a *Y*', and from 'Some *XY* is a *Z*', 'Some *X* is a *Z*'. (2) In *E* and *I* propositions, any conjunct may be transferred from either term to the other, e.g. from 'No *XY* is a *ZT*' we may infer 'No *XYZ* is a *T*' and 'No *X* is a *YZT*'. (3) In *A* and *O* propositions, the contradictory of any conjunct of the subject may be made an alternant of the predicate, and the contradictory of any alternant of the predicate a conjunct of the subject, e.g. we may pass from 'Every *XY* is a *Z*' to 'Every *X* is either a *Z* or not a *Y*', and from 'Every *X* is either a *Y* or a *Z*' to 'Every *X* that is not a *Y* is a *Z*'. These will suffice as illustrations. In de Morgan's own handling of the subject, there is rather an excess of symbolism and of technical terms, and the most lucid presentation of this part of logic is that given somewhat later by J. N. Keynes.[4]

Considerable awkwardness, to say nothing less, is introduced into this extension of the logic of categorical propositions if we still insist on not admitting 'empty terms', i.e. terms without application, as possible substitutions for our term-symbols. We

[1] *Summulae* (Bocheński's edition), 7.29.

[2] *Formal Logic*, p. 116.

[3] Ibid., pp. 119–21; *English Cyclopædia, Arts and Sciences*, vol. v, pp. 352–3.

[4] *Formal Logic*, Part IV in first three editions, and Appendix III in the fourth.

saw earlier that if this insistence is combined with the rule that if '*X*' is a term then so is 'non-*X*' (a rule implied by the substitutability of '*nb*' for a term-variable '*b*' in theses of the system), it entails that we must also keep out of our system terms which cover everything whatever. The corresponding rule for a system containing conjunctive and alternative terms would be that if '*X*' and '*Y*' are terms then so are 'at-once-*X*-and-*Y*' and 'either-*X*-or-*Y*'. But coupled with the non-admissibility of empty terms, this would mean that no true universal propositions would be expressible in our system. For (1) if 'No *X* is a *Y*' were expressible, '*X*' and '*Y*' would be among our terms, and therefore '*XY*' would be among them; therefore '*XY*' would have application, and 'No *X* is a *Y*' would be false. And (2) if 'Every *X* is a *Y*' were expressible, '*X*' and '*Y*' would be among our terms, and therefore '*X*' and 'non-*Y*', and therefore the compound 'at-once-*X*-and-non-*Y*', which would have application, and 'Every *X* is a *Y*' be consequently false.[1] Keynes simply drops the assumption that all terms have application, and frames suitable rules for determining the truth-value of propositions in which 'empty' terms occur; de Morgan in theory half retains the assumption,[2] but goes so far towards dropping it as to introduce two term-symbols '*U*' and '*u*', standing for 'Everything' and 'Nothing' (or more accurately for 'thing' and 'non-thing') respectively. By their means he formulates such theses as that 'Every *Y* is an *X*' is equivalent to 'Every real thing is either an *X* or not a *Y*', '*U*))*X*,*y*'; and 'No *Y* is an *X*' to 'Whatever is at once a *Y* and an *X* is non-existent', '*XY*))*u*'.[3] Equivalences of this sort we shall discuss more fully at a later stage.

Of the syllogisms involving complex terms with which de Morgan deals, we shall glance at one form only, after first considering an earlier version of it. Towards the end of the *Prior Analytics*,[4] Aristotle mentions a form of inference which is in a way to be contrasted with syllogism, though in another way it may be seen as a special case of it. He calls this 'induction', and it amounts to the establishment of a generalization by showing that it holds in each of its instances in turn. His own

[1] Cf. K. R. Popper, 'The Trivialization of Mathematical Logic', *Proceedings of the Tenth International Congress of Philosophy* (Amsterdam, 1949), p. 727.
[2] *Formal Logic*, pp. 110–11. [3] Ibid., p. 120. [4] Bk. II, ch. 23.

example is drawn from natural history, but apart from any objections that a zoologist might make to the statements forming its premisses and conclusion, a modern student of scientific method would question the propriety of using any example of that kind, since in natural history we are never able to examine all instances of the generalizations we make, or at all events to know that we have done so. The Aristotelian 'induction' has, however, many uses in the more abstract sciences, and we shall replace his example by one from logic itself (or perhaps it would be more accurate to say from 'metalogic'):

The substitutions $p/1$, $q/1$; $p/1$, $q/0$; $p/0$, $q/1$; and $p/0$, $q/0$, all give to the formula *CpCqp* the value 1;
But the substitutions $p/1$, $q/1$; $p/1$, $q/0$; $p/0$, $q/1$; and $p/0$, $q/0$, are all the truth-value-substitutions there are for p and q;
Therefore all the truth-value-substitutions there are for p and q give to the formula *CpCqp* the value 1.

This looks as if it might be a syllogism in the third figure with a universal conclusion. But such syllogisms are invalid—the third figure can only be used to *confute* a universal rule by bringing foward an exception, not to establish one. The appearance, however, is deceptive, for the minor premiss here is not an ordinary *A* proposition, but rather an assertion that the terms 'the substitutions $p/1$, $q/1$; $p/1$, $q/0$; $p/0$, $q/1$; $p/0$, $q/0$' and 'truth-value-substitutions for p and q' are, as Aristotle would say, 'convertible'—it asserts not only that $p/1$, $q/1$, etc., are truth-value-substitutions, but also that there are no others. It is, moreover, the second part of this assertion that is used in the inference, which may therefore be put into the first figure thus:

All the following substitutions: $p/1$, $q/1$; $p/1$, $q/0$; $p/0$, $q/1$; $p/0$, $q/0$, are ones giving *CpCqp* the value 1;
And all the truth-value-substitutions there are for p and q are the following: $p/1$, $q/1$; $p/1$, $q/0$; $p/0$, $q/1$; $p/0$, $q/0$;
Therefore all the truth-value-substitutions there are for p and q are ones giving *CpCqp* the value 1.

There remains, all the same, a difference between this and the type of first-figure syllogism which one normally encounters. In the first figure we generally argue that because some property (expressed by the major term) belongs to some wider genus (expressed by the middle term), it belongs to a species (expressed by the minor term) falling under that wider genus. But in the above we do not do this; we prove rather that the property belongs to the genus because it belongs to all the species. Calling the property the 'major', the wider genus the 'middle', and the species the 'minor', Aristotle says that whereas in ordinary syllogism we prove the major of the minor through the middle, in induction we prove the major of the middle through the minor. (In the language of Kant and Peirce, we might say that instead of proving the result in the case by the rule, we prove the rule by observing the result in all the cases.)

So Aristotle. De Morgan[1] too reduces the 'inductive syllogism' to Figure 1, but a little differently (though only a little, if we remember that what ordinary speech expresses as 'The *X*'s, the *Y*'s, and the *Z*'s are all *P*'s' would appear by a strict use of compound terms as 'Everything that is either an *X* or a *Y* or a *Z* is a *P*'). For him, the original inductive form is 'Every *P* is an *M*; every *Q* is an *M*; every *R* is an *M*; and every *X* is either a *P* or a *Q* or an *R*; therefore every *X* is an *M*'. (In our example, 'Every pair of propositions *p*, *q* in which $p = 1$ and $q = 1$ is a pair for which $CpCqp = 1$; every pair for which $p = 1$ and $q = 0$ is a pair, etc.') And what it reduces to is 'Everything that is either a *P* or a *Q* or an *R* is an *M*; and every *X* is either a *P* or a *Q* or an *R*; therefore, etc.' He classifies this form as a 'dilemma'. This is an old term applied in the first instance to inferences in the logic of propositions corresponding to such theses as *CKKCprCqrApqr* (If *p* implies *r*, and *q* implies *r*, and either *p* or *q*, then *r*) and *CKKCpqCprANqNrNp* (If *p* implies *q*, and *p* implies *r*, and either not *q* or not *r*, then not *p*), in which a combination of implicative and alternative propositions forces a single consequent upon us.[2] Menacing an opponent like some goat on a mountain path, it is sometimes called a 'horned syllogism', *syllogismus cornutus*. The only way of escaping its conclusion is either to 'take it by the horns', i.e. deny one of the implications, or 'escape between the horns', i.e. deny that the

[1] Op. cit., pp. 123, 211.

[2] For various types of dilemmas see Keynes, *Formal Logic*, 4th ed. § 318; Johnson, *Logic*, I. iii. 6. Keynes points out that an argument of this type, in which *three* alternatives (stated to be the only ones open to us) all drive us in the same direction, is strictly speaking a 'trilemma', one with four a 'tetralemma'; and so on. But the term 'dilemma' is loosely applied to them all.

alternatives presented exhaust the possibilities.[1] It is plain that inductive arguments can only be met in the same two ways—we may question whether what is said to be true in each case really does hold in some particular case, or we may question whether the listed cases are really all there are. Formally, to arrive at the principle of induction from that of the dilemma we firstly introduce a conditional element into the alternative proposition, which is transmitted to the final consequent, giving us the thesis *CKKCqsCrsCpAqrCps* (If *q* implies *s*, and *r* implies *s*, and *p* implies either *q* or *r*, then *p* implies *s*), the proof of this principle from that of the pure dilemma being as follows:

1. *CCqrCCpqCpr*
2. *CCKpqrCpCqr*
3. *CCpCqrCKpqr*
4. *CKKCprCqrApqr*
   2 *p*/*KCprCqr*, *q*/*Apq* = *C*4—5
5. *CKCprCqrCApqr*
   1 *p*/*KCqsCrs*, *q*/*CAqrs*, *r*/*CCpAqrCps* = *C*1 *q*/*Aqr*, *r*/*s*—*C*5 *p*/*q*, *q*/*r*, *r*/*s*—6
6. *CKCqsCrsCCpAqrCps*
   3 *p*/*KCqsCrs*, *q*/*CpAqr*, *r*/*Cps* = *C*6—7
7. *CKKCqsCrsCpAqrCps*.

Then by substitutions $p/\phi x$, etc., appropriate juggling, and the use of $\Pi 1$ and $\Pi 2$, we obtain the functional variant of this,

$$CKK(\Pi x C\psi x\theta x)(\Pi x C\chi x\theta x)(\Pi x C\phi x A\psi x\chi x)(\Pi x C\phi x\theta x),$$

which (apart from the number of alternatives) is de Morgan's version of induction.

[1] Dilemmas are sometimes also 'rebutted' by other dilemmas with opposite conclusions; but if the conclusions are genuinely incompatible there must be some incompatibility in the premisses. An example of a pair of rebutting dilemmas would be: (1) If 'I am now lying' is false, it is false (*Cpp*), and if it is true it is false (for that is what it says), and it must be one or the other, so it is false. But (2) if 'I am now lying' is true, it is true (*Cpp*), and if it is false it is true (for it *says* it is false), and it must be one or the other, so it is true. We can in fact escape between the horns of both of these; but the point will be dealt with in III. iii. 3.

§ 4. *Quantification of the Predicate*

It occurred to Aristotle that not only the sign of negation but also the signs of quantity might contribute to the logical form of a term as well as to that of the proposition as a whole. But he only considered the possibility in order, very curtly, to reject it. In the *De Interpretatione*,[1] to point the moral that it is the whole proposition and not a term in it which the word 'every' makes universal, he says that if we try attaching it to *both* terms we obtain a form of proposition, 'Every *B* is every *A*', which is in no circumstances true. He gives 'Every man is every animal' as an example; and then drops the matter. The Schoolmen at once underlined what their master said here, and went beyond it. They improved upon his example by considering not merely 'Every man is every animal' but 'Every man is every man', and pointed out that even in a case like this, which one might expect the law of identity to guarantee, the proposition is not true; for if every man were every man, we could infer that Socrates is every man, Plato is every man, etc.[2] But instead of dropping such forms altogether, they sought for and defended true ones of the same broad type, such as the contradictory of the previous example, 'Some man is not every man', and its contrary, 'No man is every man'.[3] They used them, even, to raise difficulties about the rules of syllogism—the writer calling himself Scotus gives, as another case of a valid syllogism with two particular premisses, 'Something that moves in a circle is every moon, and something shining is every moon, therefore something shining moves in a circle'.[4] The answer to this is that although it shows that a given inference of the form 'Some *A* is *B*, and some *C* is *B*, therefore some *C* is *A*' may have further formal features that make it valid, that does not mean that this inferential form itself is valid, i.e. safe in *every* instance and type of instance. But even more interesting than the awareness here shown that this invalid inferential form may have valid sub-forms is the awareness that a proposition of the form 'Some *B* is every *A*' may be true, and will be so if there is only one *A* and it is *B*. For it is only a step from this to the recognition that

[1] 17^b 13–16.

[2] Peter of Spain, *Summulae* (Bocheński's edition), 12.24–12.25; Burleigh, *De Puritate Artis Logicae* (ed. Boehner), pp. 101–2.

[3] Peter's *Summulae*, 12.27; Burleigh, op. cit., p. 102.

[4] *Quaestiones*, etc., q.xx.

the subalternant form so sweepingly dismissed by Aristotle may have true instances of a similarly queer sort.

The Schoolmen applied their rules of equipollence to these forms too. Peter of Spain[1] argues that if a proposition has two signs of universal negation, one before the subject and the other before the predicate, 'the former is equipollent to its contrary and the latter to its contradictory'. That is, we may simultaneously replace the first sign of universal negation by one of universal affirmation and the second by one of particular affirmation. For example, 'Nothing is nothing' is equivalent to 'Everything is something'. For by the second rule of equipollence, 'No' = 'Every not', and so 'Nothing is nothing' = 'Everything is not-nothing'; and by the first rule, 'Not no' = 'Some', so 'Everything is not-nothing' = 'Everything is something.' Similarly, 'No man is no animal' is equivalent to 'Every man is some animal', and, moreover, 'Neither is neither' is equivalent to 'Both are either'. (That is, just as 'No B is no *A*' = 'Every *B* is some *A*', so 'Neither $B1$ nor $B2$ is neither $A1$ nor $A2$' = 'Both $B1$ and $B2$ are either $A1$ or $A2$'.) Using 'Ωx' for 'For no x'[2] and 'ϕ' for 'is', we might formalize part of Peter's proof as follows (it would be completed by proving the converse implication from the converse theses):

1. $CN\Omega y\psi y\Sigma y\psi y$
2. $C\Omega x\psi x\Pi xN\psi x$
3. $CCpqCCqrCpr$

   $1\ \psi y/\phi xy \times \Pi 1 = 4$
4. $C\Pi xN\Omega y\phi xy\Sigma y\phi xy$

   $4 \times \Pi 2 = 5$
5. $C\Pi xN\Omega y\phi xy\Pi x\Sigma y\phi xy$

   $2\ \psi x/\Omega y\phi xy = 6$
6. $C\Omega x\Omega y\phi xy\Pi xN\Omega y\phi xy$

   $3\ p/\Omega x\Omega y\phi xy,\ q/\Pi xN\Omega y\phi xy,\ r/\Pi x\Sigma y\phi xy = C6\text{—}C5\text{—}7$
7. $C\Omega x\Omega y\phi xy\Pi x\Sigma y\phi xy$.

[1] *Summulae*, 1.26. Cf. Burleigh, op. cit., p. 71.

[2] For some of the effects of introducing such quantifiers into the functional calculus see C. H. Langford, *Bulletin of the American Mathematical Society*, vol. xxxii (1926), pp. 694–704, and my own paper on 'Negative Quantifiers' in the *Australasian Journal of Philosophy*, vol. xxxi (1953), pp. 107–23.

(Theses 1 and 2 here are the theses which Peter implicitly cites in his reference to the first and second rules of equipollence.)

Though this seems to be almost as far as the Schoolmen went (not quite—we shall mention some other important points shortly),[1] it is farther than anyone else went for a very long time. In the nineteenth century the 'quantification of the predicate' was advocated again, but with a quite fantastic incompetence, by the Edinburgh logician Sir William Hamilton. Hamilton used 'all' rather than 'every'—this was his undoing—and proposed the enlargement of Aristotle's four forms to the following:

(1) All *X* is all *Y*.
(2) All *X* is some *Y*.
(3) Some *X* is all *Y*.
(4) Some *X* is some *Y*.
(5) Any *X* is-not any *Y*.
(6) Any *X* is-not some *Y*.
(7) Some *X* is-not any *Y*.
(8) Some *X* is-not some *Y*.

These forms provoked considerable controversy, in which de Morgan was again to the forefront. His criticisms[2] were directed primarily against the first of the Hamiltonian forms and the last. 'All *X* is all *Y*' was put forward by Hamilton as a way of expressing the fact that *X* and *Y* are 'convertible' terms, i.e. that every *X* is a *Y* and every *Y* an *X*. But this, de Morgan points out, makes this form a conjunction of two of the other forms in the list, namely 'All *X* is some *Y*' and 'Some *X* is all *Y*', the Hamiltonian expansions of 'All *X* is *Y*' and 'Only *X* is *Y*' (or 'All *Y* is *X*'). Moreover, although the forms (2)–(7) may be arranged as pairs of contradictories, (1) has no contradictory in the list. Its contradictory is 'Either some *X* is not any *Y* or some *Y* is not any *X*'; it is certainly not (8), 'Some *X* is-not some *Y*'. For this last will be true so long as there is more than one *X* or more than one *Y*; you cannot contradict it by saying that the class of *X*'s and the class of *Y*'s are coincident. You can only contradict it by saying 'There is but one *X*, and but one *Y*,

[1] For a fuller treatment of the achievements in this field of Peter of Spain see my paper 'The *Parva Logicalia* in Modern Dress' in *Dominican Studies*, vol. v (1952).
[2] *Formal Logic*, p. 302.

and these are one and the same object'; and this contradictory also is not in Hamilton's list. De Morgan further objects to 'Some *X* is-not some *Y*' being on any list at all; he calls it a 'spurious' proposition, the circumstances under which it may be contradicted being so extraordinary. This last comment is a reactionary one; we cannot refuse to employ propositional forms for such reasons. Though de Morgan did not observe this, we may note that the offending form is equivalent to the scholastic 'Some *X* is not every *Y*', for not to be every *Y* is to have some *Y* that one is not. ($\Sigma x \Sigma y N \phi xy$, the Hamiltonian form, $= \Sigma x N \Pi y \phi xy$, the scholastic. This equivalence is stated in PM 11.5.)

De Morgan did not, however, content himself with making these criticisms, but attempted to find modifications of the Hamiltonian scheme by which they might be met. In the paper in which he does this,[1] he begins by distinguishing the 'cumular' interpretation of universal propositions suggested by the applicative 'All', and the 'exemplar' interpretation suggested by 'Every', and still more by 'Any'.[2] 'All men are mortals' makes us think of the whole class of men as being included in the whole class of mortals; 'Any man is a mortal' makes us think of the individual instances. And when extensions of the traditional set of forms are contemplated, it is important to decide whether it is the 'cumular' or the 'exemplar' forms which we wish to extend. De Morgan, by replacing the Hamiltonian 'cumular' forms by 'exemplar' ones, obtained a group of eight propositions which do fall into contradictory pairs, which he listed as follows, putting more ordinary modes of statement beside them:

(1) Any one *X* is any one *Y* (i.e. There is but one *X* and one *Y*, and *X* is *Y*.
(2) Some one *X* is not some one *Y* (i.e. There can be found some one *X* and some one *Y* which are not the same).

(3) Any one *X* is some one *Y* (i.e. All *X*'s are *Y*'s).
(4) Some one *X* is not any one *Y* (i.e. Some *X*'s are not *Y*'s).

[1] 'On the Syllogism', second paper, *Transactions of the Cambridge Philosophical Society*, vol. ix, Part I, Paper IV. See especially §§ 4 and 5. See also *English Cyclopædia, Arts and Sciences*, vol. v, pp. 349, 351.

[2] It should be noted that while 'Any *X* is a *Y*' is equivalent to 'Every *X* is a *Y*', 'Not any *X* is a *Y*' is not equivalent to 'Not every *X* is a *Y*' but rather, as we have observed earlier, to 'Not (some *X* is a *Y*)'. The convention about 'any' seems to be always so to use it that the force of the proposition as a whole will be universal.

{ (5) Some one *X* is any one *Y* (i.e. Every *Y* is *X*).
  (6) Any one *X* is not some one *Y* (i.e. Some *Y*'s are not *X*'s).

{ (7) Any one *X* is not any one *Y* (i.e. No *X* is *Y*).
  (8) Some one *X* is some one *Y* (i.e. Some *X*'s are *Y*'s).

This set of propositions does, however, still contain the objectionable form 'Some *X* is-not some *Y*', and now also contains its equally odd contradictory. Is it possible to produce anything at all resembling Hamilton's eight forms which does not? This question is worth asking even if we do not share de Morgan's distaste for the forms (1) and (2) above.

Why is it that the form 'Some *X* is-not some *Y*' is only false, and its contradictory true, under conditions into which numerical considerations enter? The reason, de Morgan says, is that the word 'is' is understood as expressing identity. 'Any one *X* is any one *Y*' asserts that no matter what *X* you take, and no matter what *Y* you take, the *X* and the *Y* will be identical; and this can only be so if only one thing is either. If the copula of identity could be replaced by one indifferently representing any relation, or perhaps any relation sharing some of the logical properties of identity without actually being identity, we might escape this result; for while there can only be one object with which any given object is identical (itself), it may be related in other ways to an indefinite number. De Morgan had already raised this possibility of alternative copulae in an earlier work, his *Formal Logic*,[1] where it is argued that the cogency of ordinary syllogisms is not due to the fact that the copula represents the relation of identity (i.e. 'Every *X* is a *Y*' means 'Every *X* has some *Y* with which it is identical'; and similarly with the others), but to the fact that the relation which it represents is what de Morgan calls 'transitive' and 'convertible'. By a 'transitive' relation he means one such that, if it holds between *A* and *B* and also between *B* and *C*, it automatically holds between *A* and *C* (e.g. 'ancestor of'—if *A* is *B*'s ancestor, and *B* is *C*'s, then *A* is *C*'s ancestor). By a 'convertible' relation he means one such that, if it holds from *A* to *B*, it automatically holds from *B* to *A* (e.g. 'fellow countryman of'—if *A* is *B*'s fellow countryman, than *B* is *A*'s). Identity has both of these properties; but so have other relations. The phrase

[1] Ch. iii.

'is tied to', for example, might be so understood that we would describe *A* as being tied to *C* if *C* were tied to *A*, and also if *A* were tied to *B* and *B* to *C*. Every valid Aristotelian syllogism, de Morgan pointed out, would remain so if the ordinary copula were replaced by 'is tied to', so understood. For example, from 'Every *Z* is tied to a *Y*' and 'No *X* is tied to a *Y*' we may infer 'No *X* is tied to a *Z*' (cf. Camestres). In the paper on the Hamiltonian forms he takes up this point again, and adds to it that such a form as 'Any one *X* is tied to any one *Y*' (i.e. Every *X* is tied to every *Y*) will have over 'Any one *X* is (identical with) any one *Y*' the advantage that it could be true if there were an indefinite number of *Y*'s and *X*'s. He therefore amends his eight forms to these:

{ (1) Each *X* is related to all the *Y*'s.
{ (2) Some *X*'s are not related to some of the *Y*'s.
{ (3) Each *X* is related to one or more *Y*'s.
{ (4) Some *X*'s are not related to any *Y*'s.
{ (5) Some *X*'s are (among them) related to all the *Y*'s.
{ (6) No *X* is related to some one or more *Y*'s.
{ (7) No *X* is related to any one *Y*.
{ (8) Some *X*'s are related to some one or more *Y*'s.

(In the contradictory pairs it is of course understood that the same relation is meant in each case.)

The Schoolmen too could handle double quantifications involving other verbs than 'is'. Thus they noticed the difference between 'Every man sees every man' and 'Every man sees himself'[1] (cf. $\Pi xy\phi xy$ and $\Pi x\phi xx$. Had J. S. Mill lived a little earlier, the example used might have been 'Every man desires-the-happiness-of every man' and 'Every man desires-the-happiness-of himself').[2] They also handled other forms of this sort without quite realizing they were doing so (much as with conjunctive terms). Thus they noted that 'Man is the noblest of creatures' does not imply 'This man is the noblest of creatures'.[3] What this amounts to is that 'Any man is-nobler-than any non-human creature' does not imply 'This man is-nobler-than any creature that is not this man' (though, we may

[1] Peter of Spain, *Summulae*, 8.16.
[2] See Mill's *Utilitarianism*, ch. iv, third paragraph.
[3] *Summulae*, 6.11.

note, it does imply 'This man is nobler than this non-human creature'). And in handling one of these disguised forms—very thinly disguised this time—they were a step ahead of de Morgan. For they noticed that (*a*) 'Both Plato and Socrates are saying something true' and (*b*) 'Something true is being said by both Plato and Socrates' are not equivalent, for if Plato were saying one true thing and Socrates another (*a*) would be true and (*b*) false.[1] Remembering that 'Both' for the Schoolmen was a variant of 'Every', we have here the distinction between 'Every *X* has some *Y* that it is *R* to' (e.g. 'Every man has something true that he says') and 'Some *Y* has every *X* being *R* to it' (e.g. 'Something true has every man saying it'. When '*X*' and '*Y*' are both the indefinite 'thing', this becomes the distinction we have noted in the functional calculus between $\Pi x \Sigma y \phi xy$ and $\Sigma y \Pi x \phi xy$. There is a hint of an awareness of this distinction in de Morgan's parenthetical 'among them' in his fifth form above; but had he been fully aware of it he would have listed not 8 forms but 12 (the six affirmatives corresponding to those in our hexagon for doubly quantified forms in Part I), and in the forms with 'is' he would have had not merely two but six 'odd' ones, e.g. 'Some *X* is every *Y*' (as in the medieval 'Something shining is every moon').

De Morgan never rectified this deficiency himself. It was clearly seen later by Peirce and his student O. C. Mitchell;[2] de Morgan pursued the subject of multiple quantification in other directions. In a later paper than this on Hamilton,[3] he occupied himself with the *composition* of relative terms, i.e. the formation from, say, 'teacher of' and 'parent of', of such complexes as 'teacher of some parent of', 'teacher of every parent of' and (a characteristically de Morgan-ish addition) 'teacher of none but parents of'. He used capitals such as *L* and *M* for relative terms; the corresponding small letters for what he called their 'contraries' (it would be more normal to

[1] *Summulae* 12.35–36. Cf. also the teaching of St. Vincent Ferrer, as summarized by I. Thomas in 'Saint Vincent Ferrer's *De Suppositionibus*', *Dominican Studies*, vol. v (1952), p. 97.

[2] See Peirce's *Collected Papers*, 2. 324, 524; 3. 396; 4. 60, 452.

[3] 'On the Syllogism, No. IV, and on the Logic of Relations', *Transactions of the Cambridge Philosophical Society*, vol. x, Part II, Paper VII. Summarized in de Morgan's article 'Relation (Logic)' in the *English Cyclopædia, Arts and Sciences*, vol. vi, pp. 1016–17.

say 'contradictories'), e.g. if L = 'teacher of', l = 'non-teacher of'; L^{-1} for the 'converse' relation to L, e.g. if L = 'teacher of', L^{-1} = 'pupil of'; LM for 'L of some M of'; LM' for 'L of every M of'; and L,M for 'L of none but M's of'. He recorded such results as that the converse of LM' (L of every M of) is M^{-1},L^{-1} (M'd only by what is L'd by), e.g. if B is a lover of every servant of A, then A is served by none but those loved by B; and that the 'contrary' of LM (L of an M of) may be stated either as lM' or as L,m, e.g. to say that B is *not* a teacher-of-some-parent of A is to say that B is a non-teacher of every parent of A, or that he is a teacher of none but non-parents of A. A transitive relation he defines as an L such that $LL))L$ ('Every L-of-an-L of anything is itself an L of it'); and he deduces a number of properties of transitive relations, such as that where $LL))L$ (e.g. an ancestor of an ancestor is an ancestor), $L))LL^{-1\prime}$, $L))l,l^{-1}$, $L))l^{-1}l'$, and $L))L^{-1},L$ (an ancestor is an ancestor of all descendants, a non-ancestor of none but non-descendants, a non-descendant of all non-ancestors, and a descendant of none but ancestors); also, where $LL))L$ there $L^{-1}))L,L^{-1}$, $L^{-1}))ll^{-1\prime}$, $L^{-1}))l^{-1},l$, $L^{-1}))L^{-1}L'$ (a descendant is an ancestor of none but descendants, a non-ancestor of all non-descendants, a non-descendant of none but non-ancestors, and a descendant of all ancestors). The reader may put into the notation for himself the further theses asserting (where L = 'ancestor') that a non-ancestor is a non-ancestor of all ancestors, and an ancestor of none but non-ancestors, while a non-descendant is a descendant of none but non-descendants, and a non-descendant of all descendants; that any descendant of a non-ancestor is a non-ancestor, and so is any non-ancestor of a descendant; and that any ancestor of a non-descendant is a non-descendant, and so is any non-descendant of an ancestor.

One of de Morgan's most intriguing theses in this paper is what he calls 'Theorem *K*', after the '*k*' of 'Baroko' and 'Bokardo' when spelt that way. By this theorem, given a statement of the form $LM))N$, 'Every L-of-an-M of anything is an N of that thing', we may infer both of the statements formed by replacing one of the antecedent relations by its converse and interchanging the contrary of the other with the contrary of the consequent relation, i.e. the statements $L^{-1}n))m$ ('Everything L'd by a non-N of anything is a non-M of it') and $nM^{-1}))l$

('Every non-*N* of something *M*'d by a thing is a non-*L* of it'). For example, from

'Every uncle-or-aunt of a parent of anyone is his great-uncle-or-aunt'

we may infer both

'Every nephew-or-niece of a non-great-uncle-or-aunt of anyone is not-his-parent'

and

'Every non-great-uncle-or-aunt of a child of anyone is not-his-uncle-or-aunt.'

The connexion with Baroko and Bokardo is this: Suppose we let *L*, *M*, and *N* be the relations between the terms expressed by '))', '((', '(·)', etc., and suppose we give names to these relations, for example, saying for 'Every *X* is a *Y*', '*X* is a species of *Y*', for 'Only *X*'s are *Y*'s', '*X* is a genus of *Y*' ('genus' is plainly the converse of 'species') and for 'Some *X* is not a *Y*', '*X* is an exient of *Y*' ('exient' is plainly the contrary of 'species'). Then we may express the principles of syllogistic reasoning by such statements as 'Every species of a species of anything is itself a species of that thing' (this means 'For any *X*, *Y*, and *Z*, if every *X* is a *Y* and every *Y* is a *Z*, then every *X* is a *Z*'); and Theorem *K* will enable us to deduce the principles of the two syllogisms derivable from the given one by indirect reduction (the 'opponent' syllogisms, as de Morgan called them). For example, from 'Species of species is species' (Barbara) we obtain by replacing the first 'species' by its converse, and interchanging the contraries of the other two, 'Genus of exient is exient'. Translating this, we have 'If only *X*'s are *Y*'s, and some *Y* is not a *Z*, then some *X* is not a *Z*'. Converting the 'only' form to its Aristotelian counterpart, and putting the premisses in the traditional order, this becomes 'If some *Y* is not a *Z*, and every *Y* is an *X*, then some *X* is not a *Z*', i.e. Bokardo. Replacing the *second* 'species' in 'Species of species is species' by its converse, and transposing the negations of the others, we obtain 'Exient of genus is exient', i.e. 'If some *X* is not a *Y*, and only *Y*'s are *Z*'s, then some *X* is not a *Z*'. The reader can turn this into Baroko for himself.

The controversy with Hamilton, as we have so far outlined it, had a sequel which we shall sketch as briefly as we can, 'for the record'. So far from welcoming de Morgan's suggested amendments to his scheme, he repudiated them with indignant scorn, and raised a number of new issues.[1] He was plainly very much wedded to the 'cumular' interpretation of universal propositions, and argued that it was what the ancient and medieval logicians had always intended in their own comparatively slight discussions of double quantification. De Morgan was easily able to show, in his final reply,[2] that this was simply nonsense. For example, Hamilton took Aristotle's objection to the proposition 'Every man is every animal' to be merely that there are in fact other animal species beside the human. But Aristotle's objection is couched much too strongly for that; he says that no proposition of this form is true, which would on Hamilton's interpretation be a denial that there are any convertible terms—a folly of which Aristotle was certainly never guilty. And to de Morgan's assertion that the form 'All *X* is all *Y*' (interpreted in Hamilton's 'cumular' manner) is a conjunction of 'All *X* is some *Y*' and 'Some *X* is all *Y*', Hamilton replies that this is so far from being the case that it is incompatible with both of them. He here discloses that in his system the word 'Some' must be taken as meaning not 'Some at least' but 'Some only'. De Morgan points out that this interpretation of 'Some' would invalidate many of the syllogisms which Hamilton constructs with his eight forms. However, he goes on, it is worth seeing what these forms mean on such an interpretation, and what can be made of them. They become (putting '*B*' and '*A*' for the terms)

(1) The whole class of *B*'s is coextensive with the whole class of *A*'s, i.e. *KAbaAab*.
(2) The whole class of *B*'s is coextensive with a portion (not the whole) of the class of *A*'s, i.e. *KAbaOab*.
(3) A portion (not the whole) of the class of *B*'s coincides with the whole class of *A*'s, i.e. *KAabOba*.

[1] *Discussions on Philosophy and Literature*, by Sir William Hamilton, Bart. (1852), Appendix II (B).

[2] 'On the Syllogism, No. V,' *Transactions of the Cambridge Philosophical Society*, vol. x, Part II, Paper XI. In the above summary I have somewhat simplified de Morgan's reasoning.

(4) A portion (not the whole) of the class of *B*'s is coextensive with a portion (not the whole) of the class of *A*'s, i.e. *KIbaKObaOab*.

(5) The whole class of *B*'s lies outside the whole class of *A*'s, i.e. *Eba* (and, of course, *Eab*).

(6) The whole class of *B*'s lies outside a portion (not the whole) of the class of *A*'s.

(7) A portion (not the whole) of the class of *B*'s lies outside the whole class of *A*'s.

(8) A portion (not the whole) of the class of *B*'s lies outside a portion (not the whole) of the class of *A*'s.

(1)–(5) here are simply the five Eulerian possibilities. But the interpretation of (6)–(8) presents difficulties. Take (6), 'The whole class of *B*'s lies outside a portion (not the whole) of the class of *A*'s'. This plainly asserts that there are some *A*'s which are not *B*'s (i.e. a portion of the class of *A*'s which the whole class of *B*'s lies outside of), and also that there are some which are (the last-mentioned portion of the *A*'s not being the whole); but does it or does it not assert that the whole class of *B*'s falls not outside, but within, this second portion of the class of *A*'s? If it does, the form becomes equivalent to (2), *KAbaOab*; if not, it just means 'Some *A*'s are not *B*'s but some are', *KOabIab*, which, though not equivalent to (2), is implied by it. Similarly, (7) is either equivalent to (3) or implied by it. And (8), most paradoxically of all, could be equivalent to (1), and if not is implied by it. (It is equivalent if it means that a portion of the class of *B*'s is distinct from a portion of the class of *A*'s, but not from the rest of the class of *A*'s, and the rest of the class of *B*'s is not distinct even from the first-mentioned portion of the class of *A*'s.) The upshot of de Morgan's final analysis is therefore that on this interpretation the Hamiltonian forms seem to reduce to the five Eulerian compounds, and if these are to be further subdivided, the way to do it is de Morgan's own way, as outlined in the first section of this chapter. 'De Morgan's final and unanswerable paper', Peirce[1] not unjustly calls this, in the controversy in which 'the reckless Hamilton flew like a dor-bug into the brilliant light of De Morgan's mind'.

[1] *Collected Papers*, 2. 533.

III

Singular and Existential Propositions

§ 1. *Singulars and Generals in Traditional and Modern Logic*

WHAT we have called 'singular' propositions, i.e. propositions about some definite individual, are not much discussed by Aristotle, though it is going too far to say, as Łukasiewicz does, that he 'does not introduce' them into his logic, and 'applies his logic only to universal terms, like "man" and "animal"'.[1] In the last chapter of the *Prior Analytics* he gives examples of inferences, including a syllogism, using singular propositions, and he notes in the *De Interpretatione* that the contradictory of a singular proposition is another singular proposition—of 'Socrates is white', 'Socrates is not white'. But the Schoolmen were much more at home with them, and used singular propositions in their most characteristic examples both of syllogism ('Every man is running, and Socrates is a man, *ergo*, etc.') and of induction ('Plato is not every man, Socrates is not every man, *et sic de singulis*, *ergo*, No man is every man'). They often discussed the syllogism in the third figure with two singular premisses ('Socrates is running, and Socrates is a white thing, therefore a white thing is running'), which they called the *syllogismus expositorius*, from an idea (possibly mistaken) that Aristotle used them in what he called proof by 'exposition' or ἔκθεσις (e.g. the proof that 'No *B* is an *A*' implies 'No *A* is a *B*' by arguing that if some *A* were a *B* then there would be something, *C*, that was a *B*, and was an *A*, so that some *B* would be an *A*; so that if 'No *A* is a *B*' is false, so is 'No *B* is an *A*', and if the latter is true, so is the former).[2] The Schoolmen were especially interested in the singular and semi-singular propositions, often rather queer ones, resulting from the substitution of singular for other terms in general propositions, and observed, beside the 'distributions' and non-distributions already noted, that from 'Some man is an animal', although we cannot infer either 'This man is an animal' or 'Some man is this animal', we may infer both 'Either this man is an animal or that man

[1] *Aristotle's Syllogistic*, p. 130.

[2] *Anal. Pr.* 25^{a} 14–16.

is or that other man is, etc.' and 'Either some man is this animal or some man is that animal, etc.' (provided it be given that the men or animals enumerated are all there are); and that from 'Every man is an animal', although we cannot infer either 'Every man is this animal' or even the disjunction 'Either every man is this animal or every man is that, etc.', we may infer the universal-with-a-disjunctive-term 'Every man is either this animal or that animal or that other, etc.'[1] (This is, of course, another illustration of their perception of the distinction between $A\Pi x\phi x\Pi x\psi x$ and $\Pi xA\phi x\psi x$, or rather between $A\Pi xC\theta x\phi x\Pi xC\theta x\psi x$ and $\Pi xC\theta xA\phi x\psi x$.)

A serious question which arises, however, both with Aristotle and the Schoolmen, is that as to how clearly and sharply they distinguished between singular and general terms and propositions. In the modern functional calculus (assuming it to be handling substantially the same material) the distinction is radical. The two kinds of term are represented by two quite different kinds of variable. Those singular terms at least which directly name, or are used (like demonstratives) to point to, their objects, are represented by the name-variables x, y, z, etc., while the nearest thing to a general term-variable in the functional calculus is the predicate-variable (ϕ, etc.)—there are no variables replaceable by words like 'man' and 'animal', but there are ones replaceable by 'is-a-man', 'is-an-animal', etc.[2] And singular propositions such as 'Socrates is-a-man' and 'Socrates is-not-a-man' are represented by the forms ϕx and $N\phi x$, while a general proposition such as 'Every man is an animal' is represented by the form $\Pi xC\phi x\psi x$, where the relation between the predicate ψ and the 'subject' ϕ is quite different from, and more complicated than, that between ϕ and x in ϕx. General terms always function as parts of predicates (even the so-called 'subject' of 'Every man is an animal' is really part of the predicate of a subordinate clause, namely the conditional clause in 'If anything is-a-man it is-an-animal'). On the other hand, singular terms, at least proper names and demonstratives, are always subjects, never predicates; and where they appear

[1] Ockham, *Summa Logicae, Pars Prima* (ed. Boehner, 1951), Cap. 70 (p. 191, ll. 52–63).

[2] On the logical superfluity of the common noun, and the sufficiency of verbs to do what we use the common noun for, see C. S. Peirce, *Collected Papers*, 2. 328, 3. 459.

to be predicates, as in 'Tully is Cicero', what is really predicated is not the singular term but a general term constructed by means of the singular term and the relation of identity. 'Tully is Cicero' means 'Tully is-an identical-of-Cicero', and so is of the same form as 'Socrates is-a man'; or more accurately it is of the same form as 'Brutus is-a murderer-of-Caesar'. Still more accurately, from the modern point of view, it is a proposition with two subjects, and the predicate is the verb '— is identical with —'. (It would not now be agreed that the copular 'is' *ordinarily* expresses identity, as de Morgan contended; it would be said rather that in singular forms it simply helps to make up the verb that is the real predicate, and in generals it represents a complex concocted out of this and implication. It does express identity in the forms in which de Morgan was most interested—'Every *B is* every *A*', etc.—but here it is less properly called a copula than a 'two-place predicate'; the true copula is the 'is' in the 'is-identical-with' to which it expands.)[1]

How far, then, does the logic of Aristotle and the Schoolmen make distinctions of this sort? For Aristotle, the answer is ambiguous. In the *Categories*, a work possibly not his but traditionally ascribed to him and in any case Aristotelian in its interests and outlook, it is said in so many words that the relation between an individual thing and the species to which it belongs is the same as that between the species and a wider genus.[2] That is, when we say that Socrates is a man we are doing the same sort of thing with the term 'Socrates' as we are doing with the term 'man' when we say that every man is an animal. On the other hand, Aristotle insists that singular terms, by contrast with general ones, can only be subjects, never predicates, and that when they appear to be predicates, as in 'A white man is Socrates', this is only a rhetorical inversion.[3] For the Schoolmen, the answer is again ambiguous. Though they freely employed syllogisms with singular premisses, they had

[1] On this point see especially Johnson, in 'The Logical Calculus', *Mind*, 1892, first article § 11. Johnson gives a weakened reproduction of his argument here in his *Logic*, I. i. 6 ('weakened' in the sense that whereas in 'The Logical Calculus'—in which Johnson is plainly and avowedly much indebted to Peirce—both common nouns and adjectives are absorbed into verbs, in the *Logic* the basic form of predication is that in which 'is' is used, still not to express identity, but to join an adjective to a proper noun, i.e. to express what Johnson calls the 'characterizing tie').

[2] *Cat.* 2^b 18–21.

[3] *An. Pr.* 43^a 25 ff.

no special vowels for such premisses in their mnemonic schemes, and tended to classify singulars as a special variety of universals or particulars, and generally as particulars. Thus Peter of Spain says that the syllogism 'Every man is every man, and Socrates is a man, therefore Socrates is every man' is in the third mood of the first figure (*in tertio primae*), i.e. in Darii.[1] Perhaps there is an oblique reflection here of Aristotle's statement in the *Prior Analytics*, that 'indefinite' propositions, i.e. propositions such as 'Man is mortal' with no expressed quantifier, are to be treated for purposes of inference as particulars;[2] how we are to consider singulars he does not say, but he perhaps thought of them, being unquantified, as a class of indefinites. But this presented problems with the *syllogismus expositorius*, for if singulars are particulars, then 'Socrates is running and Socrates is white, therefore something white is running', has two particular premisses. The writer calling himself Scotus[3] solves this one by saying that 'Socrates is running' here means 'Everything that is Socrates is running', i.e. every identical-of-Socrates is running, and so is universal; and in post-Renaissance writers singulars are usually classed as universals (though Peter Ramus, a violent sixteenth-century critic of Aristotelianism, insists on putting them, with their syllogisms, in a class apart). The Schoolmen also very freely substitute singular terms for general ones, in the predicate- as well as the subject-position. However, there are some points, especially in their theories of *suppositio*, at which they show themselves keenly aware of differences.

The Schoolmen distinguished between what a term 'meant', i.e. its *significatio*, and its *suppositio* or what it 'stood for' (*pro quo supponit*). What it means is fixed by usage, but once this meaning has been assigned, what it stands for depends on context.[4] It may be used to stand for itself as a word, as in '*Man* is a noun' (*suppositio materialis*).[5] When not so used, its supposition may be 'discrete' or 'common'. *Suppositio discreta* is reference to a definite individual; this is had by proper names and demonstratives, and such words also 'mean' the very thing they stand for.[6] This is sometimes true of general terms also; what these 'mean'

[1] *Summulae Logicales*, 12.27.
[2] *An. Pr.* 26ª 27–29.
[3] *Quæstiones*, etc., q.xi.
[4] Peter of Spain's *Summulae*, 6.01–6.03.
[5] Ockham, *Summa Logicae Pars Prima*, cap. 67.
[6] Peter of Spain, 10.02.

is never an individual thing but rather a kind-of-thing, and sometimes they stand for this too, as 'Man' does in 'Man is a species'. (It is the kind-of-thing man that is the species.) This is *suppositio simplex*;[1] but more often they stand not for the kind-of-thing that they mean, but indifferently for any thing-of-the-kind. Thus in 'A man is running', and even in 'Every man is running', it is not the human species which is said to be running, but an individual or individuals of the species. This is *suppositio personalis*;[2] it has various subdivisions which we need not enter into, though we have already touched upon one of them in connexion with the theory of 'distribution'. What lies behind the most important part of this theory is plainly the perception that the real subject of predication is almost always a concrete individual (where it is not, as in 'Man is a species', the predicate is of a peculiar sort—it is a predicate of higher order, we might say; what the Schoolmen said was that it was a term 'of second intention'). And where the subject-term does not actually 'mean' a concrete individual, then what it means is not the subject to which the predicate is really attached; having *suppositio personalis*, it is used not strictly speaking as a subject but rather as an indication of where the real subjects are to be found. Following a modern writer,[3] we might say that it serves to 'locate' what the predicate 'describes'.

This takes us well on the way to the modern viewpoint; all that is missing is a clear perception that it is precisely *by* 'describing' that a general subject-term 'locates'. It was perhaps in the nineteenth century that this came first to be quite clearly stated, in John Stuart Mill's theory that general terms (or 'general names' as he not very aptly called them) are 'connotative'.[4] A 'connotative term', Mill explains, 'is one which denotes a subject, and implies an attribute . . . The word white, denotes all white things, as snow, paper, the foam of the sea, etc., and implies, or in the language of the Schoolmen *connotes*, the attribute *whiteness* . . . . All concrete general names are connotative. The word *man*, for example, denotes Peter, Jane, John, and an indefinite number of individuals . . . But it is

[1] Ibid. 6.05. [2] Ibid. 6.08.

[3] J. Anderson, in 'Hypotheticals', *Australasian Journal of Philosophy*, May 1952, p. 3.

[4] J. S. Mill, *A System of Logic*, i. ii. 5.

applied to them, because they possess, and to signify that they possess, certain attributes.' The distinction between 'denotation' and 'connotation', as Mill indicates, is a scholastic one, and there have been disputes as to whether he has faithfully reproduced the scholastic usage. But however that may be, his meaning is plain enough—general terms refer to individuals, but not to them *as* this individual or that, but as the possessors of certain attributes, i.e. as those of whom certain things are true. (Whately's 'attributive'[1] conveys this better than Mill's 'connotative'.) Conversely, proper names *do* refer to individuals as this individual or that, and *not* as those of whom certain things are true. Mill has been much criticized at this point, but his arguments are strong, and the criticisms based for the most part on misunderstandings which he does his best to obviate.

Mill admits, for example, that when a proper name is assigned to a child, say, or to a place, there may often have been some reason for selecting that name rather than any other; but he argues that 'the name, once given, is independent of the reason', and will not cease to be correctly applicable when the reason disappears. Dartmouth will not cease to be so called (and properly so called) if it cease, through some change in the course of the river, to be at the mouth of the Dart; its being so is therefore no part of the 'signification' of its name. Mill admits also that beside proper names there are 'connotative individual names' which do convey information about the objects which they denote. These are always complex, containing a general name with additions which in one way or another restrict its application to a single individual; as 'the founder of Rome'. (We shall hear more of them later.) And distinguished both from proper names and from such 'connotative individual names' are names which merely happen—not in virtue of their meaning, but in virtue of how things are—to apply to one thing only. Such names as these, Mill insists, are not really 'individual' names at all, but general ones. The Schoolmen knew this too, and pointed out that a general name is one which is by its own nature capable of standing for many objects, even if in fact it happens to stand only for one (cf. their 'Something shining is every moon'). And Mill goes farther—a general term, he says, may have a perfectly definite meaning, and so be a genuine

[1] Whately's *Elements of Logic*, II. v. I.

general term, even if there is nothing at all to which it applies. Not only may we 'frame a class without knowing the individuals, or any of the individuals, of which it may be composed', but 'we may do so while believing that no such individuals exist'.[1]

The distinctions elaborated in his account of 'names' are used by Mill in his account of propositions, where he controverts a theory of Hobbes's that all propositions merely tell us that things referred to by one name are or are not among the things referred to by another. Mill's principal argument against this is that, by concentrating on the denotation of names and ignoring their connotation, it takes no account of *why* the names are considered applicable to the objects in question. Certainly if all men are mortal then the word 'mortal' is applicable to anything to which the word 'man' is applicable, but only because wherever the attributes which entitle a thing to be called a 'man' are found, the attribute which entitles us to call it 'mortal' is found also; and this fact about the attributes, rather than the derived fact about the names, is what 'All men are mortal' asserts.[2] Elaborating his own opposed theory, Mill begins with propositions with proper names as subjects, and says that what is asserted here is 'that the individual thing denoted by the subject, has the attributes connoted by the predicate'. And something of the same sort is true, up to a point, of propositions in which the subject is general. Here too the proposition asserts that 'the objects denoted by the subject . . . possess the attributes connoted by the predicate'. But in this case 'the objects are no longer *individually* designated. They are pointed out only by some of their attributes.' In 'All men are mortal', therefore, what is asserted 'is not . . . that the attributes which the predicate connotes are possessed by any given individual, or by any number of individuals previously known as John, Thomas, etc., but that those attributes are possessed by each and every individual possessing certain other attributes'.[3]

[1] Mill, op. cit. I. v. 3. [2] Ibid.

[3] Ibid. I. v. 4. It is a pity that Mill did not remember this when he wrote, in a note to his chapter on the functions and value of syllogism, that 'whoever pronounces the words, All men are mortal, has affirmed that Socrates is mortal, though he may never have heard of Socrates; for since Socrates, whether known to be so or not, really is a man, he is included in the words, All men, and in every assertion of which they are the subject' (note at end of II. iii. 8). If 'included in the words, All men' means 'included in their meaning', this is simply false, on Mill's own showing above.

Here the modern view that direct predication occurs only in singulars, and that universal categoricals, traditionally classified as also propositions in which a predicate is affirmed or denied of a subject, are in fact 'formal implications' of one essentially predicative term by another, is plainly laid down.

§ 2. *Existential Propositions, and the Existential Import of General Categoricals*

If what a general term 'means' is thus distinguishable from the set of things to which it is truly applicable, it is plain—as Mill saw—that it may have meaning and yet apply to nothing at all. If this is so, it is necessary to find out what would be the consequences, in the logic of categorical propositions, of removing from its theses the proviso that only terms with application shall be regarded as substitutable for its term-variables.

This restriction was in fact never strictly observed by ancient and medieval writers, and we may begin by giving some examples of ways in which they went beyond it. We are already beyond it, of course, when we so much as *discuss* whether a given term has application or not, and use propositional forms in which the fact that a term has or has not application can be conveyed. Such forms clearly lie outside any logical system which does not admit 'empty' terms or their contradictories; yet in fact Aristotle sometimes and the Schoolmen often exemplified their categorical forms by propositions making precisely this sort of assertion. For example, the Schoolmen said that the word *Nihil* (Nothing) means *Nulla res* (No thing), and classified statements beginning with it as *E* propositions.[1] Thus they treated 'Nothing is nothing' as differing only in the terms it uses from 'No man is no animal'—in the one case, subject-term and predicate-term are both 'thing'; in the other, the subject is 'man' and the predicate 'animal'. They used also the term 'existent', with its verb 'exists' or 'is'. Aristotle himself says that 'A man is' and 'A man is-not' are the simplest forms of proposition, and distinguishes this case from the one in which 'is' is used, not as the predicate, but as a 'third element' added to the subject and predicate, as in 'A man is just'.[2] The Latin logicians distinguished these as the '*est*' *secundi adiecti* ('is' added

[1] Peter of Spain's *Summulae*, 12.28.

[2] *De Int.*, ch. 10.

as a second thing) and the '*est*' *tertii adiecti* ('is' added as a third thing); we might call them the 'existential' and the 'copulative' uses of 'is' respectively.

In Aristotle, or at all events in the writer of the *Categories*, there is also a definite assignment of truth-values to propositions in which 'is' is used existentially. He says that the propositions 'Socrates is ill' and 'Socrates is well' are not true contradictories, as 'Socrates is ill' and 'Socrates is not ill' would be; and his grounds are not that the first two would both be false if Socrates were in an intermediate state of health, but that they would both be false if there were no such person. In the case of forms like the latter pair, on the other hand, 'whether the subject exists or not, one is always false and the other true. For manifestly, if Socrates exists, one of the two propositions "Socrates is ill", "Socrates is not ill", is true, and the other false. This is likewise the case if he does not exist; for if he does not exist, to say that he is ill is false, to say that he is not ill is true.'[1] Any affirmative proposition, then, at all events if it is singular, implies the existence of its subject (it may still be false even if the subject exists, but it definitely cannot be true otherwise), and any negative proposition is implied by its subject's non-existence (on the grounds, presumably, that if a thing is not even existent, then it is certainly not anything else, such as ill). These results were put by the Schoolmen into a pair of rules: (1) *ab* est *tertii ad* est *secundi adiecti valet consequentia affirmando* (in affirmatives the copulative 'is' implies the existential), and (2) *ab* est *secundi ad* est *tertii adiecti valet consequentia negando* (in negatives the existential 'is'—or rather 'is not'—implies the copulative).

This procedure, however, of introducing 'thing' or 'existent' as a term, though it is bound up with the admission of 'empty' terms into the categorical system, is otherwise very different from the procedure of the modern functional calculus. For the modern functional calculus does not introduce 'thing' as a term and so treat, say, 'Something is a Y' as the special case of 'Some X is a Y' in which X = 'thing'; on the contrary, it treats 'Some ϕ-er is a ψ-er' as the special case of 'Something ϕ's' ($\Sigma x \phi x$) in which $\phi x = K\phi x\psi x$, i.e. as being short for 'Something at once ϕ's and ψ's.' There is no term 'thing' here, for the whole

[1] *Cat.* 13^b 26–32.

analysis just does not involve 'terms' of that sort. ('Thing' cannot in fact be a description, for it is precisely 'things' that *answer to* descriptions.)

The effects on actual syllogistic theses of making 'Something ϕ's' rather than 'Some X is Y' the fundamental logical form were somewhat provocatively worked out last century by Franz Brentano.[1] Brentano in effect defined the four traditional forms as follows:

Every B is an A = Nothing is at once a B and not an A ($N\Sigma xK\phi xN\psi x$).

No B is an A = Nothing is at once a B and an A ($N\Sigma xK\phi x\psi x$).

Some B is an A = Something is at once a B and an A ($\Sigma xK\phi x\psi x$).

Some B is not an A = Something is at once a B and not an A ($\Sigma xK\phi xN\psi x$).

($N\Sigma xK\phi xN\psi x$ is of course equivalent to the more usual modern form $\Pi xC\phi x\psi x$, as Brentano himself saw.) Actually the forms on the right of Brentano's definitions do not represent his thought quite accurately; but they are near enough for formal purposes. (He regarded all judgement as acceptance or rejection of an entertained idea, simple or complex, and his version of the E form, say, might be better expressed as 'B-and-A?—No!', and of the I form, 'B-and-A?—Yes!') His interpretations, he argued, necessitate a complete revision of the traditional rules of syllogism. For they mean, to begin with, that all ordinary universal propositions are negative (denying either that anything is at once an A and a B, or that anything is at once an A and not a B) and all particulars affirmative, so that all syllogisms in which both premisses are universal will have two 'negative' premisses. Every syllogism, moreover, will contain four terms, two of them being one another's contradictories. Barbara, for example, will have the form

Nothing is at once a B and not an A,
And nothing is at once a C and not a B,
Therefore nothing is at once a C and not an A.

[1] *Psychologie vom empirischen Standpunkt* (1874), Bk. II, ch. 7, § 15.

The four terms here are *C*, non-*A*, *B*, and non-*B*. Darii will be

> Nothing is at once a *B* and not an *A*,
> And something is at once a *C* and a *B*,
> Therefore something is at once a *C* and an *A*.

The four terms here are *C*, *A*, non-*A*, and *B*. Similarly with the rest. All syllogisms, Brentano goes on, are governed by the rules that if the conclusion is 'negative', both the premisses will share its quality and contain one of its terms (see Barbara above), while if the conclusion is 'affirmative', one of the premisses will share its quality and contain one of its terms, while the other will be opposed in quality and contain the contradictory of the other term (see Darii above). A consequence of the last rule is that a particular, or as Brentano calls it an 'affirmative', conclusion must have at least one particular premiss, thus ruling out the moods Darapti, Felapton, Bramantip, and Fesapo, and all the subaltern moods. The inconsequence of such a mood as Darapti is evident if we express it in Brentano's way:

> Nothing is at once a *B* and not an *A*,
> And nothing is at once a *B* and not a *C*,
> Therefore something is at once a *C* and an *A*.

Immediate inferences by subalternation and conversion *per accidens* are also ruled out. (The syllogistic moods invalidated, it will be noted, are either subaltern ones, depending on subalternation, or ones whose names end with a '*p*', i.e. ones which involve conversion *per accidens* in their reduction.) We cannot, for example, pass to 'Something is at once a *B* and an *A*' (Some *B* is an *A*) or to 'Something is at once an *A* and a *B*' (Some *A* is a *B*) from 'Nothing is at once a *B* and not an *A*' (Every *B* is an *A*). The rules of contrariety and subcontrariety also go ('Nothing is at once a *B* and an *A*' and 'Nothing is at once a *B* and not an *A*', i.e. the *E* and *A* forms, are both true, and their contradictories both false, if nothing is a *B* at all). There do remain—though Brentano does not notice this—analogues of the laws of subalternation, contrariety and sub-contrariety with the comparatively simple forms 'Everything is an *A*', 'Nothing is an *A*', 'Something is an *A*', and 'Something is not an *A*' (the first two are incompatible, at least one of the last two must be true, and the first implies the third and the second the fourth).[1] We have these analogues, at all events, in the functional calculus as developed by means of Łukasiewicz's rules; though there are important segments of it (using other rules and with special axioms) in which even these cannot be established.

The irritation which Brentano's manner of expressing his results was calculated to produce in conservative logicians duly appeared, though the results were not in fact as novel as he imagined. We have already seen, for example, that the Schoolmen knew that a syllogism with two negative premisses might be valid if a term were *finite sumptus* in one of them and *infinite sumptus* in the other. But the invalidated moods and immediate inferences are a more serious matter. In an 'axiomatized syllogistic' of the type set out by Łukasiewicz or Bocheński it will be found that they all depend ultimately on the axiom *Iaa*. This is used to prove the two laws of subalternation from Darii and Ferio (see Ch. I, § 2); the subaltern moods depend directly or indirectly on that, and so does conversion *per accidens* (which we obtain either *via* a subaltern mood or by combining subalternation directly with the simple conversion of *I*—*CAbaIba* and *CIbaIab*; therefore, by substitution in *CCpqCCqrCpr*, *CAbaIab*). The laws of contrariety and subcontrariety depend on those of subalternation and contradiction (e.g. from *CAbaIba* we have, by substitution in *CCpqCpNNq*, *CAbaNNIba*, i.e. *CAbaNEba*). And this axiom *Iaa* itself, interpreted in Brentano's manner as 'Something is at once an *A* and an *A*', is a law only if 'Something is an *A*' is a law, which it is not if term-variables such as '*A*' may stand for terms without application.

There are, however, a number of ways in which either the whole or a large part of the Aristotelian system may be 'saved'. We may, for example, simply not attempt to translate its formulae into those of the modern functional calculus, and for the formulae thus isolated, we may lay down the rule that empty terms are not substitutable for the term-variables. Or

[1] Brentano's forms, moreover, are all equivalent to substitutions in $\Pi x\phi x$, $\Pi xN\phi x$, $\Sigma x\phi x$ and $\Sigma xN\phi x$, but—and this is the important point—not the same substitutions for *E* and *I* as for *A* and *O*. Thus *A* could be $\Pi xC\phi x\psi x$, and *I*, $\Sigma xK\phi x\psi x$; but it is no wonder that this *A* does not imply this *I*, although $\Pi x\phi x$ implies $\Sigma x\phi x$; for the Πx and the Σx do not attach to the same complex.

we may translate the formulae in a more elaborate way, thus: replace the term-variables in the Aristotelian formula systematically by ϕx, ψx, etc., the operators A and I by ΠxC and ΣxK respectively, and make each resulting formula the consequent of a conditional, in which the antecedent affirms 'existence' of each predicate involved. Thus in translating *CAbaIba* we first obtain $C\Pi xC\phi x\psi x\Sigma xK\phi x\psi x$, and then put this into an implication with $K\Sigma x\phi x\Sigma x\psi x$ as antecedent, our full translation being

$$C(K\Sigma x\phi x\Sigma x\psi x)C(\Pi xC\phi x\psi x)(\Sigma xK\phi x\psi x),$$

which is a law of the functional calculus. Or we might replace Brentano's translations of the A and O forms by the following:

$$Aba = K(N\Sigma xK\phi xN\psi x)(\Sigma x\phi x),$$
$$Oba = A(\Sigma xK\phi xN\psi x)(N\Sigma x\phi x).$$

These, it will be seen, are still contradictories (by de Morgan's Laws); but A now asserts both that nothing ϕ's without ψ-ing and that something ϕ's, and O that either something ϕ's without ψ-ing, or nothing ϕ's. This means that A, like I (which we leave alone), implies that something ϕ's (i.e. implies the existence of its subject) while O, like E, does not.[1] On these interpretations, therefore, both universal and particular affirmatives are true only if their subject-terms have application, and both the negatives are automatically true if they have none. There is some indication that Aristotle himself would have favoured a system of this sort. For (1) it extends to categoricals generally what is asserted in the *Categories* for singulars, that the copulative 'is' implies the existential, and the existential 'is not' implies the copulative, and (2) it 'saves' all the theses which Aristotle himself asserted, except *Aaa* and *Iaa*. (In one chapter of the *Prior Analytics*[2] he suggests that propositions of the forms 'Not every A is A' and 'No A is A' are always false. But on the rule just given, 'No A is A' and 'Not every A is A' would follow from 'A is not'.) It invalidates negative-to-affirmative obversion and in consequence many theses of the Boethian extension of

[1] This set of interpretations is mentioned as a possible one by Keynes (*Formal Logic*, 4th ed., pp. 219, n. 1, 226, n. 1), Johnson (*Logic*, I. ix. 3), and Popper ('The Trivialization of Mathematical Logic', *Proceedings of the Tenth International Congress of Philosophy*, pp. 726–7).

[2] Bk. II, ch. 15.

Aristotle's system, but Aristotle himself did not admit obversion of this sort.[1]

There is, however, a large element of anachronism in attributing to Aristotle himself either the last or any other satisfactory way of interpreting his forms in the modern functional calculus and at the same time 'saving' all or most of his laws. For there are grounds for suspecting that he tended to equate his *Aba* with the simple 'formal implication' $\Pi x C\phi x\psi x$, but had too poor a grasp of the logic of propositions to see that this interpretation presented any difficulties. For in one of his few excursions into propositional logic, he argues that premisses of the form *Cpq* and *CNpq* can never both be true, because together they would yield *CNqq* (*Cpq* yields *CNqNp* by transposition, and *CNqNp* and *CNpq* yield *CNqq* by syllogism), and a proposition of the form *CNqq*, he says, is an absurdity.[2] This is a mistake (*CNqq* is not bound to be false, but only bound either to be false or to have a false antecedent), but it is just the sort of mistake that *would* be made by a man who held (*a*) that *Aba* and $\Pi x C\phi x\psi x$ are equivalent forms, and (*b*) that propositions of the form *Anaa* can never be true. Whether, if his propositional logic had been corrected, Aristotle would have revised his syllogistic laws in the way suggested by Brentano, or would have preserved them by more complicated interpretations of his forms, or by declining to interpret them, is anybody's guess.

§ 3. *Venn's Diagrams, and the Quantified Logic of Properties*

When the four categorical forms are given Brentano's interpretations, their import may be exhibited in a certain type of diagram, due to John Venn. The representation of all the forms involves the use of a pair of interlaced circles:

[1] With respect to singular propositions, Aristotle's views on obversion were deduced by Pseudo-Scotus from his views on existential import (*Quæstiones super secundo libro perihermenias*, q. ii. 3).

[2] *An. Pr.* 57^b 1 ff. See Łukasiewicz, *Aristotle's Syllogistic*, pp. 49–51. It is curious that Łukasiewicz sees no connexion between Aristotle's position here and the positions he adopts within his syllogistic, but combines a determination to put the most favourable possible construction on the latter with a willingness to dismiss the former as sheer inexplicable wrong-headedness.

This as it stands, however, does not represent any proposition. It does not, in particular, like the corresponding Eulerian diagram, represent the assertion that some *B* is an *A*, some *B* is not an *A*, and some *A* is not a *B*. It merely divides the universe into four parts—the part outside the diagram which will contain anything there may be which is neither a *B* nor an *A*; the part where the circles overlap, which will contain anything there may be which is at once a *B* and an *A*; and the other two parts, which will contain respectively whatever is a *B* but not an *A* and whatever is an *A* but not a *B*. The *A*, *E*, *I*, and *O* forms are taken to assert or deny that one or other of these compartments is empty. If the emptiness of a compartment is shown by shading it in, 'Every *B* is an *A*', or 'Nothing is at once a *B* and not an *A*', will appear as

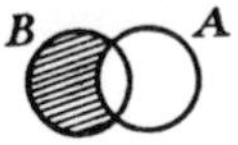

and 'No *B* is an *A*' ('Nothing is at once a *B* and an *A*') as

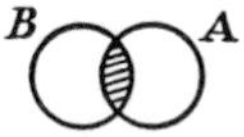

If the fact that a compartment is occupied is indicated by drawing a line across it, 'Some *B* is an *A*' will appear as

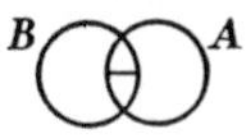

and 'Some *B* is not an *A*' as

The representation of the premisses of syllogisms involves the use of three interlaced circles, one for each term. Taking Barbara, we begin by representing 'Every *B* is an *A*' thus:

To this we add the representation of 'Every *C* is a *B*', making the whole appear as

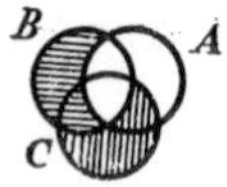

It may then be noticed that among the portions now shaded out is the part of the *C* circle which lies outside the *A* one. In other words, our shading has in effect asserted (among other things) that every *C* is an *A*—the syllogistic conclusion.

The representation of syllogisms with particular premisses is less elegant, and involves complications with which we need not here concern ourselves. But it is worth trying to express in words exactly what we have done with Barbara, and then noticing what of the same sort we may do with such a syllogism as Darii. By our first piece of shading (for 'Every *B* is an *A*') we blotted out two small compartments, thereby in effect asserting the two propositions

p. Nothing is at once a *C*, a *B*, and a non-*A*,
q. Nothing is at once a non-*C*, a *B*, and a non-*A*.

By our second piece of shading (for 'Every *C* is a *B*') we blotted out two more, thereby in effect asserting the two further propositions

r. Nothing is at once a *C*, a non-B, and an *A*,
s. Nothing is at once a *C*, a non-*B*, and a non-*A*.

We then focused our attention on the compartments whose shading asserted the propositions

p. Nothing is at once a *C*, a *B*, and a non-*A*,
s. Nothing is at once a *C*, a non-*B*, and a non-*A*,

which between them assert 'Nothing is at once a *C* and a non-*A*', i.e. 'Every *C* is an *A*.' That the four propositions *p* and *q* and *r* and *s* jointly imply the pair of propositions *p* and *s*, i.e. *CKKKpqrsKps*, is of course a tautology of the propositional calculus. Our procedure therefore was so to split up our premisses and conclusion that the implication of the latter by the former became a simple substitution in a thesis of propositional logic. And the same may be done with syllogisms into which particular as well as universal propositions enter. For example, the major premiss of Darii is equivalent to the conjunction of the two propositions

p. Nothing is at once a *C*, a *B*, and a non-*A*,
q. Nothing is at once a non-*C*, a *B*, and a non-*A*,

and its minor (Something is at once a *C* and a *B*) to the *alternation* of the propositions

r. Something is at once a *C*, a *B*, and an *A*,
Nq. Something is at once a *C*, a *B*, and a non-*A*,

while its conclusion (Something is at once a *C* and an *A*) is equivalent to the alternation of the propositions

r. Something is at once a *C*, a *B*, and an *A*,
s. Something is at once a *C*, a non-*B*, and an *A*.

So the principle of our syllogism is equivalent to a substitution in

$$CK(Kpq)(ArNq)(Ars).$$

This again is a thesis of the propositional calculus. We may show this either by truth-value calculation, or by reflection, or by proof from more evident theses. By reflection: We have in our antecedent 'Either *r* or not *q*' but the '*q*' in our other antecedent proposition, 'Both *p* and *q*', eliminates the alternative 'Not *q*' so 'Both *p* and *q*' and 'Either *r* or not *q*' jointly imply the other alternative '*r*'; and '*r*' implies 'Either *r* or *s*', so 'Both *p* and *q*' and 'Either *r* or not *q*' jointly imply 'Either *r* or *s*', i.e. *CKKpqArNqArs*.

The diagrams will not work with such syllogisms as Darapti; but they will if we add 'There are *B*'s' to the premisses. This addition amounts to the alternation of the four propositions

p. Something is at once a *C*, a *B*, and an *A*,
q. Something is at once a *C*, a *B*, and a non-*A*,
r. Something is at once a non-*C*, a *B*, and an *A*,
s. Something is at once a non-*C*, a *B*, and a non-*A*.

The major premiss of Darapti (Every *B* is an *A*) amounts to the conjunction of the two propositions

Nq. Nothing is at once a *C*, a *B*, and a non-*A*,
Ns. Nothing is at once a non-*C*, a *B*, and a non-*A*.

The minor premiss (Every *B* is a *C*) amounts to the conjunction of

Nr. Nothing is at once a non-*C*, a *B*, and an *A*, and
Ns. Nothing is at once a non-*C*, a *B*, and a non-*A*.

The conclusion (Some *C* is an *A*) amounts to the alternation of

p. Something is at once a *C*, a *B*, and an *A*, and
t. Something is at once á *C*, a non-*B*, and an *A*.

So the whole implication involved (in its 'exported' form) is

$$(CAAApqrs)C(KNqNs)C(KNrNs)(Apt).$$

This again is a thesis of the propositional calculus. (The conjuncts *Nq* and *Ns* in the major eliminate the alternatives *q* and *s* in the first antecedent, and the conjunct *Nr* in the minor adds to this the elimination of *r*, so we only have *p* left, and *p* implies *Apt*, so the antecedents together imply *Apt*.)

In thus 'reducing' theses involving quantifications to simple substitutions in theses of the propositional calculus, we tacitly employ a number of thesis which cannot be so reduced. These can, however, be derived from quite a slight basis of axioms and rules, and it is worth seeing what these are. In the first place, it is assumed that the Venn 'compartments' do not leave anything out—that everything in short is either CBA, $CB\bar{A}$, $C\bar{B}A$, $C\bar{B}\bar{A}$, $\bar{C}BA$, $\bar{C}B\bar{A}$, $\bar{C}\bar{B}A$, or $\bar{C}\bar{B}\bar{A}$. This can be easily enough justified if we have a rule to the effect that where α is a thesis of propositional logic, and $\alpha'x$ is the result of substituting ϕx, etc., for *p*, etc., in α, then $\Pi x\alpha'x$ is a thesis. Call this $R\Pi$. For example, since we have *ApNp*, we have by this rule $\Pi xA\phi xN\phi x$; since we have $AAA(Kpq)(KpNq)(KNpq)(KNpNq)$, we have

$$\Pi xAAA(K\phi x\psi x)(K\phi xN\psi x)(KN\phi x\psi x)(KN\phi xN\psi x);$$

and so on for further subdivisions of 'everything'. It is also assumed that 'Something is *B*' is equivalent to 'Either something is *BA* or something is $B\bar{A}$', and that 'Nothing is *B*' is equivalent to 'Nothing is *BA* and nothing is $B\bar{A}$.' We assume, therefore the theses

I. $E(\Sigma x\phi x)A(\Sigma xK\phi x\psi x)(\Sigma xK\phi xN\psi x)$,

II. $E(N\Sigma x\phi x)K(N\Sigma xK\phi x\psi x)(N\Sigma xK\phi xN\psi x)$.

Our procedure is to apply these until all our conjuncts or alternants contain all the predicates involved in the implication as a whole. Further, we have assumed that we can rearrange the predicates in any given conjunct or alternant into a standard order. For example, given a premiss of the form $\Sigma xK\psi x\theta x$ ('Something that ψ's, θ's'), thesis I only entitles us to equate this with $A(\Sigma xKK\psi x\theta x\phi x)(\Sigma xKK\psi x\theta xN\phi x)$, but we alter this so as in all cases to have, say, ϕ, ψ, and θ in that order, using such theses as $E(\Sigma xKK\psi x\theta x\phi x)(\Sigma xKK\phi x\psi x\theta x)$. We can obtain all theses of this kind if we lay it down as a rule of inference that if $E\alpha\beta$ is a thesis of the propositional calculus, and $E\alpha' x\beta' x$ is formed from it replacing p, q, etc., throughout by ϕx, ψx, etc., then $E\Sigma x\alpha' x\Sigma x\beta' x$ may be affirmed as a thesis. Call this $R\Sigma$. The example just given is obtainable by this rule from $E(KKqrp)(KKpqr)$. We can obtain theses I and II by this rule together with the 'law of movement'

$$E(\Sigma xA\phi x\psi x)(A\Sigma x\phi x\Sigma x\psi x),$$

our deduction being as follows:

1. $E(\Sigma xA\phi x\psi x)(A\Sigma x\phi x\Sigma x\psi x)$
2. $CEpqCEqrEpr$
3. $EpAKpqKpNq$
4. $CEpqENpNq$
5. $ENApqKNpNq$

$3\times R\Sigma = 6$

6. $E(\Sigma x\phi x)(\Sigma xAK\phi x\psi xK\phi xN\psi x)$

$2\ p/\Sigma x\phi x,\ q/\Sigma xAK\phi x\psi xK\phi xN\psi x,\ r/A\Sigma xK\phi x\psi x\Sigma xK\phi xN\psi x$
$= C6—C1\ \phi x/K\phi x\psi x,\ \psi x/K\phi xN\psi x—\text{I}$

I. $E(\Sigma x\phi x)(A\Sigma xK\phi x\psi x\Sigma xK\phi xN\psi x)$

$4\ p/\Sigma x\phi x,\ q/A\Sigma xK\phi x\psi x\Sigma xK\phi xN\psi x = C\text{I}—7$

7. $E(N\Sigma x\phi x)(NA\Sigma xK\phi x\psi x\Sigma xK\phi xN\psi x)$

$2\ p/N\Sigma x\phi x,\ q/NA\Sigma xK\phi x\psi x\Sigma xK\phi xN\psi x,$
$r/KN\Sigma xK\phi x\psi xN\Sigma xK\phi xN\psi x = C7—C5\quad p/\Sigma xK\phi x\psi x,$
$q/\Sigma xK\phi xN\psi x—\text{II}$

II. $E(N\Sigma x\phi x)(KN\Sigma xK\phi x\psi xN\Sigma xK\phi xN\psi x)$.

These give plainly the assumptions of the Venn's-diagram procedure, so that thesis 1 above ($E\Sigma xA\phi x\psi xA\Sigma x\phi x\Sigma x\psi x$),

Rules $R\Pi$ and $R\Sigma$, the definition $\Pi x = N\Sigma xN$, and the propositional calculus, form a sufficient basis for a large segment of the functional calculus. This segment is called by von Wright the 'Quantified Logic of Properties'.[1] Its theses are restricted to formulae in which the propositional components include neither propositional variables, as in $C(\Sigma xAp\phi x)(Ap\Sigma x\phi x)$, nor predicational functions with free name-variables, as in $C\phi x\Sigma x\phi x$, but only monadic predicational functions with quantifiers attached (as in the syllogistic laws verified above). This restriction means that it is not strictly necessary to use name-variables at all in this system—we could just write, say '$\Sigma\phi$' for '$\Sigma x\phi x$' and '$\Pi\phi$' for '$\Pi x\phi x$'; the law of Barbara, for example, becoming $CK(\Pi C\psi\theta)(\Pi C\phi\psi)(\Pi C\phi\theta)$, and the system's one special axiom, $E(\Sigma A\phi\psi)(A\Sigma\phi\Sigma\psi)$. Von Wright in fact uses such a notation, though of the Peano–Russellian or Hilbert–Ackermann type—he has EA for $\Sigma\phi$, $E \sim A$ for $\Sigma N\phi$, $E(A\&B)$ for $\Sigma K\phi\psi$, UA for $\Pi\phi$, $U(A \rightarrow B)$ for $\Pi C\phi\psi$, and so on. In this we may compare the system with the syllogistic one, with its unanalysed b's and a's instead of ϕx's and ψx's.

At another point, however, the Quantified Logic of Properties is very different from 'syllogistic'; for another of its limitations is that we cannot prove in it even the full functional calculus's 'simple' analogue of the law of subalternation, $C(\Pi x\phi x)(\Sigma x\phi x)$, or $C\Pi\phi\Sigma\phi$, or anything depending on this. Expressed in terms of Σ, this law would be $C(N\Sigma xN\phi x)(\Sigma x\phi x)$ which yields by transposition $C(N\Sigma x\phi x)(\Sigma xN\phi x)$ 'If the predicate ϕ has not application, then $N\phi$ has'. What the absence of such theses from this system means is that there is nothing against applying it to an 'empty universe'; i.e. a 'universe' in which there is just nothing for either ϕ or $N\phi$ to apply to. That is, considering its formulae as expressed with the name-variables inserted, its theses will hold not only if we interpret these name-variables as standing indifferently for any real thing, but also if we interpret them as standing indifferently for any man, or for any horse—or for any dragon or mermaid or chimera. We would, e.g., interpret the thesis $\Pi xC\phi x\phi x$ in the usual way as 'If anything ϕ's it ϕ's', or as 'If any man ϕ's he ϕ's', or as 'If any chimera

[1] See his Inaugural Lecture on *Form and Content in Logic* (1949), pp. 22–27. I am indebted to this lecture for the general conception, developed above, of what we do when we use Venn's diagrams.

ϕ's it ϕ's', and the theses of the system will all hold under any of these types of interpretation. But $C(N\Sigma x\phi x)(\Sigma xN\phi x)$ would not hold if we interpreted it as 'If there is no chimaera that ϕ's then there is some chimera that does not ϕ'.

At this point also the Quantified Logic of Properties is reminiscent of Venn's diagrams, for these too fail to verify, not only the thesis 'If every *B* is an *A* then some *B* is an *A*' but also the simple 'If everything is an *A* then something is an *A*'. (For if we use a single circle to represent the *A*'s, and shade out all around it to indicate the non-existence of non-*A*'s, thus:

this still does not give us

which would be required to assert that something is an *A*.) Venn himself found this worrying, as he believed that the logician *is* somehow committed to the assumption that the universe which he subdivides is not completely empty. Bradley disagreed with Venn on this point, as also did Keynes at first. Keynes, however, changed his mind, in this being perhaps influenced by Johnson.[1] In Johnson's system, $C(\Pi x\phi x)(\Sigma x\phi x)$ is easily established, since he regards $\Pi x\phi x$ as the conjunction of the singulars ϕa, ϕb, ϕc, etc., and $\Sigma x\phi x$ as their alternation, and the law follows by substitution in $CKpqApq$, itself usually proved by syllogism from $CKpqp$ and $CpApq$. Nowadays, as was indicated in Part I, this identification is not generally made; but modern proofs of $C(\Pi x\phi x)(\Sigma x\phi x)$, in systems in which this thesis occurs, have a certain similarity in pattern to that just given. The proof is generally by syllogism from $C\Pi x\phi x\phi x$ and $C\phi x\Sigma x\phi x$, 'If everything ϕ's then any given thing ϕ's' and 'If any given thing ϕ's

[1] Compare on this point Keynes's *Formal Logic*, 2nd ed. (1887), p. 145, n. 1, and 3rd ed. (1894), p. 191, n. 4. Johnson's articles on 'The Logical Calculus' appeared between these two editions (in 1892), and are referred to in connexion with an allied point in 3rd ed., p. 200, n. 1. (The problem through which Venn raises the question is slightly more complicated than that stated above.)

then something ϕ's';[1] and behind the formulation of such theses as these two is the assumption that substitutions can be made for 'x' (and of course 'ϕ', but that does not concern us here) which will turn 'ϕx' into a proposition. What this assumption amounts to is that there are such things as *names*, which there cannot be unless there are objects to be named, and it is in this way that the non-emptiness of the universe is implicit in the full functional calculus.

§ 4. *Connotative Singular Terms: The Theory of Descriptions*

In our introductory comparison between singular and general terms we have mentioned, but have as yet said no more about, a case in which the sharp modern distinction between the two seems to break down—the case of certain complex terms which are clearly singular, and yet are just as clearly descriptive or 'attributive' in character. 'The founder of Rome' or 'The King of France' would be examples. The terms are designed to identify a definite individual subject, but they 'locate' him by 'describing' him, just as a term like 'man' (or 'King' or 'founder') does. In PM[2] these terms are called 'descriptions' (in some of Russell's later writings,[3] 'definite descriptions'), and an attempt is made to analyse and symbolize them. Two main contexts are discussed in which they may occur, namely that in which we say 'The ϕ-er (Rome-founder, or whatever it may be) exists', i.e. 'There is such a thing as the ϕ-er', and that in which we say 'The ϕ-er ψ's', e.g. 'The Rome-founder is-dead.'

The existential form may be considered first. As we have already noted, there is no such predicate as 'exists' in PM, 'ϕ-ers exist' being turned into 'Something ϕ's'. Similarly, 'The ϕ-er exists' is turned into 'Something is the ϕ-er'. Since 'The ϕ-er exists' is false if nothing at all ϕ's, and also false if there are more ϕ-ers than one, but is otherwise true, we may take it that 'being the ϕ-er' means 'ϕ-ing, when there is nothing else that

[1] This proof, incidentally, brings out a connexion between the first limitation of von Wright's 'Quantified Logic of Properties' and the second. $C\Pi x\phi x\Sigma x\phi x$ cannot be proved in it because we cannot formulate in it the theses $C\Pi x\phi x\phi x$ and $C\phi x\Sigma x\phi x$, each of which contains a predicational function with a free name-variable.

[2] Introduction to first edition, ch. iii, and text, * 14.

[3] Notably his *Introduction to Mathematical Philosophy*, ch. 16.

ϕ's', and 'Something is the ϕ-er' means 'There is at least one x such that x ϕ's, and nothing other than x ϕ's', or, putting it more positively, 'There is at least one x such that x ϕ's, and anything that ϕ's is identical with x'. Using 'Iyx' for 'y is identical with x', we may put this into symbols as

(1) $\Sigma xK(\phi x)(\Pi yC\phi yIyx)$.

The more complex case, in which we say 'The ϕ-er ψ's', is analysed in the Russellian system as 'Something is-the-ϕ-er, and ψ's', i.e. 'There is an x such that (1) x ϕ's, (2) anything that ϕ's is identical with x, and (3) x ψ's, or in symbols

(2) $\Sigma xKK(\phi x)(\Pi yC\phi yIyx)(\psi x)$.

It may be observed that (1) above is obtainable by the substitution $\phi x/K\phi x\Pi yC\phi yIyx$ in the form $\Sigma x\phi x$, while (2) is obtainable by the same substitution in $\Sigma xK\phi x\psi x$, and since 'Something both ϕ's and ψ's' certainly implies 'Something ϕ's', no matter what ϕ may be, (1) logically follows from (2). That is, a statement of the form 'The ϕ-er ψ's' always implies 'The ϕ-er exists'. Thus, where the subject-term is a definite description, we may, even in Russellian logic, apply the scholastic rule that in affirmatives the copulative 'is' implies the existential. With respect to the other rule, that in negatives the existential 'is not' implies the copulative, the situation is more complicated. For the form 'The ϕ-er does not ψ' is ambiguous. It may mean 'Something is the ϕ-er, and does not ψ', i.e.

$$\Sigma xKK(\phi x)(\Pi yC\phi yIyx)(N\psi x),$$

or it may mean 'Nothing that is the ϕ-er ψ's', i.e.

$$N\Sigma xKK(\phi x)(\Pi yC\phi yIyx)(\psi x).$$

The second form is implied by 'Nothing is the ϕ-er' ('The ϕ-er does not exist'), i.e. by

$$N\Sigma xK(\phi x)(\Pi yC\phi yIyx),$$

while the first form is inconsistent with it. For example, 'The King of France is not bald' is implied by 'The King of France does not exist' if it means 'Nothing is at once the King of France and bald', but is inconsistent with it if it means 'Something is the King of France and is not bald'. The scholastic rule for negatives, therefore, applies if the form 'The ϕ-er does not ψ' is interpreted in one way, and not if it is interpreted in another.

In the Aristotelian example on which the scholastic rules are based, that about Socrates being ill, the subject-term is ostensibly not a description but a proper name. But if 'Socrates' is being used as a proper name in the strict sense, i.e. as a name which simply 'means' a certain individual, then if there is no such individual the name is meaningless, and propositions, or what are apparently propositions, which it is used to form are without a subject. In this case no sense can be made of the supposition which Aristotle considers, that Socrates does not exist. We do, however, frequently make such statements as that there is no such person as Homer, etc.; and it has been argued by Russell that in such a case what appears to be a proper name is in fact being used as a description (by 'Homer', for example, we might mean 'the author of the *Iliad*'; by 'Socrates', 'the hemlock-drinking philosopher who appears in Plato's dialogues'; etc.). Interpreted in this way, the Aristotelian example could find a place in the Russellian logic.

Before considering some of the consequences of what has been said about descriptions and existence, we may turn for a moment to the predicate '— is identical with —', which figures in the *Principia* translations of statements beginning 'The ϕ-er. . . .' In the *Principia*, the symbol corresponding to our 'I' is not a primitive one, but is introduced by the definition

$$Ixy = \Pi\phi C\phi x\phi y.$$

('x is identical with y' is an abbreviation for 'Whatever is true of x is true of y'.) This can be shown to be what de Morgan called a 'convertible' relation, by the following deduction (using Łukasiewicz's rules for Π):

Df. I: $Ixy = \Pi\phi C\phi x\phi y$.

1. Cpp

2. $CCNpNqCqp$

3. $CCpqCCqrCpr$

$1\ p/C\phi x\phi y \times \Pi 1 \phi = 4$

4. $C\Pi\phi C\phi x\phi yC\phi x\phi y$

$3\ p/\Pi\phi C\phi x\phi y,\ q/CN\phi xN\phi y,\ r/C\phi y\phi x = C4\ \phi/N\phi$—
$C2\ p/\phi x,\ q/\phi y$—5

5. $C\Pi\phi C\phi x\phi yC\phi y\phi x$

$5\times\Pi 2\phi = 6$

6. $C\Pi\phi C\phi x\phi y\Pi\phi C\phi y\phi x$

$6\times$Df. $I = 7$

7. $CIxyIyx$.

The theses $CIxyCIyzIxz$ (asserting the 'transitiveness' of identity) and Ixx are also easily provable, on the basis of this definition. And as a technical point, we may note that the definition makes the theory of identity, and by consequence the theory of descriptions, part of the higher functional calculus.

Returning to definite or singular descriptions, we have seen that these are terms of a very different sort from proper names. But it is clear all the same that there are innumerable valid inferences in which proper names and descriptions may be interchanged without the validity of the inference being affected. For example, we have 'Every undertaker is avaricious, and Callias is an undertaker, therefore Callias is avaricious', and the same with 'Callias' replaced by 'The man next door'. It is consequently convenient to have a symbol or complex of symbols for a phrase of the form 'The ϕ-er', capable of appearing in our formulae as if it were a name or name-variable. In PM the symbol-complex '$(\iota x)(\phi x)$', which may be read as 'The x such that x ϕ's', is used in this way. Thus for 'The ϕ-er ψ's' we write '$\psi(\iota x)(\phi x)$', just as for 'a ϕ's' we write 'ϕa'; and for 'The ϕ-er exists' the special form $E!(\iota x)(\phi x)$' is used. Using the Polish notation, the definitions by which these forms are introduced may be written

$$\psi(\iota x\phi x) = \Sigma xKK(\phi x)(\Pi yC\phi yIyx)(\psi y),$$

$$E!(\iota x\phi x) = \Sigma xK(\phi x)(\Pi yC\phi yIyx).$$

These, and especially the first, are simplifications. The first, as it stands, does not indicate which of the two possible interpretations mentioned above we would give to $N\psi(\iota x\phi x)$. For we may regard $N\psi(\iota x\phi x)$ as formed from $\psi(\iota x\phi x)$ either by substituting '$N\psi$' for 'ψ' or by prefixing 'N' to the whole, and if we turn to the defining formula

$$\Sigma xKK(\phi x)(\Pi yC\phi yIyx)(\psi x),$$

the substitution of '$N\psi$' for 'ψ' will give us one result, and the prefixing of 'N' to the whole quite another. To deal with this and similar ambiguities, the authors of PM introduce some complicated conventions and auxiliary symbols which we need not consider here.

Using the '$\iota x\phi x$' symbolism, the laws corresponding to our two syllogisms about undertakers may be written as

$$CK(\Pi xC\phi x\psi x)(\phi x)(\psi x)$$

$$CK(\Pi xC\phi x\psi x)(\phi\iota x\theta x)(\psi\iota x\theta x).$$

These are both provable theses; but it would not be possible to lay it down quite generally that in any thesis a description may be substituted for a name-variable. For the assumptions of existence associated with the use of descriptions often invalidate such substitutions. For example, if we substitute '$\iota x\phi x$' for 'x' in Ixx ('x is identical with itself', which holds no matter what 'x' may be the name of), we obtain

$$I(\iota x\phi x)(\iota x\phi x),$$

and since this is of the form $\psi(\iota x\phi x)$ it implies $E!(\iota x\phi x)$, and so does not hold for every ϕ, but only in cases where there is such a thing as 'the ϕ-er', i.e. for ϕ's such that at least one and only one thing ϕ's. We can, of course, obtain a genuine thesis from it by attaching $E!(\iota x\phi x)$ to it as a condition, thus

$$CE!(\iota x\phi x)I(\iota x\phi x)(\iota x\phi x).$$

The main thing to remember about '$\iota x\phi x$' is that its use is essentially predicative even when the symbolism suggests that it is functioning as a logical subject. For example, $I(\iota x\phi x)(\iota x\phi x)$, translated in accordance with the usual rule for $\psi(\iota x\phi x)$, amounts to 'Something that is-the-ϕ-er is identical with something that is-the-ϕ-er' (that is why it is not true when nothing is-the-ϕ-er). Again, when our syllogism is expanded by the definition of $\psi(\iota x\phi x)$, it amounts to 'Every undertaker is avaricious, and something that is-the-man-next-door is an undertaker, therefore etc.' (remember that the expansion of $\psi\imath x\phi x$ begins 'Σx . . .'). Russell, in fact, like the Schoolmen, puts this syllogism into Darii. It has been argued with some force[1] that in the translation of 'The ϕ-er —' as 'Something that is-the-ϕ-er . . .' the ordinary meaning of 'The ϕ-er . . .' has somehow escaped us (the apparent circularity of our verbalization of the symbols suggests this); and some writers especially emphasize the difference between the ordinary and the Russellian usage in cases in which the description turns out to have no application. Ordinarily if after having contended that the founder of Rome was a Trojan we learnt that there was no such person as the founder of Rome (i.e. if Rome turned out to have no founder, or several), the question as to whether 'he' was a Trojan would cease to interest us. We would neither admit we were wrong (about his being a Trojan) nor contend that we were right, but would just assign no truth-value at all to 'The founder of Rome was a Trojan'. The Russellian approximation to our ordinary usage does, however, give us something that is more manageable in formal systems.

An account of singular descriptions which comes closer to common usage at the point last mentioned, but which has its own oddnesses, is that of Frege.[2] Frege calls singular descriptions 'proper names', and distinguishes between their 'sense' and their 'reference'. Thus 'the Morning Star' and 'the Evening Star' have the same reference, being both proper names of Venus; but they have a different sense, and it is for this reason that 'The Morning Star is the same as the Evening Star' is not a truism like 'Venus is Venus'. Complete sentences, Frege contends, also have a reference and a sense. In most contexts their sense is the 'thought' which they express (meaning by this not anything mental—not a piece of thinking, but *what* we could be thinking), and their reference is a truth-value. 'The Morning Star is a planet' is thus a description of 'the True', while 'The father of Socrates is a planet' is a description of 'the

[1] Notably by P. F. Strawson, in 'On Referring', *Mind*, July 1950. The title indicates that the article is intended as a reconsideration of the matters dealt with in Russell's article 'On Denoting' in *Mind*, 1905, in which his characteristic theories about 'the King of France' were first put forward. See also P. T. Geach, in *Analysis* for March 1950, and in *Mind*, Oct. 1950, p. 469.

[2] Developed particularly in his 1892 article 'On Sense and Reference' (Geach and Black, *Translations from the Philosophical Writings of Gottlob Frege*, pp. 56–78).

False'. In general, the sense of a sentence with a given predicate depends on the sense of its subject-term, while its reference depends on the reference of its subject-term. Thus 'The Morning Star is a planet' and 'The Evening Star is a planet' have different senses, but both alike refer to the True. Complications sometimes arise when the subject of a sentence is itself a sentence. Thus although 'The Morning Star is a planet' and 'The Evening Star is a planet' have the same reference (the True), 'That the Morning Star is a planet is believed by Mr. *A*' could conceivably have a different reference (truth-value) from 'That the Evening Star is a planet is believed by Mr. *A*', for Mr. *A*, not knowing the identity of the Morning Star and the Evening Star, could conceivably believe that the one is a planet and the other not. Frege's solution of this is to say that in such contexts the reference of the contained sentence is not its customary reference but is rather what is ordinarily its sense. (A truth-function may then be defined as a compound in which the contained sentences *do* have their customary reference.) A corollary of this general theory is that where a singular description has no reference (as in the case of 'The present King of France'), a sentence in which it appears as subject-term has no reference either, i.e. no truth-value, though it is not without sense.

PART III

MODAL, THREE-VALUED, AND EXTENSIONAL SYSTEMS

I

The Logic of Modality

§ 1. *Modality and its Resemblance to Quantity*

A DIVISION of propositions which is given some prominence in the logic of Aristotle and the Schoolmen is that into (*a*) propositions simply asserting that something is or is not so, and (*b*) ones asserting that something must be, may be, need not be or cannot be so. The former sort are called in the Latin logics propositions *de inesse*, i.e. propositions simply concerning the predicate's 'being in' or attaching to the subject; the latter, 'modal' propositions, or propositions *cum modo*, asserting the mode or manner of this in-being. Propositions *de inesse* are also called 'pure' or 'assertoric'; and of the modals, those asserting necessity or impossibility are called 'apodeictic', and those asserting possibility, 'problematic'.

Modal propositions may in general be expressed in either of two ways: (1) with a modal adverb or auxiliary verb attached to the copula (as in '*B* is necessarily *A*', or '*B* cannot but be *A*'), or (2) with a modal adjective predicated of an entire clause or *dictum* ('That *B* should be *A*, is necessary'). In the former case the modality is said to be expressed *sine dicto*, 'without a *dictum*', in the latter case *cum dicto*, 'with a *dictum*'. (Some medieval writers argue that only in the former case is the proposition properly called a 'modal'; in the latter case it is an assertoric proposition with a modal predicate.)[1] This difference of form is sometimes used to express a difference in sense, namely that between a modality *de dicto* and a modality *de re*. The distinction

[1] So, e.g., Burleigh, *De Puritate Artis Logicae* (Boehner's edition), p. 79. John of St. Thomas (*Prima Pars Artis Logicae*, II. xxii) describes the restatement *cum dicto* of modal forms *sine dicto* as the 'reduction' of modals to simple categoricals.

here goes back to a puzzle in Aristotle's book on fallacies, the *De Sophisticis Elenchis*;[1] is it always self-contradictory to say 'A man is able to write while he is not writing', or 'A man is able to walk while he is sitting down'? The answer depends on the bracketing—'writing-while-not-writing' is not a thing that any man is able to do, but a man who is in fact not writing may still have the capacity for writing, i.e. may be able-to-write. What is involved is the 'fallacy of composition'; in 'A man is able to write-while-he-is-not-writing' the sentence is read *in sensu composito*; and 'A man is able-to-write while he is not writing' it is read *in sensu diviso*. Or we may say that in the first sense the possibility is predicated *de dicto*, of a *dictum*, for it means 'That a man should write while not writing, is possible'; while in the second sense the possibility is predicated *de re*, of an individual, for it means 'A man who is not writing is able-to-write', i.e. is 'possibly-writing'.

Considering in the meantime only modalities expressed *cum dicto*, it is important to observe that different results are obtained by 'denying the *dictum*' and by 'denying the mode'. This was noted by Aristotle. Aristotle begins his discussion of modal statements in the *De Interpretatione*[2] by remarking that although we generally form the denial of a statement by attaching a 'not' to its verb, '*B* may not be *A*' is not the denial of '*B* may be *A*'. And the reason for this, he suggests, is that 'may' is not the real 'verb' here, for '*B* may be *A*' means 'That *B* should be *A* is possible', while '*B* may not be *A*' means 'That *B* should not-be-*A* is possible', the true contradictory of the former being not this, but rather 'That *B* should be *A* is-not-possible', i.e. '*B* cannot be *A*'. So, given any *dictum* and mode, we may (1) affirm both, as in 'That Socrates should be running, is possible', or (2) deny the *dictum* and affirm the mode (i.e. affirm the mode of the denial of the *dictum*), as in 'That Socrates should not be running, is possible', or (3) affirm the *dictum* and deny the mode, as in 'That Socrates should be running, is not possible', or (4) deny both, as in 'That Socrates should not be running, is not possible'; and no two of these are equivalent.

When other modes are introduced, however, certain equipollences arise.[3] Thus 'That Socrates should not be running,

[1] 166^a 22–30. See Peter of Spain on this, *Summulae*, 7.26. [2] Chs. 12, 13.

[3] For what follows see Peter of Spain, op. cit. 1.32–37.

is not possible' is clearly equivalent to 'That Socrates should be running, is necessary.' In the later Middle Ages these equipollences were summarized by means of the four mnemonic words 'Amabimus', 'Edentuli', 'Iliace', and 'Purpurea'. In each of these, the letters *A*, *E*, *I*, and *U* respectively indicate the four combinations of affirmation and denial mentioned above; the first vowel indicates some proposition in which the modal predicate is 'possible', the second indicates the equipollent form in which the modal predicate is 'contingent', the third indicates that in which it is 'impossible', and the fourth, that in which it is 'necessary'. The word 'contingent', though it generally has another use (to be mentioned shortly), is here used as a simple synonym of 'possible'; hence in each mnemonic word the first two vowels are the same. Taking 'Amabimus' as a specimen, what this word asserts is the equipollence of the forms

A (*p*), i.e. That *B* should be *A*, is possible.
A (*c*), i.e. That *B* should be *A*, is contingent.
I (*i*), i.e. That *B* should be *A*, is not impossible.
U (*n*), i.e. That *B* should not be *A*, is not necessary.

Similarly 'Purpurea' asserts the equipollence of

U (*p*), i.e. That *B* should not be *A*, is not possible.
U (*c*), i.e. That *B* should not be *A*, is not contingent.
E (*i*), i.e. That *B* should not be *A*, is impossible.
A (*n*), i.e. That *B* should be *A*, is necessary.

The forms equated in 'Amabimus' are subalternate to those equated in 'Purpurea', and those in 'Edentuli' to those in 'Iliace'; the other ordinary relations of opposition also hold. Omitting the second line throughout as being superfluous, the logical square for these forms is as follows:

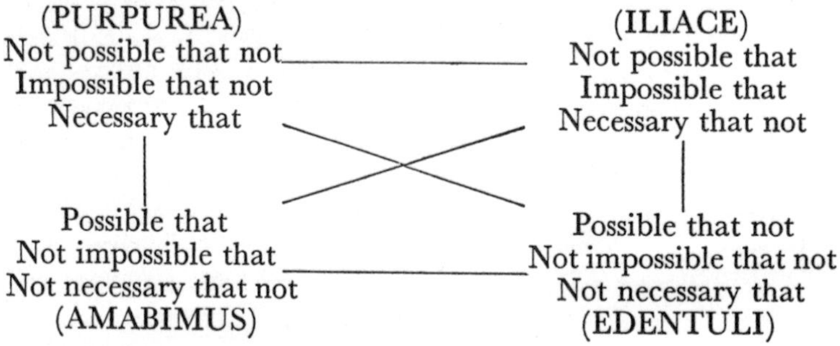

If this square be compared with that given for equipollent categoricals in II. ii. 2, it will be seen that the relations between 'possible', 'impossible', and 'necessary' exactly parallel those between 'some', 'no', and 'every'; and we may use it to define any two of the modal predicates or operators in terms of the remaining one, just as we may use the equipollences of categoricals to define *I* in terms of *A* or vice versa. In modern formalizations of the logic of modals, when a notation like that of PM is used for the 'assertoric' part of it, 'It is possible that *p*' is generally written '$\Diamond p$', and 'It is necessary that *p*' (sometimes written '$\Box p$') introduced as an abbreviation for '$\sim\Diamond\sim p$'.[1] Where a notation of the Polish type is employed, 'It is possible that *p*' is written '*Mp*' (from the German *möglich*), and 'It is necessary that *p*' (sometimes written '*Lp*', sometimes '*Sp*') defined as '*NMNp*'. The assertoric forms stand between the apodeictic and the problematic in much the same way as singulars stand between universals and particulars. Just as we have $C\Pi x\phi x\phi x$ and $C\phi x\Sigma x\phi x$, so we have *CLpp* (*a necesse esse ad esse valet consequentia*) and *CpMp* (*ab esse ad posse valet consequentia*).

We may now turn to the more usual meaning of 'contingent'. In the *De Interpretatione* Aristotle remarks that the word 'possible' is ambiguous; we would sometimes say that 'It is possible that *p*' follows from 'It is necessary that *p*', but sometimes that it is inconsistent with it. In the former sense 'possible' means simply 'not impossible'; in the latter sense, 'neither impossible nor necessary'. It is for 'possible' in this second sense that the word 'contingent' is generally used. That is, 'It is contingent that *p*' means 'Both *p* and not-*p* are possible', *KMpMNp*. Contingency in this sense stands between necessity and impossibility, but in quite a different way from that in which the simply factual stands between the necessary and the possible. It is not that necessity implies contingency, and contingency impossibility; rather, we have here three mutually exclusive alternatives which divide the field between them—either a proposition is necessary, or it is neither-necessary-nor-impossible (i.e. contingent), or it is impossible; just as, empty terms apart, either every *B* is an *A*, or some *B* is an *A* and some is not, or no *B* is an *A*.

In fact when Aldrich and Whately use the latter division of the possible cases to verify the rules of opposition, they describe

[1] The 'diamond' is thus used in Lewis and Langford's *Symbolic Logic*.

the case in which every *B* is an *A* as the case in which the inherence of the predicate in the subject is 'necessary', the case in which some but not every *B* is an *A* as that in which it is 'contingent', and the case in which no *B* is an *A* as that in which it is 'impossible'. This simple identification of modality and quantity is tempting; but in Peter of Spain's discussion of the same subject it is qualified. He uses 'natural' where the later writers use 'necessary', saying that we always have 'Every *B* is an *A*' when to be an *A* is part of the 'nature' of a *B* (part of what makes it a *B*); but we may also have 'Every *B* is an *A*' when *A* is an 'inseparable accident' of *B*, i.e. when it happens that every *B* is an *A*, though it could be otherwise.[1] The question as to whether a distinction can be made between necessary and merely factual universals is still a subject of discussion, particular attention being paid nowadays to cases in which the subject-term is empty just because the 'necessary' universal is believed to be true. Thus there are no brakeless trains precisely because it is believed that (*a*) any brakeless train would be particularly liable to accidents, and it is *not* believed that (*b*) any brakeless train would be as safe as houses. But on any view of 'existential import' the two merely assertoric universals

(*a'*) Every brakeless train is particularly liable to accidents,
(*b'*) Every brakeless train is as safe as houses,

will have the same truth-value. (If 'Every *B* is an *A*' means 'Nothing is at once a *B* and a non-*A*', both are true because in this case nothing is a *B*; if it means 'Nothing is at once a *B* and a non-*A*, but something is a *B*', both are false, for the same reason; and if 'Every *B* is an *A*' is regarded as having no truth-value when its subject-term is empty, both *a'* and *b'* have no truth-value.) Hence (*a*) and (*b*) are not respectively equivalent to (*a'*) and (*b'*), necessary and merely assertoric universals must be distinguished, and necessity is not just universality.[2]

The close parallelism between modality and quantity, however, remains, and we shall be encountering further aspects of it. For example, with respect to this division between the

[1] *Summulae*, 1.16.

[2] The brakeless train illustration is from Johnson's *Logic*, III. i. 5, where he is concerned to distinguish what he calls 'universals of law' from 'universals of fact'. More recent discussion has had as its starting-point R. M. Chisholm's article 'The Contrary-to-Fact Conditional', in *Mind*, 1946.

necessary, the contingent and the impossible, Aristotle hints[1] that the contingent may be further subdivided into what is more likely to be so than not, what is as likely to be so as not, and what is less likely to be so than not; and plainly we might go still farther and replace the threefold or fivefold distinction by an infinite series of grades of probability. And quite similarly, cases in which some *B*'s are *A*'s and some not may be subdivided into those in which most *B*'s are *A*'s, those in which half the *B*'s are *A*'s and half of them are not, and those in which most are not, and further subdivided into an infinite series of precise proportions. Both these lines of advance were investigated by de Morgan. He brought probability out of mathematics into logic; 'the theory of probabilities', he said, 'I take to be the unknown God which the schoolmen ignorantly worshipped' in their study of the properties of modals.[2] And on the side of quantity, where Hamilton stopped with such syllogisms as 'Most *B*'s are *A*'s, and most *B*'s are *C*'s, therefore some *C*'s are *A*'s', de Morgan introduced syllogisms involving all kinds of numerical proportions and percentages.

In his exhaustive study, in the *Prior Analytics*, of syllogisms with modal premisses, Aristotle regularly uses 'possible' in the second sense, i.e. as meaning 'neither impossible nor necessary'. This complicates his discussion somewhat (it is as if, in his assertoric syllogisms, he had used the form 'Some *B* is an *A* and some *B* is not an *A*' instead of the simple 'Some *B* is an *A*'), and his successor Theophrastus, working in the same field, preferred to take 'possible' in the simpler sense.[3] However, the properties of both sorts of 'possibility' are worth investigating, and one small but fruitful discovery which Aristotle made about 'contingency' is that if any proposition is contingent then so is its contradictory. Using *Qp* for 'It is contingent that *p*' (*KMpMNp*), Aristotle's thesis may be written as *CQpQNp*. The point is simple enough; since 'It is contingent that *p*' amounts to 'Both *p* and not-*p* are possible', 'It is contingent that not-*p*' amounts to 'Both not-*p* and not-not-*p* are possible', and 'Both

[1] *An. Pr.* 32^b 3–22. [2] *Formal Logic*, p. 232.

[3] On the Aristotelian 'modal syllogisms' see W. D. Ross, *Aristotle's Prior and Posterior Analytics*, Introduction, iv; I. M. Bocheński, *Ancient Formal Logic*, III. 10. On its Theophrastean modifications see I. M. Bocheński, *La Logique de Théophraste*, ch. v. A modernized system of modal syllogisms is developed by von Wright in *An Essay in Modal Logic*, Appendix I.

p and not-p are possible' implies this by double negation and the convertibility of conjunction ($Qp = KMpMNp \rightarrow KMNpMp \rightarrow KMNpMNNp = QNp$). This law may be used to show that modal functions of propositions are not truth-functions. At least, Łukasiewicz has shown that the supposition that they are, when joined with this law $CQpQNp$, has some very curious consequences. For truth-functions are governed by the law (from Leśniewski's protothetic) $C\delta pC\delta Np\delta q$, i.e. a truth-function which holds for p and also holds for Np holds for any proposition at all; and combining this, and other laws of propositional logic, with $CQpQNp$, we can argue as follows:

1. $C\delta pC\delta Np\delta q$
2. $CCpqCCpCqrCpr$
3. $CQpQNp$
   $1\ \delta/Q = 4$
4. $CQpCQNpQq$
   $2\ p/Qp,\ q/QNp,\ r/Qq = C3—C4—5$
5. $CQpQq$
   $5 \times \Sigma 1 p \times \Pi 2 q = 6$
6. $C\Sigma pQp\Pi qQq$.

That is, if any proposition is contingent then every proposition is contingent.[1] The trouble with this is, of course, 4; it is simply not true that if any proposition p is contingent, then if it is also contingent that not p, then anything at all is contingent; in other words, 'It is contingent that' is simply not the sort of operator that is substitutable for 'δ' in 1. And once again we have a parallel with quantifiers. If it be true of any predicate ϕ that $K\Sigma x\phi x\Sigma xN\phi x$, this will also be true of $N\phi$, i.e. we have

$$C(K\Sigma x\phi x\Sigma xN\phi x)(K\Sigma xN\phi x\Sigma xNN\phi x)$$

for $K(\Sigma x\phi x)(\Sigma xN\phi x) \rightarrow K(\Sigma xN\phi x)(\Sigma x\phi x) \rightarrow K(\Sigma xN\phi x)(\Sigma xNN\phi x)$. Using '$Ox\phi x$' as an abbreviation for '$K\Sigma x\phi x\Sigma xN\phi x$', we may

[1] This proof is adapted from Łukasiewicz, 'On Variable Functors of Propositional Arguments' (*Royal Irish Academy Proceedings*, 54 A 2), § 1. For an earlier version see I. M. Bocheński's *La Logique de Théophraste*, v. 42 and Note 289.

write our thesis as '*COxϕxOxNϕx*', and derive an absurdity from it thus:

1. $C\delta pC\delta Np\delta q$
2. $CCpqCCpCqrCpr$
3. $COx\phi xOxN\phi x$
   1 $p/\phi x$, $q/\psi x = 4$
4. $C\delta\phi xC\delta N\phi x\delta\psi x$
   4 $\delta/Ox = 5$
5. $COx\phi xCOxN\phi xOx\psi x$
   2 $p/Ox\phi x$, $q/OxN\phi x$, $r/Ox\psi x = C3—C5—6$
6. $COx\phi xOx\psi x$
   $6 \times \Sigma 1\phi \times \Pi 2\psi = 7$
7. $C\Sigma\phi Ox\phi x\Pi\psi Ox\psi x$.

That is, if there is any predicate ϕ of which we may say 'Something ϕ's and something does not', then we may say this of every predicate whatever, i.e. there are no true universal propositions. And the source of the trouble lies in regarding our complex quantifier '*Ox*' as substitutable for 'δ' in 4. A quantified predicational function is a function of that function, but it is not a truth-function of it; and neither are modal functions truth-functions of propositions.

It should be added that this is not the conclusion which Łukasiewicz himself draws from this reasoning. He concludes, rather, that no modal system can consistently contain an operator *Q* such that *CQpQNp*. This seems hardly reasonable; if we have a function of propositions *M*, we can surely form from it the function *KMpMNp*, and *CQpQNp* unquestionably holds if *Q* is defined as *KM'MN'*, just as *COxϕxOxNϕx* unquestionably holds if *Oxϕx* is defined as *KΣxϕxΣxNϕx*. What can be said, however, is that there is a sense in which *Ox* is not a 'quantifier', and an analogous sense in which *Q* is not an 'elementary modal operator'. We have seen earlier that for the series of quantifiers *Πx*, *ΠxN*, *NΠx*, *NΠxN*, *NNΠx*, *ΠxNN*, *NNΠxN*, etc., the following law holds:

(1) $A(\Pi\phi Cf\phi NfN\phi)(\Pi\phi CNfN\phi f\phi)$,

where '*f*' is any operator in the series just indicated. Similarly for the series of operators *M*, *MN*, *NM*, *NMN*, *NNM*, *MNN*, *NNMN*, etc., we have the law

(2) $A(\Pi pCfpNfNp)(\Pi pCNfNpfp)$,

where '*f*' is any operator in the series indicated. But where *O* is defined as above, we do not have

$$A(\Pi\phi COx\phi xNOxN\phi x)(\Pi\phi CNOxN\phi xOx\phi x).$$

For where $Ox\phi x$ holds, we always have $OxN\phi x$ also, and so do not have $C(Ox\phi x)(NOxN\phi x)$; so the first alternant is false. And where $OxN\phi x$ does not hold (i.e. when we have $\Pi x\phi x$ or $\Pi xN\phi x$), $Ox\phi x$ does not hold either, i.e. in such cases we do not have $C(NOxN\phi x)(Ox\phi x)$; so the second alternant is false. Hence if a 'quantifier' be defined as an operator for which (1) is true, *Ox* is not a quantifier. It can be similarly shown that if an 'elementary modal operator' is one for which (2) holds, *Q* is not an elementary modal operator.

§ 2. *Modality and Implication*

In post-Renaissance versions of the traditional logic the topic of modality tended to be neglected; and it was at first neglected also (except in the form of the theory of probability) in the revival and enlargement of formal logic in the nineteenth and twentieth centuries. It is not dealt with, for example, in PM. A new interest in the subject was, however, indirectly stimulated by certain of PM's characteristic theses, namely the 'paradoxical' laws *CpCqp* and *CNpCpq*, 'A true proposition is implied by any proposition' and 'Any proposition at all is implied by a false one', and others like them. As we have already remarked, for the most usual sense of 'implies' these assertions are simply not true, and the natural reaction to a system containing them was to attempt to formulate a logic in which 'implies' is used in a sense more like its usual one.

This problem is not a purely modern one. The Megaric philosophers who flourished in Aristotle's day and a little later, and from whom the Stoic propositional logic seems to have been partly derived, were occupied with the problem of what a conditional proposition means, and under what conditions it is true. One of them, Philo, gave the modern truth-functional account of the conditional, arguing that 'If *p* then *q*' is false when p is true and q false, but true in all other circumstances. His teacher Diodorus pointed out that this leads to paradoxes; it means, e.g. that 'If it is day I am conversing' is always automatically true at night-time, or when I am conversing. Diodorus's own account of the matter is that 'If p then q' is true only if it not merely does not happen that p is true and q is not, but if it is impossible that p should be true and q not. This suggests a modal definition—the replacement of $NKpNq$ by $NMKpNq$—but there are reasons for believing that Diodorus defined 'possibility' in terms of time, and meant simply that p may be said to 'imply' q when it is *never* the case that p is true but q false. But an unnamed writer, possibly the Stoic logician Chrysippus, gave a more unmistakably modal definition, arguing that p implies q only if p is 'inconsistent' with the negation of q.[1]

These alternative definitions of implication, however, give rise to paradoxes of their own. For on the Diodoran view, an implication is automatically true if its antecedent states something which is never true, or if its consequent states something which is at all times true (for in both these cases the antecedent will never be true without the consequent), and on the modal view, an implication is automatically true if its antecedent is an impossible proposition or its consequent a necessary one (for in either of these cases it will be impossible for the antecedent to be true without the consequent). These paradoxes of modal implication, as well as the paradoxes of merely assertoric implication, were well known to the later Schoolmen. In the present century the modal definition of 'If' has been adopted by C. I. Lewis, who accepts the associated paradoxes and attempts to show that they are unobjectionable. Lewis defines a relation which he calls 'strict implication', writing 'p strictly implies q' as '$p \prec q$' (the symbol is the cursive form of Peirce's '—<'), and introducing this form as an abbreviation for '$\sim \Diamond (p. \sim q)$'. If we use the form $C'pq$ for 'p strictly implies q' we may rewrite this definition in the Polish notation as

$$C'pq = NMKpNq,$$

and the two paradoxes as $C(NMp)(C'pq)$ and $C(Lq)(C'pq)$.

[1] For a full account of this discussion see B. Mates, 'Diodorean Implication', *Philosophical Review*, 1949.

Lewis regards '*p* strictly implies *q*' as equivalent in force to '*q* logically follows from *p*', and attempts to show that the paradoxes do not constitute any obstacle to this identification. He points out that if we take the impossible proposition *KpNp*, it can easily be shown that any proposition at all, say *q*, will follow from this by the following four quite ordinary and non-paradoxical rules:

(1) $Kpq \rightarrow p$,

(2) $Kpq \rightarrow q$,

(3) $p \rightarrow Apq$,

(4) $Apq, Np \rightarrow q$.

For by (1) $KpNp \rightarrow p$, and by (3) $p \rightarrow Apq$, so by (1) and (3) in succession $KpNp \rightarrow Apq$. But by (2), $KpNp \rightarrow Np$. Hence from *KpNp* we may obtain both *Apq* and *Np*, from which, by (4), we may obtain *q*.[1] A similar common-sense justification can be given for the contention that the necessary proposition *AqNq* follows from any proposition at all, say *p*. We have in fact already given this in I. ii. 2, in connexion with systems of propositional calculus without axioms; and the type of demonstration just illustrated has a place in such systems also. Complementary, in such systems, to the notion of 'demonstrability', i.e. derivability from any proposition whatever, is that of 'refutability', a 'refutable' proposition being one from which any proposition whatever may be inferred. (This use of 'refutable', like the corresponding use of 'demonstrable', is due to Popper.) What we have just shown is the 'refutability', in this sense, of *KpNp*, in any system containing rules (1)–(4).[2]

These independent proofs of the paradoxical implications have pushed Lewis's critics into some peculiar positions. A. Emch,[3] for example, suggests that since Lewis has only given

[1] Lewis and Langford, *Symbolic Logic*, pp. 250–1. The same proof was elaborated in the Middle Ages by Albert of Saxony (see P. Boehner, *Medieval Logic*, pp. 99–100, 126–7).

[2] 'Refutation' in this sense should not be confused with the 'rejection' of a formula as a thesis, i.e. Łukasiewicz's asterisk. We 'reject' a propositional form as a thesis if not-all of its exemplifications are true; but a form is 'refutable' only if all of its exemplifications are not-true. In modal terms, the difference is between 'not-necessary' and 'not-possible'.

[3] A. Emch, 'Implication and Deducibility', *Journal of Symbolic Logic*, vol. i (1936).

independent proofs for impossible and necessary propositions of the forms *KpNp* and *AqNq*, his paradoxical implications need only be regarded as holding for these. But this will not do, for in recent axiomless systems the 'refutability' of all logically impossible propositions, and 'demonstrability' of all logically necessary ones, has been clearly shown. E. J. Nelson[1] argues that 'entailment', i.e. the converse of 'following from', must consist in a definite inner connexion between antecedent and consequent, and cannot be present through some peculiarity (necessity, impossibility, truth, or falsehood) attaching to either proposition alone. (For some reason he does not consider the possibility that what Lewis's paradoxes show is precisely that necessary and impossible propositions as such *have* a definite inner connexion with all propositions whatever.) To escape Lewis's independent proofs, he denies that Both-*p*-and-*q* entails *p*. *p* entails *p*, he says, but *q* here is beside the point; and we only say that *r* is entailed by Both *p*-and-*q* when both of the conjoined propositions are necessary for *r* to follow. This decision, however, as Nelson himself sees, has an odd consequence in the theory of entailment itself. It means that we cannot say without qualification that *p*-entails-*r* is entailed by *p*-entails-*q*-and-*q*-entails-*r*; for if we let *r* here be *q*, we have '*p*-entails-*q* is entailed by *p*-entails-*q*-and-*q*-entails-*q*', which is of the forbidden form. P. F. Strawson,[2] another critic of Lewis, argues that necessary and impossible propositions are simply not capable of being terms of the entailment relation. This is rather like solving the existential paradoxes of Brentano and Venn by refusing to admit empty terms or their negations as substitutable for the term-variables in the *A*, *E*, *I* and *O* forms. It has the awkward consequence that we cannot say that 'It is necessary that *p*' entails '*p*', for if 'It is necessary that p' is true, then '*p*' is not the sort of proposition that can entail or be entailed. ('It is necessary that *p*' is not itself in this position, as Strawson takes the view that the statement that a proposition is necessary is not itself a necessary statement but a purely factual one.) In sum, it is possible to define relations which bear some resemblance to the converse of logical deducibility, and which do not give rise to the Lewis paradoxes, but there will

[1] 'Intensional Relations', *Mind*, 1930.
[2] 'Necessary Propositions and Entailment-Statements', *Mind*, 1948.

then always be some other point at which the resemblance fails; and these alternatives to strict implication all turn out to be very awkward and clumsy to handle in formal systems.[1]

Whatever be its relation to logical deducibility, the main relation of strict implication to material implication is a simple one. Just as the Russellian 'formal' implication is simply universal material implication—*ΠxCφxψx* means 'It is always the case that *φx* materially implies *ψx*'—so Lewis's strict implication is equivalent to (though it is not quite defined as) necessary material implication, *LCpq*—'It is necessarily the case that *p* materially implies *q*'. But there are other relations between strict and material implication that are a little more subtle. In particular, when two propositions together strictly imply a third, either of them strictly implies that the other materially implies the third; i.e. we have *C*(*C′Kpqr*)(*C′pCqr*) and *C*(*C′Kpqr*)(*C′qCpr*). For example, since

(*a*) All the books on this shelf are blue, and my copy of *Principia Mathematica* is a book on this shelf

strictly implies

(*b*) My copy of *Principia Mathematica* is blue,

the conjunct

(*a′*) All the books on this shelf are blue

by itself strictly implies the material implication

(*b′*) If my copy of *Principia Mathematica* is a book on this shelf, then it is blue.

A material implication may thus be filtered out, by 'exportation', from a strict implication with a conjunctive antecedent. It is important to notice that the implication thus filtered out—in our example the proposition (*b′*)—is not itself a strict but only a material one. 'My copy of *Principia Mathematica* is a book on this shelf' simply does not strictly imply 'My copy of *Principia Mathematica* is blue'; and any proposition which implied that it did would be false. For—remembering that *C′pq* = *NMKpNq*—it is not in the least impossible that 'My copy of *Principia Mathematica* is a book on this shelf' should be

[1] A useful survey of the possibilities is given by J. Bennett in 'Meaning and Implication', *Mind*, 1954.

true and 'My copy of *Principia Mathematica* is blue' be false; all that is impossible is that (*a′*) should be true and the whole implication (*b′*) be false.[1] To take another example, the conjunction 'That boy will not come back and that boy will come back', being impossible, strictly implies any proposition at all, e.g. 'I'll eat my hat'. Hence 'That boy will not come back' strictly implies the material implication 'If that boy comes back I'll eat my hat'. But 'If that boy comes back I'll eat my hat' is not itself a strict implication, and 'That boy will not come back' does not imply that it is. The law of exportation must therefore be used with caution in modal logic; though we have it in the form *C*(*C′Kpqr*)(*C′pCqr*), we do not have it in the form *C*(*C′Kpqr*)(*C′pC′qr*), or, of course, in the form *C′*(*C′Kpqr*)(*C′pC′qr*). (We do have it in the form *CCKpqrCpCqr*, where no implications are involved but material ones; hence this caution is not needed in the assertoric calculus.)

§ 3. *Iterated Modalities*

There are a variety of ways in which modal systems may be axiomatized, but when the question of the 'completeness' of a set of rules and axioms for modal logic is raised, we are confronted with a difficulty. Such a set of 'postulates' will of course be complete if it suffices to prove all formulae within the field which yield true propositions for all substitutions for their variables; but the subject is so obscure that there are many quite short formulae involving modal operators which we do not know whether to regard as always true or not. Lewis and others have consequently constructed a variety of alternative sets of rules and axioms, some of which are so weak that we cannot prove from them what most people would regard as quite obvious truths (e.g. *C′MKpqKMpMq*, 'That *p*-and-*q* is possible, strictly implies that *p* is possible and *q* is possible'), while others are strong enough to prove formulae which many people would find very dubious (e.g. *C′MpLMp*, 'If a thing is possible then it is necessarily possible').[2] With regard to all

[1] This example is discussed in G. E. Moore's important paper on 'External and Internal Relations', included in his *Philosophical Studies* (pp. 300–1).

[2] The standard reference for these systems is Lewis and Langford's *Symbolic Logic*. A particularly valuable summary of their main features is given by R. Feys in 'Les Systèmes formalisés des modalités aristotéliciennes', *Revue Philosophique de Louvain*, Nov. 1950. (The symbolism employed here is taken over from this article.)

these systems it is shown (by procedures of a kind which will be sketched in the next chapter) that the axioms are mutually consistent, that they are independent, and that in none of the systems do the modal elements just collapse, i.e. *Mp* and *Lp* cannot be proved in any of them to be simply equivalent to *p*.

An important point to note, from a metalogical point of view, is that the formula *C'pLp* ('If *p* is true it is necessary'), which if it were true for every *p* would make modal distinctions pointless, and which is therefore not a thesis in any of the systems just mentioned, is nevertheless quite consistent with them. For the assertoric calculus, into which it would make the modal calculi collapse, is itself quite a consistent system. Hence there is at least one formula not provable from the axioms of even the strongest of these systems, which yet would not result in inconsistency if joined with these axioms as a further thesis. This means that none of these systems is complete in the stronger sense mentioned in our discussion of the logic of propositions. This is similar to the qualification made to the completeness earlier claimed for the lower functional calculus as systematized by adding Łukasiewicz's two rules for *Π* to the calculus of propositions.

In the systematizing of modal logic, the most difficult formulae to decide about are those in which modal operators are 'iterated'; for example *C'MMpMp*, 'If a thing is possibly possible then it is simply possible'. The converse of this is easily provable in any system which includes as an axiom or theorem the strict consequence *ab esse ad posse*, *C'pMp*, for we obtain *C'MpMMp* from this by the substitution *p/Mp*. Similarly from the consequence *a necesse esse ad esse*, *C'Lpp*, we obtain by substitution *C'LLpLp*; but the converse implication *C'LpLLp*, 'What is necessary is necessarily necessary', does not follow from any modal thesis that is at all obvious, though it is not inconsistent with any such. But we can at least say of *C'MMpMp* and *C'LpLLp* that they stand or fall together, either being provable from the other, e.g. the second from the first as follows (3 being an easily provable law of modal equipollence):

Df. *L*: *L* = *NMN*.

1. *C'MMpMp*

2. *CC'pqC'NqNp*

3. *C′NMpLNp*
4. *CC′pqCC′qrC′pr*

   2 $p/MMNp$, q/MNp = C1 p/Np—5
5. *C′NMNpNMMNp*

   4 $p/NMNp$, $q/NMMNp$, $r/LNMNp$ = C5—C3 p/MNp—6
6. *C′NMNpLNMNp*

   6×Df. *L* = 7
7. *C′LpLLp*.

Another doubtful thesis of the same sort is *C′MpLMp*, 'If *p* is possible at all, then *p* is necessarily possible', with which we may couple *C′MLpLp*, 'If *p* is possibly necessary, then *p* is actually necessary'. As with the previous pair, there is no doubt about the converse theses. *C′LMpMp* follows from *C′Lpp* by the substitution p/Mp, and *C′LpMLp* by the substitution p/Lp in *C′pMp*. And as with the previous pair, and by the same type of proof, the two may be shown to stand or fall together. It can also be shown that the other two follow from them. We may prove *C′MMpMp* from them thus (RE′ being the rule that strictly equivalent formulae are mutually substitutable in any modal formula, the numbers after RE′ indicating the thesis asserting the equivalence used):

1. *C′MpLMp*
2. *C′MLpLp*
3. *C′Lpp*
4. *CC′pqCC′qpE′pq*

   4 p/Mp, q/LMp = C1—C3 p/Mp—5
5. *E′MpLMp*

   2 p/Mp×RE′5 = 6
6. *C′MMpMp*.

But we cannot effect the converse derivation, of *C′MpLMp* and *C′MLpLp* from *C′MMpMp* and *C′LpLLp*. We have therefore, in addition to weaker systems, a system (Lewis's S4) containing the latter but not the former pair of theses, and another (Lewis's S5) containing both pairs. In S5, all iterated modalities are equivalent to non-iterated ones, always to the modality immediately preceding the modally qualified proposition. Thus *MMp*, *LMp*, *MMMp*, *MLMp*, *LMMp*, *LLMp*, etc., are all equivalent to *Mp*; *LLp*, *MLp*, *LLLp*, *MLLp*, etc., all to *Lp*.

The following may serve as an illustration of the difference which the distinctive theses of S5 can make in a particular piece of reasoning: In certain well-known arguments for the existence of God, what is in fact shown is that the supposition that God could exist but does not necessitates something incompatible with itself, and so is necessarily false. This does not mean, however, that 'God exists' is necessarily true; and what has generally been said since Leibniz is that the argument merely shows that God's existence is necessary if it is possible. And it does show this *in sensu composito*, i.e. it shows that God's possibility would necessitate His actuality. But without the distinctive theses of S5 it does not show even this *in sensu diviso*, i.e. it does not show that if God's existence is a possible truth then it is a necessary truth. The difference is that between *LCpq* and *CpLq*, with the substitutions *p*/*Mp*, *q*/*p*. *C*(*LCpq*)(*CpLq*) is not a thesis in any modal system; but its special case *C*(*LCMpp*)(*CMpLp*) is provable in S5 as follows:

1. *E'MpLMp*
2. *C*(*LCpq*)(*CLpLq*)

    2 *p*/*Mp*, *q*/*p* = 3

3. *C*(*LCMpp*)(*CLMpLp*)

    3 × RE'1 = 4

4. *C*(*LCMpp*)(*CMpLp*).

The fact that thesis 4 is thus provable in S5 does not, of course, suffice to show that it is not also provable in some weaker system. But 4 *p*/*Mp* is *C*(*LCMMpMp*)(*CMMpLMp*); by the S4 equivalence of *MM* and *M* this reduces to *C*(*LCMpMp*)(*CMpLMp*); and the antecedent of this being an obvious law, we may detach the consequent. But nothing in S4 itself, or of course in any weaker system contained in it, will thus enable us to deduce the distinctive S5 thesis *CMpLMp*.

Von Wright[1] has recently shown that a system yielding all the 'obvious' modal laws, but not the distinctive theses of S4 or S5, may be obtained by defining *L* as *NMN*, and adding to

[1] *An Essay in Modal Logic* (1951), Appendix II.

the axioms and rules of the assertoric propositional calculus the two axioms

AB1. *CpMp*

AB2. *E*(*MApq*)(*AMpMq*),

and the two rules

RB1. $E\alpha\beta \rightarrow EM\alpha M\beta$

RB2. $\alpha \rightarrow L\alpha$.

A system equivalent to S4 is obtainable by adding to the above axioms

AC1. *CMMpMp*,

and one equivalent to S5 by adding

AC2. *CMNMpNMp*.

(The stronger forms *C'MMpMp* and *C'MNMpNMp* are obtainable from these by RB2.) But a system equivalent to S5 is obtainable much more directly by simply adding to the assertoric calculus (without any special modal axioms at all) the four rules

L1. $C\alpha\beta \rightarrow CL\alpha\beta$, unconditionally.

L2. $C\alpha\beta \rightarrow C\alpha L\beta$, provided that no propositional variable occurs in α unless it is 'modalized', i.e. is either immediately preceded by '*M*' or '*L*' or occurs as part of a propositional formula which as a whole is preceded by '*M*' or '*L*'.[1]

M1. $C\alpha\beta \rightarrow CM\alpha\beta$, provided that no propositional variable occurs in β unless it is 'modalized'.

M2. $C\alpha\beta \rightarrow C\alpha M\beta$, unconditionally.

('Modalization' here plays a part like that played by the binding of a contained name-variable in Łukasiewicz's systematization of the lower functional calculus.)[2] Alternatively

[1] Thus '*p*' is 'modalized' in *Mp* and in *MCpq*, but not in *CpMq*.

[2] Feys (op. cit. 17. 21–22) gives deduction schemata not unlike these, and related to deduction schemata for quantifiers in H. B. Curry's *A Theory of Formal Deducibility* (1950), p. 73, as these are to Łukasiewicz's rules for Π and Σ.

we may add to the assertoric calculus the rules L1 and L2 and the definition $M = NLN$, or M1 and M2 and the definition $L = NMN$. Adopting the last alternative, we may prove von Wright's AB1 and AC2 as follows:

1. *Cpp.*
   1 × M2 = AB1

AB1. *CpMp*
   1 *p*/*NMp* × M1 = AC2

AC2. *CMNMpNMp.*

Replacing his equivalence AB2 by the two implications *C*(*MApq*)(*AMpMq*) and its converse, we may prove the former as follows:

Df. *A*: *A* = *CN*.

1. *Cpp*
2. *C*(*CpCqr*)(*CKpqr*)
3. *C*(*CKpqr*)(*CqCpr*)
4. *C*(*CNpq*)(*CNqp*)
5. *C*(*CpCqr*)(*CqCpr*)
   2 *p*/*CNpq*, *q*/*Np*, *r*/*q* = *C*1 *p*/*CNpq*—6
6. *C*(*KCNpqNp*)(*q*)
   6 × M2 = 7
7. *C*(*KCNpqNp*)(*Mq*)
   3 *p*/*CNpq*, *q*/*Np*, *r*/*Mq* = *C*7—8
8. *C*(*Np*)*C*(*CNpq*)(*Mq*)
   4 *q*/*CCNpqMq* = *C*8—9
9. *C*(*NCCNpqMq*)(*p*)
   9 × M2 = 10
10. *C*(*NCCNpqMq*)(*Mp*)
   4 *p*/*CCNpqMq*, *q*/*Mp* = *C*10—11
11. *C*(*NMp*)*C*(*CNpq*)(*Mq*)
   5 *p*/*NMp*, *q*/*CNpq*, *r*/*Mq* = *C*11—12
12. *C*(*CNpq*)(*CNMpMq*)
   12 × M1 = 13

13. $C(MCNpq)(CNMpMq)$

 $13 \times$ Df. $A = 14$

14. $C(MApq)(AMpMq)$.

The converse implication is provable thus:

1. $CpCNpq$
2. $CpCqp$
3. $CCprCCqrCApqr$

 $1 \times$ M2 $= 4$

4. $CpMCNpq$

 $2\ p/q,\ q/Np \times$ M2 $= 5$

5. $CqMCNpq$

 $4 \times$ M1 $= 6$

6. $CMpMCNpq$

 $5 \times$ M1 $= 7$

7. $CMqMCNpq$

 $3\ p/Mp,\ q/Mq,\ r/MCNpq = C6—C7—8$

8. $CAMpMqMCNpq$

 $8 \times$ Df. $A = 9$

9. $CAMpMqMApq$.

Von Wright's RB1 and RB2 may be established in our system as derivative rules. RB1 thus: From a thesis of the form $C\alpha\beta$ we may derive $CM\alpha M\beta$ by first applying M2 and then M1; $CM\beta M\alpha$ is derivable from $C\beta\alpha$ similarly; hence $EM\alpha M\beta$ (i.e. the combination of $CM\alpha M\beta$ and $CM\beta M\alpha$) from $E\alpha\beta$ (the combination of $C\alpha\beta$ and $C\beta\alpha$). And RB2 thus: Let α be any thesis, and β any thesis containing no unmodalized propositional variable. Then we may always prove $L\alpha$ from α in the following manner:

1. $CpCqp$
2. $CCpqCNqNp$
3. $CCpNqCqNp$
4. α
5. β

 $1\ p/\alpha,\ q/\beta = C4—6$

6. $C\beta\alpha$

$2\ p/\beta,\ q/\alpha = C6—7$

7. $CN\alpha N\beta$

$7 \times M1 = 8$

8. $CMN\alpha N\beta$

$3\ p/MN\alpha,\ q/\beta = C8—9$

9. $C\beta NMN\alpha$

$9 \times \text{Df. } L = C5—10$

10. $L\alpha$.

The fact that the distinctive theses of S5 are obtainable in a system of this sort is, I think, something of an argument in their favour, for they appear now, not as *ad hoc* additions to the more obvious modal laws, but as by-products of the simplest way of systematizing the latter. When we see that modal logic can be systematized in this way, it is the exclusion rather than the introduction of the S5 theses which takes on an *ad hoc* air—the systems in which they are not derivable are, by comparison, clumsy.

On the other side, i.e. by way of objection to S5, the following may be offered: In any system in which we are given or may infer von Wright's rule RB2, it can be shown that whenever *x* is *in fact* identical with *y*, *x* is *necessarily* identical with *y*. The proof [1] is as follows:

Df. I: $Ixy = \Pi\phi C\phi x\phi y$.

1. $C(\Pi\phi f\phi)(f\phi)$
2. $CCpCqrCqCpr$
3. Ixx

$1\ f/C'x'y \times \text{Df. } I = 4$

4. $CIxyC\phi x\phi y$

$2\ p/Ixy,\ q/\phi x,\ r/\phi y = C4—5$

5. $C\phi xCIxy\phi y$

$3' \times \text{RB2} = 6$

[1] Due in substance to R. L. Barcan's 'The Identity of Individuals in a Strict Functional Calculus of Second Order', *Journal of Symbolic Logic*, vol. xii (1947), p. 15, Prop. 2.31. If the definition Df. *I*, used in this proof, is considered objectionable we could use a system with *I* undefined and with 3 and 4 as axioms.

6. *LIxx*

   5 ϕ/*LIx'* = *C*6—7

7. *CIxyLIxy.*

This proposition is odd, but not incredible when one reflects both on its meaning and on its proof. Any object is necessarily identical with itself, and in every case the only object that is in fact identical with a given object will be itself, i.e. the object that is necessarily identical with it. But in S5 we may draw a consequence from this proposition which is harder to accept, namely that whenever *x* is *other* than *y*, this is not a merely contingent but a necessary fact. That is, in S5 we have not only 'If *x* is identical with *y*, then it is a necessary truth that this is so', *CIxyLIxy*, but also 'If *x* is *not* identical with *y*, then it is a necessary truth that *this* is so', *CNIxyLNIxy*. The proof is as follows (using our own rule L2 for a system equivalent to S5):

1. *CIxyLIxy*
2. *CCpqCNqNp*
3. *CCpqCCqrCpr*
4. *CLpp*

   2 *p*/*Ixy*, *q*/*LIxy* = *C*1—5

5. *CNLIxyNIxy*

   5×L2 = 6

6. *CNLIxyLNIxy*

   2 *p*/*LIxy*, *q*/*Ixy* = *C*4 *p*/*Ixy*—7

7. *CNIxyNLIxy*

   3 *p*/*NIxy*, *q*/*NLIxy*, *r*/*LNIxy* = *C*7—*C*6—8

8. *CNIxyLNIxy.*

I am not sure, however, that the fault here really lies with L2, i.e. with S5. The inference 'An identical is a necessary-identical, so a non-identical is a necessary-non-identical' is one which the mind will naturally make even before L2 is brought in to formalize it, and it may be that either our premiss *CIxyLIxy* is even less innocent than it looks, or our conclusion *CNIxyLNIxy* can be given an acceptable sense. It could be defended, for example, on the ground that any system using name-variables assumes a fixed range of objects, each with its own fixed identity, for any one of which a variable may stand; so that the sense (if any) of 'might' in which we can truly say

> This thing, which is not in fact that thing, yet might have been that thing

cannot be expressed within the system.[1] And it is arguable that *CIxyLIxy* and even *LIxx* reflect the same assumption. Still, the obscurity of the issue does leave S5 under a measure of suspicion, and this must be set against our earlier argument from simplicity in its favour.

The formulae *C′LMpLp* ('What is necessarily possible is necessarily true') and *C′MpMLp* ('What is possibly true is possibly necessary') are another pair about which it may be difficult at first to make up one's mind. As in our other cases, the converse formulae are obvious laws, and the two formulae stand or fall together. But W. T. Parry has provided solid grounds for letting them fall rather than stand, by showing that they imply as a thesis the formula *C′pLp* in the presence of which (as a thesis) all modal distinctions collapse. The proof of this (using quite unexceptionable modal theses, apart from *C′LMpLp*) is as follows:[2]

1. *C′LMpLp*
2. *E′(C′pq)(LCpq)*
3. *E′(Cpq)(ANpq)*
4. *E′(NLp)(MNp)*
5. *E′(AMpMq)(MApq)*
6. *C′pMp*

   6 *p*/*Lp* × RE′2 *p*/*Lp*, *q*/*MLp* = 7

7. *LCLpMLp*

   7 × RE′3 *p*/*Lp*, *q*/*MLp* = 8

8. *LANLpMLp*

   8 × RE′4 = 9

9. *LAMNpMLp*

   9 × RE′5 *p*/*Np*, *q*/*Lp* = 10

[1] Cf. C. D. Broad, *Examination of McTaggart's Philosophy*, vol. i, ch. xiv.

[2] Adapted from Parry's 'Modalities in the *Survey* System of Strict Implication', *Journal of Symbolic Logic*, vol. iv (1939), proof of 22.8 (p. 140) and subsequent disproof of 1.9* and 1.91* (pp. 153–4).

10. *LMANpLp*

$10 \times$ RE′3 q/Lp = 11

11. *LMCpLp*

1 $p/CpLp$ = C'11—12

12. *LCpLp*

$12 \times$ RE′2 q/Lp = 13

13. *C′pLp*.

The weaker formula *CLMpLp* (with material rather than strict implication as the first operator) is, indeed, a provable thesis of an ingenious quasi-modal system recently developed by Łukasiewicz from the following two axiomatic assertions and two axiomatic rejections:

1. *CδpCδNpδq*
2. *CpMp*

*3. *CMpp*

*4. *Mp*

(where modal operators as well as ordinary truth-operators are substitutable for 'δ').[1] Given the definition '*L* = *NMN*', all the laws in the ordinary square of modal opposition and equipollence are deducible, but otherwise these axioms, considered as a basis for a modal system, yield very eccentric results. Among other things, all formulae beginning with *L*, and all formulae equivalent to these, are rejected as theses, so that *C′pMp* (being equivalent to *LCpMp*) is rejected, and the above deduction of Parry's therefore cannot be performed. Łukasiewicz points out that in this system a formula *δMp* containing *M* is a thesis if and only if the two corresponding formulae *δp* and *δCpp* are both theses. This strongly suggests that '*M*' is here being used not as a constant propositional operator, truth-functional or otherwise, but rather as a variable truth-operator with its range of values restricted to (1, 0) and (1, 1); and given this interpretation, the characteristic features of the system lose their appearance of oddity. In particular,

[1] J. Łukasiewicz, 'A System of Modal Logic', *Journal of Computing Systems*, July 1953. This system is not to be confused with the modal system which Łukasiewicz earlier developed within a 'three-valued' truth-functional logic, and which will be discussed in the next chapter.

formulae beginning with L must be rejected because when M is assigned the value (1, 1), $MN\alpha$ will have the value 1, and $NMN\alpha$ in consequence the value 0, whatever the value of $N\alpha$ may be. And $CLMpLp$ is a thesis because (i) when M has the value (1, 0), i.e. when $Mp = p$, $CLMpLp$ is equivalent to the obvious tautology $CLpLp$; and (ii) when M has the value (1, 1), both the antecedent and the consequent of $CLMpLp$ will have the value 0, since they are both of the form $L\alpha$, and it has just been shown that all propositions of this form have the value 0 for $M/(1, 1)$.

§ 4. *Combined Modality and Quantification*

Some peculiar questions may also be raised when modal operators and quantifiers are not merely compared, but employed jointly; but these admit of solution on comparatively straightforward lines, at least where only the lower functional calculus is concerned. (An odd result of modalizing the higher functional calculus has already been given in the law $CIxyLIxy$.) Let us begin with what seems obvious. When we are using both modal operators and quantifiers, it seems important, at least in certain cases, to notice the order in which the two are placed. We must distinguish, for example, between $\Pi xM\phi x$ (Everything has some chance of ϕ-ing) and $M\Pi x\phi x$ (There is some chance that everything ϕ's), and between $\Sigma xL\phi x$ (There is something which cannot but ϕ) and $L\Sigma x\phi x$ (There is bound to be something which ϕ's). Adopting the medieval terms, we might call $M\Pi x\phi x$ and $L\Sigma x\phi x$ modals *in sensu composito* or *de dicto*, and $\Pi xM\phi x$ and $\Sigma xL\phi x$ modals *in sensu diviso* or *de re*. The modal operator seems to behave here exactly like a second quantifier (like Πx, if it is L, and like Σx if it is M), and we could construct a hexagon of subalternate forms just as for double quantification.[1] A similar hexagon, we may note in passing, could be constructed for modalized conjunctive and alternative forms ($MKpq$ and $KMpMq$, etc.), analogous to that for quantifications of conjunctive and alternative predicates ($\Sigma xK\phi x\psi x$ and $K\Sigma x\phi x\Sigma x\psi x$, etc.).[2] Analogous fallacies are to be guarded

[1] The main equivalences and implications involved are given in R. L. Barcan's 'A Functional Calculus of First Order Based on Strict Implication' (*Journal of Symbolic Logic*, vol. xi, pp. 1–16), theses 37–40.

[2] For the main theses involved see again Barcan, theses 27, 29, 33, 36.

against in both fields. Chrysippus, for example, is said to have argued that since a man necessarily either does *X* or does not do it, he either necessarily does *X* or necessarily does not do it (a proof of fatalism); this is plainly on a par with the argument that since every animal is either rational or irrational, either every animal is rational or every animal is irrational. In the field of mixed modality and quantification, we have a variant of Chrysippus's argument in the belief that because there is bound to be someone whose ticket in a lottery is the winning one, there is someone whose ticket is bound to be the winning one.

There is one point, however, where the parallelism between mixed modality and quantification on the one hand, and double quantification on the other, appears to break down. The forms 'Of everything it is true that it ϕ's everything' ($\Pi x \Pi y \phi xy$) and 'Of everything it is true that everything ϕ's it' ($\Pi y \Pi x \phi xy$) are equivalent, and so are the forms 'Every *B* ϕ's every *A*' and 'Every *A* has every *B* ϕ-ing it'. But whereas there is a similar equivalence between 'Necessarily everything ϕ's' and 'Everything is under a necessity of ϕ-ing', there seems to be a difference between 'Necessarily every *B* is an *A*' and 'Every *B* is under a necessity of being an *A*'. For example, 'Necessarily every white thing is white' is true, but 'Every white thing is under a necessity of being white' is doubtful. Precisely this sort of example is in fact used by medieval writers to bring out the difference between modality *de dicto* and modality *de re*. The source of complication here is the presence, in the restricted universals of the traditional logic, of an implicative as well as a quantifying element. There are not two but three forms to be distinguished here: (1) 'It is necessarily true that everything white is white' ($L\Pi xC\phi x\phi x$); (2) 'Of everything it is necessarily true that if it is white it is white' ($\Pi xLC\phi x\phi x$); and (3) 'Of everything it is true that if it is white, then it is a necessary truth that it is white' ($\Pi xC\phi xL\phi x$). The first two are equivalent as the analogy with double quantification requires that they should be; but (2) and (3) are different (the former true and the latter false), the difference being not in the relation of the *L* to the Π, but in its relation to the *C*. What is expressed in (2) is a *necessitas consequentiae*, necessity of the consequence or implication $C\phi x\phi x$; in (3) a *necessitas consequentis*, necessity of the consequent or implied proposition ϕx. And indeed the Schoolmen did apply this last distinction to a very similar case, Aristotle's statement in the *De Interpretatione* that 'Once it is, whatever is is-necessarily, and once it is-not, whatever is-not necessarily is not'. The Schoolmen admitted that we have the *necessitas consequentiae* 'Necessarily, if anything is it is', but not that we have the *necessitas consequentis* 'If anything is, then that-it-is is necessary'.[1]

The hexagon for quantified modalities and modalized quantifications has lately been subjected by von Wright to a criticism of a different sort. Von Wright's view is not that it makes too few distinctions but that it makes too many. He suggests that, at least where 'L' means 'It is *logically* necessary that . . .' and 'M' means 'It is *logically* possible that . . .', all modal assertions *de re* 'can be translated into' modal assertions *de dicto*,[2] and that $\Sigma xL\phi x$, for example, is equivalent to $L\Sigma x\phi x$.[3] He does not demonstrate this reducibility, but indicates that his ground for asserting it is what he calls the 'principle of predication'. This principle states that all properties are of one or the other of two sorts: (*a*) 'formal' properties, which it is always either logically necessary or logically impossible that a thing should possess, and (*b*) 'material' properties, which it is never either logically necessary or logically impossible that a thing should possess. There are no properties whose inherence in some subjects is logically necessary or logically impossible, while in others it is neither. Expressed as a thesis, this would be

$$NK(\Sigma xCM\phi xL\phi x)(\Sigma xKM\phi xNL\phi x),$$

'It is never the case that both something necessarily-ϕ's-if-it-possibly-ϕ's and something (else) possibly-ϕ's-but-does-not-necessarily-ϕ.' This thesis seems on the face of it a reasonable one, but von Wright does not show how the equivalence of, say, $\Sigma xL\phi x$ and $L\Sigma x\phi x$ follows from it, and we shall demonstrate shortly, by an example, that the assertion of this equivalence

[1] For the scholastic discussions on this point see pp. 70–75 of P. Boehner's notes to his edition of Ockham's *Tractatus de Praedestinatione*, etc. (1945).

[2] *An Essay in Modal Logic*, p. 26.

[3] Ibid., p. 34. Von Wright does not directly state this equivalence, but he points out the *non*-equivalence of 'Something is known to ϕ' and 'It is known that something ϕ's' in a context in which his main point is that you can make distinctions when using 'It is known that' which you cannot make when using 'It is (logically) necessary that'.

is in any case false. Before doing so, however, we shall indicate some qualifications which von Wright himself makes in enunciating his principle.

In the first place, he admits that it only applies where it is 'logical' necessity and possibility that are under discussion. If $M\phi x$ is used to mean, not 'There would be no logical inconsistency in supposing x to ϕ', but 'x has the (natural) *power* of ϕ-ing', the 'principle of predication' does not hold. For there may be some subjects which, if they have the power of ϕ-ing, will lack the power of not ϕ-ing (i.e. which if they *can* ϕ are *bound* to do so), and others which have the power of ϕ-ing and also the power of not ϕ-ing. He also admits that, even when we confine ourselves to the 'logical' modalities, 'one can think of exceptions to the principle, e.g. among higher order properties', but adds that he is 'not convinced that they are not apparent exceptions only'. He gives no examples, but here is one: In the field of 'modalized protothetic', there are truth-operators δ such that for some p's it is either necessary or impossible that δp, while for others it is neither. N, for instance. 'N (Socrates is both dead and not dead)' is logically necessary (and consequently is either-necessary-or-impossible, i.e. necessary-if-possible,) while 'N (Socrates is dead)' is neither logically necessary nor logically impossible. That is, we have

$$K(\Sigma pCMNpLNp)(\Sigma pKMNpNLNp),$$

and so cannot lay down as a thesis, true no matter what δ may be,

$$NK(\Sigma pCM\delta pL\delta p)(\Sigma pKM\delta pNL\delta p)$$

(which would be the analogue in this field of von Wright's 'principle of predication').

Turning now to the supposed consequence of the principle, the equivalence of $\Sigma xL\phi x$ and $L\Sigma x\phi x$, it is easy to find a ϕ for which the latter is true and the former false. We may best approach the question by first considering the connected non-equivalence of $\Pi xM\phi x$ and $M\Pi x\phi x$. Consider, for example, the form $\Pi xK\phi x\Sigma xN\phi x$, i.e.

> It is true of everything both that that thing ϕ's and that something does not ϕ.

This is necessarily false; for if something does not ϕ it cannot be true of *that* thing that it ϕ's, and so cannot be true of that thing that it ϕ's-and-something-does-not-ϕ. The contradictory form $N\Pi xK\phi x\Sigma xN\phi x$ can in fact be given the following formal proof from elementary principles:

1. $CKpqp$
2. $CKpqq$
3. $CCpqCCprCpKqr$
4. $CCpqCNqNp$
5. $NK(\Pi x\phi x)(\Sigma xN\phi x)$

   1 $p/\phi x,\ q/\Sigma xN\phi x \times \Pi 1 \times \Pi 2 = 6$
6. $C(\Pi xK\phi x\Sigma xN\phi x)(\Pi x\phi x)$

   2 $p/\phi x,\ q/\Sigma xN\phi x \times \Pi 1 = 7$
7. $C(\Pi xK\phi x\Sigma xN\phi x)(\Sigma xN\phi x)$

   3 $p/\Pi xK\phi x\Sigma xN\phi x,\ q/\Pi x\phi x,\ r/\Sigma xN\phi x = C6—C7—8$
8. $C(\Pi xK\phi x\Sigma xN\phi x)(K\Pi x\phi x\Sigma xN\phi x)$

   4 $p/\Pi xK\phi x\Sigma xN\phi x,\ q/K\Pi x\phi x\Sigma xN\phi x = C8—C5—9$
9. $N\Pi xK\phi x\Sigma xN\phi x$.

Since the contradictory of $\Pi xK\phi x\Sigma xN\phi x$ is thus a logical law, a proposition of that form is not a logically possible one. That is, where ϕx has the form $K\phi x\Sigma xN\phi x$, the assertion $M\Pi x\phi x$ is false. But the assertion $\Pi xM\phi x$, where ϕx has the same form, i.e. the assertion $\Pi xMK\phi x\Sigma xN\phi x$,

> With everything it is possible that that thing should ϕ when there is something that does not ϕ,

is, for many ϕ's, perfectly true. As to $L\Sigma x\phi x$ and $\Sigma xL\phi x$, it has just been shown that $N\Pi xK\phi x\Sigma xN\phi x$ is a logical law, and since $N\Pi x\phi x$ is equipollent to $\Sigma xN\phi x$, this means that $\Sigma xNK\phi x\Sigma xN\phi x$ is a logical law, i.e. we have

$$L\Sigma x(NK\phi x\Sigma xN\phi x).$$

But it is not true of every ϕ that

$$\Sigma xL(NK\phi x\Sigma xN\phi x),$$

i.e. that there is something of which it is logically impossible that that thing should ϕ when there is something that does not ϕ.

We must conclude, therefore, that the principle of predication (unless it is itself false) does not entail that the distinction between modalities *de dicto* and modalities *de re* is not worth drawing. What has led von Wright to imagine that it does, seems to be some such line of thought as this: When we have $\Pi xM\phi x$, 'Everything possibly-ϕ's', ϕ-ing may be a 'formal' property, in which case we will also have $\Pi xL\phi x$ (for with formal properties, if it is not impossible that they should inhere in an object, it is necessary that they should do so), and this ($\Pi xL\phi x$) is equivalent to the *de dicto* assertion $L\Pi x\phi x$. Or (and this, by the principle of predication, is the only other possibility), ϕ-ing may be a 'material' or 'contingent' property, in which case $\Pi xM\phi x$ will be equivalent to $\Sigma xM\phi x$, for where ϕ-ing is a 'material' property, both the possibility of ϕ-ing and the possibility of not ϕ-ing are present in everything and we will not have $\Sigma xM\phi x$ without also having $\Pi xM\phi x$. But $\Sigma xM\phi x$ is equivalent to the *de dicto* assertion $M\Sigma x\phi x$. So we may lay it down that $\Pi xM\phi x$ is either equivalent to $L\Pi x\phi x$ or to $M\Sigma x\phi x$, i.e.

(1) $A[E(\Pi xM\phi x)(L\Pi x\phi x)][E(\Pi xM\phi x)(M\Sigma x\phi x)]$.

We may also lay it down that $\Sigma xL\phi x$ always either has the same truth-value as $L\Pi x\phi x$ (this will be the case when ϕ-ing is a 'material' property, when both $\Sigma xL\phi x$ and $L\Pi x\phi x$ will be false) or has the same truth-value as $M\Sigma x\phi x$ (this will be the case when ϕ-ing is a formal property, when it will be possible that something ϕ's, i.e. there will be something that possibly-ϕ's, only when there is something that necessarily-ϕ's). That is, we may lay down

(2) $A[E(\Sigma xL\phi x)(L\Pi x\phi x)][E(\Sigma xL\phi x)(M\Sigma x\phi x)]$.

There is, however, no one *de dicto* proposition to which either $\Pi xM\phi x$ or $\Sigma xL\phi x$ is equivalent in all cases. As we have seen, $\Pi xM\phi x$ is certainly not always equivalent to $M\Pi x\phi x$, nor $\Sigma xL\phi x$ to $L\Sigma x\phi x$. Nor is either of them always equivalent to 'Either $L\Pi x\phi x$ or $M\Sigma x\phi x$', i.e. we do not have as laws either of the equivalences

(1′) $E(\Pi xM\phi x)A(L\Pi x\phi x)(M\Sigma x\phi x)$

(2′) $E(\Sigma xL\phi x)A(L\Pi x\phi x)(M\Sigma x\phi x)$.

We may be tempted to think that (1′) follows from (1) and (2′) from (2), but

$$C(AEpqEpr)(EpAqr)$$

is not a logical law, and is false for $p/0$, $q/1$, $r/0$, and for $p/0$, $q/0$, $r/1$. For example, let ϕ-ing be a 'material' or 'contingent' property. Then $\Sigma xL\phi x$ will be false, $L\Pi x\phi x$ will be false, and $M\Sigma x\phi x$ will be true; $A(L\Pi x\phi x)(M\Sigma x\phi x)$ will be true because $M\Sigma x\phi x$ is, and the false proposition $\Sigma xL\phi x$ will thus not be equivalent to it. There are thus no *de dicto* forms which can replace these *de re* forms in theses which hold for all predicates whatever, but only forms which may replace them in theses holding for all 'formal' predicates, and other forms which may replace them in theses holding for all 'material' predicates.

§ 5. *Extensions of the Notion of Modality*

We have hitherto used the words 'mode' and 'modality' in a comparatively restricted sense; it has also been given by many writers a more extended one. Thus in Peter of Spain[1] 'mode' is used in a broad sense for any sort of qualification of anything, adjectival or adverbial; but more strictly for adverbial qualifications, and most strictly of all for qualifications of the manner of connexion between the subject and the predicate, which is what he takes the ordinary modes of necessity, etc., to be. Other 'adverbial' modes express time-distinctions, or take us right outside propositions in the strict sense altogether; the distinction between indicative and imperative sentences, for example, being classifiable as a 'modal' one. (The grammatical word 'mood' comes from the Latin *modus* as well as the logical word 'mode'.) The eighteenth-century logician Isaac Watts (better known as a hymn writer) having dealt with necessity, impossibility, possibility, and contingency, says, 'Let it be noted that this quadruple Modality is only an enumeration of the *natural Modes* or Manners wherein the Predicate is attached to the Subject: We might also describe several *moral* or *civil Modes* of connecting two Ideas together (*viz.*) *Lawfulness* and *Unlawfulness*, *Conveniency* and *Inconveniency*, etc. whence we may form such *modal Propositions* as these: . . . *It is lawful for Christians to eat Flesh in* Lent. . . There are several other *Modes* of speaking whereby a Predicate is connected with a Subject: Such as, *it is*

[1] *Summulae*, 1.28.

certain, it is doubtful, it is probable, it is improbable, it is agreed, it is granted, it is said by the ancients, it is written, etc. all which will form other Kinds of *modal Propositions*.'[1] Whately, who tends to regard modal signs as simply disguised signs of quantity, suggests that undisguised ones might be regarded as modal too. 'Every sign of universality or particularity may be considered as a *Mode*', and may be expressed as an adverbial modification of the predicate, e.g. 'No injustice is expedient' as 'Injustice is *in no case* expedient'.[2]

Contemporary writers have suggested similar enlargements of this field. J. N. Findlay, for example, observes that there is a 'calculus of tenses' which 'should have been included in the modern development of modal logics', and gives some specimen formulae which such a calculus might include, the last of these being '*Πx*(*x* past) future', which he reads as 'All events (past, present, and future) will be past'.[3] (Medieval logicians laid down a few rules on this subject; thus Ockham states that, with certain qualifications, what may now be said truly in the present tense may for ever afterwards be said truly in the past tense, and even God's absolute power will be unable to alter it.[4] We shall encounter this law again in the next chapter.) The logic of imperative sentences[5] and Watts's 'moral modes' have been quite widely studied; and there are even logicians of distinction who have taken something like Watts's 'It is written' quite seriously as a modal operator, and have discussed 'theological modes' such as those expressed by 'It is *de fide* . . .' and 'It is heretical. . . .'[6] Von Wright, whose work on the 'moral' modes we shall glance at shortly, has also studied the 'epistemic' modes expressed by 'It is known that . . .', 'It is not known to be false that . . .', etc. (cf. Watts's 'It is certain'), and has described

[1] I. Watts, *Logick*, II. ii. 4.

[2] *Elements of Logic*, II. iv. I.

[3] J. N. Findlay, 'Time: A Treatment of Some Puzzles' (1941), reproduced in A. G. N. Flew's *Logic and Language*, first series (see p. 52, n. 1).

[4] *Tractatus de Praedestinatione*, etc. (Boehner's edition), p. 4.

[5] On this see A. Hofstadter and J. C. C. McKinsey, 'On the Logic of Imperatives', *Philosophy of Science*, 1939, pp. 446 ff.; A. Ross, 'Imperatives and Logic', ibid. 1944, pp. 30 ff.; H. G. Bohnert, 'The Semiotic Status of Commands', ibid. 1945; R. M. Hare, 'Imperative Sentences', *Mind*, 1949, pp. 21 ff., and *The Language of Morals* (1952), Part I; A. E. Duncan-Jones, 'Assertions and Commands', *Proc. Arist. Soc.* 1951–2.

[6] I. Thomas, 'Logic and Theology', *Dominican Studies*, Oct. 1948; I. M. Bocheński, 'Logical Remarks on A-Sentences', ibid. July 1949.

quantifications as 'existential modalities' (cf. Whately).[1] Other writers also have touched upon the logical peculiarities of such operators as 'It is believed that . . .', 'It is asserted that . . .'. As far back as 1918, W. E. Johnson noted the distinction between the *de dicto* and *de re* forms in which 'It is asserted that . . .' is combined with quantification.[2]

There is probably an embarrassment of riches here. We can hardly count all the 'modal' operators mentioned by these old and new writers as strictly belonging to the logical form of the propositions into which they enter, and so as constituting the subject-matter of a special branch of logic. For example, it seems obvious that Watts's 'It is said by the ancients that . . .' is not a purely formal operator; and few logicians would hesitate to say the same of 'It is *de fide* that . . .'. We might perhaps compare modal logic in this wider sense with the logic of relations or dyadic predicates. The logician is quite properly interested (1) in the general propositional form 'x ϕ's y'; but there are not many particular dyadic ϕ's which are of special interest to him. It is no part of his task, for example, to find out what conditions would verify a proposition of the form 'x hits y', and what would verify one of the form 'x loves y'. (2) There are, however, exceptions. The specific dyadic ϕ '— is identical with —', for example, may properly be given a chapter in a logic-book. And (3) there are certain logical properties which are found in some dyadic predicates but not in others, e.g. transitiveness in '— is an ancestor of —', but not in '— is a parent of —', and the logician may work out what would be the consequences of a relation's possessing such a property, regardless of what relations (if any) do possess it and what do not. According to what is called the 'formalist' school of mathematical philosophy it is precisely the pursuit of inquiries of this last kind that constitutes pure mathematics.[3]

[1] *An Essay in Modal Logic*, i, ii, iv, and vi.

[2] 'Analysis of Thinking', *Mind*, 1918, p. 139.

[3] To illustrate this view of mathematics, let us take the formula

$$CK(\psi b)(\Pi yzCK\phi zy\psi y\psi z)(\Pi xC\theta x\psi x)$$

and read 'b' as the number 0, 'ϕ' as 'is the successor of', and 'θ' as 'is an integer'. The formula then asserts that if a property ψ attaches to 0 and also attaches to y's successor whenever it attaches to y itself, then it will attach to anything which is an integer. This would normally be regarded as stating a truth about integers. But on the 'formalist' account of the matter, the pure mathematician is not

Exactly the same points may be made about the general modal form 'It is *Φ* that *p*'. In the first place, the logician is interested in this form itself as a distinct propositional form, and also in allied forms, such as the dyadic modal form 'That *p* *Φ*'s that *q*' (e.g. 'That *X* is *Y* causes it to be the case that *Z* is *W*'). Or perhaps it would be accurate to say that he ought to be interested; in fact this field has not been much cultivated. Russell emphasized in 1919 the need to recognize as a distinct logical form the 'proposition with two verbs', such as 'I believe that *X* is *Y*',[1] but he did not follow up this hint. And in recent years there has been a tendency to reduce propositions of this sort to the ordinary predicative form by saying that in a complex sentence of the form 'It is *Φ* that *p*', the subordinate sentence '*p*' is not *used* to refer to objects outside itself in the normal way but is merely *mentioned* as a sentence (as the Schoolmen would put it, in all such cases the proposition is taken in 'material supposition'). On this view, all that we have here is a statement about a form of words. Ordinary modal assertions, for example, are treated in this way by P. F. Strawson.[2] This does not seem to me plausible even in the case of ordinary modal assertions—when I say that it is impossible

interested in whether there are any such things as integers, successors, and the number 0, or in whether it is possible to find any ϕ, θ, and b at all for which the above formula holds. The one question that concerns him is this: If there *were* any ϕ, θ, and b for which the above formula held, together with one or two others, what further formulae would also hold (as logical consequences of the given ones) for such a ϕ, θ, and b? This is, of course, quite different from the view (to be sketched in a later chapter) that mathematics is an *extension* of logic, i.e. that its concepts are definable in terms of logical concepts (predication, quantification, identity, etc.) and its theses deducible from logical theses. The pure mathematician as the formalist conceives him is not concerned either to affirm or deny that there are *logical* properties, relations and objects for which his formulae hold. Quite similarly, we could trace the consequences of Łukasiewicz's axioms for 'syllogistic' without concerning ourselves at all with the question as to whether there are any properly logical operators and variables which yield true formulae when substituted for '*A*', '*E*', '*I*' and '*O*' and for '*a*', '*b*', '*c*', etc., respectively; and we can proceed similarly with, say, the axioms of Lewis's S5. Whether or not it is properly described as 'Mathematics', this application of logic to an unidentified subject-matter is a useful and often illuminating exercise, and some exercises allied to it will be performed in the first section of the next chapter.

For the embedding of formulae of number-theory in Łukasiewicz's formulae for propositional calculus see his 'Sur la Formalisation des Théories Mathématiques', in the *Proceedings of the* 1950 *Colloque de Logique Mathématique at Paris.*

[1] 'The Philosophy of Logical Atomism', *Monist*, 1919, p. 61.

[2] 'On Necessary Propositions and Entailment-Statements', *Mind*, 1948.

that Socrates should be dead without being dead I am not talking about the sentence 'Socrates is dead without being dead'; it would be impossible for Socrates to be dead without being dead even if there were no such phenomenon as speech and no such thing as a sentence. In other cases this treatment is even more obviously inadequate. It is quite plain, for example, that I am not talking about the sentence 'Socrates is dead' when I say 'I wish that Socrates were dead'. ('It is wished-by-me that Socrates be dead.') The form 'It is Φ that p', then, offers itself for systematic logical consideration, and there seems no good reason for refusing it.

Secondly, although specific terms that may be substituted for 'Φ' in 'It is Φ that p' may not be of special interest to the logician, in very many cases they are. The 'necessary', 'possible', etc., of ordinary modal logic are a case in point. 'It is not the case that p' is another specific exemplification of 'It is Φ that p' which is of obvious logical importance, and indeed truth-functions generally may be regarded as a special case of this type of form. (Perhaps we have already suggested as much in our introduction of 'truth-operators' as a sub-group within the genus 'propositional operators'.) Thus 'If p then q' could be written 'That p implies that q' (e.g. 'That I am in implies that I am not out'), which is of the form 'That p Φ's that q'. Frege's reflections on the difference between truth-functions and other functions of propositions (the contained sentences retaining their 'customary reference' to truth-values in the one case and not in the other) belong to this field, but it would seem to be an error to suppose that truth-functions are the only functions with propositional arguments in which the logician has a special interest. (There are also, at least, the ordinary modal functions.)

Finally, we may classify operators of the form 'It is Φ that . . .' according to their possession or lack of certain logical properties analogous to transitiveness, convertibility, etc., in relations, and we may work out the consequences of an operator's possessing such a property. Thus just as we may say of some dyadic predicates, but not of others, that for any x and y, if x ϕ's y then y ϕ's x, so we may say of some 'modalities' that for any p, if it is Φ that p then it is not Φ that not p. I do not know of any name for this property, but quite a number of propositional operators possess it. For example, 'It is necessary that p' always implies 'It is not necessary that not p', 'It is known that p' always implies 'It is not known that not p', and 'It is obligatory that A be done' always implies 'It is not obligatory that A be not done', though in none of these cases does the converse hold for every p or A. The possession of this property has as its logical consequence the possession of others; for example, if 'It is Φ that p' implies 'It is not Φ that not p', then 'It is Φ that not p' implies 'It is not Φ that p' ('It is necessary that not p' implies 'It is not necessary that p'; 'It is known that not p' implies 'It is not known that p'; 'It is obligatory that A be not done', i.e. forbidden that A be done, implies 'It is not obligatory that A be done'). Von Wright's studies of moral (or as he calls them 'deontic') and 'epistemic' modes, and also Thomas's and Bocheński's studies of 'theological modes', are perhaps to be regarded as studies in logical consequences of this kind, worked out with certain specific non-logical operators especially in view. (It is as if one presented a study of transitiveness under the guise of a 'logic' of the relation of ancestorhood.)

§ 6. *Deontic Logic*

To illustrate how these non-logical 'modes' may be logically handled—made the subject, in fact, of formal calculi—we may take some examples from the logic of obligation. The analogies which this presents with the logic of modality proper and with the logic of quantification are numerous and obvious.[1] For example, if we take the three moral modes 'obligatory', 'permissible', and 'forbidden', we may construct a square of opposition and equipollence exactly like those for modal and quantified forms, thus:

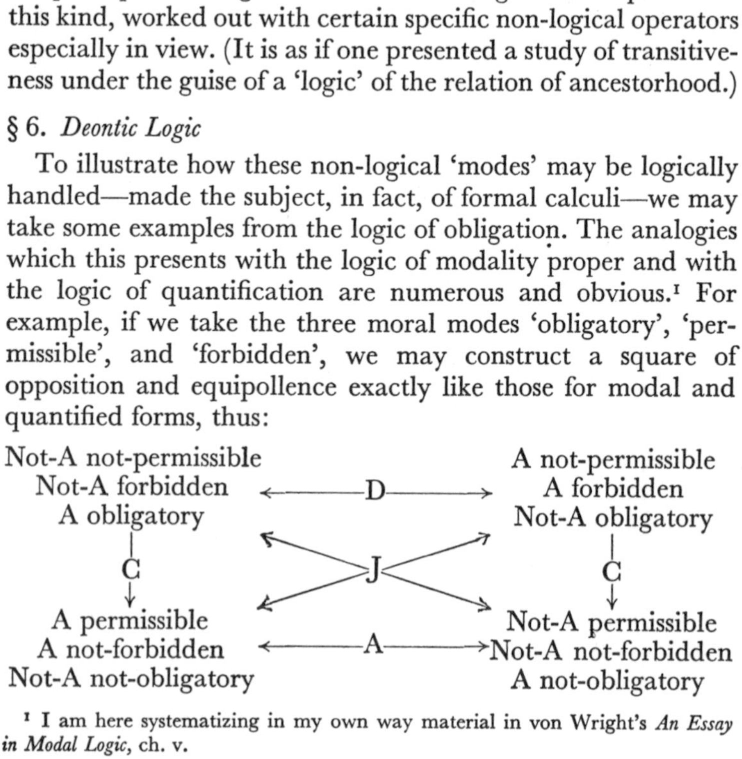

[1] I am here systematizing in my own way material in von Wright's *An Essay in Modal Logic*, ch. v.

We may also make a threefold division of moral operators analogous to that between 'All', 'Some but not all', and 'None', or between 'necessary', 'contingent', and 'impossible'; namely the division into 'obligatory', 'indifferent', and 'forbidden'. Then there are 'laws of movement' of deontic operators analogous to those of ordinary modal operators and quantifiers. Thus just as 'Possibly both *p* and *q*' implies but is not implied by 'Possibly *p* and possibly *q*', so 'It is permissible to do both *A* and *B*' implies but is not implied by 'It is permissible to do *A* and permissible to do *B*'.

Using '*a*', '*b*', '*c*', etc., for assertions of the form 'An act of the sort *A* is done', '*P*' for 'It is permissible that (such-and-such an act be done)', and '*O*' for 'It is obligatory that', quite a substantial 'deontic logic' may be built up by dovetailing into the propositional calculus the two special axioms

AD1. *COaPa*

AD2. *E*(*PAab*)(*APaPb*),

the definition

Df. *O*: *O* = *NPN*,

and the rule

RD1. $E\alpha\beta \rightarrow EP\alpha P\beta$.

These, which are restatements of a set of 'principles' listed by von Wright, are very like the axioms AB1 and AB2, the rule RB1 and the definition '*L* = *NMN*' used in the same writer's axiomatization of ordinary modal logic, mentioned in § 3. The main difference is that here AB1, *CpMp*, is not replaced by its exact deontic analogue *CaPa*, 'If *A* is done it is permissible that *A* be done', but by the analogue of the weaker thesis *CLpMp*. For '*A* is done' does not imply '*A* is permissible', nor is it implied by '*A* is obligatory', in the way that it implies 'It is possible that *A* should be done' and is implied by '*A* cannot but be done'.

Von Wright's systematization of ordinary modal logic, we may further note, involves a second metalogical rule RB2, $\alpha \rightarrow L\alpha$, 'If "$\alpha$" expresses a logical law, then it is a logical law that α is necessary'. This seems a reasonable rule, but there is no evident reasonableness about what would be its deontic analogue,

RD2. $\alpha \rightarrow O\alpha$,

'If the assertion that a certain sort of act is done expresses a logical law, then we have a moral obligation to act in that manner.' (We always have a moral obligation, e.g. to either-go-out-or-not-go-out.) It has, however, been shown by J. Hintikka[1] that this rule is derivable from RB1 and the axioms, if we add to the latter the further axiom *NΠbPb*, 'Not everything is permissible'. For given that the action-formula α expresses a logical law, and that the act-variable *b* does not occur freely in α, we may always prove $O\alpha$ as follows:

1. α
2. *CpCNpq*
3. *CKpqq*
4. *CCpqCCqpEpq*
5. *CEpqCpq*
6. *CCpqCCqrCpr*
7. *CCpqCNqNp*
8. *CPKabPa*
9. *NΠbPb*

    2 p/α, $q/KbN\alpha$ = C1—10

10. $CN\alpha KbN\alpha$

    4 $p/N\alpha$, $q/KbN\alpha$ = C10—C3 p/b, $q/N\alpha$—11

11. $EN\alpha KbN\alpha$

    11 × RD1 = 12

12. $EPN\alpha PKbN\alpha$

    5 $p/PN\alpha$, $q/PKbN\alpha$ = C12—13

13. $CPN\alpha PKbN\alpha$

    6 $p/PN\alpha$, $q/PKbN\alpha$, r/Pb = C13—C8 a/b, $b/N\alpha$—14

14. $CPN\alpha Pb$

    14 × Π2 = 15

[1] See von Wright, *An Essay in Modal Logic*, pp. 38–39.

15. $CPN\alpha\Pi bPb$

$7\ p/PN\alpha,\ q/\Pi bPb = C15—C9—16$

16. $NPN\alpha$

$16 \times \text{Df. } O = 17$

17. $O\alpha$.

(Here 2–7 are simple laws of the propositional calculus, while 8 is easily provable from von Wright's basis.)

A weaker rule, '$\alpha \rightarrow P\alpha$', is derivable from von Wright's basis without the assistance of $N\Pi bPb$. For given this basis, we may always deduce $P\alpha$ from a thesis α as follows:

1. α
2. $CCNpqApq$
3. $CEpqCqp$
4. $CpCqp$
5. $ANpp$
6. $CCpqCCqpEpq$

AD1. $COaPa$

AD2. $E(PAab)(APaPb)$

$\text{AD1} \times \text{Df. } O = 7$

7. $CNPNaPa$

$2\ p/PNa,\ q/Pa = C7—8$

8. $APNaPa$

$3\ p/PANaa,\ q/APNaPa = C\ \text{AD2}\ a/Na,\ b/a—C8—9$

9. $PANaa$

$4\ p/ANaa,\ q/\alpha = C5\ p/a—10$

10. $C\alpha ANaa$

$4\ p/\alpha,\ q/ANaa = C1—11$

11. $CANaa\alpha$

$6\ p/\alpha,\ q/ANaa = C10—C11—12$

12. $E\alpha ANaa$

$12 \times \text{RD1} = 13$

13. $EP\alpha PANaa$

$3\ p/P\alpha,\ q/PANaa = C13—C9—14$

14. $P\alpha$.

This derivative rule '$\alpha \to P\alpha$', 'If α expresses a logical law, then it is a law that α is permissible', might be rendered more freely as

What I cannot but do, I am permitted to do.

As this applies to negative as well as to positive 'doings', we may infer from it

What I cannot but omit, I am permitted to omit.

This amounts to

What I cannot do, I am not obliged to do,

and this yields by transposition the Kantian principle 'What I ought, I can'.

Of the wealth of theorems deducible from his axioms, even when RD2 is not used, von Wright gives a number connected with what he calls 'commitment'. He defines 'Doing *A* commits us to doing *B*' as 'It is obligatory that if we do *A* we do *B*', *OCab*; and he mentions such theorems as *CK*(*Oa*)(*OCab*)(*Ob*), 'If doing what we ought commits us to doing something else, then we ought to do this something else', and *CK*(*OCaAbc*)(*KNPbNPc*)(*NPc*), 'If doing *A* commits us to doing either *B* or *C*, and both *B* and *C* are not permitted, then *A* is not permitted'. Also provable from this basis, though not mentioned by von Wright, are analogues of the paradoxes of strict implication—(*CNPa*)(*OCab*), 'Doing what is not permitted commits us to doing anything whatever', and *C*(*Ob*)(*OCab*), 'Doing anything whatever commits us to doing what is obligatory'. As with Lewis's paradoxes, these appear less startling when the definitions of the terms used are considered. *OCab*, 'Doing *A* commits us to doing *B*', amounts simply to *ONKaNb*, 'We are obliged not to do *A* in conjunction with the omission of *B*', and this would follow naturally enough from *NPa*, i.e. from our being obliged not to do *A* at all.

An alternative and perhaps more natural formula for 'Doing *A* commits us to doing *B*' would be *CaOb*, 'If we do *A* we are obliged to do *B*'.[1] This gives us the second of the above two paradoxes in the form *C*(*Ob*)(*CaOb*) simply by substitution in *CpCqp*, but does not give us the first, which with this new

[1] This alternative was suggested to me as a possibility by Professor G. E. Hughes.

definition of commitment would be *C*(*NPa*)(*CaOb*). There are, however, not only paradoxes but quite plain truths about 'commitment' in this sense which do not seem to be provable in von Wright's system; for example, *C*(*Oa*)*C*(*CaOb*)(*Ob*), 'If we are obliged to do *A*, then if our doing *A* implies that we are obliged to do *B*, we are obliged to do *B*'. And if this be accepted we can deduce *CNPaCaOb* as follows:

1. *CCpCqrCqCpr*
2. *CNpCpq*
3. *CCpqCCqrCpr*
4. *CpNNp*
5. *CNPaONa*
6. *COaCCaObOb*

   1 *p*/*Oa*, *q*/*CaOb*, *r*/*Ob* = *C*6—7
7. *CCaObCOaOb*

   3 *p*/*Na*, *q*/*CaOb*, *r*/*COaOb* = *C*2 *p*/*a*, *q*/*Ob*—*C*7—8
8. *CNaCOaOb*

   3 *p*/*a*, *q*/*NNa*, *r*/*CONaOb* = *C*4 *p*/*a*—*C*8 *a*/*Na*—9
9. *CaCONaOb*

   1 *p*/*a*, *q*/*ONa*, *r*/*Ob* = *C*9—10
10. *CONaCaOb*

    3 *p*/*NPa*, *q*/*ONa*, *r*/*CaOb* = *C*5—*C*10—11
11. *CNPaCaOb*.

Another law beside *COaCCaObOb* which does not seem provable in von Wright's system (and which therefore constitutes a further indication that his rules and axioms are not sufficient for the derivation of all the laws that are formulable with *O* and *P*) is *OCOaa*, 'We ought to do-what-we-ought-to-do', a proposition which is trivial enough but which must be distinguished from the mere identity *COaOa*, 'We ought-to-do what we ought-to-do.'[1] In von Wright's ordinary modal system the analogues

[1] We have here, we might say, the two meanings of 'A thing's being obligatory commits us to doing it'. In von Wright's sense of 'commits', i.e. with the *OCab* definition, this is *OCOaa*; with the *CaOb* definition, it is *COaOa*.

of both of these laws—*CLpCCpLqLq* and *LCLpp*—are easily provable as follows:

1. *CCNpqCNqp*
2. *CCpqCCqrCpr*
3. *CCpCqrCqCpr*

AB1. *CpMp*

   1 *q*/*MNp* = *C* AB1 *p*/*Np*—4

4. *CNMNpp*

   4×Df. *L* = 5

5. *CLpp*

   2 *p*/*Lp*, *q*/*p*, *r*/*Lq* = *C*5—6

6. *CCpLqCLpLq*

   3 *p*/*CpLq*, *q*/*Lp*, *r*/*Lq* = *C*6—7

7. *CLpCCpLqLq*

   5×RB2 = 8

8. *LCLpp*.

But these proofs depend on AB1, *CpMp*, and the deontic analogue of this, *CaPa*, does not hold. There is, however, a deontic analogue of the related thesis *LCpMp* which both implies and is implied by *OCOaa*, namely *OCaPa*, 'It is obligatory that if we do *A* we be permitted to do *A*'. The force of this is clearer if we read it 'We are obliged to confine our doings to what is permissible'; it is not to be confused with 'If we do *A*, it is obligatory that we be permitted to do *A*', *CaOPa*.[1]

Deontic operators and ordinary modal operators may be combined to form a system in which, for example, Kant's 'What I ought I can' may be expressed not only as a rule of deduction but as a thesis, *COaMa*. But in this field we need to work very carefully. One principle which would be formulable in such a wider system, and which is not without a certain intuitive plausibility, is *C*(*C*′*Kabc*)(*CKaObOc*),

> If the doing of *A* and *B* jointly necessitates the doing of *C*, then if we do *A* and are obliged to do *B*, we are obliged to do *C*.

[1] *OCaPa* is again a 'commitment' in von Wright's sense, while *CaOPa* would express the same 'commitment' ('Doing *A* commits us to *A*'s being permissible') in the other sense.

This principle was laid down by Grelling in one of the earliest attempts to formalize the logic of obligation. In criticism of it, it was pointed out by Reach that if we substitute '*C*' for '*A*' and 'not-*C*' for '*B*' we obtain

> 'If doing both-*C*-and-not-*C* necessitates doing *C*, then if we do *C* but ought not to do *C*, we ought to do *C*.'

But the antecedent of this is true, for doing both-*C*-and anything at all necessitates doing *C*, so we must accept the consequent also, i.e.

> 'If we do *C* but ought not to do *C*, then we ought to do *C*.'

We might call this the 'principle of the *fait accompli*'.[1] Formalized, its proof runs as follows (the logic is impeccable):

1. $C(C'Kabc)(CKaObOc)$
2. $C'Kpqp$

   $1\ a/c,\ b/Nc = C2\ p/c,\ q/Nc—3$

3. $CKcONcOc$.

But if we accept this conclusion we must either deny that anyone ever does what he ought not to do, or deny the rule of subalternation *CONaNOa*, 'If we are obliged not to do *A* we are not obliged to do *A*'. Again, if we substitute '*a*' for '*c*' in Grelling's rule, we may show that either nothing at all is obligatory or whatever we are doing is obligatory, thus:

1. $CC'KabcCKaObOc$
2. $C'Kpqp$
3. $CCKpqrCqCpr$
4. $CCpqANpq$

   $1\ c/a = C2\ p/a,\ q/b—5$

5. $CKaObOa$

   $3\ p/a,\ q/Ob,\ r/Oa = C5—6$

6. $CObCaOa$

   $6 \times \Sigma 1b \times \Pi 2a = 7$

[1] Grelling's and Reach's papers are summarized by F. B. Fitch in the *Journal of Symbolic Logic*, vol. v (1940), p. 39.

7. $C\Sigma bOb\Pi aCaOa$

$$4\ p/\Sigma bOb,\ q/\Pi aCaOa = C7\text{—}8$$

8. $AN\Sigma bOb\Pi aCaOa$.

We might call this the 'principle of continuous moral rectitude'.[1]

A still richer system becomes possible if instead of using the variables '*a*', '*b*', etc., for assertions '*A* is done', '*B* is done', etc., we use the form 'αx', for 'The individual action *x* (e.g. the next thing we do) has the character α', and 'βx', 'γx' etc., similarly, and '$O\alpha x$' for 'The action *x* (e.g. the next thing we do) ought to have the character α'. Quantifiers may then be used to distinguish between what we might call 'perpetual' obligations, and obligations which only lie upon us on a particular occasion. Consider, for example, the assertion-form 'If doing *A* necessitates doing *B*, then if we ought to do *A* we ought to do *B*'. This seems reasonable until we consider such examples as

> If loving God and our neighbour necessitates riding a bicycle, then if we ought to love God and our neighbour we ought to ride a bicycle.

It may well be felt that even in circumstances in which loving God and our neighbour does necessitate riding a bicycle (and such circumstances do arise), riding a bicycle is not an 'obligation' in the same sense as loving God and our neighbour is. And we might perhaps bring out the distinction which is obscured here by means of the two formulae

(1) $\Pi xC(C'\alpha x\beta x)(CO\alpha xO\beta x)$

(2) $\Pi xC(C'\alpha x\beta x)(C\Pi xO\alpha x\Pi xO\beta x)$.

If $\alpha =$ loving God and our neighbour, and $\beta =$ riding a bicycle, (1) will assert that if any given action's being one of love to God, etc., necessitates that action's being a ride on a bicycle, then if that action ought to be one of love, etc., it ought to be one of riding a bicycle. (2), on the other hand,

[1] I owe this phrase, as well as the above use of this principle as a *reductio ad absurdum* of Grelling's rule, to a paper by Professor G. E. Hughes. I understand that an early attempt to axiomatize 'deontic logic' by E. Mally ended in a similar fatality.

asserts that if any given action's being one of love, etc., necessitates its being a ride on a bicycle, then if love to God, etc., ought to characterize every action whatever, being a ride on a bicycle ought to characterize every action whatever. It is (2) which is clearly false, but (1) does not imply it, and so far as I can see is true.

NOTE, 1960

I cannot now regard so complacently the proposition *CNPaCaOb* on p. 225. As A. R. Anderson has pointed out, this means that if anything forbidden is done, then everything whatever is obligatory; so that if we lay it down (as we well might) that not everything is obligatory, we can conclude that nothing forbidden is done, i.e. *CNPaNa*, and so also *COaa*. And since this is quite unacceptable, the 'plain truth' *COaCCaObOb*, from which *CNPaCaOb* is deduced on p. 225, is unacceptable too. Putting *C,ab* for 'Doing *a* commits us to doing *b*', Anderson points out that intuitively we want both *COaCC,abOb* and *CaCC,abOb*, that the former is unacceptable with the definition *C,ab* = *CaOb*, and the latter with von Wright's definition. His own suggestion is to introduce modality and define *C,ab* as *C′aOb*. Professor Hughes tells me that what he also had in mind was not *CaOb* but the same with some stronger implication-functor.

The law *OCOaa* of pp. 225–6, about which there has been some discussion in the literature, was originally suggested to me by Mrs. J. F. Bennett (in 1953 or 1954) as an example of a synthetic *a priori* proposition.

II

Three-valued and Intuitionist Logic

§ 1. *Two-valued and Three-valued Arithmetic*

Let us turn back for a short time from the modal to the pure or assertoric propositional calculus, and especially to the symbolic apparatus which we have employed here for the development of this branch of logic. This symbolic apparatus (and the same would be true of other notations, e.g. that of PM) could quite easily have been put to other uses, some of them not strictly logical at all. For example, we could use them to express certain arithmetical truths about the numbers 0 and 1. We have already noted that if '0' and '1' were given their usual senses, the symbol 'K', defined by means of the equations $K11 = 1$ and $K10 = K01 = K00 = 0$, could quite well represent ordinary multiplication. And it is not difficult to find arithmetical operations which could similarly replace our other truth-operators. For example, we would obtain the equations $N1 = 0$ and $N0 = 1$ if we interpreted 'N' as the operation of subtracting from 1. For $1-1 = 0$ and $1-0 = 1$. And since we know that Cpq has the same value as $NKpNq$, we could use these results to find an arithmetical interpretation for 'C'. It would be

$$Cpq = 1-p(1-q)$$

(i.e. 'C' is the operation of subtracting the second number from 1, then multiplying the first number by what we now have, and finally, subtracting the result of this from 1). We can easily see that this gives the required properties for 'C', for

$$C11 = 1-1(1-1) = 1-0 = 1$$
$$C10 = 1-1(1-0) = 1-1 = 0$$
$$C01 = 1-0(1-1) = 1-0 = 1$$
$$C00 = 1-0(1-0) = 1-0 = 1.$$

And if we interpret Łukasiewicz's axioms for the C–N calculus as asserting that

(1) $CCpqCCqrCpr = 1$, (2) $CCNppp = 1$, and (3) $CpCNpq = 1$

(where '*p*', '*q*', and '*r*' are variables which may stand indifferently for '0' and for '1', but not for any other numbers, and '*C*' and '*N*' are interpreted as above) these axioms will remain true. (Ordinary truth-value calculations, reinterpreted, prove this.) Moreover, all theses derivable from these three by substitution and detachment, and interpreted similarly, will be true also. For it has been shown that if the values of a variable *p* are confined to 0 and 1, the values of *Np* will be confined to 0 and 1, and that if the values of *p* and *q* are confined to 0 and 1, the values of *Cpq* will be confined to 0 and 1. Hence the values of all complexes constructed by means of *C* and *N* in the usual way will be confined to 0 and 1. Hence if any thesis holds for all *p*'s, *q*'s, etc., whose values are confined to 0 and 1, it will continue to hold if these *p*'s, *q*'s, etc., are replaced by any complexes constructed by means of *C* and *N* in the ordinary way. That is, the rule of substitution will be valid for this interpretation of our symbols. Again, if we have $C\alpha\beta = 1$ and $\alpha = 1$, we will have $\beta = 1$, for when $\alpha = 1$, $C\alpha\beta = 1$ only when $\beta = 1$ ($C11 = 1$, but $C10 = 0$). So the rule of detachment will be valid also.

Such reinterpretations of the symbols of a deductive system are useful in proving the system's consistency, that is, in showing that it is not possible in the system to prove any formula together with its contradictory. From the above reinterpretation, in particular, we can prove that the propositional calculus as axiomatized by Łukasiewicz is consistent if ordinary arithmetic is consistent. For the derivability of formulae by substitution and detachment from the three used by Łukasiewicz as axioms does not depend on how we interpret the symbols (the rules are quite mechanical). Hence if we could derive theses of the forms 'α' and '$N\alpha$' respectively when we had the propositional interpretation in mind, we would be equally able to derive them when we had the arithmetical interpretation in mind. But if ordinary arithmetic is consistent, we cannot derive from true propositions and by valid rules a pair of assertions equating the same number with 1 and with 0, which is what we would be in effect doing if we derived theses of the forms 'α' and '$N\alpha$' from the above axioms, interpreted arithmetically. Hence we cannot derive contradictory theses by substitution and detachment from the above set of axioms.

It is possible to give many other arithmetical interpretations of the symbols of the propositional calculus which will preserve the truth of its axioms and the validity of its rules. Some of these, like that just mentioned, involve only the numbers 0 and 1, but some involve other numbers as well. I shall not immediately give an example of the latter, but I shall give something a little like it. Suppose we let our variables stand indifferently for any of the three numbers 0, 1, and $\frac{1}{2}$. And suppose we let 'N' be an arithmetical operator such that $N1 = 0$, $N\frac{1}{2} = \frac{1}{2}$, and $N0 = 1$. It could again represent, for example, the operation of subtracting from 1. For we then have

$$N1 = 1-1 = 0, \quad N\tfrac{1}{2} = 1-\tfrac{1}{2} = \tfrac{1}{2}, \quad N0 = 1-0 = 1.$$

Suppose, further, that we let 'C' be an arithmetical operator on two numbers such that when the numbers are drawn from the three 0, $\frac{1}{2}$, and 1, $Cpq = 1$ when the second number is equal to or greater than the first, $= 0$ when the first number is 1 and the second 0, and $= \frac{1}{2}$ in other cases. That is, let it be an operator with the following matrix

C	1	$\frac{1}{2}$	0
1	1	$\frac{1}{2}$	0
$\frac{1}{2}$	1	1	$\frac{1}{2}$
0	1	1	1

Cpq could be,[1] for example, $\frac{2}{3}(q-p)^4 - 7/6(q-p)^2 + \frac{1}{2}(q-p) + 1$. Let our formulae again be constructed by means of 'C' and 'N' in the usual way; and let our theses be taken to assert that the formula in question $= 1$ whatever be the values of its variables (provided they be drawn from the three 0, $\frac{1}{2}$, and 1). In a system thus interpreted, the rules of substitution and detachment will again apply. For it is clear that anything constructed by means of 'C' and 'N' in the usual way out of variables standing only for 0, $\frac{1}{2}$, and 1 will itself have one of the values 0, $\frac{1}{2}$, and 1, and so will be substitutable for variables in theses; and from the top line of the matrix for 'C' we may infer that the rule of detachment will apply also, for when $\alpha = 1$, $C\alpha\beta = 1$ only when $\beta = 1$ ($C1\frac{1}{2} = \frac{1}{2}$ and $C10 = 0$). As to the axioms, calculation shows that $CCpqCCqrCpr = 1$ always, and that $CpCNpq = 1$ always. When, however, we take Łukasiewicz's

[1] I am indebted for this, as a function from elementary algebra meeting the requirements, to Mr. W. W. Sawyer.

second axiom *CCNppp*, calculation does not give 1 for all three values of *p*; for when $p = \frac{1}{2}$, $CCNppp = CCN\frac{1}{2}\frac{1}{2}\frac{1}{2} = CC\frac{1}{2}\frac{1}{2}\frac{1}{2} = C1\frac{1}{2} = \frac{1}{2}$. We cannot, therefore, use these interpretations to prove the consistency of Łukasiewicz's axioms and rules from the consistency of ordinary arithmetic.

There is something, all the same, that this second interpretation does show us about Łukasiewicz's rules and axioms, namely that the second axiom is not provable from the other two. For since the rules of substitution and detachment are mechanical in character (i.e. we can apply them without considering what the theses mean), if we could prove the second *C–N* axiom from the other two, we could prove, by ordinary arithmetic, that if $CCpqCCqrCpr = 1$ and $CpCNpq = 1$ then $CCNppp = 1$, when '*C*', '*N*', and the variables are given the interpretations suggested in the last paragraph. But, on the contrary, ordinary arithmetic shows that with these interpretations, although $CCpqCCqrCpr = 1$ and $CpCNpq = 1$ for all values of *p*, *q*, and *r*, there is a case in which $CCNppp \neq 1$, for there is a case in which $CCNppp = \frac{1}{2}$. Other interpretations may be found to show in a similar way that the first axiom is not provable from the second and the third, nor the third from the first and the second. This is the method regularly used for establishing the 'independence' of the axioms in a given set, i.e. for showing that no axiom in the set is superfluous, in the sense of being derivable from the others as a theorem. (It does not show, of course, that an entire set of axioms is not derivable from some smaller set. There are, for example, various single *C–N* axioms from which all of Łukasiewicz's three may be derived despite the fact that no one of them is derivable from the others.)

The same method is used for showing that a set of axioms is not complete. We find some interpretation of our symbols which will make the axioms true but some known tautologous thesis false, and thus show that the axioms are insufficient to prove the thesis. We noted in I. iv. 4, for example, that in a system in which '*Cpq*' is defined as short for '*NKpNq*', Łukasiewicz's three axioms—which then become abbreviations of

(1) *NKNKpNqNNKNKqNrNNKpNr*

(2) *NKNKNpNpNp*

(3) *NKpNNKNpNq*

—do not suffice to prove the law *CKpqNCpNq*, which in such a system would be an abbreviation of

(4) *NKKpqNNNKpNNq*.

This may be shown by interpreting '*K*' and '*N*' as numerical operators with the following matrices:[1]

K	1	½	0
1	1	1	0
½	½	½	0
0	0	0	0

N	
1	0
½	1
0	1

Calculation shows that formulae (1), (2), and (3) have the value 1 for all distributions of the values 1, ½, and 0 among their arguments, and that the rule of detachment in the form

$$(\alpha = 1), (NK\alpha N\beta = 1) \rightarrow (\beta = 1)$$

holds for these operators, but that formula (4) has the value 0 when $p = 1$ and $q = \frac{1}{2}$.

Other points also may be noted about our second arithmetical system, involving the three numbers 0, 1, and ½. In the first place, although not all formulae which express theses in the propositional calculus will also express theses of this second system, the converse does hold—all formulae which express theses in our second arithmetical system will also express theses in the propositional calculus. We may show this as follows: If we take the two matrices

C	1	½	0
1	1	½	0
½	1	1	½
0	1	1	1

N	
1	0
½	½
0	1

and consider only those cases in which $p = 1$ or 0 and $q = 1$ or 0, i.e. the top and bottom cases with *N* and the four corner cases with *C*, we will notice that the equations yielded are the ordinary ones—$C11 = C01 = C00 = 1$, $C10 = 0$, $N1 = 0$ and $N0 = 1$. Now if any formula expresses a thesis in our second arithmetical system, it must be equal to 1 in these cases as well as in the others; and if it holds in these cases, it would hold in

[1] Adapted from Łukasiewicz, 'On the Intuitionistic Theory of Deduction', *Nederl. Akad. Wetensch. Proc. Ser. A* 55 (1952), p. 203.

On the general topic of the use of 'interpretations' to prove consistency, independence, and incompleteness see A. Tarski's *Introduction to Logic*, Part I, ch. vi.

a system which included these cases only, and which had the above equations for them. It would hold, that is to say, in our *first* arithmetical system, and so in the propositional calculus. Our second arithmetical system is therefore an analogue of a *part* of the propositional calculus.

Our second arithmetical system can, moreover, be axiomatized, and of course its axioms, like its other theses, will be capable of expressing theses of the propositional calculus. Wajsberg found in 1932 that the following four formulae,

1. *CpCqp* 2. *CCpqCCqrCpr* 3. *CCCpNppp* 4. *CCNpNqCqp*,

will yield by substitution and detachment all formulae equalling 1 for all distributions of the values 0, ½, and 1 among their variables, when *C* and *N* are interpreted as in our second system. For example, *Cpp* is derivable as follows:

1 *q*/*CpNp* = 5

5. *CpCCpNpp*

2 *q*/*CCpNpp*, *r*/*p* = *C*5—*C*3—6

6. *Cpp*.

Considered as theses in the propositional calculus, axioms 1 and 2 are quite familiar, 4 is one of the laws of transposition, and 3 is a modification of *CCNppp*—it does not assert 'If not-*p* implies *p*, then *p*', but 'If *p*'s implying not-*p* implies *p*, then *p*'. (We shall be looking more closely into this difference later.) Between them, these four axioms form in a sense a complete basis for the 'three-valued' system. There is, however, a sense in which they do not. The theses for which they form a complete basis are only those which can be formulated by means of '*C*' and '*N*' and operators definable in terms of them, but while in a system dealing only with 1 and 0 all other operators *are* definable in terms of these two, in a system dealing with 1, 0, and ½ this is not the case. Consider only the 'monadic' operators. For 1 and 0 there are four of these; for 1, 0, and ½ there are twenty-seven. Using the form $(x, y, z)p$ for a function of p such that it has the value x when $p = 1$, y when $p = \frac{1}{2}$, and z when $p = 0$, the first nine monadic operators on 1, ½, and 0 are (1, 1, 1), (1, 1, ½), (1, 1, 0), (1, ½, 1), (1, ½, ½), (1, ½, 0), (1, 0, 1), (1, 0, ½), and (1, 0, 0). Replace the first '1' in these by '½', and we have another nine; and replace it by '0', and we have the remainder.

Of these, $(0, \frac{1}{2}, 1)$ is our '*N*', and many others are definable in terms of '*N*' and '*C*'. E.g. $(1, 1, 0)p$ could be *CNpp*, for

$$CN11 = C01 = 1, \quad CN\tfrac{1}{2}\tfrac{1}{2} = C\tfrac{1}{2}\tfrac{1}{2} = 1, \quad CN00 = C10 = 0.$$

But there are other functions such as $(\frac{1}{2}, \frac{1}{2}, \frac{1}{2},)p$, which cannot be arrived at by any combination of the operations represented by '*C*' and '*N*'; and many dyadic functions of which the same is true. Słupecki found in 1936, however, that we can arrive at all of them by combinations of the operations represented by '*C*', '*N*', and '*T*', where '*T*' is a monadic operator producing functions with the value $\frac{1}{2}$, whether *p* be 0, $\frac{1}{2}$, or 1. That is, '*Tp*' is '$(\frac{1}{2}, \frac{1}{2}, \frac{1}{2})p$.' ('*T*-ing' could be the operation of subtracting a number from itself and adding $\frac{1}{2}$.) This operator has no analogue in propositional logic; at least, it has none in the kind of propositional logic which we have so far considered. Słupecki found, further, that all formulae which we can construct by means of *C*, *N*, and *T*, and which equal 1 for all distributions of the values 0, $\frac{1}{2}$, and 1 among their variables, are derivable by substitution and detachment from Wajsberg's four axioms together with the following two:

5. *CTpNTp* 6. *CNTpTp*.

The Wajsberg–Słupecki axioms form a complete basis for this field in the strong sense of 'complete'—any *C–N–T* formula which is not provable from them by substitution and detachment will, if treated as a thesis, make the system inconsistent, i.e. will make it possible to deduce in the system the simple variable *p*, and so any formula whatever. For example, if *CCNppp* be added to the Wajsberg–Słupecki axioms, we may deduce *p* as follows:

1. *CpCqp*
2. *CCNpNqCqp*
3. *CTpNTp*
4. *CNTpTp*
5. *CCNppp*

 5 *p*/*Tp* = *C*4—6

6. *Tp*

 3 = *C*6—7

7. *NTp*

 1 *p*/*NTp*, *q*/*Np* = *C*7—8

8. *CNpNTp*

 2 *q*/*Tp* = *C*8—*C*6—9

9. *p*.

Wajsberg's four *C–N* axioms alone are not complete in this strong sense even for the *C–N* part of the three-valued system. For completeness of this sort is a property of sets of formulae which is independent of their interpretation, so that if the simple variable *p* could be deduced by substitution and detachment from the combination of, say, *CCNppp* with Wajsberg's four axioms when *C* and *N* are given our second ('three-valued') arithmetical interpretation, it would also be derivable when they are given our first ('two-valued') arithmetical interpretation, or the ordinary truth-functional ones. But when *C* and *N* are interpreted in either of these latter ways, *CCNppp* is a law as well as Wajsberg's four. Wajsberg's system is complete only in the sense that his axioms yield all *C–N* formulae which hold on a certain interpretation; and if we wish to describe this completeness without referring to interpretations at all we can only do so by looking beyond purely *C–N* formulae and saying that Wajsberg's axioms yield all such formulae which can be consistently combined with both *CTpNTp* and *CNTpTp*. This condition automatically restricts the possible interpretations of *C* and *N*; and in particular it precludes both our first arithmetical interpretation and the ordinary truth-functional one, for on neither of these can there be an α such that both $C\alpha N\alpha$ and $CN\alpha\alpha$.[1]

This is not, of course, the only way in which this part of the arithmetic of 1, $\frac{1}{2}$, and 0 may be axiomatized. An alternative method with some interesting features was described by Słupecki in 1946. In this system the undefined operators are *C″*, *N″*, and *R* with the following matrices:

C″	1	$\frac{1}{2}$	0
1	1	$\frac{1}{2}$	0
$\frac{1}{2}$	1	1	1
0	1	1	1

N″	
1	0
$\frac{1}{2}$	1
0	1

R	
1	$\frac{1}{2}$
$\frac{1}{2}$	1
0	0

All other 'three-valued' operators are definable in terms of these; and all expressions having the value 1 so long as the values of the variables are confined to 1, $\frac{1}{2}$, and 0 are obtainable

[1] If, in the ordinary propositional calculus, *Tp* were the tautologous function (1, 1)*p* we would have *CNTpTp* as a thesis but not *CTpNTp*, while if it were the contradictory function (0, 0)*p* we would have *CTpNTp* but not *CNTpTp*.

by substitution and detachment from the following nine:

1. $C''C''pqC''C''qrC''pr$
2. $C''C''N''ppp$
3. $C''pC''N''pq$
4. $C''RpN''p$
5. $C''RC''pqRq$
6. $C''pC''RqRC''pq$
7. $C''RRpp$
8. $C''pRRp$
9. $N''RN''p$.

What is interesting about this systematization is that the underived formulae 1–3 are simply Łukasiewicz's axioms for the propositional calculus with C and N replaced by C'' and N''; and this time we have all three of them. Hence in the segment of this system which employs only the operators C'' and N'' we have a complete arithmetical counterpart of the propositional calculus.

Another arithmetical counterpart of the full propositional calculus was shown in 1949, by the Chinese logician Tzu-Hua Hoo,[1] to be obtainable within Słupecki's 1936 C–N–T calculus by using the operators (C) and (N) defined as follows:

$$(N)p = CTpNp$$
$$(C)pq = C(N)q(N)p.$$

The equations for (N) work out as

$$(N)1 = CT1N1 = C\tfrac{1}{2}0 = \tfrac{1}{2}$$
$$(N)\tfrac{1}{2} = CT\tfrac{1}{2}N\tfrac{1}{2} = C\tfrac{1}{2}\tfrac{1}{2} = 1$$
$$(N)0 = CT0N0 = C\tfrac{1}{2}1 = 1,$$

while similar calculations for (C) give the matrix

(C)	1	$\frac{1}{2}$	0
1	1	$\frac{1}{2}$	$\frac{1}{2}$
$\frac{1}{2}$	1	1	1
0	1	1	1

The formulae corresponding to Łukasiewicz's three axioms—$(C)(C)pq(C)(C)qr(C)pr$, $(C)(C)(N)ppp$, and $(C)p(C)Npq$—are all

[1] '*m*-valued sub-systems of $(m+n)$-valued propositional calculus', *Journal of Symbolic Logic*, vol. xiv (1949), pp. 177–81.

derivable from Słupecki's six *C–N–T* axioms and the definitions of (*C*) and (*N*), and the formulae corresponding to the rest of the propositional calculus are derivable from these three in the usual way.

A comparison of the matrices for Tzu-Hua Hoo's (*C*) and (*N*) and those for Słupecki's *C″* and *N″* suggests the following metatheorem: All laws for two-valued implication and negation will hold for any three-valued implication and negation such that $C\alpha\beta \neq 1$ when $\alpha = 1$ and $\beta \neq 1$, but $C\alpha\beta = 1$ in all other cases, and $N\alpha \neq 1$ when $\alpha = 1$, but $N\alpha = 1$ in both other cases. Using the symbol $\bar{1}$ for 'Not 1', the general form of such matrices will be

C	1	$\frac{1}{2}$	0
1	1	$\bar{1}$	$\bar{1}$
$\frac{1}{2}$	1	1	1
0	1	1	1

N	
1	$\bar{1}$
$\frac{1}{2}$	1
0	1

This might be proved as follows:

(i) For the formula *CCpqCCqrCpr* we have

(*a*) $CCp1CC11Cp1 = C1C11 = C11 = 1$,

(*b*) $CCp1CC1\bar{1}Cp\bar{1} = C1C\bar{1}\beta = C11 = 1$,

(*c*) $CC\bar{1}qCCqrC\bar{1}r = C1C\alpha 1 = C11 = 1$,

(*d*) $CC1\bar{1}CC\bar{1}rC1r = C\bar{1}\beta = 1$.

These cover all cases, so this formula expresses a law.

(ii) For the formula *CCNppp* we have

(*a*) $CCN111 = CC\bar{1}11 = C11 = 1$,

(*b*) $CCN\bar{1}\bar{1}\bar{1} = CC1\bar{1}\bar{1} = C\bar{1}\bar{1} = 1$.

These cover all cases so this formula expresses a law.

(iii) For the formula *CpCNpq* we have

(*a*) $C1CN1q = C1C\bar{1}q = C11 = 1$,

(*b*) $C\bar{1}CN\bar{1}q = C\bar{1}\beta = 1$.

These cover all cases, so this formula expresses a law.

(iv) The rule of detachment holds for any C of the given type, since when $\alpha = 1$, $C\alpha\beta = 1$ only when $\beta = 1$.

§ 2. *The Sea-Battle Tomorrow*

Considered as slightly odd exercises in arithmetic or algebra, the 'two-valued' and 'three-valued' systems discussed in the last section are quite plain sailing. Some of the relations between these systems and the ordinary propositional calculus are also clear. The symbols used to express our theses about the two numbers 0 and 1 may also be used to express theses of the propositional calculus, and all formulae expressing theses with either interpretation will express them with the other. Those theses about 0, $\frac{1}{2}$, and 1 which use only Łukasiewicz's operators C and N, or others definable by means of them, will when reinterpreted form a limited segment of the propositional calculus. And analogues of the entire propositional calculus may be found within the wider three-valued system employing the undefined operator T as well as C and N. A question which we may now raise is whether the entire three-valued calculus can be given, as well as its obvious arithmetical interpretation, an interpretation in terms of the logic of propositions. When the symbols 0, $\frac{1}{2}$, and 1 are used in its associated matrices, what is clearly suggested is a logic in which propositions are thought of as being able to take a third truth-value intermediate between truth and falsity. It was precisely such an interpretation which Łukasiewicz had in mind when he first turned his attention to the three-valued calculi which Wajsberg and Słupecki later axiomatized.

That there is such a third truth-value was suggested by Aristotle himself, in the ninth chapter of the *De Interpretatione*. This chapter is concerned with propositions in the future tense about matters whose outcome is not yet determined. That there are such matters he is convinced, for otherwise 'there would be no need to deliberate or to take trouble, on the supposition that if we should adopt a certain course, a certain result would follow, while, if we did not, the result would not follow'. And 'since propositions correspond to facts', i.e. their truth or falsehood depends on their relation to facts, 'it is evident that when in future events there is a real alternative, and a potentiality in contrary directions, the corresponding affirmation and denial have the same character', i.e. have a potentiality both of being true and of being false, but are not actually either. For, Aristotle argues, it is not really possible to hold at one and the same time (*a*) that whether or not there will be a sea-battle tomorrow is as yet undetermined, and (*b*) that it is already either definitely true or definitely false that tomorrow a sea-battle will occur. For what is the case already has by that very fact passed out of the realm of alternative possibilities into the realm of what cannot be altered. 'Once it *is*, that which is is-necessarily, and once it is-not, that which is-not necessarily-is-not', i.e. when it passes from the future into the present and so into the past, a thing's chance of being otherwise has disappeared. This is the original context of the statement which we have already encountered as a subject of discussion by the Schoolmen, and we shall later consider whether this context puts a new complexion upon it. In the meantime the moral drawn from it is clear—what is not yet determined cannot be a matter of present fact, by which the truth or falsehood of a proposition uttered now can be measured. Aristotle thinks, all the same, that although neither of its parts is either true or false, the entire disjunction 'Either there will be a sea-battle tomorrow or there will not' is definitely true.

If there really are propositions which are neither true nor false but just 'potentially either', this clearly means that the logic of truth-functions, as developed in Part I, cannot be applied without modification to fields in which such propositions arise. Among medieval writers, this was perceived at least by Ockham, who in his commentary on the *De Interpretatione* tries to work out what *consequentiae* involving 'neuter' propositions Aristotle would have admitted, and what he would have rejected.[1] He takes his examples from theology, medieval writers being interested in the bearing of the three-valued theory on the doctrine of God's omniscience. What he gives us is in fact a fascinating blend of three-valued logic and theological (or theo-epistemic) modalities. Since whatever is known can be expressed in a true proposition, if there are matters about which it is not at present possible to frame either

[1] See Boehner's edition of Ockham's *Tractatus de Praedestinatione*, etc., pp. 112–13.

true propositions or false ones, it would seem that there are questions to which God cannot yet be said to 'know' the answer. Consider, then, the two propositions '*A* will occur' and 'God knows that *A* will occur', where *A* is a contingent, i.e. undetermined, future event. Can we say in such a case, on the Aristotelian view, 'If God knows that *A* will occur, then *A will* occur'? Ockham thinks we can, for the antecedent in this case is simply false, and the consequent is 'neuter', and it is fitting that we should regard false propositions as implying neuter propositions, just as they imply true ones. We have, then, $C0\frac{1}{2} = 1$, just as we have $C01 = 1$. And this means (Ockham does not pursue this explicitly, but the question plainly lies behind his actual inquiry) that 'If God knows that *A* will occur, then *A will* occur' can be laid down as true no matter what sort of event *A* may be. For if it is already determined that it will not occur, the consequent will be definitely false, and so will the antecedent, for one cannot be said to 'know' that *A* is going to happen when it is in fact not going to happen. So for this case we will have $C00$, which $= 1$ in the ordinary way. The only remaining case is that in which it is already determined and therefore true that *A* will occur, in which case God (being God) will know it, so that we will have $C11$, which also $= 1$.

Ockham also considers the converse implication, 'If *A* is going to occur, God knows that it is'. Here again, if the antecedent is false the consequent will be false, and if true, true, and in either case the whole will be true. But if the antecedent be neuter, the consequent will be false, and what will the whole be then? Ockham thinks that in this case the *consequentia* will not hold ($C\frac{1}{2}0 \neq 1$), but sees a difficulty in this conclusion. For even an Aristotelian, it might be argued, would agree that '*A* is going to occur' and 'God does not know that *A* is going to occur' cannot be true together; but in that case how can we deny that '*A* is going to occur' implies 'God knows it'? Ockham's answer is that a believer in neuter propositions would have to say that in this subject-matter 'Not both *p* and not *q*' does not always imply 'If *p* then *q*'.

The problem of constructing a truth-functional logic which allows for Aristotelian 'neuter' propositions was taken up again in 1920 by Łukasiewicz, who dealt with it much more systematically. He suggested for '*N*', '*C*', '*A*', '*K*', and '*E*' the following matrices:

N	
1	0
$\frac{1}{2}$	$\frac{1}{2}$
0	1

C	1	$\frac{1}{2}$	0
1	1	$\frac{1}{2}$	0
$\frac{1}{2}$	1	1	$\frac{1}{2}$
0	1	1	1

A	1	$\frac{1}{2}$	0
1	1	1	1
$\frac{1}{2}$	1	$\frac{1}{2}$	$\frac{1}{2}$
0	1	$\frac{1}{2}$	0

K	1	$\frac{1}{2}$	0
1	1	$\frac{1}{2}$	0
$\frac{1}{2}$	$\frac{1}{2}$	$\frac{1}{2}$	0
0	0	0	0

E	1	$\frac{1}{2}$	0
1	1	$\frac{1}{2}$	0
$\frac{1}{2}$	$\frac{1}{2}$	1	$\frac{1}{2}$
0	0	$\frac{1}{2}$	1

The ones for *N* and *C* are those already considered in the last section. As we there noted, the three-valued *Np* resembles the two-valued in being true if and only if *p* is false, and false if and only if *p* is true; while *Cpq* in both systems is true if and only if the value of *q* is at least as great as that of *p*, and false if and only if *p* is true and *q* false. In the other matrices, the corner values are the usual ones for the corresponding two-valued operators, and in both the three-valued and two-valued systems, *Apq* is true if and only if at least one of the alternatives is true, and false if and only if both are false; *Kpq* is true if and only if both its parts are true, and false if and only if at least one of them is false; and *Epq* is true if and only if both its parts have the same truth-value, and false if and only if it has one part true and the other false. With these matrices, *Kpq* is definable as *NANpNq* and *Epq* as *KCpqCqp*; *Apq* is not, however, definable as *CNpq*, but it is definable, as in an 'implicational' calculus, as *CCpqq*. (In the three-valued system, *CNpq* and *CCpqq* are not equivalent.)[1] We could also, with the above matrices, define *Np* as *Cp*o. (The last column of the '*C*' matrix, i.e. the column for *Cpq* when $q = 0$, is the same as the single column for *Np*.)

As we have noted when considering this system simply as an arithmetical exercise, all the laws involving the '*C*' and '*N*' which have the above matrices are also interpretable as laws

[1] For an enlargement of this point see my 'Three-valued Logic and Future Contingents', in the *Philosophical Quarterly*. The difference between the two systems is put to an interesting use by Z. Zawirski in 'Les Rapports de la logique polyvalente avec le calcul des probabilités', *Actes du Congrès International de Philosophie Scientifique*, Paris, 1935, vol. iv, p. 41.

of the two-valued *C–N* calculus, and similarly with laws involving operators defined in terms of '*C*' and '*N*' in the above ways. But, as we also noted before, many laws of the two-valued propositional calculus cease to hold when the operators are given the above meanings; for example, Łukasiewicz's second *C–N* axiom, *CCNppp*. Another law that ceases to be a thesis in the three-valued system is the law of excluded middle, *ApNp*. For when $p = \frac{1}{2}$, $ApNp = A\frac{1}{2}N\frac{1}{2} = A\frac{1}{2}\frac{1}{2} = \frac{1}{2}$. At this point there is therefore a divergence between Łukasiewicz's system and that suggested in the *De Interpretatione*; for Aristotle held that even when neither 'There will be a sea-battle tomorrow' nor its negation is definitely true, the alternation 'Either there will be a sea-battle or there will not' is definitely true. We could remove this discrepancy by giving a different meaning to '*A*'; for example, by defining it as *CN*. This would give to $A\frac{1}{2}\frac{1}{2}$ the value 1. But it is doubtful whether this alteration would really express Aristotle's intentions. For his ground for asserting that 'Either there will or there will not be a sea-battle tomorrow' is true was almost certainly not that an alternation is to be automatically counted true if both its components are 'neuter'. It is not because its components are both neuter, but because they are contradictories, that Aristotle affirms this disjunction. There is thus something non-truth-functional about it, and what it is would seem to be this: Aristotle has here confused two rather different propositions. The first is 'Either there will or there will not be a sea-battle tomorrow', taken as a truth-function which is true if and only if at least one of its components is true. In this sense the alternation in question is *not* true, since *ex hypothesi* neither of its components is true. The second is 'It will be the case tomorrow that either there is a sea-battle or there is not'. This is not purely truth-functional, the truth-functional 'either' being governed by the non-truth-functional operator 'It will be the case tomorrow that . . .'. There is no such operator in Łukasiewicz's three-valued system; but that system, as we shall see later, does afford grounds for considering this second proposition as true.

Ockham does not come off quite so lightly. Łukasiewicz's matrices do incorporate his ruling that $Co\frac{1}{2} = 1$, and so support his view that in all circumstances 'God knows that *A* will occur' implies '*A* will occur'. They also incorporate his ruling that $C\frac{1}{2}0 \neq 1$, and his consequent decision that when '*A* is going to occur' is a neuter proposition, the implication 'If *A* is going to occur then God knows that it is' will not be true. They do not, however, support his view that $NK\frac{1}{2}N0$ is true even though $C\frac{1}{2}0$ is not, and the solution which they suggest for his difficulty about denying the implication 'If *A* is going to occur then God knows that it is' is that although this is not true when its antecedent is neuter (and its consequent therefore false), its negation is not true either, both of them being neuter, and similarly with '*A* is going to occur but God does not know that it is' under the same circumstances. ($C\frac{1}{2}0 = NC\frac{1}{2}0 = \frac{1}{2}$ and $K\frac{1}{2}N0 = NK\frac{1}{2}N0 = \frac{1}{2}$.) The fact seems to be that Ockham just did not consider the possibility of attaching the third truth-value to *consequentiae*.[1] If this be done, in Łukasiewicz's manner, the solution of the medieval problem 'If there are neuter propositions can God be omniscient?' would seem to be as follows: Let '*Gp*' be used for 'God knows that *p*'. Then 'God is omniscient', i.e. 'For any *p*, if *p* then God knows that *p*', will be $\Pi pCpGp$. If there are neuter propositions, this will amount to $KK(C1G1)(C\frac{1}{2}G\frac{1}{2})(C0G0)$. Theology and epistemology supply us with the equations $G1 = 1$, $G\frac{1}{2} = 0$, $G0 = 0$. (Because God is what He is, He knows whatever is true, and because knowledge is what it is, neither He nor anyone else knows that which is neuter or false.) We therefore have, with *C* and *K* interpreted as in Łukasiewicz,

$$\begin{aligned} & KK(C1G1)(C\tfrac{1}{2}G\tfrac{1}{2})(C0G0) \\ = {} & KK(C11)(C\tfrac{1}{2}0)(C00) \\ = {} & KK1\tfrac{1}{2}1 \\ = {} & K\tfrac{1}{2}1 \\ = {} & \tfrac{1}{2}. \end{aligned}$$

Thus if there are neuter propositions, that God is omniscient is one of them.[2]

We may now turn to a slightly different point. We suggested in Chapter I that it is impossible to regard the modal operators

[1] Boehner (op. cit., pp. 64–65) credits Ockham with doing this, but the text does not seem to bear him out.

[2] Unless the true theology is the atheist one, in which case $G1 = 0$, $C1G1 = C10 = 0$, and $\Pi pCpGp = KK(C1G1)(C\frac{1}{2}G\frac{1}{2})(C0G0) = KK0\frac{1}{2}1 = K01 = 0$.

'It is possible that. . . .', etc., as truth-operators; but we reached this conclusion by considering a characteristic thesis of a purely two-valued truth-functional logic, the thesis *CδpCδNpδq* from Leśniewski's 'protothetic'. In a three-valued logic this thesis simply does not hold. For example, *CpApNp* and *CNpApNp* are both theses in three-valued logic (they can easily be verified by calculation), so that if *CδpCδNpδq* were a thesis we could prove *ApNp* thus:

1. *CδpCδNpδq*
2. *CpApNp*
3. *CNpApNp*

    1 δ/C'*ApNp* = C2—C3—4

4. *CqApNp*

    4 q/*CpApNp* = C2—5

5. *ApNp*.

But *ApNp*, as we have seen, is not a law in this system. And in any case the thesis *CδpCδNpδq* quite patently depends for its truth on the assumption that for any *p*, propositions with the truth-value of *p* and propositions with that of *Np* cover between them all the propositions there are, an assumption which only holds if one's logic is two-valued. The possibility therefore arises that in a three-valued logic this objection to regarding modal operators as truth-functional may collapse, and that we may in fact interpret them as truth-operators in this new system.

With considerations of this sort in mind, Łukasiewicz has suggested that we interpret '*M*', 'It is possible that . . .', as a three-valued truth-operator such that $M1 = 1$, $M\frac{1}{2} = 1$, and $M0 = 0$, defining the other modal operators by the usual equipollences—'It is impossible that . . .' as *NM*, and 'It is necessary that . . .' as *NMN*. Tarski has pointed out, further, that *Mp* may itself be defined in terms of the fundamental operators as *CNpp*. In a two-valued system, 'If not *p* then *p*', with the 'if' interpreted materially, both implies *p* and is implied by it; but in three-valued logic, while we have *CpCNpp* (this follows by the substitution *q*/*Np* in the first of Wajsberg's axioms, *CpCqp*), we have not *CCNppp*. In both systems, the implicative form 'If *p* then *q*' is true quite generally so long as *p* is no closer to truth than *q* is, so that 'If not *p* then *p*' is true so long as not-*p* is no closer to truth than *p* is; but whereas in two-valued logic the only way for this to be so is by *Np* being false and *p* being true, in three-valued logic *Np* is also 'no closer to truth than *p*' when they are both equally close but neither of them right there, i.e. when both have the value $\frac{1}{2}$. What does imply *p*, in the three-valued system, by Wajsberg's third axiom (*CCCpNppp*), is not *CNpp* but *CCpNpp*. Since *CpNp* can be shown equivalent to *CNNpNp*, i.e. to *MNp*, what this axiom says instead of 'If not-*p* implies *p*, then *p*' may be rendered 'If the very possibility of not-*p* implies *p*, then *p*.'

We may summarize the properties of the modal operators by introducing some abbreviations and some matrices. We shall use *Ip* for *NMp* ('It is impossible that *p*'), *Sp*[1] for *NMNp* ('It is necessary that *p*') and *Qp* for *KMpMNp* ('It is contingent that *p*', or 'Both *p* and not-*p* are possible'). These, with what we already have for *Mp*, give us the matrices

p	*Mp*	*Ip*	*Sp*	*Qp*
1	1	0	1	0
$\frac{1}{2}$	1	0	0	1
0	0	1	0	0

From these we may easily read off the ordinary laws of modal systems. We have, for example, *CpMp* (this is the thesis *CpCNpp* already mentioned) and *CSpp*; Lewis's 'paradoxical' laws *CIpSCpq* and *CSqSCpq*; and the Aristotelian law of contingency *CQpQNp* (which, in the absence of *CδpCδNpδq*, has no paradoxical consequences). We have also (defining *C′pq* as *SCpq*) the reduction theses *C′SpSSp* and *C′MMpMp* of Lewis's *S4*, and the further pair *C′MpSMp* and *C′MSpSp* of his *S5*. But unless we remember the character of the system we are handling, some features of the matrices for these operators will seem very peculiar. For example, *S*1 = 1, i.e. if *p* is a true proposition, then it is *ipso facto* true that it is necessary; and *I*0 = 1, i.e. if *p* is a false proposition, it is *ipso facto* true that it is impossible. The justification for these equations is that in this system a proposition is counted definitely true (assigned the value 1) only (*a*) when it is already determined that the event which it

[1] Not '*Lp*' as before, as it will be contended later that the 'necessity' now being considered is not interpretable as 'logical' necessity. (*Sα* is always true when *α* expresses a logical necessity; but *α* does not always express a logical necessity when *Sα* is true.)

refers to shall turn out as it says, or (*b*) when the event referred to has passed from the future into the present or the past, and so has lost the potentiality it had, while it was still future, of turning out otherwise. It is only propositions which are in this sense 'necessary' which are definitely true, and only propositions which are in an analogous sense 'impossible' which are definitely false. A proposition is definitely false only when any chance it may have had of being true has gone.

If this is the kind of 'necessity' which Aristotle had in mind when he said that 'once it is, whatever is is-necessarily', the medieval criticism of him as confusing *necessitas consequentiae* and *necessitas consequentis* is beside the point. The criticism would only be valid if what he intended were the necessity which consists in a proposition's exemplifying a logical law. (It is quite true that whereas the entire proposition 'Whatever is, is' exemplifies a logical law, it is not the case that whenever a thing is, the proposition that it is exemplifies a logical law.) It is in any case important to distinguish the 'necessity' which is expressed by the monadic three-valued truth-operator (1, 0, 0) from the necessity which consists in exemplifying a logical law. The latter, of course, cannot be a truth-function in any system at all—it is rather a consequential characteristic of certain truth-functions, consisting in the fact that all truth-functions formed in the same way, whatever their arguments, are true. For example, the assertion

'It is logically necessary that if Socrates is dead, he is dead'

is not automatically made true by its argument 'If Socrates is dead he is dead' having the truth-value that it does have, namely truth; it is true, rather, because this argument is of the form 'If p then p', and all propositions of this form are true. On the other hand

'(1, 0, 0) If Socrates is dead he is dead'

is true simply because its argument is true; that is, it is true for exactly the same reason as

'(1, 0, 0) Socrates is dead'

is true, though 'Socrates is dead' does not exemplify a logical law at all.

It should also be noted that the equations $S1 = 1$ and $I0 = 1$

cannot be translated into theses of the system as *CpSp* and *CNpIp* respectively. Certainly when *p* is a true proposition, *Sp* will be a true proposition, and so will *CpSp*, for it will be an implication with a true consequent. *CpSp* will also be true when *p* is false, as it will then be an implication with a false antecedent. But when *p* is a 'neuter' proposition, *Sp* will be false, and *CpSp*, having a neuter antecedent and a false consequent, will itself be a neuter proposition. Or to put it another way, the implication *CpSp* holds in the sense that from the truth of *p* we may always infer the truth of *Sp*; but not in the sense that from the falsehood of *Sp* we may infer the falsehood of *p*, for *Sp* is also false when *p* is neuter. Thus even though the truth of 'It is necessary that *p*' follows from the truth of *p*, as well as vice versa (*CSpp* is a logical law), we nevertheless commit ourselves to more when we use the modal form. For if we say 'There will necessarily be a sea-battle tomorrow' (assuming the matter of the sea-battle to be contingent) we will be definitely wrong, whereas if we say only 'There will be a sea-battle tomorrow' our statement will be 'neuter'. The logical laws that do correspond to the equations $S1 = 1$ and $I0 = 1$ are *CpCpSp* and *CNpCNpIp*, which come very close to Aristotle's '*Once it is*, whatever is is-necessarily' and '*Once it is-not*, whatever is-not necessarily-is-not'.

A peculiarity of the modal functions is that they never take the third truth-value. 'It is possible that *p*' is definitely true not only when *p* is definitely true but also when it only has the 'potentiality' of being true and false, i.e. when it is 'neuter'; 'It is impossible that *p*' is definitely false under both these conditions; and similarly with the others. This peculiarity accords well enough with our intuitive notion of a 'possibility' as that which is somehow real even when that of which it is a possibility is not yet so; and it has the effect of giving a two-valued character to the modal part of the three-valued system. Thus although *ApNp*, 'Either *p* or not-*p*', is not a law of this system, it is a law that any proposition either is or is not possible, *AMpNMp*. For we have

$$AM1NM1 = A1N1 = A10 = 1$$
$$AM\tfrac{1}{2}NM\tfrac{1}{2} = A1N1 = A10 = 1$$
$$AM0NM0 = A0N0 = A01 = 1.$$

Similarly it is a law that any proposition either is or is not necessary, *ASpNSp*. And with propositions about matters of present fact, their affirmation, and the affirmation of their 'necessity', are equivalent.[1] If *A* has now happened, then that it has now happened is necessary, i.e. beyond the possibility of alteration, and conversely; and if it has not now happened, that it has not now happened is necessary in the same sense, and conversely. (With matters of present fact, the third truth-value is 'out'; and similarly with matters of timeless fact, e.g. the truths of mathematics.) Hence the statement 'Either there is a sea-battle going on now or there is not' is equivalent to 'Either there is a sea-battle necessarily (irrevocably) going on now, or there is not', and this exemplifies the logical law *ASpNSp*. We can therefore justify the Aristotelian application of the law of excluded middle to the sea-battle to the extent of agreeing that it will be the case tomorrow that there either is or is not a sea-battle going on. And should the view that there are 'neuter' propositions be accepted, not only the law of excluded middle but the whole structure of two-valued propositional logic can be preserved by the understanding that the 'propositions' substitutable for its variables are only those referring to matters of present, past or otherwise determinate fact.

§ 3. *The Intuitionist Calculus*

The system just outlined is capable of enlargement and modification in a variety of ways. For example, 'logics' (or 'algebras', however we care to regard them) involving not merely three but an indefinite number of 'values' have been developed and studied by various workers; and within the three-valued limit it is possible to work with other types of implication, negation, etc., than those so far mentioned. For example, we might use '*N*', '*C*', '*A*', '*K*', and '*E*' for operators with the following matrices:

N	
1	0
$\frac{1}{2}$	0
0	1

C	1	$\frac{1}{2}$	0
1	1	$\frac{1}{2}$	0
$\frac{1}{2}$	1	1	0
0	1	1	1

A	1	$\frac{1}{2}$	0
1	1	1	1
$\frac{1}{2}$	1	$\frac{1}{2}$	$\frac{1}{2}$
0	1	$\frac{1}{2}$	0

K	1	$\frac{1}{2}$	0
1	1	$\frac{1}{2}$	0
$\frac{1}{2}$	$\frac{1}{2}$	$\frac{1}{2}$	0
0	0	0	0

E	1	$\frac{1}{2}$	0
1	1	$\frac{1}{2}$	0
$\frac{1}{2}$	$\frac{1}{2}$	1	0
0	0	0	1

[1] Hence the appearance in this system of the reduction theses of Lewis's *S5*. The question as to the possibility of *p* is a question of present fact; so that if *p* is possible at all, it is 'necessarily' possible.

Here *A* and *K* are as before, *Np* = *Cp*o and *Epq* = *KCpqCqp*, but *C* is different and consequently *N* and *E*. The new *N* is in fact the *I* of the previous system, and because of its difference from the other *N*, *Kpq* is no longer equivalent to *NANpNq*, though *Apq* is equivalent to *KCCpqqCCqpp*. Łukasiewicz has shown that all formulae constructed by means of these operators and having the value 1 for all distributions of the three values among their variables are deducible from the following twelve axioms:

1. *CpKpp*	7. *CpApq*
2. *CKpqKqp*	8. *CApqAqp*
3. *CCpqCKprKqr*	9. *CKCprCqrCApqr*
4. *CKCpqCqrCpr*	10. *CNpCpq*
5. *CqCpq*	11. *CKCpqCpNqNp*
6. *CKpCpqq*	12. *CCNpqCCCqpqq*.

Formulae not holding in this system include not only the law of excluded middle, *ApNp*, but also the law of double negation—at least, *CpNNp* holds, but not *CNNpp*.[1] This is a little like the Aristotelian system in which we may obvert affirmatives to negatives but not vice versa; the affirmation implies the negation of the negation, but the negation of the negation does not imply the affirmation. This new negation is as it were stronger than ordinary negation (it is, we may remember, like the 'It is impossible that . . .' of the other system)—*Np* positively conflicts with *p*, so that we cannot have the two of them together (*CpNNp*), but the negation of the negation may take us not precisely back to *p* but somewhere on the other side of it (so not *CNNpp*). The law of triple negation, however, holds, i.e. we have both *CNpNNNp* and *CNNNpNp*. In two-valued logic, we might obtain these two by performing the substitution *p*/*Np* in *CpNNp* and *CNNpp*; and in fact if we perform this substitution (and similar substitutions for the other variables) in any thesis at all of two-valued logic, the resulting formula will be a thesis, in the system now being considered. The reason is, of course, that the function *Np*, like the modal functions of the other

[1] There are other formulae which do hold in the present system but do not hold in that of the last section, for example *CCpCpqCpq*. (If this held in the other system, we could use it to deduce *CpSp*, which is not a thesis of that system, from *CpCpSp*, which is.)

system, only takes the two ordinary truth-values, so that if we prefix N to all variables, the third truth-value falls out of consideration after the first move in our truth-value calculations. We may observe this in the following for $CNpNNNp$:

$$CN1NNN1 = C0NN0 = C0N1 = C00 = 1$$
$$CN\tfrac{1}{2}NNN\tfrac{1}{2} = C0NN0 = C0N1 = C00 = 1$$
$$CN0NNN0 = C1NN1 = C1N0 = C11 = 1.$$

The present system is of some interest because if we remove its twelfth axiom and leave the rest, we have the theses used by A. Heyting to axiomatize what is called the 'intuitionist' calculus. 'Intuitionism' is a logical theory due to L. E. J. Brouwer which has arisen not from an interest in the problems of time and determinism, but from a desire to remove certain paradoxes and contradictions in the mathematics of infinite collections. They are removed—and a great deal else along with them—by a systematic refusal to employ, at least in certain fields, proofs based on the law of excluded middle and on the law of double negation in the form $CNNpp$. What Heyting has attempted to do is to provide an axiomatized propositional calculus whose implicative theses, translated into rules of inference, will justify only those forms of proof which the theory of Brouwer will admit as valid in this branch of mathematics. A peculiarity of this calculus to which Gödel has drawn attention, and which is connected with certain features of Brouwerian mathematics, is that no formula of the form 'Either α or β' is provable in it unless at least one of its components is provable. This distinguishes Heyting's theory of deduction not only from the classical theory, in which $ApNp$ is a thesis although neither the simple variable p nor the simple negation Np is a thesis, but also from Łukasiewicz's three-valued system in which $AMpNMp$ is a thesis although neither Mp nor NMp is one.

All theses of Heyting's calculus are of course theses of the three-valued system in which the operators have the matrices given at the beginning of the present section.

But (owing to the omission of axiom 12) not all theses provable in this system are provable in Heyting's calculus.[1] One which

[1] That axiom 12 would suffice to remedy this was pointed out by Łukasiewicz in his contribution to F. Gonseth's *Entretiens de Zürich* (1941).

is not is the equivalence of *Apq* to *KCCpqqCCqpp*. In fact there are no equivalences which one could use to define any of Heyting's five operators except *E* in terms of any of the others.[1] Moreover, there is no set of matrices with a finite number of elements (like 0, 1, or 0, $\frac{1}{2}$, 1, or a larger group) which would give us a many-valued logic for which Heyting's 11 axioms would be a complete basis, though some with an infinite number would. (This is another result due to Gödel's work on the intuitionist calculus in 1932.) There is much to be said for regarding Heyting's operators as not truth-functional at all but modal, and Tarski and McKinsey[2] have found a number of possible interpretations for them within Lewis's *S4*. For example, if in a thesis of Heyting's calculus we replace every simple propositional variable α by $L\alpha$, *N* by *NM*, and *C* by *C'*—i.e. if we regard his calculus as applying solely to assertions of necessity, his implications as all being strict ones, and his negation-sign as meaning impossibility—and leave his *A* and *K* alone, the result will always be a law in S4; and conversely, a formula which becomes a law of S4 when thus translated, will be a law in Heyting's calculus. Thus *CpNNp* becomes on this interpretation *C'LpNMNMLp*, i.e. *C'LpLMLp*, 'If anything is necessary, then it is necessarily possible that it should be necessary', which is a law in S4;[3] but *CNNpp* becomes *C'LMLpLp*, 'If it is necessarily possible that a thing is necessary, then it *is* necessary', which is not a law in S4, though it is in S5. This reduces the problem of interpreting intuitionist logic within classical to that of interpreting Lewis's S4.

[1] This result (for which an extremely elegant proof is given by J. C. C. McKinsey in the *Journal of Symbolic Logic*, vol. iv, 1939, pp. 155 ff.) is quite in accordance with the general spirit of intuitionist mathematics, which is not afraid to multiply indefinables. Like the 'formalist' theory sketched in an earlier note, intuitionism is opposed to the view that mathematical concepts are definable in terms of logical ones, and mathematical theses provable from logical ones. But whereas the formalist is not concerned to interpret the distinctive theses which he adds to his purely logical ones, but simply says that if there is any interpretation which fits then it will fit all other formulae which are logically derivable from them, the intuitionist insists that *his* non-logical formulae express known truths about a discernible subject-matter. The formalist, moreover, does not restrict his underlying logic in the ways described above; he employs, for example, the thesis *CNNpp*.

[2] 'Some Theorems about the Sentential Calculi of Lewis and Heyting', *Journal of Symbolic Logic*, vol. xiii (1948), pp. 13–14.

[3] For in S4 we have *C'LpLLp*; and hence (by the substitution *p/Lp*) *C'LLpLLLp*; hence (by syllogism) *C'LpLLLp*; hence (by subalternation) *C'LpLMLp*.

It is also possible, instead of interpreting intuitionist logic as a fragment of classical modal logic, to interpret the classical truth-functional logic as a fragment of the intuitionist logic. For it has been found (again by Gödel in 1932) that all theses of the ordinary propositional calculus which involve no operators but *N* and *K* are theses in Heyting's calculus also.[1] For example, *NKNNpNp*, i.e. 'Not both not-not-*p* and not *p*', or 'Not not-not-*p* without *p*', is provable from his axioms, although 'If not-not-*p* then *p*' and 'Either not *p* or *p*' are not. Consequently all theses whatsoever of the ordinary propositional calculus will hold in Heyting's also if all other operators occurring in them are defined in terms of *N* and *K*, and in particular if *C* and *A* are not identified with the undefined 'if' and 'or' of his axioms, but are separately introduced by definition, *Cpq* as an abbreviation for *NKpNq*, and *Apq* as one for *CNpq* in this sense, i.e. for *NKNpNq*. *CNNpp* and *ANpp*, for example, *are* theses in this system if we use these forms simply as abbreviations for *NKNNpNp*, and represent the undefined 'if' and 'or' of the axioms by other symbols.

This last fact suggests that ordinary truth-functional logic might be regarded as just that portion of the intuitionist calculus which exhibits directly or indirectly the properties of 'and' and 'not'; and this is a conclusion to which unsophisticated logical feeling gives some support. Unsophisticated logical feeling at all events suggests that truth-functional logic is that portion of *some* wider logic which studies the properties of 'and' and 'not'. ('And' and 'not' are the only operators which are quite unambiguously truth-functional in ordinary speech; truth-functional interpretations of other ordinary-speech connectives all wear at times an air of artificiality.) If this suggestion were taken seriously we would have to say that the differences between the intuitionist and the classical systems are not due to the employment in the former of a particularly 'strong' kind of negation, but rather to its employment of particularly strong kinds of implication and alternation. The matter is not, however, quite as straightforward as this. Both the 'classical' and the intuitionist calculi are designed for use in making inferences;

[1] See B. Sobociński, *An Investigation of Protothetic*, p. 11; J. Łukasiewicz, 'On the Intuitionistic Theory of Deduction', *Nederl. Akad. Wetensch. Proc. Ser. A* 55 (1952).

and in particular the classical logician claims for his '*C*', as the intuitionist does for his, that where $C\alpha\beta$ expresses a logical law, it is always legitimate to infer β from α. But what the classical logician means by this is that where $NK\alpha N\beta$ is a logical law, it is always legitimate to infer β from α; or at least he means something that implies this. But in intuitionist logic the rule of detachment is only laid down for the undefined '*C*' of the axioms, not for $C\alpha\beta$ in the sense of $NK\alpha N\beta$. The fact that *CNNpp*, for example, is a thesis even for the intuitionist if we take it to be short for *NKNNpNp*, does not mean that the intuitionist logic permits us to infer α from $NN\alpha$ no matter what α may be. It does not mean, to be more concrete still, that we can infer *ApNp*, in the undefined sense of *A*, from *NNApNp* (which does follow from Heyting's axioms). The intuitionist would only admit this if *CNNpp* were a thesis in the *other* sense of '*C*'—which, in his logic, it is not. He would also admit, however, that the rule

$$\alpha,\ NK\alpha N\beta \rightarrow \beta$$

does hold if the formulae α and β themselves contain no propositional operators but *N* and *K* (or ones definable in terms of them); and it could perhaps be argued that formulae constructed by means of the distinctively intuitionist operators *A* and *C* are 'propositions' only in a wider sense than that intended in classical logic, so that they may be beyond the scope of the rule without any violation of classical principles.

The point of view just sketched has been elaborated formally by Łukasiewicz,[1] but with modifications due to his desire to present the classical system which he finds embedded in the intuitionist one in a *C–N* rather than a *K–N* form. Łukasiewicz's axioms *CCpqCCqrCpr*, *CCNppp*, and *CpCNpq* suffice for the classical calculus only if all propositional operators other than *C* and *N* are defined in terms of these two, e.g. *Kpq* as *NCpNq*. If it is *K* and *N* which we have at the outset, and *C*, for example, is defined as *NKpNq*, our axiomatization will need to be different.[2] Łukasiewicz accordingly does not identify the intuitionist conjunction, in terms of which classical implication is defined, with classical conjunction; instead, using *Fpq*, *Tpq*,

[1] 'On the Intuitionistic Theory of Deduction', *Nederl. Akad. Wetensch. Proc. Ser. A* 55 (1952), pp. 202–12.

[2] Cf. I. iv. 4, and § 1 of the present chapter.

Opq, and *Np* for intuitionist implication, conjunction, alternation, and negation, he defines the classical implication *Cpq* as *NTpNq*, and then defines the classical conjunction *Kpq* as *NCpNq*, i.e. *NNTpNNq*. From ten *F–T–O–N* axioms equivalent in force to Heyting's eleven, he deduces his own three *C–N* axioms, together with the further theses *FCpqFpNNq*, *FCpNqFpNq* and *FCpCqrFpCqr*. These last, together with the axiom *FpFNpq*, he employs in showing that the rule of detachment holds not only for '*F*' but for '*C*', so long as what is detached is a purely *C–N* formula. Any such formula will be either a simple variable, say *q*, or a negation of some formula, say $N\gamma$, or a classical implication of one formula by another, say $C\delta\epsilon$. The following proof-schemata will show how, using the above four theses and the rule of detachment for '*F*' only, we may obtain a formula of any of these three sorts when given a classical implication of which it is a consequent, together with the antecedent α of this implication:

1. *FCpqFpNNq*
2. *FpFNpq*
3. *FCpNqFpNq*
4. *FCpCqrFpCqr*
5. $C\alpha q$
6. $C\alpha N\gamma$
7. $C\alpha C\delta\epsilon$
8. α

 $1\ p/\alpha = F5—F8—9$

9. *NNq*

 $2\ p/NNq = F9—F9\ q/Nq—10$

10. *q*[1]

 $3\ p/\alpha,\ q/\gamma = F6—F8—11$

11. $N\gamma$

 $4\ p/\alpha,\ q/\delta,\ r/\epsilon = F7—F8—12$

12. $C\delta\epsilon$.

[1] This deduction is of course only of use when either $C\alpha q$ or α is *not* a thesis, and when we are showing that the adjunction of one of them to the axioms results in inconsistency.

The restriction of the rule of *C*-detachment thus established to *C–N* formulae still of course leaves it sufficient, in conjunction with the rule of substitution, for the derivation of all formulae of the classical calculus from the three formulae *CCpqCCqrCpr*, *CCNppp*, and *CpCNpq*. There is thus a sense in which the entire classical *C–N* system—not only all its theses but even its mode of deriving them—is contained within Heyting's *F–T–O–N* system, rather than vice versa.

The intuitionist propositional calculus, like the classical, can be made the subject of all kinds of diminutions and extensions. We can, for example, axiomatize its purely implicational segment; or we can enlarge it by the introduction of predicational functions and quantifiers. Heyting has given some attention to this latter point, i.e. to the modifications which must be made to the theory of quantification when the underlying propositional logic is of the kind which he has systematized.[1] Since *NNp* does not imply *p*, in the intuitionist sense of 'imply', it cannot be assumed, for example, that $\Sigma xNN\phi x$ will be equivalent (in the intuitionist sense) to $\Sigma x\phi x$, or either of these to $NN\Sigma x\phi x$ or to $NN\Sigma xNN\phi x$. Heyting does not define Σ in terms of Π or vice versa, but works with a set of axioms and rules for the two quantifiers which, if combined with the ordinary propositional calculus, would yield the ordinary equipollences—$E(\Pi x\phi x)(N\Sigma xN\phi x)$, $E(\Sigma x\phi x)(N\Pi xN\phi x)$ and so on. But when combined with his own restricted calculus, while they yield some of the normal equivalences (e.g. $EN\Sigma x\phi x\Pi xN\phi x$), in a number of cases they only yield implications. Among other results, $\Pi x\phi x$ implies $NN\Pi xNN\phi x$ but not vice versa, and this means that even if we did define Σx as $N\Pi xN$, Πx would not then be equivalent to $N\Sigma xN$ (which would, of course, enlarge by this definition to $NN\Pi xNN$). Similarly his results show that if we took Σx as undefined and defined Πx as $N\Sigma xN$, Σx would not be equivalent in his calculus to $N\Pi xN$. Instead of the usual four non-equivalent quantifiers constructible by means of Πx, Σx, and N (Πx, Σx, ΠxN, and ΣxN), Heyting has ten. F. B. Fitch[2] has obtained analogous results with the introduction

[1] His work and that of others on this point is neatly wound up in his article 'On Weakened Quantification' in the *Journal of Symbolic Logic*, vol. xi (1946), pp. 119 ff.

[2] 'Intuitionistic Modal Logic with Quantifiers', *Portugaliae Mathematica*, 1948.

of modal operators into a propositional calculus of Heyting's sort; e.g. even if *M* is defined as *NLN*, *L* will not be equivalent to *NMN*, nor *M* to *NLN* even if *L* is defined as *NMN*. (In each case the form without negations implies but is not implied by the one with two, as with the quantifiers.)

Turning to systems which result from Heyting's propositional calculus by contraction rather than expansion, we obtain some striking results if we replace Heyting's eleven axioms by Łukasiewicz's equivalent ten, which consist of

(*a*) Two involving implication only: *FpFqp*, *FFpFqrFFpqFpr*.
(*b*) Three involving only implication and conjunction: *FTpqp*, *FTpqq*, *FpFqTpq*.
(*c*) Three involving only implication and alternation: *FpOpq*, *FqOpq*, *FFprFFqrFOpqr*.
(*d*) Two involving only implication and negation: *FFpNqFqNp*, *FpFNpq*.

It has been found that no thesis of the system from which any of the four symbols is absent requires for its proof any axiom of this set in which the symbol is present. (This result was first obtained by Wajsberg[1] for a slightly different set of axioms, with *FFpqFFprFpTqr* instead of *FpFqTpq* and *FFpNpNp* instead of *FFpNqFqNp*.) Thus all intuitionist theses involving implication alone are derivable from the two implicative axioms alone, this segment of Heyting's calculus forming what Hilbert and Bernays have called 'positive logic'; all involving implication and negation only are derivable from the two purely implicative axioms and the two implicative-negative ones; and so on. If we drop the second axiom involving negation, *FpFNpq*, we may also drop the first and obtain an equivalent system (equivalent, that is, to the system without *FpFNpq*) by using a constant false proposition ϕ and defining *Np* as *Fp*ϕ, without further axioms. (For *FFpNqFqNp*, considered as an abbreviation for *FFpFq*ϕ*FqFp*ϕ, is derivable by substitution in *FFpFqrFqFpr*, which follows from the purely implicative axioms alone.) 'Positive logic' supplemented by *FFpNqFqNp*, or by the definition *Np* = *Fp*ϕ, is equivalent to a non-classical calculus developed by the Russian logician A. Kolmogorov in 1925. The entire calculus without *FpFNpq*, or with both the axioms

[1] Summarized in the *Journal of Symbolic Logic*, vol. iii (1938), p. 169.

of negation removed and *Np* introduced as *Fpφ*, is equivalent to the 'minimal calculus' of I. Johannson. Johannson's original form of this[1] was obtained by dropping the similar axiom *FNpFpq* from Heyting's eleven; and an interesting feature of it is that it retains one of the paradoxes of implication—that a true proposition is implied by any proposition, *FpFqp*—but not the other. (This is only possible in a system which lacks the law of double negation, for *FpFqp* yields *FpFNpNq* by syllogism and transposition, the latter yields *FpFNpNNq* by the substitution *q/Nq*, and from this we could derive *FpFNpq*, given *FNNqq*.)

Unsophisticated logical feeling lends some support to this omission—that a true proposition is implied by any proposition, does tend somehow to be less shocking than that a false proposition implies every proposition. This difference is even more definitely felt with some of the derivative paradoxes. For example, where 'formal implication' is concerned, the proposition *CΠxφxΠxCψxφx*,

'If everything whatever φ's, then what does anything at all φ's'

is not a paradox at all, but

'If nothing whatever φ's, then what φ's does anything at all'

will not be assented to without careful explanation. Again, that whatever we do 'commits' us to doing what is right, is not nearly so incredible as that doing what is wrong 'commits' us to doing whatever we please. The 'minimal calculus' is one in which the implicative operator employed formally exhibits this felt asymmetry. And in it, as in the full propositional calculus of Heyting, all the classical *C–N* theses are derivable if we do not use '*C*' for the system's undefined 'if' but define it in terms of 'and' and 'not'; though we are no longer able, as we are in Heyting's calculus, to deduce from all *C–N* formulae which are not theses the simple variable '*p*'.[2]

[1] Summarized in the *Journal of Symbolic Logic*, vol. ii (1937), p. 47.

[2] If the reader glances back at Łukasiewicz's proof of the restricted rule of detachment for *C* within Heyting's system, he may observe the appeal made to the axiom *FpFNpq* in showing that the simple *q* is deducible from α and *Cαq*. But *FpFNpq* is not used in the derivation either of the three *C–N* axioms or of the theses used to show the derivability of *Nγ* from α and *CαNγ*, and of *Cδε* from α and *CαCδε*.

III

The Logic of Extension

§ 1. *The Logic of Classes*

THE material to be set out in the present chapter will be somewhat concentrated, and it will be as well to state clearly at the outset what its main aims are, so that we can see where the exposition is tending. Its subject is the logic of classes and relations in extension, considered as a foundation upon which arithmetic, or something very like it, may be built. Particular attention will therefore be paid in the first two sections, and especially in the second, to conceptions which are involved in this provision of logical foundations for arithmetic. In this first section we shall also give some consideration to the connexions between what we are now studying and what we have done already. And in § 3 there will be a discussion of certain rather vexing problems which have arisen in this field.

For the branch of logic we are now entering, no better symbolism (on the whole) has been devised than that of PM, which we shall accordingly for the most part employ; together, of course, with the associated notation for the propositional and functional calculi. To refresh the memory on the latter, we make the following list of the main notations, with their Łukasiewicz equivalents beside them:

$$
\begin{array}{rcl}
\sim p & \ldots & Np \\
p \vee q & \ldots & Apq \\
p \supset q & \ldots & Cpq \\
p \,.\, q & \ldots & Kpq \\
p \equiv q & \ldots & Epq \\
(x)\phi x & \ldots & \Pi x \phi x \\
(\exists x)\phi x & \ldots & \Sigma x \phi x \\
(x, y)\phi(x, y) & \ldots & \Pi xy \phi xy \\
(\exists x, y)\phi(x, y) & \ldots & \Sigma xy \phi xy.
\end{array}
$$

For bracketing, dots are generally used, and the larger the

number of dots the more comprehensive is the bracketing intended. There are special conventions for cutting down the number of dots in special cases, but with these we shall not trouble ourselves. And we will relapse into the Polish notation when formalizing the proofs of theses in the higher functional calculus on which the theory of classes depends. (We shall find that the logic of classes is simply a segment of the higher functional calculus more or less conveniently disguised.)

Of the symbols above listed, the truth-operators '$\sim$', '$\vee$', '$\supset$', etc., are used for forming propositions out of other propositions. The predicates 'ϕ', 'ψ', etc., form propositions out of names. And the quantifiers '(x)' and '$(\exists x)$' form propositions out of predicates (or out of predicational functions). We are now to consider an operator for forming names out of predicates. One such operator we have already encountered, namely (ιx), which combined with the predicational function ϕx forms 'The ϕ-er' or 'The thing that ϕ's', $(\iota x)(\phi x)$. Our new one is '$\hat{x}$', '$\hat{x}(\phi x)$' meaning not 'The ϕ-er' but 'The class of ϕ-ers', 'The ϕ-ers', 'The things that ϕ', or in some contexts just 'ϕ-er'. We have also several operators for forming propositions out of class-names. In the first place, one for expressing the membership of an individual in a class, 'ϵ'. In common speech this is 'is-a'; '$x \epsilon \hat{x}(\phi x)$' may be read '$x$ is a ϕ-er'. For the compound proposition '$x \epsilon \hat{x}(\phi x) . y \epsilon \hat{x}(\phi x)$', i.e. '$x$ is a ϕ-er and y is a ϕ-er' we have the abbreviation '$x, y \epsilon \hat{x}(\phi x)$', which may be read '$x$ and y are ϕ-ers'. Similarly '$x, y, z \epsilon \hat{x}(\phi x)$' means '$x$, y, and z are ϕ-ers'. We also abbreviate '$\sim . x \epsilon \hat{x}(\phi x)$', 'It is not the case that x is a ϕ-er', to '$x \sim \epsilon \hat{x}(\phi x)$', '$x$ is not a ϕ-er.' We shall not attempt at the moment to analyse the meaning either of 'class' or of 'membership' in a class, but will turn to this question later, and in the meantime our ordinary rough intuitive notions of what these terms mean will do.

We may define in terms of 'ϵ' another proposition-forming operator which, however, expresses a relation not between an individual and a class but between one class and another. For abbreviation in contexts in which it is not necessary to indicate the predicate from which the class is formed, we shall use 'α', 'β', 'γ', etc., as class-symbols instead of '$\hat{x}(\phi x)$', '$\hat{x}(\psi x)$', etc. When every member of the class α is a member of the class β, or more briefly when whatever is an α is a β, i.e. when we have

$(x) . x \in \alpha \supset x \in \beta$, we say that the class α is included in the class β, or that the α's are included in the β's, and write this '$\alpha \subset \beta$'. It is important to observe that '$\in$' and '$\subset$' do not express the same relation. The difference is not simply that the first term of the relation of membership must be an individual while the first term of the relation of inclusion must be a class; it is in fact possible for a class to be a member—of a class of classes. And it is just in this type of case that the difference between the two relations is most obvious. Consider, for example, the class of pairs that may be formed from the four individuals, x, y, z, and t. This class will have as its members the pairs (x, y), (x, z), (x, t), (y, z), (y, t), and (z, t). And it will itself be included in the class of two-membered classes, i.e. will be a sub-class of this class; but it will not itself *be* a two-membered class (for the number of its members is not two but six); that is, it will not be a *member* of the class of two-membered classes.[1]

We also have operators for constructing classes out of other classes. '$-\alpha$' is the 'remainder' to the class of α's, i.e. the class of things that are not α's, or $\hat{x}(x \sim\in \alpha)$. '$\alpha \cap \beta$' is the 'logical product' or common part of the class of α's and the class of β's, i.e. the class of things that are at once α's and β's, or $\hat{x}(x \in \alpha . x \in \beta)$. For the class of things that are at once α's and not β's, i.e. $\hat{x}(x \in \alpha . x \sim\in \beta)$ or $\alpha \cap -\beta$, we may use the abbreviation '$\alpha - \beta$'. '$\alpha \cup \beta$' is the 'logical sum' of the class of α's and the class of β's, i.e. the class of things that are either α's or β's, $\hat{x}(x \in \alpha \vee x \in \beta)$. Thus just as '$\subset$' is defined in terms of the propositional operator '$\supset$', so '$-$', '$\cap$', and '$\cup$' are defined in terms of the propositional operators '$\sim$', '$.$', and '$\vee$'; but not in the same way, for '$\alpha \subset \beta$' is a proposition, while '$-\alpha$', '$\alpha \cap \beta$', and '$\alpha \cup \beta$' are classes. In some more recent systematizations of class theory than PM,[2] it has been found convenient to employ a symbol '$\ni$' related to '$\supset$' exactly as '$-$', '$\cap$', and '$\cup$' are related to '$\sim$', '$.$', and '$\vee$'. That is, '$\alpha \ni \beta$' is used to mean the class of things whose being α's implies their being β's, $\hat{x}(x \in \alpha \supset x \in \beta)$. This is the same as the class of things which are not α's without being β's, i.e. the remainder to the class $\alpha - \beta$.

[1] This type of argument for the distinction between class-membership and class-inclusion was used by Frege in 1895 in a review of Schröder (Geach and Black, *Translations from the Philosophical Writings of Frege*, p. 96. Cf. also PM *51, introductory summary).

[2] Notably that in W. V. Quine's *A System of Logistic* (1934).

The extremely difficult question of what 'class' and 'member' mean may now be raised.[1] Two laws which both seem to be involved in the ordinary use of the terms 'class' and 'member' are these:

(1) $x \epsilon \hat{x}(\phi x) . \equiv . \phi x$

(2) $(x) . x \epsilon \hat{x}(\phi x) \equiv x \epsilon \hat{x}(\psi x) : \supset : \hat{x}(\phi x) = \hat{x}(\psi x)$.

(1) states that x is a ϕ-er if and only if x ϕ's; (2) that if the class of ϕ-ers and the class of ψ-ers have the same members (literally, 'if for every x, x is a ϕ-er if and only if x is a ψ-er'), then the class of ϕ-ers and the class of ψ-ers are one and the same class. In other words, (1) means that x belongs to a given class if and only if it has the predicate that marks off the class, and (2) means that different predicates may mark off one and the same class, and will do so if they attach to exactly the same objects. It is, however, very difficult to find meanings for '$\hat{x}(\phi x)$' and for 'ϵ' for which both (1) and (2) will be true. The difficulty comes out particularly clearly when we introduce modal notions. In illustrating this, we will use the symbol '$\Box$' for 'It is (logically) necessary that. . . .' One obvious and simple modal rule is that we may prefix a symbol with this meaning to any logical law. Hence if (1) were such, this rule would immediately lead us from it to the modal thesis

(3) $\Box : x \epsilon \hat{x}(\phi x) . \equiv . \phi x$.

Another very reasonable and very useful modal rule is that if the formulae F and F' are necessarily equivalent, we may replace either by the other in any logical law in which it occurs. We shall use this rule, with (3) in mind, at a later stage. Let us now turn to (2). In the consequent of (2), '$\hat{x}(\phi x) = \hat{x}(\psi x)$', the symbol '$=$' is the ordinary PM symbol for identity. The symbol for definition is distinguished from it by writing 'Df' at the end of a defining formula, thus:

$$p \supset q : = : \sim p . \vee . q \quad \text{Df.}$$

(Here the whole complex '$=$ . . . Df.' means 'means the same as';

[1] What now follows might be described as an introduction to and commentary on PM *20.

'$=$' alone simply means '*is* the same as'.) It will be recalled that in PM identity is defined as follows:

$$x = y : = : (\phi) . \phi x \supset \phi y. \quad \text{Df.},$$

or as we had it in our other notation,

$$Ixy = \Pi\phi C\phi x\phi y.$$

This definition has sometimes been criticized on the grounds that it is logically possible (though not likely to be true) that two distinct things might be exactly similar, so that everything true of either would be true of the other without their being identical. But whatever be the truth about this, it must be admitted that the converse is not possible, i.e. it must be admitted that if x and y are one and the same, whatever is true of either is true of the other. (Even if we do not admit what has been called the 'identity of indiscernibles', we must admit the indiscernibility of identicals.) So even if we reject the above definition, we must admit the implication

$$x = y : \supset : (\phi) . \phi x \supset \phi y,$$

or in our other notation

$$CIxy\Pi\phi C\phi x\phi y.$$

Applying this to $\hat{x}(\phi x)$ and $\hat{x}(\psi x)$, we obtain

$$(4)\ \hat{x}(\phi x) = \hat{x}(\psi x) : \supset : (f) . f[\hat{x}(\phi x)] \supset f[\hat{x}(\psi x)],$$

i.e. if the class of ϕ-ers and the class of ψ-ers are one and the same class, then whatever is true of the class of ϕ-ers will be true of the class of ψ-ers. From this and (2), if (2) were a thesis, we could obtain

$$(5)\ (x) . x \epsilon \hat{x}(\phi x) \equiv x \epsilon \hat{x}(\psi x) : \supset : (f) . f[\hat{x}(\phi x)] \supset f[\hat{x}(\psi x)],$$

i.e. if the class of ϕ-ers and the class of ψ-ers have the same members, then whatever is true of the class of ϕ-ers will be true of the class of ψ-ers. Now let us apply this to the case in which the class of ϕ-ers is the logical product of two classes; let it be, say, the class of things that are at once χ-ers and ϕ-ers. (5) then gives us

$$(6)\ (x) . x \epsilon \hat{x}(\chi x) \cap \hat{x}(\phi x) \equiv x \epsilon \hat{x}(\psi x) : \supset : (f) . f[\hat{x}(\chi x) \cap \hat{x}(\phi x)] \supset f[\hat{x}(\psi x)],$$

i.e. if the class of things that are at once χ-ers and ϕ-ers has the same members as the class of ψ-ers, anything true of the former will be true of the latter. For example, if it is true of the former class that it is necessarily included in the class of χ-ers, this will be true of the latter class also, or in symbols,

$$(7)\ (x) . x \epsilon \hat{x}(\chi x) \cap \hat{x}(\phi x) \equiv x \epsilon \hat{x}(\psi x) . : \supset : . \Box . \hat{x}(\chi x) \cap \hat{x}(\phi x) \subset \hat{x}(\chi x) : \supset : \Box . \hat{x}(\psi x) \subset \hat{x}(\chi x).$$

By the definitions of '$\cap$' and '$\subset$' the two parts of the main consequent of this expand respectively to

$$\Box(x) : . x \epsilon \hat{x}(\chi x) . x \epsilon \hat{x}(\phi x) : \supset : x \epsilon \hat{x}(\chi x),$$

and

$$\Box(x) . x \epsilon \hat{x}(\psi x) \supset x \epsilon \hat{x}(\chi x).$$

And the necessary equivalence of '$x \epsilon \hat{x}(\phi x)$' and '$\phi x$', which we have in (3) above, entitles us to perform substitutions turning these respectively into

$$\Box(x) : . \chi x . \phi x : \supset : \chi x,$$

and

$$\Box(x) . \psi x \supset \chi x,$$

and (7) as a whole into

$$(8)\ (x) :: . \chi x . \phi x : \equiv : \psi x . :: \supset :: . \Box(x) : . \chi x . \phi x : \supset : \chi x :: \supset :: \Box(x) . \psi x \supset \chi x,$$

or in our other symbolism

$$C(\Pi x E K \chi x \phi x \psi x) C(L \Pi x C K \chi x \phi x \chi x)(L \Pi x C \psi x \chi x)$$

i.e. 'If whatever both χ's and ϕ's also ψ's, and whatever ψ's also both χ's and ϕ's, then if it be a necessary truth that whatever both χ's and ϕ's χ's, it will also be a necessary truth that whatever ψ's χ's.' And this is clearly false. To take a concrete example, (8) would mean that if (*a*) whatever is both rational and animal is a featherless biped, and whatever is a featherless biped is both rational and animal (as might very well be true), then if (*b*) it is a necessary truth that whatever is both rational and animal is rational (and this *is* a necessary truth), it is also a necessary truth that whatever is a featherless biped is rational (but this is *not* a necessary truth).

Before sketching the PM solution of this type of puzzle, we may delimit the class of cases in which such puzzles arise. Assertions or assertion-forms into which predicates enter are of two main sorts: (*a*) those whose truth-value is unaffected if the given predicate is replaced by any 'formally equivalent' predicate, i.e. by any predicate applying to exactly the same subjects; and (*b*) those for which this is not the case. The assertion 'Something ϕ's', for example, will not have its truth-value altered if we replace 'ϕ' by any other predicate applying to the same objects; for

$$(x).\phi x \equiv \psi x : \supset : (\exists x)\phi x \equiv (\exists x)\psi x,$$

or in the Polish notation

$$C(\Pi xE\phi x\psi x)E(\Sigma x\phi x)(\Sigma x\psi x),$$

is a law of the functional calculus (it is PM 10.281). Similarly the assertion 'If anything ϕ's it χ's' will remain true if we replace 'ϕ' by any other predicate applying to the same objects, for

$$(x).\phi x \equiv \psi x .:\supset:.(x).\phi x \supset \chi x : \equiv : (x).\psi x \supset \chi x$$

or

$$C(\Pi xE\phi x\psi x)E(\Pi xC\phi x\chi x)(\Pi xC\psi x\chi x)$$

is a law of the functional calculus. On the other hand, 'It is logically necessary that if anything ϕ's it χ's' could have its truth-value altered by such substitution. For

$$(x).\phi x \equiv \psi x .:\supset:.\Box(x).\phi x \supset \chi x : \equiv : \Box(x).\psi x \supset \chi x,$$

or what comes to the same thing

$$(x).\phi x \equiv \psi x .:\supset:(x).\phi x \multimap \chi x : \equiv : (x).\psi x \multimap \chi x,$$

or in our other notation

$$C(\Pi xE\phi x\psi x)E(\Pi xC'\phi x\chi x)(\Pi xC'\psi x\chi x)$$

is not a law in any modalized functional calculus. Assertions of the first kind involving predicates are called 'extensional' functions of predicates, or, more often, 'extensional' functions of (predicational) functions. Others are sometimes called 'intensional' functions of functions.[1] Truth-functions, which have their truth-value unaltered if their arguments are replaced by other arguments of the same truth-value, are often analogously called 'extensional' functions of propositions; and all functions of functions constructed purely by means of truth-operators and quantifiers are extensional. It is only with 'non-extensional' functions of functions that difficulties arise in connexion with laws (1) and (2).

From any non-extensional function of functions $f(\phi x)$ we may easily construct an extensional one, for whether 'f' itself be extensional or not, the function

$$(\exists\psi) : . (x) . \psi x \equiv \phi x : f(\psi x),$$

or in the Polish notation

$$\Sigma\psi K(\Pi x E\psi x\phi x)(f\psi)$$

will always be an extensional function of ϕ. In words, this function is 'There is some predicate ψ, applying to the same objects as ϕ, for which $f(\psi)$ holds'. Clearly if ϕ here be replaced by any other predicate χ applying to the same objects, the truth-value of this will be unaltered; for if χ applies to the same objects as ϕ, then ψ will apply to the same objects as χ if and only if it applies to the same objects as ϕ, and the rest of the function (the conjunct '$f\psi$' and the introductory '$\Sigma\psi K$') will not be changed by the replacement.

Where the function $f\phi$ is itself already an extensional function of ϕ, the 'associated extensional function'

$$\Sigma\psi K(\Pi x E\psi x\phi x)(f\psi),$$

will be equivalent to it. For (*a*) whether $f\phi$ be extensional or not it implies that there is at least one predicate, namely ϕ itself, which applies to the same objects as ϕ does and of which f is true. And (*b*), if $f\phi$ be extensional, we will have

$$C(\Pi x E\psi x\phi x)(Cf\psi f\phi),$$

[1] The distinction between 'extension' and 'intension' is broadly the same as Mill's between 'denotation' and 'connotation'. (For some useful secondary distinctions see Keynes, *Formal Logic*, Part I, ch. ii.)

and from this we will be able to prove the converse implication as follows:

1. $C\Pi xE\psi x\phi xCf\psi f\phi$

2. $CCpCqrCKpqr$

$2\ p/\Pi xE\psi x\phi x,\ q/f\psi,\ r/f\phi = C1\text{—}3$

3. $CK\Pi xE\psi x\phi xf\psi f\phi$

$3\times\Sigma 1 = 4$

4. $C\Sigma\psi K\Pi xE\psi x\phi xf\psi f\phi$.

But where *f* is not extensional, it will not be thus equivalent to the 'associated extensional function' (obviously, for if it were, it would itself be extensional).

Returning to classes, in PM '$\hat{x}(\phi x)$' and 'ϵ' are so defined that (*a*) every assertion about the class $\hat{x}(\phi x)$ is equivalent to one about the predicational function ϕx, and (*b*) to find this equivalent assertion we proceed in two stages. First we replace '$x\epsilon\hat{x}(\phi x)$' by 'ϕx' (all other operators on classes being defined in terms of 'ϵ'), and then we replace the resulting function $f(\phi x)$ by the associated extensional function $(\exists\psi).:(x).\psi x\equiv\phi x:f(\psi x)$. (The precise definition by which this result is achieved is somewhat odd and artificial,[1] but that is unimportant.) In view of what has been said in the last paragraph, the second step in the 'reduction' is not necessary where $f(\phi x)$ is already extensional, but in other cases it is important. For example, the assertion

$$\Box.\hat{x}(\psi x)\subset\hat{x}(\chi x),$$

[1] '$\hat{x}(\phi x)$' is defined (PM 20.01) by saying that to make any statement about $\hat{x}(\phi x)$ is to make the extensional statement associated with *the same* statement about predicates, it being thus assumed that we can say such things as 'ϕ's is included in ψ's', 'x is a ϕ's', etc. A definition is then given, not for '$x\epsilon\hat{x}(\phi x)$', but for '$x\epsilon\phi x$', 'x is a ϕ's.' This is said to mean 'x ϕ's' (PM 20.02). From this and the definition of '$\hat{x}(\phi x)$' it follows that '$x\epsilon\hat{x}(\phi x)$', 'x is a ϕ-er', means

$$(\exists\psi).:(x).\psi x\equiv\phi x:\psi x,$$

and since 'ϕx' is an extensional function of ϕ (for we have

$$(x).\phi x\equiv\psi x:\supset:\phi x\equiv\psi x,$$

by the law of identity and $\Pi 1$) we may infer that '$x\epsilon\hat{x}(\phi x)$' is equivalent to 'ϕx' simply (PM 20.3).

'The class of ψ-ers is necessarily included in the class of χ-ers', is not really equivalent to

$$\Box(x).\psi x \supset \chi x,$$

'ψ-ing necessarily implies χ-ing', but rather to the associated extensional function

$$(\exists\theta).:(x).\theta x \equiv \psi x:\Box(x).\theta x \supset \chi x,$$

'Some predicate which applies to exactly the same objects as ψ does, necessarily implies χ-ing'. And this does follow from 'The predicate Both-χ-and-ϕ applies to exactly the same objects as ψ does' and 'At-once-χ-ing-and-ϕ-ing necessarily implies χ-ing'. So 'The class of ψ-ers is necessarily included in the class of χ-ers', properly interpreted, does follow from 'The class of things that are at once χ-ers and ϕ-ers has the same members as the class of χ-ers' and 'The class of things that are at once χ-ers and ϕ-ers is necessarily included in the class of χ-ers.'[1] In fact all inclusion is necessary inclusion, on this interpretation of it; for whenever all that ψ's χ's, the ψ-ers will coincide with the things which at once ψ and χ, so that there will always be at least one predicate—Both-ψ-ing-and-χ-ing—applying to the same objects as ψ does, and such that it will be a tautology to say that whatever does this thing χ's. To put it in another way, when modal operators (and non-extensional operators generally) are prefixed to assertions about classes, their meaning is so 'flattened' that it becomes a matter of indifference whether one attaches them or not. The whole 'class' language is in fact simply a device for making extensional assertions about predicates, and its rules of interpretation are such that we just cannot make any other sort of assertion about predicates in this language.

[1] In dealing with long formulae like those used in deriving our modal paradox, where '$x \in \hat{x}(\phi x)$' occurs within statements which are themselves within other statements, which in turn also count as being in a sense 'statements about $\hat{x}(\phi x)$', it is difficult to know how large a bit to take hold of to begin the 'translation'; and the rules of translation are such that one obtains different results by starting from different bits. We encountered this same difficulty in connexion with singular descriptions; in both cases it is met in PM by elaborate and awkward conventions to remove the ambiguity. Modal paradoxes, incidentally, can be constructed with singular descriptions as well as with classes. (See W. V. Quine, 'The Problem of Interpreting Modal Logic', *Journal of Symbolic Logic*, vol. xii (1947), pp. 43–48, and the answer to this by F. B. Fitch, 'The Paradox of the Morning Star and the Evening Star', *Philosophy of Science*, vol. xvi (1949), pp. 137–41.)

This being understood, the equivalence of '$(x) . x \in \alpha \equiv x \in \beta$' to '$\alpha = \beta$' (PM 20.43) may be granted,[1] and we shall hereafter employ '$\alpha = \beta$' as if it were an abbreviation for '$(x) . x \in \alpha \equiv x \in \beta$' just as '$\alpha \subset \beta$' is an abbreviation for '$(x) . x \in \alpha \supset x \in \beta$'. In view of the relation between equivalence and implication

$$(p \equiv q : \equiv : p \supset q . q \supset p;\ EEpqKCpqCqp),$$

a law which we may lay down here is

$$\alpha = \beta : \equiv : \alpha \subset \beta . \beta \subset \alpha$$

(PM 22.41), and also, in view of another relation between equivalence and implication ($p \supset q . : \equiv : . p : \equiv : p . q$; $ECpqEpKpq$),

$$\alpha \subset \beta . \equiv . \alpha = \alpha \cap \beta$$

(PM 22.621). Other laws may be stated when we have symbols for two new notions. The class of objects which are identical with themselves, $\hat{x}(x = x)$, is called the 'universal class', and symbolized by 'V'. Its remainder ('$-$V'), i.e. the class of objects which are not identical with themselves, $\hat{x}(x \neq x)$, is called the null class, and symbolized by 'Λ'. It is plain that everything belongs to the former class and nothing to the latter, and it will often be convenient to read 'V' as 'Everything' and 'Λ' as 'Nothing'. It must be remembered, however, that 'thing' and 'non-thing' are not class-names in PM; we only have operators corresponding to the whole phrase 'Everything is a . . .' and 'Nothing is a . . .' We might put it this way: In the propositional calculus we may introduce a 'standard false proposition', say *Πpp*; but we cannot introduce a proposition whose whole meaning consists in its being false—it must already have a meaning before we can judge that it *is* false. Similarly, in our present field we can introduce a 'standard empty class'; but we cannot introduce a class defined simply by its being

[1] '$(x) . x \in \alpha \equiv x \in \beta$' is obviously *implied* by '$\alpha = \beta$', i.e. by '$(f) . f\alpha \supset f\beta$'. That it also *implies* it, has really been shown earlier. For the definitions of '$=$' and '$\hat{x}(\phi x)$' first turn

$$(x) : x \in \hat{x}(\chi x) . \equiv . x \in \hat{x}(\phi x) . : \supset : . \hat{x}(\chi x) = \hat{x}(\phi x)$$

into $$(x) : x \in \hat{x}(\chi x) . \equiv . x \in \hat{x}(\phi x) . : \supset : . (f) . f[\hat{x}(\chi x)] \supset f[\hat{x}(\phi x)]$$

and then turn the consequent of this into the same statement about the extensional functions of χx and ϕx 'associated' with $f(\chi x)$ and $f(\phi x)$; and that these are equivalent when χ and ϕ apply to the same objects—i.e. that they *are* extensional—has already been shown.

empty—some criterion for marking off a class's members must be already given before we can judge that it has none.

By means of the operators 'Everything is a . . .' and 'Nothing is a . . .', we can of course express the universality of the universal class and the nullity of the null class; the former by '$(x) x \in V$' (PM 24.104) and the latter by '$\sim(\exists x) x \in \Lambda$'. '$(\exists x) x \in \alpha$', '$\alpha$ has members', being sometimes abbreviated to '$\exists ! \alpha$', we may also express the nullity of the null class by '$\sim \exists ! \Lambda$' (PM 24.54). And with 'V' and 'Λ' at our disposal, we may set down the following equivalences:

$$\alpha \subset \beta . \equiv . \alpha - \beta = \Lambda . \equiv . -\alpha \cup \beta = V$$

(PM 24.3 and 24.31). The 'class' locution for the paradoxical law 'If nothing ϕ's, then everything that ϕ's ψ's' is 'If a class is empty it is included in any class at all', $\sim \exists ! \alpha . \supset . \alpha \subset \beta$; from which, along with $\sim \exists ! \Lambda$, we may infer $\Lambda \subset \beta$, 'The null class is included in every class' (PM 24.12).

The nineteenth-century 'logical algebra' of Boole (which Venn's diagrams were designed to illustrate) was an early 'calculus of classes'. This was thus the first branch of logic to be put into the 'calculus' form. In Boole's writings the universal class and the null class (undefined) are represented by '1' and '0'. These symbols cannot be used in this way in PM, as they are required for another purpose, in fact for their ordinary purpose. For the main aim of PM is to show that the conceptions of arithmetic are at bottom logical ones, definable in purely logical terms, and its laws deducible from logical laws. Some of the beginnings of this derivation we may now sketch.

Just as there are classes with no members at all, so there are classes with only one, called 'unit classes'. Given any individual x, we can construct a unit class, namely the class of individuals identical with x, $\hat{y}(y = x)$, generally abbreviated to $\iota ' x$. By this means any assertion of class membership may be equated with an assertion of class inclusion, for

$$x \in \alpha . \equiv . \iota ' x \subset \alpha$$

(PM 51.2. Cf. Pseudo-Scotus's equation of 'Socrates is running' with 'Everything that is Socrates is running', in dealing with the *syllogismus expositorius*). And a unit class may be defined as any α for which there is some individual x such that α coincides with the class of individuals identical with x. In expressing this definition formally, what is defined is the *class* of unit classes, and this is identified with the number 1. (To say 'α is a unit class' is to say 'α is a one'; 'one' is the general term which applies to all such classes.) '1', then, is defined as follows:

$$1 = \hat{\alpha}[(\exists x)\alpha = \iota`x] \text{ Df.}$$

(PM 52.01). An important thesis concerning 1 is this:

$$\alpha \in 1 \cup \iota`\Lambda \,.:\equiv:.\, (x, y):x, y \in \alpha \,.\supset.\, x = y$$

(PM 52.4). On the left-hand side, $\iota`\Lambda$ is 'the class of classes identical with the null class', or the class of no-membered classes. $1 \cup \iota`\Lambda$ is therefore the class of classes which are either one-membered or no-membered; and $\alpha \in 1 \cup \iota`\Lambda$ may be read 'α is at most one-membered'. The right-hand side reads 'For every x and y, if x and y are α's, then x is identical with y'. This is simply the scholastic 'Every α is (identical with) every α', and what PM 52.4 asserts is that this is the case if and only if α has at most one member. De Morgan's conclusion, it may be recalled, was that 'Every α is every α' holds only when α has exactly one member; but de Morgan's logic did not admit empty classes.

Just as the number 1 is identified in PM with the class of one-membered classes, so the number 0 is identified with the class of no-membered classes, $\hat{\alpha}(\alpha = \Lambda)$, or $\iota`\Lambda$ (PM 54.01), and the number 2 with the class of two-membered classes ('α is a two' means 'α is a pair'). To give the definition in non-numerical terms, a '2' is a class α for which there are objects x and y such that x and y are not the same and any member of α is either identical with x or identical with y; in symbols,

$$2 = \hat{\alpha}[(\exists x, y):x \neq y \,.\, \alpha = \iota`x \cup \iota`y] \quad \text{Df.}$$

(PM 54.02). But it is not at this stage asserted that 0, 1, and 2, thus defined, are numbers; that cannot be said until 'number' has been defined, and much more ground must be covered before this is possible.

§ 2. *Relations in Extension and the Foundations of Arithmetic*

If we arrange the objects, *A*, *B*, *C*, etc., in the universe in pairs in all possible ways, we obtain an array like this:

$A{:}A$,	$B{:}A$,	$C{:}A$,	$D{:}A$,	etc.
$A{:}B$,	$B{:}B$,	$C{:}B$,	$D{:}B$,	etc.
$A{:}C$,	$B{:}C$,	$C{:}C$,	$D{:}C$,	etc.
$A{:}D$,	$B{:}D$,	$C{:}D$,	$D{:}D$,	etc.
etc.	etc.	etc.	etc.	

And just as we may regard monadic predicates as dividing the universe of objects into two parts, the 'class' of objects to which the predicate attaches, and the remainder to this class, so we may regard a dyadic predicate as similarly dividing the 'universe of pairs' into two parts, the class of pairs such that the first member is related to the second in the way that the predicate indicates, and the rest. A class of pairs thus marked off by a dyadic predicate constitutes the 'extension' of the predicate, just as the class of individuals marked off by a monadic predicate constitutes its extension; and such a class of pairs may be called a 'relation in extension'. In PM it is usually just called a 'relation'.

By analogy with the symbolism for classes, the class of pairs x, y such that x ϕ's y is denoted by '$\hat{x}\hat{y}[\phi(x,y)]$'. Where it is not necessary to indicate the dyadic predicate used to mark off the relation, we may symbolize it by a single letter such as 'R' or 'S'. And corresponding to the statement-form '$x \epsilon \alpha$', 'x is an α', in class theory, we have in the theory of relations the statement-form 'x is an R (e.g. a ϕ-er) of y', written 'xRy'. Between relations, as between classes, there are relations of inclusion and identity, indicated by the same symbols as in class theory, with a dot added in a suitable place. '$R \mathrel{\dot{\subset}} S$', 'The relation R is included in the relation S', means 'If anything is an R of anything then it is an S of that thing', $(x,y) . xRy \supset xSy$. '$R \doteq S$', 'The relation R is identical with the relation S', is equivalent to $(x,y) . xRy \equiv xSy$, 'If and only if a thing is an R of something, it is an S of that thing'. Like classes, relations have remainders, logical sums, and logical products. $\dot{-}R$, the remainder to R, is definable as $\hat{x}\hat{y}\,({\sim}\, xRy)$, 'the pairs x, y such that x is not an R of y'. R $\mathrel{\dot{\cap}}$ S, the logical product of R and S, is $\hat{x}\hat{y}(xRy . xSy)$; and $R \mathrel{\dot{\cup}} S$, the logical sum of R and S, is $\hat{x}\hat{y}(xRy . \vee . xSy)$. The remainder to the relation 'teacher' is 'non-teacher'; the logical product of 'teacher' and 'parent', 'teacher-and-parent'; and their logical sum, 'teacher or parent'. The universal relation $\dot{V}$ is the class of pairs x, y such that x is identical with itself and y is identical with itself, $\hat{x}\hat{y}(x = x . y = y)$; and the null relation $\dot{\Lambda}$ is the remainder to this. That a relation R is not null, i.e. that $(\exists x, y)xRy$, is expressed by the formula $\dot{\exists}!R$.

To every thesis in the calculus of classes, there corresponds a thesis in the calculus of relations. Thus we have in the calculus of relations the equivalences

$$R \mathrel{\dot{\subset}} S : \equiv : R \mathrel{\dot{-}} S \doteq \dot{\Lambda} : \equiv : \dot{-}R \mathrel{\dot{\cup}} S \doteq \dot{V}.$$

But associated with the logic of relations are a number of conceptions which have no parallel in the logic of classes. There are, for example, other special relations beside $\dot{V}$ and $\dot{\Lambda}$; in particular the pair I and J. I is the relation of identity, $\hat{x}\hat{y}(x = y)$; in our diagrammatic array of pairs, it is the set of pairs going down diagonally from the top left corner—A:A, B:B, C:C, etc. J is its remainder. The four relations $\dot{V}$, $\dot{\Lambda}$, I and J (differently symbolized) figure prominently in the work of Peirce, who developed, and Schröder, who systematized, the logic of relations after de Morgan. A relation in which identity is included, i.e. a relation R such that

$$(x, y) . xIy \supset xRy,$$

or a relation which everything has to itself (to 'its identical'), is called 'reflexive'. A relation which is included in diversity, i.e. a relation R such that

$$(x, y) . xRy \supset xJy,$$

or a relation which a thing has only to 'its Others', and never to itself, is called 'irreflexive'. 'Fellow-countryman' is an example of the former, 'father', of the latter. Some relations are neither; e.g. not everybody is a shaver of himself, but some are. These are sometimes called 'non-reflexive'.

There are, again, ways of forming relations out of other relations which have no analogues among the ways of forming classes out of other classes. In particular, there are the two studied by de Morgan—the formation of the converse of a relation, and of what is now called the 'relative product' of two relations. The converse of R, written $\breve{R}$, is defined as $\hat{x}\hat{y}(yRx)$, and the relative product of R and S, written $R|S$ (R of an S), as $\hat{x}\hat{y}[(\exists z):xRz.zSy]$. These definitions give the obvious equivalences

$$x\breve{R}y \equiv yRx$$

$$xR|Sy.:\equiv:.(\exists z):xRz.zSy.$$

We can now put de Morgan's Theorem K (see II. ii. 4) into the PM notation as

$$R|S \subset T: \equiv :\breve{R}|\dot{-}T \subset \dot{-}S: \equiv :\dot{-}T|\breve{S} \subset \dot{-}R.$$

His use of it to derive Bocardo and Baroco from Barbara amounts to the substitution for R, S, and T of the particular relation $\hat{\alpha}\hat{\beta}(\alpha \subset \beta)$. As in de Morgan, a 'convertible' (or as it is now called 'symmetrical') relation is defined as an R such that $\breve{R} \doteq R$, and a 'transitive' one as an R such that $R|R \subset R$. The method of definition is similar to that for defining 'unit class'. The class of transitive relations is written 'Trans', and this is defined (PM 201.01) by writing

$$\text{Trans.} = .\hat{R}(R|R \subset R) \quad \text{Df.}$$

Aristotle and the Schoolmen thought of the relation between a relation and its converse (or as they said, its 'correlative') as a form of 'opposition',[1] and it has at least one important feature in common with negation, namely the fact that two applications of it bring us back where we began. Just as $\dot{-}\dot{-}R \doteq R$, so $\breve{\breve{R}} \doteq R$. To the other function, the relative product, Peirce added a number of other 'relative' analogues of arithmetical functions. For the relative sum of R and S, $R\dagger S$, he chose a function related to $R|S$ in the same way as the logical sum is related to the logical product by de Morgan's Laws. That is, he chose a function such that

$$R\dagger S. \doteq . \dot{-}(\dot{-} R|\dot{-}S)$$

The relative sum of 'parent' and 'teacher' is thus identical with the relation 'not-a-(non-parent-of-a-non-teacher)'; we might read it 'parent of every non-teacher'.[2] Peirce also regarded de

[1] *Categories*, ch. 10; *Topics*, 109 b, 18–20.
[2] *Collected Papers* of C. S. Peirce, 3. 332 ff.

Morgan's '*R* of every *S*' as a raising of *R* to the power *S*—we might write it as 'R^S'.[1] Just as we have in arithmetic $x^{y+z} = (x^y)(x^z)$, so we have in the logic of relations

$$R^{S \dot{\cup} T} \doteq R^S \dot{\cap} R^T$$

('parent of every servant or teacher' = 'parent of every servant and parent of every teacher'). And just as $x^{yz} = (x^y)^z$, so

$$R^{S|T} \doteq (R^S)^T$$

('parent of every servant-of-a-teacher' = 'parent-of-every-servant of every teacher'). In PM there is not the same profusion of arithmetical analogues, as the authors are too interested in arriving at arithmetic itself.[2] Ordinary numerical 'powers' of relations are considered, however. R^2 is obviously $R|R$. R^3 is $R^2|R$, and so on. R^1 is R itself; is there anything that R^0 might be? In arithmetic, $x^0 = 1$; 1 is the number which, multiplied by x, gives x^1 in the same way as $x^1 \times x$ gives x^2, etc. What is it which is related to 'parent' itself as 'parent' is related to 'parent of a parent', 'parent of a parent' to 'parent of a parent of a parent', etc? What, of a parent, is a parent? Plainly an identical of a parent is a parent; so $R^0 \doteq I$. (This requires a slight qualification,[3] but that need not be given here.)

Another peculiarity of the logic of relations is that when we form the descriptive function $(\iota x)(xRy)$, 'the *R* of *y*', we may regard this not only as a name or quasi-name formed out of the predicate *Ry*, but also as a name or quasi-name formed out of the name *y*. Thus considered, 'the *R* of *y*' is written $R\text{`}y$, and called a 'descriptive function' of the argument *y*. Descriptive functions are very common in mathematics—the square of *y*, the cube of *y*, etc.—and also in logic itself (whether mathematics be simply a continuation of logic or not). Thus 'the class of all classes included in α' is a descriptive function of α, and may be written $Cl\text{`}\alpha$. On this subject PM has the following theorem:

$$63{\cdot}55.\ Cl\text{`}\alpha = Cl\text{`}\beta\,.\equiv.\,\alpha = \beta$$

i.e. 'the class of classes included in α is the same as the class of

[1] *Collected Papers* of C. S. Peirce, 3. 77 ff.

[2] A useful article which covers ground neglected in PM is A. Tarski's 'On the Calculus of Relations', *Journal of Symbolic Logic*, vol. vi (1941), pp. 73 ff.

[3] See PM 90.15.

classes included in β if and only if α is the same class as β’. Replace the identities here by inclusions, and we have

$$Cl‘\alpha \subset Cl‘\beta . \equiv . \alpha \subset \beta$$

i.e. ‘the class of α’s sub-classes is included in the class of β’s sub-classes if and only if α is included in β’, which is a way of stating the Theophrastean thesis that ‘All of anything, all of which is α, is β’ (i.e. ‘For any γ, if all γ’s are α’s then all γ’s are β’s’) is equivalent to ‘All α’s are β’s’.

A simpler logical example of a descriptive function is ‘The converse of the relation R’, for which we may write *Cnv‘R*. This notation is particularly convenient when we wish to speak of the converse of a complex relation, such as $R|S$. Thus we may write down the law

$$Cnv‘R|S \doteq \breve{S}|\breve{R}$$

(PM 34.2); e.g. the converse of ‘parent of a teacher of’ is ‘pupil of a child of’. Some important descriptive functions of relations are not themselves relations but classes. For example, the *domain* of *R*, *D‘R*, is the class of objects such that they have something they are *R*’s of; e.g. the domain of ‘parent’ is the class of parents. In symbols,

$$D‘R = \hat{x}[(\exists y)xRy]$$

(PM 33.11).[1] The converse domain of *R*, *D‘R*, is the class of objects such that they have something that is an *R* of them; e.g. the converse domain of ‘parent’ is the class of children. The domain and the converse domain together constitute the relation’s field, *C‘R*. One thesis which turns out to be of some importance is that both the domain and the converse domain of the null relation are the null class, i.e.

$$D‘\dot{\Lambda} = Ɑ‘\dot{\Lambda} = \Lambda.$$

This is proved in PM (33.241) as follows: If either the domain or the converse domain of a relation has members, then there are objects related by that relation. Hence, by transposition, if there are no objects related by a relation, neither the domain nor the converse domain of that relation has members.

[1] This is not a definition in PM, because what is defined in PM is the relation *D*, ‘domain of’, and 33.11 is deduced from this and the definition of *R‘y*.

In PM, it may be noted, the descriptive function $R`y$, being an abbreviation for $(\iota x)(xRy)$, is a special case of $(\iota x)(\phi x)$. Statements containing $(\iota x)(\phi x)$ are equated with statements containing no descriptive functions but only predicational ones, e.g. $E!(\iota x)(\phi x)$ with $(\exists x):.\phi x:(y).\phi y \supset y = x$. Hence in the system of PM the notion of a predicational function is fundamental, and that of a descriptive function is derived from it. In the mathematical logic of Frege, who produced a derivation of arithmetic from logic some time before Russell did, this relation between these two conceptions is reversed, and predicational functions are treated as a special class of descriptive ones. This inversion is connected with Frege's view, to which we have earlier referred, that sentences 'refer to' their truth-values in the same way as singular descriptions refer to objects. Thus. 'The square of 2 is an even number' refers to or describes the True in the same way as 'The square of 2' itself refers to or describes the number 4. On this view we can say that the predicate '—is an even number' expresses a 'function' of whatever subject it is attached to in the same way as 'The square of —' expresses a function of whatever subject it is attached to. What object (the True or the False) is referred to by '*x* is an even number' depends on what object *x* is, in just the same way as what object is referred to by 'The square of *x*' depends on what object *x* is. A function which thus refers to a truth-value when its argument is fixed is called by Frege a 'concept'.[1]

Returning to relations in extension as they are discussed in PM, a relation *R* is sometimes such that if *x* is an *R* of anything, then nothing else is an *R* of that thing. (For example, if *x* is *y*'s father, then no one else is *y*'s father.) It is then called 'one-many', the class of one-many relations being symbolized as '$1 \rightarrow Cls$'. The fundamental property of such relations is given by the theorem

$$R \epsilon 1 \rightarrow Cls :: \equiv :: (x, y, z) :. xRz . yRz : \supset : x = y,$$

'*R* is a one-many relation if and only if whenever *x* is an *R* of *z* and *y* is an *R* of *z*, *x* and *y* are one and the same' (PM 71.17).[2]

[1] See Frege's paper 'Function and Concept' (1891), in Geach and Black's *Translations*, pp. 21–41.

[2] This is not a definition in PM because what is defined (70.01) is the general expression '$\alpha \rightarrow \beta$', which '$1 \rightarrow Cls$' exemplifies.

Technically, it should be noted, the null relation is one-many. For we can say of the null relation that for any *x*, *y*, and *z*, if both *x* and *y* stand in that relation to *z*, *x* is identical with *y*. We can say this because in fact no *x* and *y* stand in that relation to any *z*, and a formal implication with an antecedent which is always false is itself always true. (The point is plain if we express the implication thus: 'There is no set *x*, *y*, *z* such that *x* and *y* stand in the null relation to *z* without being identical.' This is true because there is no set *x*, *y*, *z* such that *x* and *y* stand in the null relation to *z*.) A 'many-one' relation, $Cls \rightarrow 1$, is an *R* such that if *x* is an *R* of any given thing then it is not an *R* of anything else. (For example, if *x* is a limb of *y*, then *x* is not anyone else's limb.) The key theorem here is

$$R \epsilon Cls \rightarrow 1 :: \equiv :: (x, y, z) : .xRy.xRz : \supset : y = z$$

(PM 71.171). The null relation is many-one for the same sort of reason as it is one-many. If, whenever *x* is an *R* of *y*, nothing else is an *R* of *y* and *x* is an *R* of nothing else, *R* is said to be a one-one relation, $1 \rightarrow 1$. A relation is clearly one-one when it is at once many-one and one-many (71.103). The null relation, therefore, is a one-one relation (72.1).

If one class is the domain and the other the converse domain of a one-one relation, the two classes are said to be 'similar'. To take the standard example, if complete monogamy could be assumed, the relation 'husband' would be one-one, and its domain (the class of husbands) and converse domain (the class of wives) would be consequently 'similar'. Similar classes always have the same number of members, for the one-one relation pairs off every member of either class with one and only one member of the other. This fact is used in PM to define 'number'. The 'cardinal number of' a given class is defined as the class of classes similar to it, or in symbols

$$Nc\text{`}\alpha . = . \hat{\beta}(\beta \text{ sm } \alpha)$$

(PM 100.1).[1] And an object is said simply to be 'a cardinal number' if there is some class *of* which it is the cardinal number, in the sense just defined (PM 100.02, 100.4). To prove that, say,

[1] This is not a definition in PM, what is defined being the relation *Nc*, 'cardinal number of'. For Frege's elaboration of a similar view of number see his *The Foundations of Arithmetic* (trans. J. L. Austin), §§ 62–73.

0 is a number, we must therefore show there is some class such that 0 is a class of classes similar to it. It is in fact the class of classes similar to the null class (73·48). For the null class is the only class which it contains, and is similar to itself, and nothing else is similar to it (73·46, 73·47). It is similar to itself because it is both the domain and the converse domain of a one-one relation; for, as we have shown above, it is both the domain and the converse domain of the null relation, and the null relation is one-one. Hence 0, in the sense of PM, is a number, in the sense of PM; or in symbols

$$0 \epsilon NC$$

(PM 101.11. *NC* is the class of cardinal numbers. It is a class of classes of classes).

The importance of the proof just sketched lies in the fact that its conclusion, '0 is a number', is one of five propositions from which Peano showed that the whole of ordinary arithmetic could be deduced, and '0' and 'number' (defined in PM in purely logical terms) are two of the three notions in terms of which Peano said that all other notions of arithmetic could be defined. Peano's third notion was 'successor', and this also is given a purely logical definition in PM, and his four other propositions proved. Whitehead and Russell, in sum, if they have not succeeded precisely in deriving arithmetic from logic (in particular, it has often been questioned whether a class of similar classes is exactly what we mean by a 'number' when we are doing arithmetic), have at all events constructed out of purely logical materials an exact formal analogue of arithmetic —a set of concepts, that is, the laws of which are exactly analogous to the laws of numbers, so that the symbols employed can be used to stand for numbers and their relations without the truth-value of the system being altered.[1] Nor is it only an analogue of some part of arithmetic which Whitehead and Russell have constructed—that much we have, as we have seen, even in the propositional calculus—but an analogue, it would seem, of the whole. Or nearly the whole; for there are certain fields of arithmetic in which the theorems only follow from the *Principia* basis conditionally, the condition being in some cases that there are an infinite number of individuals (the so-called

[1] Cf. A. Tarski, *Introduction to Logic* (English translation, 1946 edition), p. 130.

'axiom of infinity') and in some cases a more complicated hypothesis called the 'multiplicative axiom' or 'axiom of choice'. But with these exceptions, all number-theory has been provided by Whitehead and Russell with (at the least) an analogue which, when defined symbols have been removed, falls within the higher functional calculus.

To bring this point finally home, let us see how we might express in the symbolism of this calculus the statement that a certain class of classes $\hat{\alpha}(f\alpha)$ is a 'number'. In the language of predicates, this will amount, not to an assertion about such objects as the numbers 0, 1, 2, 3 (these belong to the 'class' locution, and are dispensable), but to an assertion about such functions of predicates as 'Precisely ten objects ϕ', 'Precisely twenty objects ϕ', etc. Calling these 'numerical' functions of predicates, what we have to express is the assertion that $f\phi$ is such a function. To do this fully, we need similar 'translations' of 'α is the domain of R', 'α is the converse domain of R', and 'R is a one-one relation'. For 'The ϕ-ers form the domain of $\hat{x}\hat{y}(\psi xy)$' we may give this (using the Polish notation):

$$\Pi x E \Sigma y \psi xy \phi x,$$

'For all x, x ψ's something if and only if x ϕ's.' (This is the predicate equivalent of 'For all x, x is a ψ-er of something if and only if x is a ϕ-er.') For 'The ϕ-ers form the converse domain of $\hat{x}\hat{y}(\psi xy)$' we may similarly give

$$\Pi y E \Sigma x \psi xy \phi y.$$

For '$\hat{x}\hat{y}(\psi xy)$ is one-one', we may give

$$\Pi xyz C \psi xy K C \psi zy Izx C \psi xz Izy,$$

'For all x, y, z, if x ψ's y, then if z ψ's y then z is identical with x, and if x ψ's z then z is identical with y'. ('Izx' and 'Izy' may of course be further expanded to '$\Pi\phi C\phi z\phi x$' and '$\Pi\phi C\phi z\phi y$', but we will content ourselves with the abbreviations.) '$\hat{x}(\phi x)$ is similar to $\hat{y}(\theta y)$', i.e. 'There is a relation $\hat{x}\hat{y}(\psi xy)$ such that $\hat{x}(\phi x)$ is its domain and $\hat{y}(\theta y)$ is its converse domain, and it is one-one', now clearly turns into

$$\Sigma\psi KK(\Pi x E \Sigma y \psi xy \phi x)(\Pi y E \Sigma x \psi xy \theta y)\text{-}$$
$$\text{-}(\Pi xyz C \psi xy K C \psi zy Izx C \psi xz Izy).$$

Finally, '$\hat{\alpha}(f\alpha)$ is a number', i.e. 'There is a class $\hat{y}(\theta y)$ such that $\hat{\alpha}(f\alpha)$ is the class of all classes similar to $\hat{y}(\theta y)$', or 'There is a class $\hat{y}(\theta y)$ such that if any class $\hat{x}(\phi x)$ is in $\hat{\alpha}(f\alpha)$, then $\hat{x}(\phi x)$ is similar to $\hat{y}(\theta y)$', turns into 'There is a predicate θ such that for any predicate ϕ, if $f\phi$, then $\hat{x}(\phi x)$ is similar to $\hat{y}(\theta y)$', i.e.

$$\Sigma\theta\Pi\phi Cf\phi[\Sigma\psi KK(\Pi xE\Sigma y\psi xy\phi x)\text{-}$$
$$\text{-}(\Pi yE\Sigma x\psi xy\theta y)(\Pi xyzC\psi xyKC\psi zyIzxC\psi xzIzy)].$$

For example, '$N\Sigma x\phi x$ (Nothing ϕ's) is a numerical function of ϕ' means

$$\Sigma\theta\Pi\phi C(N\Sigma x\phi x)(\Sigma\psi KK \ldots \text{etc.}),$$

i.e. 'There is a predicate θ such that for any predicate ϕ, if nothing ϕ's, then the class of ϕ-ers is similar to the class of things that θ'. And this is true; for there is the predicate '— is not identical with itself', of which we may say that, whatever ϕ-ing may be, if nothing ϕ's, then the class of ϕ-ers will be similar to the class of things not identical with themselves. This in turn is true because if we let our dyadic predicate ψxy be 'x is not identical with x, nor y with y', $KNIxxNIyy$, then if nothing ϕ's, we may truly say

(a) x ψ's something if and only if x ϕ's (for nothing ψ's anything, and nothing ϕ's), i.e. $\hat{x}(\phi x)$ is the domain of $\hat{x}\hat{y}(x \neq x . y \neq y)$.

(b) y is ψ'd by something if and only if y θ's, i.e. is not identical with itself (similar reason), i.e. $\hat{y}(y \neq y)$ is the converse domain of $\hat{x}\hat{y}(x \neq x . y \neq y)$.

(c) If anything ψ's anything, then nothing else ψ's the latter or is ψ'd by the former (true because nothing ψ's anything), i.e. $\hat{x}\hat{y}(x \neq x . y \neq y)$ is one-one.

This reproduces in the 'predicate' language the proof that 0 is a number. To have done it quite exactly we should have taken for our $f\phi$, not $N\Sigma x\phi x$, 'Nothing ϕ's', but $\Pi xE\phi xNIxx$, 'A thing ϕ's if and only if it is not identical with itself', this being the function of predicates that strictly corresponds to 'The class of ϕ-ers is one of those coextensive with the null class', i.e. 'is a 0'. However, 'Nothing ϕ's' is a 'numerical' function of predicates too, in the sense defined, and is 'extensionally' the same function as $\Pi xE\phi xNIxx$; that is, it holds for the same arguments.

Another 'numerical' function of ϕ—i.e. another which would yield a true proposition if substituted for '$f\phi$' in the above expansion of '$f\phi$ is a numerical function of ϕ'—would be '*ΣyΠxEφxIxy*', 'There is some *y* such that a thing ϕ's if and only if it is identical with *y*', which amounts to 'Precisely one thing ϕ's'; and another, '*ΣyzK(NIyz)(ΠxEφxAIxyIxz)*', 'There are a *y* and a *z* such that *y* is not identical with *z* and a thing ϕ's if and only if it is identical either with *y* or with *z*', i.e. 'Precisely two things ϕ'. '$1 \epsilon NC$' and '$2 \epsilon NC$' are proved along with '$0 \epsilon NC$' in PM *101.

§ 3. *The Paradoxes and the Theory of Types*

In the proof that 0 is a number, the concluding step is the passage from

> '0 is the class of classes similar to the null class'

to

> 'There is at least one class such that 0 is the class of classes similar to it.'

To justify this inference, we need the thesis

$$f\alpha . \supset . (\exists\beta) f\beta,$$

in which we can substitute 'Λ' for 'α' and '$0 = \hat{\alpha}(\alpha \text{ sm } \ldots)$' ('0 is the class of classes similar to . . .') for 'f'. But this thesis is not to be found in PM, the procedure of the authors being to appeal in such cases simply to theorem 10.24, i.e.

$$\phi y . \supset . (\exists x) \phi x.$$

This suggests that it is quite legitimate to substitute 'Λ' for 'y' and '$0 = \hat{\alpha}(\alpha \text{ sm} \ldots)$' for '$\phi$' in this formula. And such a liberty would in fact be very useful in this field.[1] But if we do consider ourselves thus free to substitute, e.g., classes for name-variables whenever we please, we will find ourselves in trouble.

For suppose we take a class-symbol 'β' and define 'β' as the class of all classes which are not members of themselves, thus:

$$\beta . = . \hat{\alpha}(\alpha \sim\epsilon \alpha) \quad \text{Df.}$$

[1] Russell has pointed out (*Introduction to Mathematical Philosophy*, pp. 134–5) that if we could proceed in this way without restriction the axiom of infinity could easily be given a logical basis.

We may then take the basic equivalence of class theory,

$$y \epsilon \hat{x}(\phi x) . \equiv . \phi y,$$

and by substituting 'β' for 'y' and '$\alpha \sim\epsilon\, \alpha$' for '$\phi x$', obtain

$$\beta \epsilon \hat{\alpha}(\alpha \sim\epsilon \alpha) . \equiv . \beta \sim\epsilon \beta$$

('β is a member of the class of classes which are not members of themselves, if and only if β is not a member of β'). But since 'β' is simply, by definition, an abbreviation for '$\hat{\alpha}(\alpha \sim \epsilon\alpha)$', we may substitute it for this in the last equivalence, and obtain

$$\beta \epsilon \beta . \equiv . \beta \sim\epsilon \beta$$

i.e. the class (β) of all classes which are not members of themselves is a member of itself if and only if it is not a member of itself. Reflection on the verbal statement of the case suggests the same conclusion. But since '$\beta \sim\epsilon \beta$' means '$\sim(\beta \epsilon \beta)$', our conclusion is of the form '$p \equiv \sim p$', i.e. '$p \supset \sim p . \sim p \supset p$'. But by the law of *reductio ad absurdum* (the first thesis proved in PM, 2.01), the conjunct '$p \supset \sim p$' implies '$\sim p$'; and by the *consequentia mirabilis* (PM 2.18), the other conjunct '$\sim p \supset p$' implies 'p'. So if the above substitutions are permissible the system of PM is one in which we can draw contradictory conclusions.

This paradox, however, is Russell's own; and a great deal of verbal explanation and symbolic machinery in PM is expressly devoted to preventing it and similar paradoxes from appearing. The essence of the PM view is that, although classes are in a sense objects—we can make true and intelligible statements about them, such as that one class is included in another, or that a class has such and such a number of members—they are not objects in the same sense as individuals are, and classes of classes are similarly not objects in the same sense as classes of individuals are. The subjects of our predications in fact fall into an infinite hierarchy of 'logical types'—individuals, classes of individuals, classes of classes of individuals, classes of classes of classes of individuals, and so on—and what can intelligibly be said about objects of one type cannot be said about objects of another type. Type-distinctions must be particularly attended to when forming propositions by means of logical operators and connectives, for some of these, such as identity, can only connect objects of the same logical type, while others, such as membership, can only connect objects whose logical types differ in certain specific ways. Thus we may write '$x = y$' or '$\alpha = \beta$', but not '$x = \beta$' or '$\alpha = y$'; and we may write '$x \epsilon \alpha$', and also '$\alpha \epsilon \kappa$', where 'κ' is a class of classes, but not '$x \epsilon y$' or '$\alpha \epsilon \beta$' or '$\kappa \epsilon \kappa$'. Nor may we say that the result of writing, say, '$x \epsilon y$', is simply false, for in that case it would be legitimate to write '$x \sim\epsilon y$'; the fact is rather that neither '$x \epsilon y$' nor '$x \sim\epsilon y$' is a genuine proposition. The same applies to '$x \epsilon \kappa$' and '$x \sim\epsilon \kappa$', for although here the logical type of the right-hand term κ is higher than that of the left-hand term x, as ought to be the case when the connective is 'ϵ', it is not one type higher but two types higher, and this produces nonsense also. (We shall illustrate this shortly.) It follows from this that the simple substitution of, say, class-variables for name-variables is never legitimate, and will always turn sense into nonsense. It is not legitimate, for example, to substitute 'Λ' for 'y' in

$$`\phi y . \supset . (\exists x) \phi x'.$$

'ϕy' is a formula which could represent such a proposition as 'Socrates smokes'; but 'The null class smokes' is neither true nor false; it is not a proposition at all. Two substitutions which separately make nonsense may, however, together make sense. For example, if in ϕy we simultaneously substitute 'Λ' for 'y' and '$(x) . x \sim\epsilon$ . . .' for 'ϕ . . .', we obtain a quite genuine and obviously true proposition about the null class. We might say that the thesis '$f\alpha . \supset . (\exists \beta) f\beta$' is an 'analogue' of 10.24, and Whitehead and Russell treat 10.24 as if it stated itself and all its analogues at once. (They let their symbols be 'systematically ambiguous' as to their logical type.) We might also say that the most serious logical sin committed in the proof of the paradoxical thesis $\beta \epsilon \beta . \equiv . \beta \sim\epsilon \beta$ is not the substitution of β for y in the thesis $y \epsilon \hat{x}(\phi x) . \equiv . \phi y$, but the use of such a formula as '$\alpha \sim\epsilon \alpha$' in the first place. It is nonsense to talk of a class as either being a member of itself or not being a member of itself.

In the first edition of PM this theory of type-distinctions among logical subjects was complicated by having dovetailed into it a theory of distinctions of 'order' among logical predicates. Even between predicates attaching to subjects of the same logical type, Whitehead and Russell argued, there are sometimes differences radical enough to be a barrier to substitution. Consider, for example, the two predicates '— is temperamental' and '— has all the characteristics of a great artist'. Both are predicates attaching to individuals, but if we call the former a 'first-order' predicate we must call the latter a 'second-order' predicate, because it contains an implicit reference to all predicates of the first sort. '— has all the characteristics of a great artist' means 'If any characteristic belongs to a great artist, then — has it'. The characteristics here mentioned, according to the 'ramified' theory of types propounded in the first edition of PM, cannot without a sort of circularity include this very characteristic of having-all-the-characteristics-of-a-great-artist, or any others like it. This restriction was found, however, to invalidate certain very fruitful mathematical procedures, and to save these Whitehead and Russell introduced into their system a mitigating 'axiom of reducibility', to the effect that for any predicate of higher order there may be found a 'formally equivalent' predicate of the lowest order. For example, there is (according to this axiom) some first-order characteristic present in all those, and only those, who have the second-order characteristic of having all the characteristics of a great artist. On the face of it, the axiom of reducibility, even if true, would express a fact of nature rather than a law of logic, and it was an early target of criticism. F. P. Ramsey attempted to remove this blemish in the system of PM by excising that part of the theory of types which seemed to make it necessary, i.e. the part relating to predicates of different 'orders'. He argued[1] that the distinction of 'orders' is not one between actual characteristics, but only one between the symbols by which we represent them. For example, 'If any characteristic is one belonging to every great artist, then it belongs to y' is just a particular way (a very convenient way, and owing to our limitations the only way open to us) of writing down the conjunction of first-order assertions 'If every great artist ϕ's then y ϕ's, and if every great artist ψ's then y ψ's, and if every great artist θ's then y θ's', and so on until all first-order predicates have been used. According to a theory of Wittgenstein's adopted by Ramsey at this time, 'Both

[1] *The Foundations of Mathematics*, pp. 20–21, 32–39.

A and *A*' and '*A*', being tautologously equivalent, are just different ways of saying the same thing; hence 'Both *A* and *B*, and both *A* and *B*' and '*A*, and *B*, and both *A* and *B*', have exactly the same meaning as 'Both *A* and *B*'; so if, having written down the above list of first-order characters, we add to them the entire list, what the new list means is exactly what the old one did. We may therefore without circularity include 'having all the characteristics of a great artist' among the characteristics of great artists; its inclusion is just like adding 'and both *A* and *B*' to '*A*, and *B*', and leaves things exactly as they were. This 'deramification' of the theory of types plainly involves some questionable assumptions (the identity of meaning of 'Both *A* and *A*' and '*A*', and especially the equation of universal quantification with prolonged conjunction),[1] but with the conclusion that at most the 'simple' theory of types is necessary for the avoidance of paradoxes, most logicians are now in agreement.

The theory of orders, like the theory of types, was put forward in order to eliminate paradoxes; what Ramsey argued was that the paradoxes in question differ from Russell's about the class $\hat{\alpha}(\alpha \sim\epsilon\, \alpha)$ in being all of them concerned with the relation between symbols and their meaning rather than with the proper subject-matter of logic and mathematics. On this point he would seem to be right; but it is worth glancing at these other paradoxes and seeing exactly how the paradox about $\hat{\alpha}(\alpha \sim\epsilon\, \alpha)$ is related to them. A particularly clear example is one which is not actually among those considered in PM, having been constructed since that work appeared, Grelling's paradox about 'heterological'. Suppose we classify adjectives into those which apply to themselves ('English', for example, is itself an English word), and those which do not (like 'German', which is not itself a German word), and suppose we describe the latter as 'heterological' adjectives. The question now arises, 'Is "heterological" heterological or not?' If it is, by the meaning of 'heterological', it does not apply to itself, and so is *not* heterological; while if it is not heterological, it does not apply to

[1] This perhaps amounts in itself to a kind of 'axiom of reducibility'. An odd result of it to which Ramsey draws attention (pp. 59–61) is that it makes the axiom of infinity either tautologous or self-contradictory (while leaving us no way of knowing which of the two it is).

itself, and so, by the meaning of 'heterological', *is* heterological. Here we have clearly a case in which a principle of non-substitutability of predicates of different 'orders' would be useful, while distinctions of type alone are of no help. For 'heterological' is the same kind of *subject* as, say, 'English'—it is a word, and an adjective, and moreover an adjective to be applied to words—but as a predicate, it is of a higher 'order' than 'English', for '*W* is heterological' in effect says 'For any predicate, if *W* means that predicate, it does not have it', and if we are not allowed to include this predicate of *W* among the predicates intended, the paradox cannot arise.

A similar paradox is the very old one of the Liar (generally attributed to the early Megarian Eubulides), which runs as follows: From ' "The sun is shining" is true' we may validly infer that the sun is shining, and vice versa; and similarly with other statements. But consider the statement 'What I am now saying is false'. If this statement is true, it will follow that what it says is the case, i.e. that the statement is false; while if it is false what it says will be the case, so it will be true. Calling the statement *x*, '*x* is false' and '*x* is true' turn out in this case to be equivalent, so that if either is true the other will be, and either way we shall have a contradiction. This was often included in the collections of so-called *Insolubilia* discussed by medieval logicians, and presented with variations (e.g. 'Suppose that all that Socrates says is "What Plato says is false", and all that Plato says is "What Socrates says is true" ').[1] It is not so obvious in this case that the 'ramified' theory of types would solve the puzzle while the 'simple' theory will not; but we might put the matter in this way: Whether any proposition '*S* is *P*' is true or false is determined by whether or not *S* is in fact *P*, and this 'determination' is an essentially one-sided relation—whether or not *S* is in fact *P* is *not* 'determined' in the same sense

[1] Cited from Albert of Saxony in Boehner's *Medieval Logic* (1952), p. 13. Albert seems to have been a better logician than Mr. P. E. B. Jourdain, who suggested in *The Philosophy of Mr. B*rtr*nd R*ss*ll* (1918), p. 72, that the paradox of the liar, if 'spread out a little, . . . becomes an amusing hoax or an epigram. Thus, one may present to a friend a card bearing on both sides the words: "The statement on the other side of this card is false." ' Here each 'statement' in effect simply asserts its own truth and the falsity of the other; which of them is true is quite undecidable, but neither leads to its own contradictory. But leave one side of the card as Jourdain suggests, and put on the other 'The statement on the other side of this card is *true*', and we do have the paradox of the liar reproduced.

by whether '*S* is *P*' is true or false.[1] By the same token, i.e. the essential one-sidedness of this 'determining', whether the proposition '*S* is *P*' is true or false is not determined by whether the proposition '*S* is *P*' is true or false—what is determined by that is not whether the proposition '*S* is *P*' is true or false, but whether the proposition ' "*S* is *P*" is true' is true or false. But if we attempt to construct a proposition by letting our *S* be 'what I am now saying' (i.e. the proposition itself that we construct) and our *P* be 'false', we are attempting to construct an '*S* is *P*' such that whether '*S* is *P*' is true or false will be determined by whether '*S* is *P*' is true or false. (For whether 'What I am now saying is false' is true or false would be determined, in the usual way, by whether or not *S*, i.e. what I am now saying, is *P*, i.e. false; and since what I am now saying is 'What I am now saying is false', this would be to make it depend on whether or not 'What I am now saying is false' is false, i.e. on whether this is false or true.) Determination of truth and falsity, however, just will not work this way; so what we have constructed just cannot *be* true or false, i.e. is not a proposition. A similar one-sided determination is involved in the use of 'heterological'. Whether or not 'English' is heterological is determined by whether or not 'English' is English, but there is nothing by which whether or not 'heterological' is heterological could be determined in the same way.[2] The

[1] No one is clearer on this point than Aristotle, or the Aristotelian (if it was not Aristotle) who wrote the *Categories*. In this work, at the end of ch. 12, it is pointed out that although 'the fact of the being of a man carries with it the truth of the proposition that he is and the implication is reciprocal (for if a man is, the proposition wherein we allege that he is is true, and conversely, if the proposition wherein we allege that he is is true, then he is)' nevertheless 'the true proposition . . . is in no way the cause of the being of the man, but the fact of the man's being does seem somehow to be the cause of the truth of the proposition, for the truth or falsity of the proposition depends on the fact of the man's being or not being.'

[2] Cf. G. Ryle, 'Heterologicality', *Analysis*, Jan. 1951, esp. pp. 65, 67. Ryle's development of this point is marred by being embedded with a quite different and not at all plausible explanation of the fallacy. On this other view of his, the trouble with the statement ' "Heterological" is heterological' is not that 'heterological' is a *dependent* 'philological epithet', but that it is not a 'philological epithet' at all, i.e. not a word descriptive of words. Apart from being untrue, his account of the matter has as a corollary that the application to words of quite ordinary non-philological epithets, like 'thatched' (as in ' "thatched" is thatched') results not in falsity but in nonsense (so that we cannot say ' "thatched" is not thatched' either). This sweeping restriction is not justified by any demonstration that paradoxes result from not observing it, but merely by a vague appeal to linguistic 'propriety' —' "thatched" is not thatched' is nonsense because it has an air of oddity.

ramified theory of types is just an attempt to put into formal rules this necessary respect for the one-sidedness of what we have called 'determination' (Whitehead and Russell themselves describe it as directed against 'Vicious-circle Fallacies');[1] but it is too sweeping. It might well seem that whether or not *X* has all the characteristics of a great artist is 'determined' in a one-sided way by whether or not the first-order characteristics ϕ, ψ, etc., which are all the characteristics of great artists, are all possessed by *X*; but in fact the matter is not nearly so clear in this case as it is in those which involve a linguistic element.

We may now turn back to the paradox of the class $\hat{\alpha}(\alpha \sim\in \alpha)$, which Whitehead and Russell at first assimilated to those just considered. It does unquestionably resemble them, and the resemblance is not merely superficial. Up to a point, it may be dealt with on quite similar lines; but only up to a point. There *is* a 'vicious-circle fallacy' in this paradox—a relation of 'determination' the one-sidedness of which is not respected. For talk about class-membership is only a way of talking about the possession of characters, and whether or not anything is a member of a specified class is determined by whether or not it possesses the defining characteristic of the class and not vice versa. When we turn to the supposed class of all classes not members of themselves, and ask whether or not this class is a member of itself, we find that this depends on whether or not it possesses its own defining characteristic; but this defining characteristic is 'not being a member of itself' (this is the attribute that a class must have if it is to belong to this class of classes); hence whether or not this class is a member of itself depends on whether or not it is a member of itself, which is as repugnant to the notion of class-membership as the dependence of a proposition's truth or falsehood upon its truth or falsehood is to the notions of truth and falsehood. This, however, is only half the story, for the paradox may be reproduced if we talk solely in terms of predicates, and drop the 'class' locution altogether. For consider the predicate '— is not predicable of itself', i.e. the predicate ψ such that to say that any predicate ϕ ψ's is to say that ϕ does not ϕ. We may write down this definition symbolically as follows:

$$\psi\phi . = . \sim \phi\phi \quad \text{Df.}$$

[1] See especially the Introduction to the First Edition, ch. ii.

From this definition and $p \equiv p$ we obtain the equivalence

$$\psi\phi \equiv \sim\phi\phi.$$

Substitute 'ψ' for 'ϕ' in this, and we obtain

$$\psi\psi \equiv \sim\psi\psi$$

('Non-self-predicability is non-self-predicable if and only if non-self-predicability is not non-self-predicable').

There is no cure for the paradox in this last form—where it is cleared of linguistic accretions—but to say that a predicate of individuals is one thing and a predicate of predicates another, that neither is substitutable for the other in a logical law, and that to predicate a predicate-of-individuals of predicates is meaningless. (Like the symbol 'ϵ', the juxtaposition that symbolizes predication can only join objects of different logical types.) By the former prohibition we cannot substitute ψ (which is introduced as a predicate of predicates) for ϕ (which is introduced as a predicate predicated-of) in $\psi\phi$; and by the latter, neither of the predicational functions $\phi\phi$ and $\sim\phi\phi$ may be formed at all. Ordinary language itself suggests that these prohibitions are reasonable; for although in the above exposition we have verbalized '$\psi\phi$' as 'ϕ ψ's' and '$\sim\phi\phi$' as 'ϕ does not ϕ', these translations will not really do. Remembering that 'ϕ' is a symbol for a verb, we ought to have said 'ϕ's ψ's' and 'ϕ's does not ϕ', and that this means nothing seems clear. Moreover, although in the first case our 'subject' ought to have been read not as 'ϕ' but as 'ϕ's', our predicate ought *not* to have been read 'ψ's', for the functions of predicates which we do in fact form are not themselves predicational, but are functions like '$(\exists x)\phi x$'—not 'ϕ does something', or even 'ϕ's does something', but 'Something ϕ's.' Or we might have 'Nothing ϕ's' or (moving further into arithmetic) 'Twenty things ϕ', or 'Exactly as many things ϕ as ψ.'[1] It is therefore not at all surprising that one sort of proposition-forming operator should not be substitutable for another.

This 'argument from grammar' is only to be pressed lightly.

[1] Cf. Frege, 'On Concept and Object' (1892), p. 201 (Geach and Black's *Translations*, pp. 50–51): 'Second-level concepts, which concepts fall under, are essentially different from first-level concepts, which objects fall under. The relation of an object to a first-level concept that it falls under is different from the (admittedly similar) relation of a first-level to a second-level concept.'

It does help to show the reasonableness of the restrictions which the paradoxes show to be necessary, but grammar is a very flexible instrument, and it is easy to construct secondary locutions in which what is normally said by means of a verb is said by means of a noun. The 'class' locution is one such; and there are others. For example, we can give a function of predicates the appearance of a predicational function by means of the verbal noun ending in '-ing' (and in many cases by an ordinary noun of the 'abstract' sort). Thus although we cannot read '$(\exists x)\phi x$' either as 'ϕ does something' or as 'ϕ's does something', we can read it as 'ϕ-ing is done by something'; similarly '$(x) . \phi x \supset \psi x$' turns easily into the dyadic quasi-predicational function 'ϕ-ing always implies ψ-ing.' 'That . . .' clauses will do the same for functions of propositions, giving us 'That p implies that q' for 'If p then q', and 'It is necessary that X should be Y' for 'Necessarily, X is Y'. Where quantifications of higher order are involved, the urge to proceed in this manner is almost irresistible. '$(\phi) . \phi x \supset \phi y$' may be read roughly 'For all ϕ, if x ϕ's then so does y', but in ordinary speech it would be something more like 'Whatever ϕ-ing may be, if x does it so does y'. We can only retain the verbal form of predicates in cases of this sort by complicating the quantifier—we might say 'That a thing ϕ's—let that be what it may, if x ϕ's then y ϕ's'. And the turning of forms like '$(p)p$' and '$(\exists p)p$' into idiomatic speech is practically impossible, though logic would be vastly the poorer without them, and they lead in themselves to no paradoxes. What we can say is simply that the higher-type functions have synonyms which are not predicational even in appearance; while the point about quantifiers is that they can in principle be attached to functions of any kind, predicational or not, though we only have idiomatic speech-forms for their attachment to functions which are at least in appearance predicational.

Although the $\hat{\alpha}(\alpha \sim\epsilon\, \alpha)$ paradox is not as like the old *Insolubilia* as was at first supposed, the theory of types that was evolved to deal with it did have its ancient and medieval adumbrations. Ryle has suggested that the puzzles and discussions in Plato's *Parmenides* point towards something like it,[1] and so does the Aristotelian theory of 'categories' of being,

[1] G. Ryle, 'Plato's *Parmenides*', two articles in *Mind*, 1939. See also the same writer's 'Categories', *Proc. Arist. Soc.* 1937–8.

for which the *Parmenides* may have paved the way. According to the Aristotelian doctrine, things, qualities, relations, times, places, numbers, etc., may all be said in a sense to 'be' or to be real, but not in the same sense: 'being' is not a single generic category with all the others as species. Also a given thing or quality or relation or number, etc., may be said to be 'one' (itself, and not another thing, quality, etc.), but 'one' too is not used in the same sense, but only analogically, in the different cases.[1] There is a hint here not only of the theory of types but also of the fact that *quantification* 'makes sense' when applied at all levels, though a slightly different sense in each case. Of the formal details of the theory of types, some are foreshadowed in the medieval rules of 'supposition', such as that we may not pass from a term in 'simple' supposition to the same term in 'personal' supposition.[2] For example, we may not pass from 'Man is a species' to 'Some man is a species'. In modern symbolism this would be a passage from '$\alpha \epsilon \kappa$' to '$(\exists x) : x \epsilon \alpha . x \epsilon \kappa$', where '$x \epsilon \kappa$' is nonsense because only classes (not individuals) can be members of classes of classes.

§ 4. *Ontology and Mereology*

A little has already been said of the formalist and intuitionist alternatives to the PM conception of the relation between logic and arithmetic, and a little should be said also of an alternative to the PM view of something more basic, namely the relation of the logic of classes to the logic of predicational functions. Instead of introducing 'classes' as merely a notational device for handling the higher functional calculus, it is also possible to deal with them as a special kind of real object, with a distinct logic of their own. One form of this approach has been given very systematic development by the school of Leśniewski (notably Leśniewski himself and Sobociński).[3]

The basis of Leśniewski's logic is the 'protothetic', i.e. propositional calculus enriched with functorial variables and

[1] *Metaphysics*, 998^b 22–28 (see Bocheński's comment on this, *Ancient Formal Logic*, pp. 34–35), 1045^b 1–7.

[2] Peter of Spain's *Summulae*, 6.06.

[3] A valuable source of information on this subject is Sobociński's series of articles on 'L'analyse de l'antinomie russellienne par Leśniewski' in *Methodos*, vols. i (1949) and ii (1950). See also Łukasiewicz, 'The Principle of Individuation', *Proc. Arist. Soc.*, suppl. vol. xxvii (1953), pp. 77–80.

quantifiers, on which we have already touched, and on this he builds two further disciplines called 'ontology' and 'mereology'. The metalogical apparatus by which Leśniewski develops all these systems is somewhat different from the usual; but we shall arrive at the substance of his 'ontology' if we begin from the following considerations: In the calculus of predicational functions as it is ordinarily interpreted, the name-variables 'x', 'y', etc., are understood as keeping a place for expressions which simply 'mean' the individual objects which they indicate. The whole calculus would, however, remain structurally unaltered if they stood instead, like the variables of the Aristotelian syllogistic, for *common nouns*, like 'man', 'horse', etc., and for proper names somehow treated as a species of common nouns (so that it makes sense to talk of 'The Socrates . . .' 'Every Socrates . . .', etc.).[1] And that is, in effect, how the name-variables (or 'term-variables') of the predicate calculus are interpreted in Leśniewski's ontology.

When the name-variables of the predicate calculus are thus reinterpreted, it is of course necessary to give a corresponding reinterpretation to the predicate-variables 'ϕ', 'ψ', etc. These no longer stand for simple verbs, like '— smokes', or '— detests —', or '— gives — to —', but for operators which can be intelligibly attached to common nouns, such as the Aristotelian 'Every — is a —' and 'Some — is a —'. Some of these are of sufficient logical interest to appear as formal constants, but in ontology the only undefined constant operator on terms is the operator 'ϵ', which may be rendered verbally as 'The — is a —'. Of operators which may be defined in terms of this one, the most important are the dyadic operator 'I', which we may read as 'The — is identical with the —', or simply 'The — is the —', and which is defined thus:

$$DI\colon Iab = K\epsilon ab\epsilon ba$$

and the monadic operators '$\exists!$' and '$E!$', which may be read respectively as 'A — exists' and 'The — exists', being respectively defined by

$$D\exists!\colon \exists!a = \Sigma b\epsilon ba$$

$$DE!\colon E!a = \Sigma b\epsilon ab.$$

[1] In other words, no distinction would be made in this interpretation between a proper name and a common noun applying to a single object only. This typically ontological approach to singular, plural, and empty terms clearly underlies Łukasiewicz's discussion of them in *Aristotle's Syllogistic*, p. 4.

According to *D∃!*, 'An *a* exists' is short for 'For some *b*, the *b* is an *a*', or 'There is something that is an *a*', while 'The *a* exists' is short for 'For some *b*, the *a* is a *b*', or 'There is something that the *a* is.' That 'The *a* exists' implies 'An *a* exists', *CE!a∃!a*, is a law of the system.

The system is developed by engrafting on to the axioms and rules of protothetic a single special axiom of ontology, and by various metalogical devices of which the most important, 'ontological definition', will be illustrated shortly. A number of different formulae have been used by Leśniewski and Sobociński as the single special axiom (all of them yielding equivalent systems), the easiest to work with, though not the shortest, being the following:

(1) $E(\epsilon ab)(K\Pi cC\epsilon ca\epsilon cbK\Sigma c\epsilon ca\Pi cdCK\epsilon ca\epsilon da\epsilon cd)$.

This axiom asserts that a proposition of the form 'The *a* is a b' (ϵab) is true if and only if (i) every *a* is a *b*, (ii) something is an *a* and (iii) for any *c* and *d*, if the *c* is an *a* and the *d* is an *a* then the *c* is a *d*. This last condition can only be met if there is only one *a*.[1] A law which is derivable from this one, and which we shall find useful later, is

(2) $C\epsilon ab\epsilon aa$,

'If the *a* is a *b*, the *a* is an *a*'.[2] Using 'cons (1)' for 'the consequent (or second equivalent) in (1)' and 'ant (1)' for 'the antecedent in (1)', we may set out its proof from (1) as follows:

1. *CpCqp*
2. *Cpp*
3. *CCpqCKprKqr*
4. *CCpqCErpCEsqCrs*

$1\ p/C\epsilon ca\epsilon ca = C2\ p/\epsilon ca$—5

[1] These three conditions for the truth of the form ϵab may be compared with the three components of the Russellian definition of $\psi(\imath x\phi x)$. Ontology can in fact be interpreted within the Russellian calculus as a systematized theory of descriptions, just as the Russellian calculus may be interpreted within ontology as the general theory of functions of terms.

[2] That 'ϵaa' is not a senseless expression in ontology, as '$\alpha\epsilon\alpha$' is in the Russellian class calculus, does not mean that Leśniewski would admit such forms as '$\phi\phi$'. 'ϵaa' is not ostensibly of the form '$\phi\phi$' (but rather of the form, 'ϕa'), and for Leśniewski it is not disguisedly so either.

5. $C q C \epsilon c a \epsilon c a$

$5\ q/Cpp \times \Pi 2c = C2—6$

6. $\Pi c C \epsilon c a \epsilon c a$

$1\ p/\Pi c C \epsilon c a \epsilon c a,\ q/\Pi c C \epsilon c a \epsilon c b = C6—7$

7. $C \Pi c C \epsilon c a \epsilon c b \Pi c C \epsilon c a \epsilon c a$

$3\ p/\Pi c C \epsilon c a \epsilon c b,\ q/\Pi c C \epsilon c a \epsilon c a,\ r/K \Sigma c \epsilon c a \Pi c d C K \epsilon c a \epsilon d a \epsilon c d$
$= C7—8$

8. C cons (1)—cons (1) b/a

$4\ p/$cons (1), $q/$cons (1) b/a, $r/$ant (1), $s/$ant (1) b/a
$= C8—C$ (1)—C (1) b/a—(2)

(2) $C \epsilon a b \epsilon a a$.

From this we may prove the law previously mentioned, $CE!a\exists!a$, as follows:

1. Cpp
2. $CCpqCCqrCpr$

$(2) \times \Sigma 1b = 3$

3. $C \Sigma b \epsilon a b \epsilon a a$

$1\ p/\epsilon b a \times \Sigma 2b = 4$

4. $C \epsilon b a \Sigma b \epsilon b a$

$2\ p/\Sigma b \epsilon a b,\ q/\epsilon a a,\ r/\Sigma b \epsilon b a = C3—C4\ b/a—5$

5. $C \Sigma b \epsilon a b \Sigma b \epsilon b a$

$5 \times DE! \times D\exists! = 6$

6. $CE!a\exists!a$.

From (2) we may also prove that 'The *a* is an *a*' and 'The *a* exists' are equivalent. That $\epsilon a a$ is implied by $E!a$, i.e. by $\Sigma b \epsilon a b$, is Proposition 3 in the last proof; that it implies it may be shown thus:

1. Cpp

$1\ p/\epsilon a b \times \Sigma 2b = 2$

2. $C \epsilon a b \Sigma b \epsilon a b$

$2\ b/a = 3$

3. $C \epsilon a a \Sigma b \epsilon a b$.

Special terms and special types of terms may be introduced by 'ontological definition', i.e. by giving an equivalent for the formula 'ϵat', where 't' is the special term or type of term introduced. This is not a definition in the strict sense, since it gives no equivalent for 'ϵtb' and so does not enable us to replace the special term 't' by undefined terms in all contexts in which it may occur. And an unrestricted use of this type of definition could easily lead to contradictions. For suppose we introduced a term '$\wedge$'—read it 'non-object'—by the definition

$$(D \wedge): \epsilon a \wedge = N\epsilon aa.$$

We could then deduce a contradiction thus:

1. Epp

   $1\ p/\epsilon a \wedge \times (D \wedge) = 2$

2. $E(\epsilon a \wedge)(N\epsilon aa)$

   $2\ a/\wedge = 3$

3. $E(\epsilon \wedge \wedge)(N\epsilon \wedge \wedge)$.

No such contradiction can occur, however, if we lay it down that the right-hand side of an ontological definition must always contain the assertion that what is said on the left-hand side to be a t is something that exists.[1] This assertion could be made in the direct form '$E!a$', or in the form 'ϵaa', which we have just shown to be equivalent to that. No contradiction arises, for example, if we introduce the term 'non-object' by the ontological definition

$$D \wedge : \epsilon a \wedge = K\epsilon aaN\epsilon aa.$$

What does follow from this definition is that it is always self-contradictory, and therefore false, to assert that anything is a non-object, or that the non-object is anything—even itself. (It is not anything precisely *because* it is not itself, since by (2) whatever is anything is itself.)

The definition $D \wedge$ thus succeeds in introducing into the system that which is demonstrably not itself ($N\epsilon \wedge \wedge$ being provable from $D \wedge$ and $NKpNp$), but it introduces this without paradox. We cannot argue that since the $\wedge$ is not itself, and

[1] This restriction does not apply to such definitions as our DI, $D\exists!$, and $DE!$, which are not ontological definitions of terms but straightforward definitions of proposition-forming operators.

'what is not itself' is what ' $\wedge$ ' *means*, it therefore *is* itself; for 'what is not itself' is not *all* that ' $\wedge$ ' means—it also means, what any term at all means, 'what *is* itself', and it is just this part of its own description which it does not answer to. This is very similar in logical style to a solution favoured by Peirce[1] for the paradox of the liar. Every proposition, Peirce held, makes a claim to be true, so that he who says 'I am lying' is also implicitly saying '— and I am not' ('I am not lying' being what we implicitly say along with every statement we make). This makes the liar's statement simply false because self-contradictory; and its falsehood does not imply its truth, that is its truth as a whole, but only the truth of that part of it which is uttered.

Another consequence of the law $N\epsilon a \wedge$ is that if we wish to express the non-existence of, say, the King of France, it will not do to say 'The King of France is a non-object', for it is a peculiarity of the term 'non-object' that it is false to say of anything at all that it is a non-object, and therefore as false to say this of the (*ex hypothesi* non-existent) King of France as it is to say it of the (*ex hypothesi* existent) Queen of England. We can bring out the different ontological status of the two monarchs, however, by pointing out that to say that something is a King of France is always equivalent to saying that it is a non-object (both being in all cases false), while to say that something is a Queen of England is not always equivalent to saying that it is a non-object (the former being true and the latter false in the case of the Queen of England). In short, of the non-existent we may truly affirm nothing and deny anything, if by 'affirming something of *a*' we mean making a statement of the form ϵab and by 'denying something of *a*' making a statement of the form $N\epsilon ab$; though since the wider predicational form ϕa covers the forms ϵab and $N\epsilon ab$ alike (and also the form $E\epsilon ab\epsilon a\wedge$), we may make true affirmations even of the non-existent, if by 'affirming something of *a*' we mean simply making any statement at all in which *a* occurs. Note too that while for any proposition-forming operator on terms we may introduce another which simply means the negation of the first (e.g. we could introduce an operator ' $\wedge$!' simply meaning '$N\exists$!'), we cannot introduce a *term* 'non-*b*' such that 'The *a* is a non-*b*' simply means 'The *a*

[1] *Collected Papers*, 2. 618, 5. 340.

is not a *b*', but only one such that 'The *a* is a non-*b*' means 'The *a* is not a *b*, and the *a* is an *a*'. And in this sense of 'non-*b*', there will be *a*'s, namely the non-existent ones, for which 'The *a* is a non-*b*' is always false and 'The *a* is not a *b*' always true. At this point ontology is thoroughly Aristotelian.

The third of Leśniewski's disciplines, mereology, is obtained by adding to protothetic and ontology the notion of an 'element' of the *a*, 'μa', with a characteristic axiom. Correlative to this notion of an 'element', and definable in terms of it, is that of a 'class'. In mereology, the class of *b*'s, κb, is thought of, not as a mere 'logical construction' out of predicational functions, but as a single collective object literally made up of all the *b*'s. Thus we have

(3) $C(\epsilon a\kappa b)(\epsilon aa)$,

'That the *a* is the class of *b*'s implies that the *a* is an object'. Also, if there are no *b*'s for the class of *b*'s to be made up of, there is no such object as the class of *b*'s; that is,

(4) $C(\epsilon a\kappa b)(\Sigma c\epsilon cb)$.

Also, of course, 'The *a* is the class of *b*'s' implies that if anything is a *b* it is a member or element of the *a*, i.e.

(5) $C(\epsilon a\kappa b)(\Pi cC\epsilon cb\epsilon c\mu a)$.

The converse, however, is not the case; that is, it is not the case that if the *c* is an element of the class of *b*'s it is bound to be a *b*. For a 'class' in this sense, being made up of its elements, is equally made up of the elements of those elements, e.g. the class of piles (more than one high) of sheets of paper in my room is 'made up' not only of the piles, but also of the individual sheets (which are not themselves piles). And further than this, it has elements which are neither piles of sheets nor individual sheets, but groups of sheets drawn from different piles. We can say, however, that if the *c* is an element of the class of *b*'s', then there must be some *b* with which the *c* has an element in common, i.e.

(6) $C(\epsilon a\kappa b)(\Pi cC\epsilon c\mu a\Sigma deK\epsilon dbK\epsilon e\mu d\epsilon e\mu c)$.

The case in which the *c* *is* a *b*, and the only *b*, is covered by this, because everything is an element of itself, so that the *c*, *d*, and *e* of the last formula could all be the same object. These four implications of the *a*'s being the class of *b*'s are jointly equivalent to it, and may therefore together make up the right-hand side of an 'ontological definition' of 'κ' in terms of 'μ'. (3)—(6) will follow from this definition, since what is equivalent to a conjunction of four propositions, as $\epsilon a \kappa b$ is by this definition, will imply each several one of them. Strictly speaking, it may be noted, what will be defined here will not be 'The *a* is *the* class of *b*'s', but 'The *a* is *a* class of *b*'s', but it is provable from the one axiom of mereology, together with this definition, that if the term 'κb' has any application at all its application is unique.

Since in this system every object is an element of itself, there is no class which is not an element of itself, and therefore no such object as the class of such classes. Hence it is (not meaningless but) simply false to say of any object that it is a class of such classes, and simply false to say of the class of such classes that it is anything at all, even that it is a class of such classes or a member of the class of such classes. It will, therefore be (again not meaningless but) simply true to deny all these things. Formally, the position is that we cannot introduce the term 'what is not a member of itself' by the definition

$$(D*): \epsilon a* = N\epsilon a\mu a,$$

but only by the definition

$$D*: \epsilon a* = K\epsilon aaN\epsilon a\mu a;$$

and since we have as a law of mereology

(7) $E(\epsilon aa)(\epsilon a\mu a)$,

the right-hand side of this is equivalent to $K\epsilon aaN\epsilon aa$, so that $\epsilon a*$ is always false. And since, by (4), $\epsilon a\kappa*$ implies $\Sigma a\epsilon a*$, $\epsilon a\kappa*$ is always false too. Hence, by substitution, $\epsilon\kappa*\kappa*$ is false; and so, by (7), $\epsilon\kappa*\mu\kappa*$ is false, and $N\epsilon\kappa*\mu\kappa*$ is true.

APPENDIX I

Postulate Sets for Logical Calculi

(Revised 1960)

1. Classical Propositional Calculus: *C–N* Systems.
2. Classical Propositional Calculus: *C* and *C*–1 Fragments.
3. Classical Propositional Calculus: *C*–0 and other Completions from *C*–Pure.
4. Rules for Quantifiers.
5. Extended Classical Propositional Calculus (*C*–Π).
6. Classical Propositional Calculus: *A–N*, *K–N*, and *D* Systems.
7. Classical Propositional Calculus with Functor-Variables and *C* Primitive.
8. Classical Propositional Calculus: Equivalential Fragments and Completions.
9. Leśniewskian Systems.
10. Formalized Syllogistic.
11. Modal Systems.
12. Intuitionist Propositional Calculus with Sub-Systems and Extensions.

(*Note*: Substitution for variables is assumed as a rule throughout all sections, and other rules understood as added to this.)

§ 1. *Classical Propositional Calculus: C–N Systems*

Rule throughout Sections 1–3: Detachment (α, $C\alpha\beta \rightarrow \beta$)

Definitions throughout this section: Df. *A*: *A* = *CN*
Df. *K*: *Kpq* = *NCpNq*
Df. *E*: *Epq* = *KCpqCqp*

1.1. The System of Frege's *Begriffschrift* (1879).

Axioms: (1) *CpCqp* (4) *CCpqCNqNp*
(2) *CCpCqrCCpqCpr* (5) *CNNpp*
(3) *CCpCqrCqCpr* (6) *CpNNp*

((3) not independent: Łukasiewicz, 1929. But (3) is independent of (1) and *CCqCprCCpqCpr*, which with (1) and (3) will yield (2)—Meredith.)

1.2. System in Russell's *Theory of Implication* (1906).

Axioms: *Cpp* (superfluous), *CpCqp*, *CCpqCCqrCpr*, *CCpCqrCqCpr*, *CNNpp*, *CCpNpNp*, *CCpNqCqNp*.

1.3. System of Hilbert (1922).

Axioms: *CpCqp*, *CCpCpqCpq* (superfluous: Łukasiewlcz, 1924), *CCpCqrCqCpr*, *CCqrCCpqCpr*, *CpCNpq*, *CCpqCCNpqq*.

1.4. 3-Axiom *C–N* Systems.

Axioms: (*a*) *CCpqCCqrCpr*, *CpCNpq*, *CCNppp* (Łukasiewicz, 1924)
or (*b*) *CCCpqrCNpr*, *CCCpqrCqr*, *CCNprCCqrCCpqr* (Łukasiewicz, 1929)

or (*c*) *CpCqp*, *CCpCqrCCpqCpr*, *CCNpNqCqp* (Łukasiewicz, 1930; cf. 1.1)
or (*d*) *CNpCpq*, *CpCqCrp*, *CCNprCCqrCCpqr* (Sobociński, 1953)
or (*e*) *CCpqCNqCpr*, *CpCqCrp*, *CCNpqCCpqq* (Sobociński, 1954)

((*a*) has shortest total length; (*e*) shortest possible length of longest axiom; (*b*) simply equates, as to their logical force, *CCpqr* and the pair *CNpr*, *Cqr*.)

1.5. Single-Axiom *C–N* System (Meredith, 1953).
Axiom: *CCCCCpqCNrNsrtCCtpCsp*
(On earlier single axioms, see Tarski 2, pp. 44–45 and notes.)

§ 2. *Classical Propositional Calculus*: *C and C–1 Fragments*

2.11. Implicational Calculus (Restricted Propositional Calculus) (Tarski–Bernays).
Axioms: (1) *CpCqp*
(2) *CCpqCCqrCpr*
(3) *CCCpqpp*

(In 1921 Tarski used (1), (2), and (3′) *CCCpqrCCprr* with quantifiers to give full p.c. as in 5.3; in 1926 proved their sufficiency for r.p.c.; Bernays replaced (3′) by (3) in 1928.)

2.12. Łukasiewicz Generalization of Tarski–Bernays (1950).
Axioms: (1) Any of the form *CpCαβ*
(2), (3) as in 2.11.

2.13. Alternative 3- and 4-Axiom Sets.
(*a*) *CCCpqrCCprr*, *CCCpqrCqr*, *CCCprrCCqrCCpqr* (Prior, verified Thomas, 1960) (cf. 1.4(*b*), 6.12(*a*))
(*b*) *CpCCpqq*, *CCpqCCqrCpr*, *CCpCpqCpq*, *CCCpqqCCqpp* (Meredith) (no unconnected variables)

2.14. Two-Axiom Implicational Calculi.
10–*C* Axiom Pairs (Wajsberg, 1925–6)
(*a*) *CpCqCrp*, *CCCpqrCCsrCCprr*
(*b*) *CCCpqpp*, *CCCCpqrsCCqrCps* (cf. 12.7)
9–*C* Axiom Pairs
(*c*) *CpCqp* with *CCCCpqrsCCqsCps* (Łukasiewicz)
or *CCCCpqrqCCqsCps* (Prior, 1960)
(*d*) *CCqrCqCpr*, *CCCpqrCCrpp* (Meredith, 1957)
(*e*) *CCCrCpqpp* with *CCqrCCpqCpr* or *CCpqCCqrCpr* (Meredith)
(*f*) *CCCpqpCrp*, *CCpqCCqrCpr* (Wajsberg, 1939)
(*g*) *CCCpqpp* with *CCpqCsCCqrCpr* (Wajsberg, 1939) or *CCpqCCqrCsCpr* or *CCpqCCqrCpCsr* (Meredith, 1958); or with *CsCCpqCCqrCpr* (direct corollary of 2.12)
8–*C* Axiom Pair
(*h*) *Cpp*, *CCCpqrCCrpCsCtp* (Meredith, 1960)

2.15. Single-Axiom Implicational Calculi.
Axiom: (*a*) *CCCpqCCrstCCuCCrstCCpuCst* (Wajsberg, 1926)
or (*b*) *CCCpqCrsCtCCspCrp* (Łukasiewicz, 1930)
or (*c*) *CCCpqCrsCCspCtCrp* (Łukasiewicz, 1932)
or (*d*) *CCCpqrCCrpCsp* (Łukasiewicz, 1936)

2.2 Single-Axiom *C*–1 (Meredith, 1957).
Axiom: *CCCpqCrC*1*sCCspCrCtp*, or *CCCpqC*1*rCsCCrpCtCup*
(The simple 1, i.e. constant true proposition, provable and replaceable in the axiom by any formula completing the full propositional calculus from the implicational, as in 3.12 and 3.3.)

§ 3. *Classical Propositional Calculus*: *C*–0 *and other Completions from C–Pure*

3.11. Full Calculus in *C* and 0 (Peirce, 1885).
Axioms: (1) *Cpp* (4) *C*0*p*
(2) *CCpCqrCqCpr* (5) *CCCpqpp*
(3) *CCpqCCqrCpr*
((1) not independent: Prior, 1958).
Definition for 3.11–13: Df. *N* : *Np* = *Cp*0.

3.12. Full Calculus in *C* and 0 (Wasjsberg, 1937).
Axioms: Any complete for *C*–Pure, plus *C*0*p*.

3.13. Single-Axiom *C*–0 System (Meredith, 1953).
Axiom: *CCCCCpqCr*0*stCCtpCrp*
or *CCCpqCC*0*rsCCspCtCup*.

3.2. 'Tiered' System in *C–K–A–N* (Variations of Kanger, 1955).
(1) Axioms in *C*: Any set from 2.11 to 2.15
(2) Axioms in *C–K*: (*a*) *CKpqp*, *CKpqq*, *CCpqCCprCpKqr*
or (*b*) *CKpqp*, *CKpqq*, *CpCqKpq*
or (*c*) *CCKpqrCpCqr*, *CCpCqrCKpqr*
(3) Axioms in *C–A*: *CpApq*, *CqApq*, *CCprCCqrCApqr*
(4) Axioms in *C–N*: *CCpNpNp*, *CpCNpq*

(Theorems in any functor require only those axioms which contain it and those in *C*; i.e. (1) is complete for *C*, (1)+(2) for *C–K*, (1)+(3) for *C–A*, (1)+(2)+(3) for *C–K–A*, (1)+(4) for *C–N*, etc. Cf. 12.5.)

3.3. Implicational Calculus with Implicational Definitions (Lejewski, 1954).
Axiom(s): Any sufficient for implicational calculus
Rule of definition: We may adjoin to the system at any stage either a pair of theses of the forms *C*$\alpha\beta$, *C*$\beta\alpha$, or a single thesis of the form *CCC*$\alpha\beta$*CC*$\beta\alpha\gamma\gamma$, where
(*a*) γ is a single propositional variable not occurring in α
(*b*) All variables in α occur in β and vice versa, and none occurs in α more than once
(*c*) α is an implication, its antecedent being a function not previously occurring in the system (e.g. *Np*, *Kpq*) and its consequent a single variable
(*d*) β is an implication, its consequent being the same as that of α, and its antecedent containing no expressions which have not previously occurred in the system.

(The application of this rule with *CNpq* for α and *CCpqq* for β gives the full calculus in *C–N*. It will also give it with weaker implicational bases, e.g. the set 12.71; and if the 2-thesis definition-form is used, with weaker ones still, e.g. 12.7.)

§ 4. *Rules for Quantifiers*

Where new types of variables are introduced, appropriate substitution rules are introduced along with them; and where there are quantifiers substitutions must be made *for* free occurrences of variables only, and only *of* variables (or expressions containing free occurrences of variables) which do not occur bound by any quantifier introducing a sub-formula in which the variable to be replaced occurs freely (e.g. we may not replace x by y in either $C\Pi x\phi x\Pi z\phi z$ or $CK\Pi z\phi z\psi x\Pi yK\phi y\psi x$, or ϕ by Iy' in $\Sigma y\Pi xC\phi y\phi x$, though we may replace the third x by y both in $C\Pi x\phi x\phi x$ and in $C\Pi x\phi xA\phi x\Pi y\psi y$). Nor, when substituting for a functor-variable, may we substitute an expression in which there is a quantifier binding a variable which already occurs as an argument of the functor for which we are substituting. For example, we cannot make the substitution '$\phi/\Sigma xNIx$' in $C\Pi y\phi y\phi x$ (or in $C\phi y\Sigma x\phi x$), and so obtain $C\Pi y\Sigma xNIxy\Sigma xNIxx$ (or $C\Sigma xNIxy\Sigma x\Sigma xNIxx$).

Of possible rules for introducing quantifiers, we list only those (of the Warsaw school) used in the text, which are so framed below as to allow for the appearance of 'vacuous' quantifications, i.e. expressions in which the variable bound by the quantifier either does not occur in the formula which follows, or is already bound in it (e.g. Πxp, $\Pi x\phi y$, $\Sigma x\Sigma xNIxx$). All such expressions may be proved equivalent to the corresponding expressions with all the vacuous bindings omitted (p, ϕy, $\Sigma xNIxx$). The rules are in all cases subjoined to axioms, definitions and rules for the propositional calculus; and the x occurring in a rule may be understood as a variable of any type occurring in the calculus in which the rules are used.

4.1. Π and Σ both undefined.

$\Pi 1$: $C\alpha\beta \rightarrow C\Pi x\alpha\beta$ (or $C\alpha\Pi x\beta \rightarrow C\alpha\beta$)
$\Pi 2$: $C\alpha\beta \rightarrow C\alpha\Pi x\beta$, for x not free in α
$\Sigma 1$: $C\alpha\beta \rightarrow C\Sigma x\alpha\beta$, for x not free in β
$\Sigma 2$: $C\alpha\beta \rightarrow C\alpha\Sigma x\beta$ (or $C\Sigma x\alpha\beta \rightarrow C\alpha\beta$).

4.2. With Π undefined.

Definition: Df. Σ: $\Sigma x = N\Pi xN$
Rules: $\Pi 1$, $\Pi 2$ as in 4.1.

4.3. With Σ undefined.

Definition: Df. Π: $\Pi x = N\Sigma xN$
Rules: $\Sigma 1$, $\Sigma 2$ as in 4.1.

§ 5. *Extended Propositional Calculus* (C–Π)

(The implicational calculus of § 3 supplemented with quantifiers binding propositional variables and a definition of N in terms of them, enabling us to prove the full system of § 1.)

5.1. The System of Russell's *Principles of Mathematics* (1903).

Axioms: (1) $CKpqp$ (4) $CCKpqrCpCqr$
(2) $CKCpqCqrCpr$ (5) $CKCpqCprCpKqr$
(3) $CCpCqrCKpqr$ (6) $CCCpqpp$

Definitions: Df. K: $Kpq = \Pi rCCpCqrr$
Df. A: $Apq = CCpqq$
Df. N: $Np = \Pi qCpq$

Rules not clearly stated (apart from detachment as in 1–3), but Π postulates of 5.2 below would make the above sufficient, (3) and (5) indeed superfluous. Without Π, but with detachment, the axioms are complete for *C–K*.

5.2. System in Russell's *Theory of Implication* (1906).

Axioms: (1), (2), (3) of 2.11 plus the superfluous pair *Cpp* and *CCpCqrCqCpr*

Definitions: Dff. *K* and *A* as in 5.1

Df. 0: $0 = \Pi pp$

Df. *N*: $Np = Cp\Pi pp$ ($= Cp0$)

Rules: Detachment as in 1–3, plus postulates for Π equivalent to those of § 4, viz. $\alpha \rightarrow \Pi x\alpha$ and the axiom-forms $C\Pi xf(x)f(y)$ (case of this: Cop) and $C\Pi xCpf(x)Cp\Pi xf(x)$ (functions of free x not substitutable for p) (legitimate cases: $C\Pi qCCp\Pi qqCpqCCp\Pi qq\Pi qCpq$; $C\Pi qCpqCp\Pi qq$).

5.3. Extended Propositional Calculus (Tarski and Łukasiewicz).

Axioms: Any sufficient for *C*-pure

Definitions: As in 5.2

Rules: Detachment as in 1–3; $\Pi 1$, $\Pi 2$.

(These definitions and rules also give full p.c. from some weaker implicational bases, e.g. 8.7.)

§ 6. *Classical Propositional Calculus: A–N, K–N, and D Systems*

6.11. The System of *Principia Mathematica* (Russell, 1908).

Axioms: (1) *CAppp* (3) *CApqAqp* (5) *CCqrCApqApr*

(2) *CqApq* (4) *CApAqrAqApr*

((4) not independent; Łukasiewicz, 1924, and Bernays, 1926)

Definitions for 6.11–6.2: Df. *C*: $C = AN$

Df. *K*: $Kpq = NANpNq$

Df. *E*: as in 1

Rule for 6.11–14: Detachment (α, $AN\alpha\beta \rightarrow \beta$).

6.12. Three-Axiom *A–N* Systems.

Axioms: (*a*) *CCApqrCpr*, *CCApqrCqr*, *CCprCCqrCApqr* (Łukasiewicz, 1929; cf. 1.4 (*b*))

or (*b*) *CAppp*, *CpApq*, *CCpqCArpAqr* (Götlind, 1947, with superfluous *Cpp* removed by Rasiowa, 1948)

or (*c*) *ApNApp*, *CpApq*, *CAqNpCArpAqr* (Rose, 1949)

or (*d*) *CAppp*, *ApCpq*, *CApqCCqrApr* (Meredith, 1951)

or (*e*) *CApqAqApr*, *CpCqArp*, *CApqCCpqq* (after Jáskowski; cf. 1.4 (*e*))

6.13. Two-Axiom *A–N* System (Meredith, 1953).

Axioms: *CpApq*, *CApAqrCCqpArp*.

6.14. Single-Axiom *A–N* Systems (Meredith, 1953).

Axiom: *CCCpqArAstCCspArAtp*

or *CCCpqArAstCCtsArAps*

or *CCCpqArAstCCrpAtAsp*.

6.2. *A–N* System with *Modus Tollendo Ponens* (Reichbach, 1952).
Axioms: (1) Any set sufficient for *A–N* with usual rule, with each axiom preceded by *NN*
(2) *ANpp* (3) *CApqApNNq*
Rule: $N\alpha$, $A\alpha\beta \rightarrow \beta$.

6.3. *K–N* Systems.
Axioms: (*a*) *NKNpKpq*, *NKNqKpKrq*, *NKNKNprKNKNqrKNKpqr*, *CNKpqCpNq* (Sobociński, 1939; cf. 1.4 (*d*)
or (*b*) *CpKpp*, *CKpqp*, *CCpqCNKqrNKrp* (Rosser, 1942 or 1946, removing superfluous *Cpp* from set of 1939)
or (*c*) the preceding with *CKpqp* replaced by *CKpqq*, *NKKNpqp* or *NKKqNpp* (Meredith).
Definition: Df. *C*: *Cpq* = *NKpNq*
Rule: Detachment (α, $NK\alpha N\beta \rightarrow \beta$).

6.4. Single-Axiom Systems in *D*.
Axiom: *DDpDqrDDtDttDDsqDDpsDps* (Nicod, 1918)
or *DDpDqrDDsDssDDsqDDpsDps* (Łukasiewicz, 1925)
or *DDpDqrDDDsrDDpsDpsDpDpq* (Wajsberg, 1931)
or *DDpDqrDDpDrpDDsqDDpsDps* (Łukasiewicz, 1931)
Definitions: Df. *N*: *Np* = *Dpp*
Df. *K*: *K* = *ND*
Df. *C*: *Cpq* = *DpNq*
Df. *A*: *Apq* = *DNpNq*
Rule: Detachment (α, $D\alpha D\beta\gamma \rightarrow \gamma$).

§ 7. *Classical Propositional Calculus with Functor-Variables and C Primitive*

(In all cases, besides substitution for both types of variables, there is detachment as in 1–3.)

7.1. *C–N* Calculus with Functor-Variables (Meredith, 1953).
Axiom: $C\delta pC\delta Np\delta q$
Definitions as in 1.

7.2. *C*–o Calculus with Functor-Variables.
Axiom: $C\delta CooC\delta o\delta p$ or $C\delta oC\delta Coo\delta p$ (Łukasiewicz, 1951)
or $C\delta\delta o\delta p$ (Meredith, 1951)
Definitions as in 3.1 (and 1 = *N*o).

7.3. Implicational Fragment of Propositional Calculus with Functor-Variables (Meredith, 1951).
Axiom: $C\delta pCq\delta\delta q$
or $CpC\delta q\delta\delta p$
or $C\delta p\delta\delta Cqq$.

7.4. Propositional Calculus with Functor-Variables and Quantifiers (Meredith, 1951).
Axiom: As in 7.3; or $C\delta\delta\Pi pp\delta p$
Definitions: As in 5.2
Rules: To substitution and detachment add Π1, Π2 as in 4.1.

(*Note*: All the above systems with functor-variables are obtainable from the corresponding systems without them by subjoining to any adequate basis for the latter the 'law of extensionality' *CEpqCδpδq*, and substitution for the new variables (Łukasiewicz, 1953); and conversely yield such a basis and this law. These systems therefore assume that the range of δ is confined to extensional functors of propositions in the sense of p. 267.)

§ 8. *Classical Propositional Calculus: Equivalential Fragments and Completions*

(In all cases the sole rule beside substitution is *E*-detachment: α, $E\alpha\beta \rightarrow \beta$.)

8.11. Two-Axiom Equivalential Calculus (Leśniewski, 1929).
Axioms: *EEpqEqp*, *EEEpqrEpEqr*.

8.12. Single-Axiom Equivalential Calculus (Łukasiewicz, 1933).
Axiom: *EEpqEErqEpr*, *EEpqEEprErq* or *EEpqEErpEqr*.
(Also *EEEpqrEqErp*, *ErEEqErpEpq*, *EpEEqErpEqr*, *EEpEqrErEpq*, *EEpqErEEqrp*, *EEpqErEErqp*, *EEEpEqrrEqp*, *EEEpEqrqErp*: Meredith, first two 1951.)

8.2. Equivalential Calculus with Negation (Mihailescu, 1937).
Axioms: (1) Any sufficient for *E* only
(2) *EENpNqEpq*
Definition: Df. *J*: *Jpq* = *EpNq* (or *NEpq*).

(*Note*: Though the pure *E*-calculi 8.11 and 8.12 are strongly complete, no *E–N* system can be so. In an *E–N* formula, either (i) no propositional variable occurs an odd number of times, and *N* does not occur an odd number of times; or (ii) at least one propositional variable occurs an odd number of times; or (iii) no propositional variable occurs an odd number of times, but *N* does. All *E–N* tautologies are of type (i), and all such are provable in 8.2; any formula of type (ii), if tried as an extra axiom, is disprovable by deriving the simple *p* as a thesis; but those of type (iii) are neither provable nor thus disprovable, though if any one type (iii) formula be added to the system all other such formulae will follow.)

8.3. Equivalential Calculus with Exclusive Alternation.
Axioms: (1) Any sufficient for *E* only
(2) *EEJpqJrsEEpqErs* (Mihailescu, 1938)
or *EEpqEJrqJpr* (Rasiowa, 1948)
Definition: Df. *N* : *Np* = *EpJpp*
Metalogical remarks under 8.2 apply with *N* replaced by *J*.

8.4. *E*–o Calculus (Rose, 1955).
Axioms: Any sufficient for *E* only
Definition: Df. *N*: *Np* = *Ep*o
Df. *J* as in 8.2
8.2 (2) and 8.3 (2) are obtainable as theorems.

8.5. *E*–μ Calculus (Meredith, 1959).
Let μ stand for any 'one-hole functor', i.e. taking such substitutions as *E'p* and *Ep'* (also the plain '), but not such as *E''*. With this substitution-rule for μ, and substitution for *p* and detachment as in the rest, a sufficient single axiom (yielding, for example, 8.11 and 8.12) is

E$\mu\mu$*pp*, or *Ep*$\mu\mu$*p*.

8.6. *E–K–F* Full Calculus (Lejewski, 1954).
Axioms: *EEpqEEprErq* (from 8.2), *EKEpqrEKprEKqrr*,
EKpKqKrsKpKpKKqrs, *EKpKqrKpKrq*, *EFqrKpFqr*
(Here *Fpq* is the contradictory function of *p* and *q*)
Axiomatic Rejection: **Fpp*
Rules of Rejection: (1) Reject any formula with a rejected substitution
(2) $*\alpha$, $E\alpha\beta \rightarrow *\beta$
Definitions: Df. *C*: *Cpq* = *EpKpq*
Df. *N*: *Np* = *EpFpp*.

8.7. Ambiguous *E–C* Calculus (Rasiowa, 1955).
Axioms: *CCpqCCqrCpr*, *CqCpCpq*, *CCCpqCCpqpp*
Rule: *C* detachment as in 1–3.
(Covers all laws which hold regardless of whether *C* be read as implication or as equivalence. Complete implicational calculus derivable if any thesis added which holds for *C* but not *E*; and complete *C–Π* with *Π*1, *Π*2.)

§ 9. *Leśniewskian Systems*

Here the only quantifier is the universal (*Σx* below just abridges *NΠxN*), all variables are bound, there are no vacuous quantifications, and definitions are equivalences introduced by special rules. Variables of a given 'semantical category' not appearing in the axioms cannot be used until some expression substitutable for them has been introduced by definition, and we may then lay down a law of extensionality for functions of the category concerned. The remaining rules are substitution for variables where bound by an initial quantifier (with adjustment of the variables in that quantifier), e.g. from *ΠδpEδpδp* we may infer *ΠpENpNp* and *ΠδpqEδEpqδEpq*; *E*-detachment; and the rule that in any quantified equivalence we may transfer variables from the initial quantifier to quantifiers (introduced, if necessary) before the arguments of the main *E* (omitting them where those arguments do not themselves contain them), e.g. from *ΠpqEEpqEqp* we may infer *ΠqEΠpEpqΠpEqp*, *ΠpEΠqEpqΠqEqp* and *EΠpqEpqΠpqEqp*; from *ΠpqEpEpEqq*: *ΠqEΠppΠpEpEpq*, *ΠpEpΠqEpEqq*, *EΠppΠpqEpEqq*.

In 9.1 δ is a dyadic truth-operator variable except in Tarski's Df. *K*, where it is monadic. In Leśniewski's own notation the scope of a functor is indicated by brackets put round its arguments (as we have done for the variable functor in 9.1), functors with arguments of different logical types having differently shaped brackets.

9.1. Protothetic (*E* undefined).
Axiom: *ΠpqEEpqΠδEδ(p,δ(p,Πuu))ΠrEδ(q,r)Eqp* (Sobociński, 1954)
Definitions: Df. *N*: *ΠpEEpΠuuNp*
Df. *K*: *ΠpqEΠδEpEδ(p)δ(q)Kpq* (Tarski, 1923) or *ΠpqEΠδEδ(p,q)δ(q,Epq)Kpq* (Sobociński, 1939)
Df. *C* as in 8.6
(For earlier axioms, and other definitions, see Sobociński 2.)

9.21. Ontology (ϵ undefined).

(Understood as subjoined to protothetic)

Axiom: $\Pi abE\epsilon abK\Sigma c\epsilon c\epsilon caK\Pi cdCK\epsilon ca\epsilon da\epsilon cd\Pi cC\epsilon ca\epsilon cb$ (Leśniewski, 1920)

or $\Pi abE\epsilon abK\Sigma cK\epsilon ca\epsilon cb\Pi cdCK\epsilon ca\epsilon da\epsilon cd$ (Leśniewski, 1921)

or $\Pi abE\epsilon abK\Sigma cK\epsilon ca\epsilon cb\Pi cC\epsilon ca\epsilon ac$ (Sobociński, 1929)

or the pair $\Pi abC\epsilon ab\Sigma c\epsilon ca$, $\Pi abcCK\epsilon ab\epsilon ca\epsilon cb$ (Sobociński, 1929)

or $\Pi abE\epsilon ab\Sigma cK\epsilon ac\epsilon cb$ (Leśniewski, 1929)

Definitions: Df. ex: $\Pi aE\Sigma b\epsilon ba$exa

Df. ob: $\Pi aE\Sigma b\epsilon ab$oba

Df. sol: $\Pi aE\Pi bcCK\epsilon ba\epsilon ca\epsilon bc$sola

Df. U: $\Pi abE\Pi cC\epsilon ca\epsilon cbUab$

Df. I: $\Pi abEK\epsilon ab\epsilon baIab$.

(Here 'ex' and 'ob' are the $\exists$! and E! of the text; 'sol a' means 'There is at most one a'; Uab, 'Every a is a b'; and Iab, 'The a is the b'. With the 1920 axiom the definitions yield $\Pi abE\epsilon abKK$exasolaUab.)

9.22. Ontology (U undefined).

Axiom: $\Pi aUaa$ (Lejewski, 1960)

Definitions: Df. ex: $\Pi aE\Sigma bNUab$exa

Df. sol: $\Pi aE\Pi bcCUbaAUabUbc$sola (Sobociński)

Df. ob: ΠaEoba$K$exasola

Df. ϵ: $\Pi abE\epsilon abK$obaUab.

(But note that the 'ontological definitions' of p. 297, formulated in terms of U, are considerably more complicated than those of ϵ-primitive ontology.)

§ 10. *Formalized Syllogistic*

(All systems understood as subjoined to the full classical propositional calculus, with substitution for term-variables.)

10.11. System not admitting Empty Terms, and without Negative Terms but with Rejection (Łukasiewicz–Słupecki, 1951) (A and I undefined).

(Subjoined to 1.4(a). In special rule below, A, E, I, O forms are counted as elementary, and if α is an A, E, I, or O form and β is elementary, $C\alpha\beta$ is elementary; and there are no other elementary forms.)

Axioms (Łukasiewicz, 1929):

(1) Aaa (3) $CKAbcAabAac$ (Barbara)

(2) Iaa (4) $CKAbcIbaIac$ (Datisi)

Definitions: Df. E: $E = NI$

Df. O: $O = NA$

Axiomatic Rejection: $*CKAcbAabIac$

Rejection Rules: (1) Reject any formula with a rejected substitution

(2) $*\beta, C\alpha\beta \rightarrow *\alpha$

Special Rejection Rule (Słupecki): $*C\alpha\gamma$, $*C\beta\gamma \rightarrow *C\alpha C\beta\gamma$, if α and β are E or O forms and γ is elementary.

10.12. Eulerian System without Negative Terms (Thomas, 1957, improving on Faris, 1955).

(Operators *1*, *2*, *3*, *4*, *5* relating terms as in the diagrams (α), (β), (δ), (γ), (ε) of p. 108; *1*, *2*, *5* undefined.)

Axioms: (1) *1aa*
(2) *N2aa*
(3) *N5aa*
(4) *C1abC1cb1ac*
(5) *C2abC2bc2ac*
(6) *C1abC2bc2ac*
(7) *C1abC2cb2ca*
(8) *C1abC5cb5ac*
(9) *C2abC5bc5ac*

or alternatively
(10) *Aaa*
(11) *Iaa*
(12) *CAabCAbcAac*
(13) *CAabCEcbEac*
(14) *C1ab1ba*
(15) *CAabN2ba*

Definitions: Df. *4*: *4ab* = *2ba*
Df. *3*: *3ab* = *KN1abKN2abKN4abN5ab*
Df. *A*: *Aab* = *CN1ab2ab*
Df. *E*: *E* = *5*
Df. *I*: *I* = *NE*.

(All theses of 10.11 are provable in 10.12, and theses of 10.12 provable in 10.11 given the definitions *1ab* = *KAabAba*, *2ab* = *KAabOba*, *3ab* = *KOabKObaIab*, *4ab* = *2ba*, *5* = *E*.)

10.21. *A–n* System not admitting Empty or Universal Terms (Thomas, 1949. *na* for 'non–*a*').
Axioms: *Aaa*, *Iaa*, *CKEbcIabOac* (Ferio)
Definitions: Df. *E*: *Eab* = *Aanb* (*I* = *NE*, *O* = *NA*)
Special Rule: *nna* and *a* are interchangeable.

10.22 *A–n* System not admitting Empty or Universal Terms (Wedberg, 1949).
Axioms: (1) *Aanna*
(2) *Annaa*
(3) *CAabAnbna*
(4) *CKAabAbcAac*
(5) *CAabNAanb* (or *NAana*; Shepherdson, 1955)
Definitions as in 10.21
No special rule for negative terms.
(Equivalent to 10.21.)

10.23. *E–n* System not admitting Empty or Universal Terms (Meredith, 1957).
Axioms: *Eana*, *NEaa*, *CKEanbEbcEca* (Camenes)
Definitions: Df. *A*: *Aab* = *Eanb* (*I* = *NE*, *O* = *NA*)
No special rule for negative terms.
(Equivalent to 10.21 and 10.22.)

10.3. Aristotelian System admitting Empty Terms, but without Negative Terms (Słupecki, 1946. *A*, *I* undefined).
Axioms: *CAabIab*, *CIabIba*, *CKAbcAabAac* (Barbara), *CKAbcIabIac* (Darii)
Definitions as in 10.11

Interpretations rendering Axioms provable within Ontology (9.21):

$$Aab = K\Pi cC\epsilon ca\epsilon cb\Sigma c\epsilon ca$$
$$Iab = \Sigma cK\epsilon ca\epsilon cb.$$

(All Aristotelian laws but *Aaa* and *Iaa* provable.)

10.4. Brentano-Style System admitting Empty Terms, but without Negative Terms (Shepherdson, 1955. *A*, *I* undefined).

Axioms: (1), (3), (4) of 10.11 with (2) replaced by the pair *CIabIaa*, *CNIaaAab*

Definitions as in 10.11

Interpretations rendering Axioms provable within Ontology:

$Aab = \Pi cC\epsilon ca\epsilon cb$ (cf. Df. *U*, 9.21)

$Iab = \Sigma cK\epsilon ca\epsilon cb.$

(The system has all laws in *A*, *I* which hold with this interpretation. It has *Aaa* but not *Iaa*, nor laws of subalternation, contrariety, sub-contrariety, conversion *per accidens* or syllogisms with 'p' in mood-name.)

10.5. Brentano-Style *A-n* System admitting Empty Terms (Wedberg, 1949).

Axioms: (1), (2), (3), (4) as in 10.22, but (5) replaced by *CAanaAab*

Definitions as in 10.21.

10.6. Brentano-Style *A–n* System admitting Empty Terms but excluding Empty Universe (Shepherdson, 1955).

Axioms: As for 10.5, plus *CAanaNAnaa*.

§ 11. *Modal Systems*

11.1. The Lewis (*N–K–M*) Systems (S3, 1918; others 1932; amended). (Rules and definitions the same in all.)

Definitions: Df. *L*: *L* = *NMN*

Df. *C'*: *C'pq* = *NMKpNq*

Df. *E'*: *E'pq* = *KC'pqC'qp*

Rules: (1) Adjunction ($\alpha, \beta \rightarrow K\alpha\beta$)

(2) Detachment ($\alpha, C'\alpha\beta \rightarrow \beta$)

(3) Interchangeability of strict equivalents

Axioms for S1:	(1) *C'KpqKqp*	(4) *C'KpKqrKqKpr*
	(2) *C'Kpqp*	(5) *C'KC'pqC'qrC'pr*
	(3) *C'pKpp*	(6) *C'pMp*
Axioms for S2:	(1)–(6) plus	(7) *C'MKpqMp*
Axioms for S3:	(1)–(6) plus	(8) *C'C'pqC'MpMq*
Axioms for S4:	(1)–(6) plus	(9) *C'MMpMp*
Axioms for S5:	(1)–(6) plus	(10) *C'MpLMp*
Axioms for S6:	(1)–(7), i.e. as for S2, plus (11) *MMp*	
Axioms for S7:	(1)–(8), i.e. as for S3, plus (11) *MMp*	
Axioms for S8:	(1)–(8), i.e. as for S3, plus (12) *LMMp*.	

(*Note*: The Lewis systems are so framed that the unmodalized *C* and *E* do not occur in the axioms and rules; though they could be introduced by definition as in the *K–N* systems 6.3. With these definitions, the full classical propositional calculus is provable in all the systems.)

11.21. The Gödel Systems (*L* undefined) (1933).

(These are all understood as subjoined to some complete basis for the classical propositional calculus, e.g. any from § 1 or § 3 or § 6.)

Definition: Df.*M*: *M* = *NLN*

Rule: α → *L*α

Axioms for Common Basis: (1) *CLpp*, (2) *CLCpqCLpLq*

Axioms for S4: (1) and (2), plus (3) *CLpLLp*

Axioms for S5: (1) and (2), plus (4) *CNLpLNLp*.

((1) and (2) alone, with the definition and rule, yield a system—Feys's system T—equivalent to what we would obtain by adjoining the rule α → *L*α to S1; a system contained in S4, containing S2, and independent of S3.)

11.22. The von Wright Systems (*M* undefined) (1951).

(For subjunction to classical propositional calculus)

Definition: Df. *L*: *L* = *NMN*

Rules: (1) α → *L*α

(2) *E*αβ → *EM*α*M*β

Axioms for System M: (1) *CpMp*, (2) *EMApqAMpMq*

Axioms for System M′: (1) and (2), plus (3) *CMMpMp*

Axioms for System M″: (1) and (2), plus (4) *CMNMpNMp*.

(System M is equivalent to the system T of 11.21; M′ to S4; M″ to S5.)

11.23. S5 without Added Axioms (Prior, 1953, with correction by Łukasiewicz and Bausch, 1955).

(For subjunction to the classical propositional calculus)

Rules: L1: *C*αβ → *CL*αβ

L2: *C*αβ → *C*α*L*β, if all α's variables are modalized

M1: *C*αβ → *CM*αβ, if all β's variables are modalized

M2: *C*αβ → *C*α*M*β

(*p* is modalized if and only if it is the whole or a part of a propositional formula prefixed by *L* or *M*.)

Or L1 and L2, with Df. *M* as in 11.21

Or M1 and M2, with Df. *L* as in 11.22.

11.24. S5 with Contingency Primitive (Lemmon and Gjertsen, 1959).

(For subjunction to the classical propositional calculus. *Qp* for '*p* is neither necessary nor impossible')

Definitions: Df. *L*: *Lp* = *KpNQp*

Df. *M* as in 11.21

Rule: α → *NQ*α

Axioms: (1) *EQpQNp* (3) *CQCpqCNQpp*

(2) *CNQEpqCQpQq* (4) *NQCpQp*.

11.25. Gödel-type Versions of S1–S4 (Lemmon, 1956. *L* undefined).

Rules selected from

(*a*) α → *L*α

(*a*′) α → *L*α if α is a tautology or axiom

(*b*) *LC*αβ → *LCL*α*L*β

(*b*′) Interchangeability of strict equivalents

Axioms: (1) *CLpp* plus one of
(2) *CLCpqLCLpLq*
(2′) *CLCpqCLpLq*
(3) *CKLCpqLCqrLCpr*

For S1 use (*a*′), (*b*′), (3)
For S2 use (*a*′), (*b*), (2′)
For S3 use (*a*′), (2) (cf. T, which has (*a*), (2′))
For S4 use (*a*), (2).

11.3. Systems between S4 and S5 (1957).
Axioms to be subjoined to sufficient basis for S4 or (Lemmon) S3
S4.2: *CMLpLMp* (Geach)
S4.3: *AC′LpLqC′LqLp* (Lemmon) or *AC′LpqC′Lqp* (Geach) or *CKMpMqAMKpMqMKqMp* (Hintikka).

11.41. Rule-simplified S3 and S4 (Simons, 1952).
Definitions as in 11.1
Rule: Material detachment (α, $C\alpha\beta \rightarrow \beta$)
Axioms for S3: (1) *C′pKpp* (2) *C′Kpqq* (3) *C′KKrpNKqrKpNq* (4) *CNMpNp* (5) *C′pMp* (6) *C′C′pqC′NMqNMp*
For S4: (1)–(6) plus (7) *C′MMpMp*.

(*Note*: This and the systems following to 11.71 are not for subjunction to the propositional calculus but, except for 11.61, contain it in the manner of 11.1.)

11.42. Rule-simplified S5 (Anderson, 1956).
Definitions and Rule as in 11.41
Axioms: (1)–(6) of 11.41 plus *C′C′LpMpC′pLMp*.

11.43. Rule-simplified M (Anderson, 1956).
Axioms: (1), (2) as in 11.41
(3) *C′NNKNNKrpNNNKqrNNKpNq*
(4) *CC′LppCC′pqC′Lpq*
(5) *CLpp*
(6) *C′C′pqCNMqNMp*

Definitions: Df. *L* as in 11.1.
Df. *C*: *C′pq* = *LCpq*

Rule: α, $CL\alpha\beta \rightarrow \beta$
(Equivalent to M of 11.22.)

11.44. S3 and S4 in *D* and *D′* (Ishimoto, 1956).
Axioms for S3: *C′pp*, *C′D′DqrC′DsqDps*, *C′D′pDqrC′D′sqD′ps*, *C′D′KpqKpqD′pq*, *CD′pqDpq*, *C′D′pqDpq*
Axioms for S4: *C′pp*, *D′D′pDqrDC′DsqDpsC′D′tuDtu*, *D′D′pDqrDC′D′sqD′psC′D′KtuKtuD′tu*, *DD′pqDDpqC′D′rrD′MrMr*

Definitions: Df. *C′*: *C′pq* = *D′pDqq*
Df. *C*: *Cpq* = *DpDqq*
Df. *N*: *Np* = *Dpp*

Df. K: $K = NDD$

Df. M: $Mp = ND'pp$

Rule: α, $D\alpha D\beta\gamma \rightarrow \beta$.

11.51. System of 'Rigorous' Implication (Ackermann, 1956).

(We write C here not for material but for 'rigorous' implication, for which we have neither $CpCqp$, $CpCNpq$ nor even—unlike 'strict' implication—$CqCpp$ and $CKpNpq$; in fact no laws of the form $C\alpha\beta$ where α and β have no common variables.)

Axioms:	(1) Cpp	(8) $CpApq$
	(2) $CCpqCCqrCpr$	(9) $CqApq$
	(3) $CCqrCCpqCpr$	(10) $CKCprCqrCApqr$
	(4) $CCpCpqCpq$	(11) $CKpAqrAqKpr$
	(5) $CKpqp$	(12) $CCpqCNqNp$
	(6) $CKpqq$	(13) $CpNNp$
	(7) $CKCpqCprCpKqr$	(14) $CNNpp$
Rules:	(a) α, $C\alpha\beta \rightarrow \beta$	(c) α, $AN\alpha\beta \rightarrow \beta$
	(b) α, $\beta \rightarrow K\alpha\beta$	(d) β, $C\alpha C\beta\gamma \rightarrow C\alpha\gamma$.

11.52. System E of Entailment (Anderson and Belnap, 1958) (C for entailment).

Axioms and Rules: 11.51 without (c); or (equivalently) without (c) or (d) but with (1) replaced by $CCKCppCqqrr$

Definitions: Df. L: $Lp = CCppp$

Df. M: $Mp = NLNp$

($CLqCpq$ and $CNMpCpq$ not provable.)

Axioms for C-pure fragment, with Rule (a) (Belnap, 1960):

$CCCppqq$, $CCpqCCqrCpr$, $CCpCpqCpq$

11.61. Strict-Implication Fragment of S5.

(We write C here not for material but for strict implication; and P, Q for the strict implications Crp, Crq.)

Rule: Strict detachment (α, $C\alpha\beta \rightarrow \beta$)

Definitions: Df. L: $Lp = CCppp$

Df. M: $Mp = CCpLpp$ (or $CCpLpLp$)

4-Axiom Base (Lemmon, 1956): $CCpqCCqrCpr$, $CCCPqPP$, $CPCqP$, Cpp

3-Axiom Base (Meredith, 1956): (a) $CCpqCCqrCpr$, $CCCPqPP$, $CqCpp$; or (b) $CCpqCCqrCpr$, $CCCCpqrqCpq$, Cpp

2-Axiom Base (Meredith, 1956): (a) $CqCpp$, $CCCCpqrqCCqsCps$; or (b) Cpp, $CCCCpqrqCCqsCtCps$

2-Axiom Base (Prior, 1958): (a) $CqCpp$, $CCCCpqrsCCqsCps$ (cf. 2.14 (c); or (b) Cpp, $CCCCpqrsCCqsCtCps$

1-Axiom Base (Meredith, 1956): $CCCCCttCpqCrsCCspCuCrp$.

11.62. S3, S4, S5 in N–K–C' (Lemmon, 1956).

Notation and Rule as in 11.61

Definitions: Df. L: $Lp = CNpp$

Df. M: $Mp = NLNp$

Axioms in *C*:

For S3: (1) *CCpqCCqrCpr*, (2) *CQCpp*, (3) *CCpCpqCpq*
For S4: (1), (2)′ *CqCpp*, (3)
For S5: (1), (2)′, (3)′ *CCCPqPP*

Remaining Axioms (common to S3–5):

(4) *CKpqp*	(7) *CCpqCNqNp*
(5) *CKpqq*	(8) *CpNNp*
(6) *CCpqCCprCpKqr*	(9) *CNNpp*

(10) *CKpNKpNqq*.

(*Note*: (1), (2)′, (3) give the strict-implication fragment of S4. Equivalent set, Kripke, 1958: *Cpp*, *CPCqP*, *CCpqCCpCqrCpr*. Cf. 12.1.)

11.71. Łukasiewicz Modal Logic with δ (1953).

(Understood as subjoined to 7.1, with *M*, *L*, etc., substitutable for δ; either *M* or *L* undefined, and subjoined axioms given in terms of the undefined functor. *C* now reverts to its normal use.)

Special Axiom: *CpMp*, or *CLpp*
Axiomatic Rejections: **CMpp*, **Mp*; or **CpLp*, **NLp*
Definition: Df. *L* as in 11.1 or Df. *M* as in 11.21
Rejection Rules as in 10.11.

11.711. One-axiom Ł-Modal (Meredith, 1953).
Impossibility (*I*) and (*C*) sole primitives.
Definitions: Df. *N*: *Np* = *CpIp*
Df. *M*: *Mp* = *NIp*
Axiom: *CpCδδIpδq*
Axiomatic Rejections: **CpIIp*, **CIpp*
Rules as in 11.71.

11.72. S5 in *C–L–*o with δ (Meredith, 1953).
Rules as in 7.1
Axioms: (1) *LCδCCpoCqrδCCrpCqp*
(2) *CLpCδCpqδq*
(3) *CδoCδCooδLp*.

(Also obtained by subjoining to any adequate basis for S5 the weak law of extensionality *CE′pqCδpδq* and substitution for the new variables. But, not being subjoined to 7.1, does not contain the stronger *CEpqCδpδq*.)

11.73. S5 with δ and *n* (Meredith, 1953).

(*n* is a contingent propositional constant, equivalent to the logical product of all true propositions.)

Rules as in 7.1
Axioms: (1), (2), (3) of 11.72, together with
(4) *n*, (5) *CpLCnp*, (6) *CLnp*
or drop (6), define o as *Ln*, and replace
(3) by *CδoCδCopδq*.

§ 12. *Intuitionist Propositional Calculus with Sub-Systems and Extensions*

(Each system has, with its implication functor, the rule of detachment as in 1.1.)

12.1. Positive Implicational Calculus.
4-Axiom Base (Hilbert, 1922):
CCpCpqCpq, *CCqrCCpqCpr*, *CCpCqrCqCpr*, *CpCqp*
3-Axiom Base (Hilbert, 1930): *CCpCpqCpq*, *CCpqCCqrCpr*, *CpCqp*
2-Axiom Base: *CpCqp*, *CCpCqrCCpqCpr* (Łukasiewicz); or *CpCqp*, *CCpqCCpCqrCpr* (Wajsberg, 1939)
1-Axiom Base (Meredith):
CCCpqrCsCCqCrtCqt, or *CtCCpqCCCspCqrCpr*.

12.2. Full Positive Logic (Variations of Hilbert-Bernays, 1934).
Axioms: Any of the sets in 12.1 plus sets (2) and (3) of 3.2.

12.3. Minimal Calculus (Variations of Johannson, 1936).
Axioms: (1) Any set in 12.2
(2) *CCpqCCpNqNp*; or *CCpNqCqNp*; or simply add the constant 0 with Df. *N*: *Np* = *Cp*0.

12.4. Kolmogorov's Calculus (Variations of Kolmogorov, 1925).
Axioms: (1) Any set in 12.1
(2) as in 12.3.

12.5. Full Intuitionistic Calculus (Variations of Heyting, 1930).
Axioms: Add to any set in 12.2 the (4) of 3.2; or add to 12.3 either *CpCNpq* or (if 12.3 is axiomatized with 0 and Df. *N*) *C*0*p*.

(*Note*: 12.2–12.5 all have the 'tiered' character of 3.2. But if in 12.5 *CpCNpq* is replaced by *CNNpp*, or *C*0*p* by *CCCp*00*p*, we will have the full classical propositional calculus, but not in a 'tiered' form, as the axioms for *N* or 0 will now yield formulae in pure *C*, e.g. *CCCpqpp*, not derivable from the pure *C* axioms, i.e. from 12.1. Cf. Hilbert and Bernays 1.)

12.6. Weak Positive Implicational Calculus (Church, 1951).
Axioms: (1) *CCpCpqCpq* (3) *CCpCqrCqCpr*
(2) *CCqrCCpqCpr* (4) *Cpp*.

(*Note*: In 12.1–4, *CpCNpq* is not a thesis but *CpCqp* is. In 12.6, with or without Df. *N*, neither *CpCNpq* nor *CpCqp* is provable.)

12.7. System B–C–I (Meredith, 1956).
Following certain 'combinatory logicians', put B for (2), C for (3), I for (4) of 12.6, P for *CCpqCCqrCpr* and T for *CpCCpqq*. Then the set B,C,I (with substitution and detachment) is equivalent to
(*a*) T,I and either B or P; and to
(*b*) I together with any one of
CCpCqrCCsqCsCpr
CCsqCCpCqrCsCpr
CCCCpqrsCCqrCps
CCqrCCCCpqrsCps.

12.71 System B–C–K (Meredith).
Replace I in preceding by *CpCqp*
Equivalent Single Axiom: *CCCpqrCCsCrtCqCst*.

12.8. Systems between Intuitionist and Classical Propositional Calculus (Dummett, 1958).

(These correspond to the systems of 11.3 as the intuitionist calculus does to S4; see p. 253.)

System KC (corresponding to S4.2):

12.5+*ANpNNp*

System LC (corresponding to S4.3):

12.5+(*a*) *ACpqCqp*

or (*b*) *CCCpqrCCqprr*

System LC′ (equivalent to LC):

12.5 less the *A* axioms

+(*b*) and Df. *A*: *Apq* = *KCCpqqCCqpp*

12.1+(*b*) are complete for the pure *C* fragment of LC (Bull, 1959).

(Let propositions take values represented by 1, 0, and all proper fractions; let *Cpq* = 1 if $p \leqslant q$, and = q if $p > q$, and let *Kpq* be min(p, q), *Apq* be max(p, q), and *Np* be *Cp*0. Then laws of LC are all those formulae, and only those formulae, which always = 1 with this interpretation.)

Note: For Łukasiewicz many-valued systems, which all contain 12.7 and 12.71 but neither contain nor are contained in any others in this section, see Tarski 2, Paper IV.

APPENDIX II (1960)

Some Methods of Proof

§ 1. *Propositional Calculus; Condensed Detachment*

FOLLOWING Meredith, let us write *Dxy* for the most general result of detachment with *x*, or some substitution in *x*, for our *Cαβ*, and *y*, or some substitution in *y*, for our α ('most general' in the sense of having no unnecessary identifications of variables. For example, with 1. *Cpp* and 2. *CpCqp*, D21 is *CqCpp*, not *CpCpp* or *CqCqq*, though these also are obtainable by detachment with substitutions in 2 for our *Cαβ* and 1 or a substitution in it for our α).

With this method of abridgement we give, firstly, a proof of the Tarski–Bernays axioms, i.e. 2.11 of previous Appendix, from the *C*-pure axioms in Peirce's 3.11:

1. *Cpp*		3. *CCpqCCqrCpr*
2. *CCpCqrCqCpr*		4. *CCCpqpp*
D33	=	5. *CCCCqrCprsCCpqs*
D55	=	6. *CCpCqrCCsqCpCsr*
D23	=	7. *CCqrCCpqCpr*
D72	=	8. *CCsCpCqrCsCqCpr*
D87	=	9. *CCqrCpCCpqr*
DD393	=	10. *CCqrCCCCpqrsCps*
D2.10	=	11. *CCCCpqrsCCqrCps*
D11.4	=	12. *CCqpCpp*
D2.12	=	13. *CpCCqpp*
D6.13	=	14. *CCqCrpCpCqp*
D2.1	=	D9.1 = 15. *CpCCpqq*
D14.15	=	16. *CpCqp*

The Tarski–Bernays set are 3, 4, 16. 1 is not independent, since it is D12.4, and is not itself used in the proof of 12. In the remaining three axioms, 2 is replaceable by 15, since D6.15 = 2, and the 'synthetic theorem' 6 (= DD33D33) follows from 3 alone. Since 3, 4, 15 are thus a sufficient set, so is the pair 4, 11 (2.14 (*b*) of previous Appendix); for DD11.4.4 = 1, and (see set 12.7) DD11.11.1 = 3 and DD11.1.1 = 15.

That 3, 4 and 15 suffice for *C*-pure was noted by Wajsberg; and Łukasiewicz's more general result, the sufficiency of set 2.12, is demonstrated as follows:

		1. *CpCαβ*	
		2. *CCCpqpp*	
		3. *CCpqCCqrCpr*	
D33	=	4. *CCCCqrCprsCCpqs*	By 3
D44	=	5. *CCpCqrCCsqCpCsr*	By 3
D3D43	=	6. *CCCCCprsCCqrstCCpqt*	By 3
D45	=	7. *CCqrCCpqCCrsCps*	By 3
D57	=	8. *CCtCpqCCqrCtCCrsCps*	By 3

D72	= 9. *CCpCCsqsCCsrCpr*	By 2.3
D79	= 10. *CCpCtCCsqsCCCCsrCtruCpu*	
DD317	= 11. *CpCCqαCCβrCqr*	By 1.3
DD3.11.3	= 12. *CpCCCCβrCqrsCCqαs*	
DD10.12.5	= 13. *CpCCsCCCβrCqrqCCqtCst* (α eliminated)	
DD10.13.9	= 14. *CpCCsrCCCsqsr* (β eliminated)	
D8.14	= 15. *CCCCCsqsrtCpCCtuCCsru*	
D6.15	= 16. *CCCsqtCpCCCCtsruCCsru*	
D2.16	= 17. *CpCCCCtpruCCpru*	
DD17.2.2	= 18. *CCCCCprppqq*	
DD10.16.18	= 19. *CCCprpCqp*	
DD9.17.19	= 20. *CpCqp*	

Frege's third axiom (set 1.1) is proved from his first two thus:

1. *CpCqp*	2. *CCpCqrCCpqCpr*
DD2D121	= 3. *CCqrCCpqCpr* (Frege)
DD2DD332D11	= 4. *CCpCqrCqCpr* (Łukasiewicz)

If, on the other hand, we take as axioms 1. *CpCqp*, 2. *CCqCprCCpqCpr*, 3. *CCpCqrCqCpr*, we obtain Frege's 2 as DD2D3D123.

When thus investigating the deductive possibilities of different formulae, it is handy to refer to the more important of them by nicknames, e.g.

Simp, *CpCqp*	Duns Scotus, *CpCNpq*
Modus Ponens, *CpCCpqq*	Clavius, *CCNppp*
Comm, *CCpCqrCqCpr*	Peirce, *CCCpqpp*
Comm Comm, *CqCCpCqrCpr*	Frege, *CCpCqrCCpqCpr*
Syll, *CCpqCCqrCpr*	Hilbert, *CCpCpqCpq*
Weak Syll or Comm Syll, *CCqrCCpqCpr*	Tarski or Dilemma, *CCCpqrCCprr*
Syll Simp, *CCCpqrCqr*	Roll, *CCCpqrCCrpp*

'Simp' is for Simplification, and Dilemma is so called because with *q*/o it becomes *CCNprCCprr*. Note that Comm and Comm Comm, i.e. D(Comm) (Comm), are interdeducible—put X for the latter, and Comm is DDXXX (cf. Łukasiewicz, *Aristotle's Syllogistic*, p. 107). Syll Simp, i.e. D(Syll) (Simp), is a useful thesis—with Clavius or Peirce it gives Identity, *Cpp*; with *CCNqNpCpq*, *CNpCpq*; with *CCCpqpCCpqq* or with Roll, Modus Ponens.

§ 2. *Suppositional Proof in Ontology*

In developing their various characteristic disciplines, Leśniewski and his school often set out their proofs in 'suppositional' form, first listing the various components of the antecedent of the thesis to be proved, and then showing step by step how its consequent follows, gathering each formula proved into a continually enlarging conjunctive consequent, with the required consequent as the final conjunct.

We may illustrate this method by using it to set out (following B. Sobociński) the proofs involved in the derivation of Leśniewski's original ontological axiom of 1920 from his much abridged one of 1929 (see Appendix I, 9.21). General principles from propositional logic and quantification theory, such as *CEpqCqp* or *CCΣaf(a)pΠaCf(a)p*, are simply assumed without being stated (those two, for example, in the proof of T1).

A1. $\Pi ab E \epsilon ab \Sigma c K \epsilon ac \epsilon cb$
T1. $\Pi abc C K \epsilon ab \epsilon ca \epsilon cb$ (A1 a/c, c/a)
T2. $\Pi ab C \epsilon ab \Sigma c K \epsilon ac \epsilon cb$ (A1)
D1. $\Pi abc E K \epsilon ab \epsilon ca \epsilon a {*} bc$ (Ontological definition)

T3. $\Pi abcd C K \epsilon ab K \epsilon ca \epsilon da \epsilon cd$
Proof (Tarski, 1921):
$\Pi abcd$
(1) $CK\epsilon ab$
(2) $K\epsilon ca$
(3) ϵda
(4) $K\epsilon a{*}bc$ (D1; 1; 2)
(5) $K\epsilon d{*}bc$ (T1 $b/{*}bc$, c/d; 4; 3)
ϵcd (D1 a/d; 5)

T4. $\Pi ab C \epsilon ab \epsilon aa$
Proof: Πab
(1) $C\epsilon ab$
$K\Sigma c$
(2) $K\epsilon ac$ (T2; 1)
(3) ϵcb
ϵaa (T3 a/c, c/a, d/a; 3; 2; 2)

(Note how the existential quantification falls away when the variable which it binds disappears from the conclusion of the inference made from premisses within its scope. This is a frequent move in proofs of this type.)

T5. $\Pi abc C K \epsilon ab \epsilon ca \epsilon ac$
Proof: Πabc
(1) $CK\epsilon ab$
(2) ϵca
(3) $K\epsilon aa$ (T4; 1)
ϵac (T3 c/a, d/c; 1; 3; 2)

D2. $\Pi ab E \epsilon ab (\epsilon' b) a$

This definition merits a little comment. Leśniewskian systems do not assume at the outset an infinity of types of variables for which appropriate substitutions may be made, if necessary by 'apostrophe'; e.g. a variable ϕ for monadic proposition-forming functors of terms, such that by the substitution $\phi/\epsilon' b$ we may pass from ϕa to ϵab. The procedure is rather first to define a functor ϵ' such that its application to a term b forms a functor $(\epsilon' b)$ whose application to the term a forms a proposition equivalent to ϵab. (This is D2 above; propositions of such forms as $(\epsilon' b)a$ are described as 'many-link functions', as they are formed by means of functors which are themselves functions.) We may then, and only then, having a particular expression of the category of monadic proposition-forming functors of terms, introduce variables of this category, for which we can make substitutions (but not apostrophic ones; though it is clear that the actual effect of performing the substitution $\phi/\epsilon' b$ in ϕa may be obtained by performing the substitution $\phi/(\epsilon' b)$ and then passing form $(\epsilon' b)a$ to ϵab by D2). In this way the system becomes richer in its 'semantic categories' as well as in its theses as we go along; and for each newly introduced category we may lay down its own law of extensionality, as T6 below for the category of $(\epsilon' b)$.

T6. $\Pi abE\Pi cE\epsilon ca\epsilon cb\Pi\phi E\phi a\phi b$

T7. $\Pi abcCK\epsilon caK\Pi cdCK\epsilon ca\epsilon da\epsilon cd\Pi cC\epsilon ca\epsilon cb\epsilon ab$

Proof (Sobociński, 1929):

Πabc

(1)	$CK\epsilon ca$	
(2)	$K\Pi cdCK\epsilon ca\epsilon da\epsilon cd$	
(3)	$\Pi cC\epsilon ca\epsilon cb$	
(4)	$K\epsilon cb$	(3; 1)
(5)	$K\Pi dC\epsilon dc\epsilon da$	(T1 a/c, b/a, c/d; 1)
(6)	$K\Pi dC\epsilon da\epsilon dc$	(2; 1)
(7)	$K\Pi dE\epsilon dc\epsilon da$	(5, 6)
(8)	$K\Pi\phi E\phi c\phi a$	(T6 a/c, b/a; 7)
(9)	$K(\epsilon' b)c$	(D2 a/c; 4)
(10)	$K(\epsilon' b)a$	(8 $\phi/(\epsilon' b)$; 9)
	ϵab	(D2; 10)

(The remaining steps are Leśniewski's, 1929)

T8. $\Pi abC\epsilon ab\Sigma c\epsilon ca$

Proof: Πab

(1)	$C\epsilon ab$	
(2)	$K\epsilon aa$	(T4;1)
	$\Sigma c\epsilon ca$	(2)

T9. $\Pi abE\epsilon abKK\Sigma c\epsilon ca\Pi cdCK\epsilon ca\epsilon da\epsilon cd\Pi cC\epsilon ca\epsilon cb$
(T8; T3; T1; T7)

§ 3. *Suppositional Proof in Propositional Calculus*

The procedure of deriving the consequent of a thesis from its antecedents and affirming the whole implication on the basis of this derivation, is clearly capable of wider use, and in 1934, following a suggestion made by Łukasiewicz in 1926, S. Jaśkowski set up a system of rules for such derivations which could be used for establishing the propositional calculus in *C* and *N*. In sketching his procedure, I shall use some of the devices employed by later writers in connexion with the richer 'natural deduction' systems of G. Gentzen.

We write premisses and conclusions as numbered lines, putting at the left the number or numbers of the premiss or premisses ('suppositions') on which the given formula ultimately depends, and on the right the rule by which, and premiss or premisses from which, the line is immediately derived. Jaśkowski's four rules for *C*–*N* are then in effect the following:

(i) Rule of Premisses (P): Any formula may be laid down as a consequence of itself or of any set of assumptions including itself.

(ii) Rule of *C*-Introduction, Conditionalization, or Conditional Proof (CP): If a formula β is derivable from assumptions which include α, then we can derive $C\alpha\beta$ from any further assumptions on which β may depend.

(iii) Rule of *C*-Elimination, Detachment, or *Modus Ponens* (MP): α, $C\alpha\beta \rightarrow \beta$. β will then depend on any assumptions on which either α or $C\alpha\beta$ may depend.

(iv) Rule of *N*-Elimination (NE): Given derivations of both β and $N\beta$ from an assumption $N\alpha$, we may derive α from any further assumptions on which either β or $N\beta$ may depend.

Illustrative deductions:

1	(1) *q*	P
1, 2	(2) *p*	P
2	(3) *Cqp*	2, 1 CP
—	(4) *CpCqp*	3, 2 CP
5	(5) *CpCqr*	P
6	(6) *Cpq*	P
7	(7) *p*	P
5, 7	(8) *Cqr*	7, 5 MP
6, 7	(9) *q*	7, 6 MP
5, 6, 7	(10) *r*	9, 8 MP
5, 6	(11) *Cpr*	10, 7 CP
5	(12) *CCpqCpr*	11, 6 CP
—	(13) *CCpCqrCCpqCpr*	12, 5 CP
14	(14) *Np*	P
14, 15	(15) *q*	P
16	(16) *CNpNq*	P
14, 16	(17) *Nq*	14, 16 MP
15, 16	(18) *p*	14, 15, 17 NE
16	(19) *Cqp*	18, 15, CP
—	(20) *CCNpNqCqp*	19, 16 CP

Of the three conclusions which here emerge as not depending on any particular supposition, (4) and (13) form Łukasiewicz's basis for the positive implicational calculus (12.1), and in fact a suppositional proof or series of proofs using Rules (i)–(iii) above provides one of the most straightforward ways of showing that a formula is in that calculus. We may often sketch such proofs by tabulating the antecedents of a formula and indicating by arrows how its final consequent follows from them, thus (for the proof of (13)):

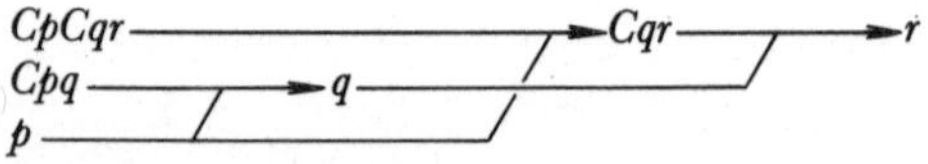

With (20) added, (4) and (13) give one of Łukasiewicz's bases for classical *C–N* (1.4(*c*)). Jaśkowski noted also that if in his rule (iv) the assumption $N\alpha$ is replaced by α, and the conclusion α by $N\alpha$, the rules no longer yield classical *C–N* but do yield Kolmogorov's calculus (12.4). (iv) with this change is in fact an exact counterpart of Kolmogorov's own axiom *CCpqCCpNpNp* for subjunction to *C*-positive.

The rule CP, when occurring as a derived rule in a system in which the originally given rules are different, is called the 'deduction theorem'.

APPENDIX III

Select Bibliography

(Revised 1960)

The following abbreviations are used for periodicals:

AJP for *Australasian Journal of Philosophy*.
BJPS for *British Journal of Philosophy of Science*.
DS for *Dominican Studies*.
JCS for *Journal of Computing Systems*.
JSL for *Journal of Symbolic Logic*.
NDJFL for *Notre Dame Journal of Formal Logic*.
PAS for *Proceedings of the Aristotelian Society*.
PSASA for the *Yearbook* of the Polish Society of Arts and Sciences Abroad (London).
RPL for *Revue philosophique de Louvain*.
SL for *Studia Logica*.
ZML for *Zeitschrift für mathematische Logik und Grundlagen der Mathematik*.

References to systems use the numbering of Appendix I.

ABAELARDUS, PETRUS (1079–1142)

1. *Dialectica*. First complete edition of the Paris manuscript by L. M. de Rijk (Van Gorcum, Assen, 1956). The beginning, to all intents and purposes, of the great medieval flowering of logic.

ACKERMANN, WILHELM (1896–   )

1. 'Begründung einer strengen Implikation', *JSL*, xxi (1956), pp. 113–28. System 11.5.
   See Anderson and Belnap 1; Hilbert and Ackermann.

AJDUKIEWICZ, KASIMIERZ (1890–   )

1. 'Die syntaktische Konnexität', *Studia Philosophica*, i (1935), pp. 1–27. Mimeographed English translation available at the University of Chicago. Develops, under the influence of Leśniewski, a hierarchy of 'parts of speech', functioning like the simple theory of types.

ANDERSON, ALAN ROSS (1925–   )

1. *The Formal Analysis of Normative Concepts*, Technical Report No. 2, U.S. Office of Naval Research Contract No. SAR/Nonr-609 (16), 1956.
   See Hamblin 2 and 3; Prior 7, 11, 14.

ANDERSON, A. R., and BELNAP, NUEL DINSMORE, JNR. (1930–   )

1. 'The Pure Calculus of Entailment', *JSL*, xxvi (1960).

ANDERSON, A. R., BELNAP, N. D., and WALLACE, JOHN ROY (1938–   )

1. 'Independent Axiom-schemata for the Pure Theory of Entailment', *ZML*, vi (1960), pp. 93–5.

ARISTOTLE (384–321 B.C.)

1. *The Works of Aristotle Translated into English*, vol. i (Oxford University Press, 1928).
2. *Aristotle's Prior and Posterior Analytics*: A Revised Text with Introduction and Commentary by W. D. Ross (Clarendon Press, 1949). The notes contain useful elucidations and tabulations of Aristotle's arguments; see, for example, the notes to *An. Pr.* i. 46, ii. 2–7, 22, 23.

BARCAN, RUTH (MRS. J. A. MARCUS) (1921–)

1. 'A Functional Calculus of First Order Based on Strict Implication', *JSL*, xi (1946), pp. 1–16.
2. 'The Identity of Individuals in a Strict Functional Calculus of Second Order', *JSL*, xii (1947), pp. 12–15.

BAUDRY, LÉON (–)

1. *La Querelle des futurs contingents* (J. Vrin, Paris, 1950). Documents from a fifteenth-century controversy involving 3-valued logic, centring around the contentions of the Louvain scholar Peter de Rivo, with a lucid introductory account by Baudry of preceding medieval discussions. Peter's arguments are very acute, and this is the most instructive book so far published on this topic.

See Cicero, Ockham.

BENNETT, JONATHAN FRANCIS (1930–)

1. 'Meaning and Implication', *Mind*, 1954, pp. 451–63.

See Smiley 1.

BOCHENSKI, INNOCENTIUS M. (1902–)

1. *La Logique de Théophraste* (Librairie de l'Université de Fribourg en Suisse, 1947).
2. 'On the Categorical Syllogism', *DS*, i (1948), pp. 35–37. See Thomas 1.
3. *A Précis of Mathematical Logic* (D. Reidel, Dordrecht). 1959 translation of a 1948 French text.
4. *Formale Logik* (Karl Alber, Freiburg/München, 1956). A collection, with interstitial comments, of ancient, medieval, modern-mathematical, and Indian sources. An English translation in preparation.

See also Petrus Hispanus.

BOEHNER, PHILOTHEUS (1901–55)

1. *Medieval Logic*: An Outline of its Development from 1250 to *c.* 1400 (Manchester University Press, 1952).

See also Burleigh; Ockham; Thomas 3.

BOETHIUS, ANICIUS MANLIUS TORQUATUS SEVERINUS (455–526)

1. *Opera Omnia*, Tomus Posterior, being vol. 64 of J. P. Migne's *Patrologia Latina* (1891). See esp. *Introductio ad Syllogismos Categoricos* (pp. 761–72) and *De Syllogismo Hypothetico* (pp. 831–76).

BRENTANO, FRANZ (1838–1917)

1. *Psychologie vom empirischen Standpunkt* (Leipzig, 1874); French translation by Maurice de Gandillac, *Psychologie du point de vue empirique* (Aubier, Paris, 1944), bk. ii, ch. 7, esp. §§ 7, 15.

BULL, ROBERT ANSLEY (1939–)

1. 'The Implicational Fragment of Dummett's LC', *JSL*. System 12.8.

BURLEIGH, WALTER (1237–1345)

1. *De Puritate Artis Logicae Tractatus Longior*, with a revised edition of the *Tractatus Brevior*, edited by Philotheus Boehner (Franciscan Institute, St. Bonaventure, N.Y., 1955). The most attractive, readable, and 'modern' of the medieval general logical textbooks so far reprinted. See Prior 14.

CARROLL, LEWIS (CHARLES LUTWIDGE DODGSON, 1832–98)

1. *Symbolic Logic* and *The Game of Logic* (bound in one, Dover Edition, 1955). See Prior 14.
2. 'A Logical Paradox', *Mind*, 1894, pp. 436–8. See Johnson 2 and 3; Sidgwick 1 and 2.
3. 'What the Tortoise said to Achilles', *Mind*, 1895, pp. 278–80. Answer to Sidgwick 2?

CHURCH, ALONZO (1903–)

1. *A Bibliography of Symbolic Logic* (Association for Symbolic Logic). Covers the period 1666–1935. The *JSL* has aimed, in its reviews, at a complete coverage of the period from 1936 onwards, and also has occasional supplementations of Church's *Bibliography* for the earlier period.
2. 'The Weak Theory of Implication', in *Kontrolliertes Denken* (Kommissions-Verlag Karl Alber, Munich, 1951). System 12.6.
3. *Introduction to Mathematical Logic*, I (Princeton, 1956). Outstanding for copious references, meticulous exposition, and incorporation of major historical results in exercises.

CICERO, MARCUS TULLIUS (106–43 B.C.)

1. *De Fato*. Included, with English translation by H. Rackham, in the second volume of Cicero's *De Oratore*, Loeb Classical Library (Heinemann, London, and Harvard University Press, Cambridge, Mass., 1942). A principal source for the Stoic-Epicurean controversy about the Law of Excluded Middle. Much cited, for example, in Baudry 1.

COUTURAT, LOUIS (1868–1914)

1. *La Logique de Leibniz d'après des documents inédits* (Alcan, Paris, 1901). See especially the discussion of syllogistic logic, ch. i, §§ 1–10 (cf. Thomas 5), and of algebraic interpretations of propositional forms, ch. viii (cf. de Morgan 3).

CURRY, HASKELL BROOKS (1900–), and FEYS, ROBERT

1. *Combinatory Logic*, I (Amsterdam, 1956). A work suggesting many of the directions of the logic of the future. Contains some but not all of the material in Feys 2, with much further matter. See especially chs. 5 (presupposing 3B) and 8, and section 9E1.

DE MORGAN, AUGUSTUS (1806–78)

1. *Formal Logic* (London, 1847; reprinted by Open Court Publishing Co., 1926, with original page-numbering incorporated in the text).
2. 'On the Structure of the Syllogism, and on the Application of the Theory of Probabilities to Questions of Argument and Authority', *Transactions of the Cambridge Philosophical Society*, viii (1849), pp. 379–408.
3. 'On the Symbols of Logic, the Theory of the Syllogism, and in Particular of the Copula, and the Application of the Theory of Probabilies to some Questions of Evidence', ibid. ix (1856), part i, pp. 79–127.
4. 'On the Syllogism, No. III, and on Logic in General', ibid. x (1864), pp. 173–230.
5. 'On the Syllogism, No. IV, and on the Logic of Relations' (with Appendix 'On Syllogisms of Transposed Quantity'), ibid., pp. 331–8.
6. 'On the Syllogism, No. V, and on Various Points of the Onymatic System', ibid., pp. 428–87.
7. Articles 'Logic' and 'Relation (Logic)', in *The English Cyclopedia*, Arts and Sciences Division, v (1860), pp. 340–54, and vi (1861), pp. 1016–17.

See Couturat; Keynes.

DUGUNDJI, JAMES (–)

1. 'Note on a Property of Matrices for Lewis and Langford's Calculi of Propositions', *JSL*, v (1940), pp. 150–1. Shows that if these calculi are treated as many-valued logics, they must involve an infinite number of values.

DUMMETT, MICHAEL ANTHONY EARDLEY (1925–)

1. Review of Frege 2 in *Mind*, 1954, pp. 102–5.
2. 'Frege on Functions: A Reply', *Philosophical Review*, lxiv (1955), pp. 96–107.
3. 'A Propositional Calculus with Denumerable Matrix', *JSL*, xxiv (1959), pp. 97–106. System 12.8.

DUMMETT, M. A. E., and LEMMON, E. J.

1. 'Modal Logics between S4 and S5', *ZML*, v (1959), pp. 250–64. Systems 11.3 and 12.8.

FARIS, JOHN ACHESON (1913–)

1. 'The Gergonne Relations', *JSL*, xx (1955), pp. 207–31. Syllogistic with relations expressed by Euler's circles as primitive. Cf. Thomas 8.

FEYS, ROBERT (1889–)

1. 'Les Logiques nouvelles des modalités', *Revue néoscholastique de philosophie* (Louvain), 1937, pp. 517–33; 1938, pp. 217–52. See Sobociński 5.
2. 'Le Technique de la logique combinatoire', *RPL*, 1946, pp. 74–103, 237–70.
3. 'Les Méthodes récentes de déduction naturelle', ibid. 1946, pp. 340–400; 1947, pp. 60–72.
4. 'A Simple Notation for Relations', *Methodos*, i (1949), pp. 79–83.
5. 'Les Systèmes formalisées des modalités aristotéliciennes', *RPL*, 1950, pp. 478–509. System 11.1.

See Curry and Feys 1; Gentzen 1.

FREGE, GOTTLOB (1848–1925)

1. *Die Grundlagen der Arithmetik* (Breslau, 1884; reprinted with English translation by J. L. Austin, *The Foundations of Arithmetic*, Basil Blackwell, Oxford, 1950).
2. *Translations from the Philosophical Writings of Gottlob Frege*, edited by Peter Geach and Max Black (Basil Blackwell, Oxford, 1952).

See Church 3; Dummett 1 and 2; Geach 1.

GEACH, PETER THOMAS (1916–)

1. 'Subject and Predicate', *Mind*, 1950, pp. 461–82.
2. 'On *Insolubilia*', *Analysis*, Jan. 1955, pp. 71–72.
3. 'Imperatives and Deontic Logic', *Analysis*, Jan. 1958, pp. 49–56.
4. 'Entailment', *P.A.S.*, Supp. Vol. xxxii (1958), pp. 157–72.
5. 'History of a Fallacy', *Journal of the Philosophical Association* (India), v (1958), pp. 111–22.

GENTZEN, GERHARD (1909–45)

1. *Recherches sur la déduction logique* (Paris, 1955). Translation of *Untersuchungen über das logische Schließen* (1934) by Jean Ladrière, with notes by Jean Ladrière and R. Feys.

HALLDÉN, SÖREN (1923–)

1. 'On the Semantic Non-completeness of Certain Lewis Calculi', *JSL*, xvi (1951), pp. 127–9.
2. *On the Logic of 'Better'* (Gleerup, Lund & Munksgaard, Copenhagen, 1957).

HAMBLIN, CHARLES LEONARD (1922–)

1. 'Questions', *AJP*, Dec. 1958, pp. 159–68.
2. Review of Prior 7 and Anderson 1, ibid., pp. 232–4.
3. 'The Modal "Probably" ', *Mind*, April 1959, pp. 234–40.

HENKIN, LEON (1921–)

1. 'Fragments of the Propositional Calculus', *JSL*, xiv (1949), pp. 42–47. Systematic method of adding to the *C*-pure calculus adequate axioms for any further functor, given its truth-table. See Thomas 11, 12.

HILBERT, DAVID (1862–1943), and ACKERMANN, WILHELM

1. *Principles of Mathematical Logic* (Chelsea Publishing Co., N.Y., 1950; translation of *Grundzüge der theoretischen Logik*, edition of 1938).

HILBERT, DAVID, and BERNAYS, PAUL (1888–)
1. *Grundlagen der Mathematik* (Berlin, 1934 and 1939).

HINTIKKA, KAARLO JAAKKO JUHANI (1929–)
1. 'Identity, Variables, and Impredicative Definitions', *JSL*, xxi (1956), pp. 225–45.
2. 'Quantifiers in Deontic Logic', *Societas Scientiarum Fennica Commentationes Humanarum Litterarum*, xxiii. 4 (1957), pp. 3–23.
3. 'Modality as Referential Multiplicity', *Ajatus*, xx (1957), pp. 49–64.

ISHIMOTO, ARATA (1917–)
1. 'A Set of Axioms of the Modal Propositional Calculus Equivalent to S3', *The Science of Thought* (Tokyo), i (1954), pp. 1–11.
2. 'A Note on the Paper 'A Set of Axioms, etc.'' ', ibid. ii (1956), pp. 69–72.
3. 'A Formulation of the Modal Propositional Calculus Equivalent to S4', ibid., pp. 73–82.

Systems 11.44.

JOHNSON, WILLIAM ERNEST (1858–1931)
1. 'The Logical Calculus', *Mind*, 1892, pp. 3–30, 235–50, 340–57.
2. 'A Logical Paradox', ibid. 1894, p. 583. Answer to Carroll 2.
3. 'Hypotheticals in a Context', ibid. 1895, pp. 133–4. Answer to Sidgwick 2.
4. *Logic* (Cambridge University Press; Part I, 1921; Part II, 1922; Part III, 1924). Mill and Keynes on singular and general terms carried further in I. vi, vii, ix. 1, 2; II. i. 4–6, iv. 4; Keynes on existential import in I. ix. 3, 4; see also discussion of functions in II. iii and vi, and of fact and law in III. i.

Many of Johnson's logical reflections also appear in footnotes to the later editions of Keynes 1.

JORDAN, ZBIGNIEW (1911–)
1. *The Development of Mathematical Logic and of Logical Positivism in Poland between the Two Wars*, being Polish Science and Learning No. 6 (Oxford University Press, 1945).

KANGER, STIG GUSTAV (1924–)
1. 'A Note on Partial Postulate-sets for Propositional Logic', *Theoria*, xxi (1955), pp. 99–104. System like 3.2.

KEYNES, JOHN NEVILLE (1852–1949)
1. *Studies and Exercises in Formal Logic* (Macmillan; 1st ed. 1884; 2nd ed. 1887; 3rd ed. 1894; 4th ed. 1906). See especially his development of Mill's views on singular and general terms in I. ii, iii; II. vi; his discussion of existential import in II. viii; and of complex terms (in the tradition of de Morgan) in Appendix C (references to 4th ed.).

KNEALE, MARTHA (1909–)

KNEALE, WILLIAM CALVERT (1906–)
1. *The Development of Logic* (Clarendon Press, 1961).

KRIPKE, SAUL AARON (1940–)

1. 'A Completeness Theorem in Modal Logic', *JSL*, xxiv (1959), pp. 1–14.

LEJEWSKI, CZESŁAW (1913–)

1. 'Logic and Existence', *BJPS*, v (1954), pp. 104–19.
2. 'A Contribution to Leśniewski's Mereology', *PSASA*, 1954–5, pp. 43–50.
3. 'A New Axiom of Mereology', *PSASA*, 1955–6, pp. 65–70.
4. 'Proper Names', *PAS* Supp. Vol. xxxi (1957), pp. 229–56.
5. 'On Implicational Definitions', *SL*, viii (1958), pp. 189–205. System 3.3.
6. 'On Leśniewski's Ontology', *Ratio*, Dec. 1958, pp. 150–76.

(These papers, especially 6, form the most instructive introduction to Leśniewskian systems available in English.)

LEMMON, EDWARD JOHN (1930–)

1. 'Alternative Postulate Sets for Lewis's S5', *JSL*, xxi (1956), pp. 347–9. Proof in S5 of 11.23.
2. 'New Foundations for Lewis Modal Systems', *JSL*, xxii (1957), pp. 176–86. System 11.25. See also review by Yonemitsu, *JSL*, xxiii (1958), pp. 346–7.

See also Dummett and Lemmon.

LEONARD, HENRY S. (1905–), and GOODMAN, NELSON (1906–)

1. 'The Calculus of Individuals and its Uses', *JSL*, v (1940), pp. 45–55. A system akin to Leśniewski's mereology.

LEWIS, CLARENCE IRVING (1883–), and LANGFORD, COOPER HAROLD (1895–)

1. *Symbolic Logic* (New York, 1932. Reprinted Dover, 1959, with Appendix incorporating some results of Parry 1).

ŁUKASIEWICZ, JAN (1878–1956)

1. *Elementy logiki matematycznej* (Warsaw, 1929; republished 1958). This little book is full of valuable material even for those who do not know Polish—the symbolism at least can be followed. It develops the system of 1.4(*a*), with proofs of consistency, independence, and completeness, and many glances aside at historical points and at other systems, including the 3-valued one; 5.3 is set up and 1.4(*a*) developed within it; and finally the rudiments of 10.11. Some of its contents are presented anew in 4 below and in the joint paper in Tarski 2.
2. 'The Shortest Axiom of the Implicational Calculus of Propositions', *Proceedings of the Royal Irish Academy*, 52 A 3 (Hodges, Figgis & Co., Dublin, 1948). System 2.15.
3. 'On Variable Functors of Propositional Arguments', *Proceedings of the Royal Irish Academy* (Dublin, 1951). System 7.2. See Meredith 1.
4. *Aristotle's Syllogistic* (Clarendon Press, Oxford, 1951; 2nd ed. 1957). System 10.11. See Meredith 2; Thomas 3 and 4.

5. 'On the Intuitionistic Theory of Deduction', Koninkl. Nederl. Akademie van Wetenschappen, *Proceedings*, Series A, 55, No. 3, and *Indagationes Mathematicae*, 14, No. 3 (North-Holland Publishing Co., Amsterdam, 1952).
6. 'Sur la formalisation des théories mathématiques', in *Les Méthodes formelles en axiomatique*: Colloques Internationaux du Centre National de la Recherche Scientifique, No. 36 (published by the Centre, Paris, 1953).
7. 'A System of Modal Logic', *JCS*, vol. i, No. 3 (July 1953), pp. 111–49. Systems 7.1, 11.71. See Prior 7, 12; Thomas 6.
8. 'The Principle of Individuation', *PAS*, Supp. Vol. xxvii (London, 1953), esp. pp. 77 ff.

MCKINSEY, JOHN CHARLES CHINOWECH (1908–53)

1. 'Proof of the Independence of the Primitive Symbols of Heyting's Calculus of Propositions', *JSL*, iv (1939), pp. 155–8.
2. 'Proof that there are Infinitely Many Modalities in Lewis's System S2', *JSL*, v (1940), pp. 110–12.

See McKinsey and Tarski.

MCKINSEY, J. C. C., and TARSKI, ALFRED

1. 'Some Theorems about the Sentential Calculi of Lewis and Heyting', *JSL*, xiii (1948), pp. 1–15.

MATES, J. R. BENSON (1919–)

1. *Stoic Logic* (University of California Press, 1953).

MEREDITH, CAREW ARTHUR (1904–)

1. 'On an Extended System of Propositional Calculus', *Proceedings of the Royal Irish Academy*, 54 A 3 (Hodges, Figgis & Co., Dublin, 1951). System 7.2.
2. 'The Figures and Moods of the *n*-Term Aristotelian Syllogism', *DS*, vi (1953), pp. 42–47.
3. 'Single Axioms for the Systems (*C*, *N*), (*C*, *O*) and *A*, *N*) of the Two-valued Propositional Calculus', *JCS*, vol. i, No. 3 (July 1953), pp. 155–64. Systems 1.5, 3.13, 6.13, 6.14.
4. 'A Single Axiom for Positive Logic', ibid., pp. 169–70. System 12.1.

MILL, JOHN STUART (1806–73)

1. *A System of Logic* (1st ed. 1843, final edition the 8th). Mill's characteristic views on singular and general terms are developed in I. ii. 3, 5; v. 1–4; vi; vii. 1; II. ii and iii.

See Whately; Keynes; Johnson 4; Brentano.

MOH SHAW-KWEI

1. 'The Deduction Theorem and Two New Logical Systems', *Methodos*, ii (1950), pp. 56–75.
2. 'Logical Paradoxes for Many-valued Systems', *JSL*, xix (1954), pp. 37–40. See Geach 2; Prior 2.

MOODY, ERNEST ADDISON (1903–)

1. *Truth and Consequence in Mediaeval Logic* (North-Holland Publishing Co., Amsterdam, 1953).

NAGEL, ERNEST (1901–), and NEWMAN, JAMES ROY (1907–)

1. *Gödel's Proof* (Routledge & Kegan Paul, London, 1959). A superb popularization of a very difficult subject.

OCKHAM, WILLIAM OF (*c.* 1285–1349)

1. *Tractatus de Praedestinatione et de Praescientia Dei et de Futuris Contingentibus*, edited with a Study on the Medieval Problem of a Three-valued Logic by Philotheus Boehner (Franciscan Institute, St. Bonaventure, N.Y., 1945). See also Baudry.

PARRY, WILLIAM TUTHILL (1908–)

1. 'Modalities in the *Survey* System of Strict Implication', *JSL*, iv (1939), pp. 137–54. See Feys 4; Lemmon 2.
2. 'A New Symbolism for the Logical Calculus', ibid. xix (1954), pp. 161–8. Contains in § 3 an explanation of Leśniewski's wheel symbolism for truth operators, mentioned in Sobociński 2.

PEIRCE, CHARLES SANDERS (1839–1914)

1. *Collected Papers of Charles Sanders Peirce*, vols.. i–vi, edited by Charles Hartshorne and Paul Weiss (Harvard University Press, 1931–5). Of particular value to the formal logician are the following items and passages: On his own development, 4.2–4; on the history of logic, 4.21–37; on various aspects of the traditional syllogism, 2.445–516, 619–31, 3.154–97, 407–14, 5.320–32; on truth-operators, 4.12–20, 257–65; on implication, 2.344–56, 3.154–97, 365–91, 440–8, 4.69–73 (3.171 and 182 ff. employ a 'natural deduction' technique like that of Appendix II, § 3; system 3.1 is sketched in 3.376–84); on the logic of relations, 3.45–149, 328–58, 416–22 (on nouns and verbs), 571–608, 4.453; on 'not' as a relation, 2.550, 597–9, 3.407–14; on logic systematically viewed as the theory of implication with lower- and higher-order quantification, 3.365–403M; on higher-order quantification, 4.80–84; on logical puzzles and paradoxes, 2.618, 4.78, 546, 5.333–40.
2. Ibid., vols. vii, viii, edited by Arthur W. Burks (Harvard University Press, 1958). On the text of Aristotle, 7.233–55; Peirce bibliography 8.
3. Article 'Syllogism', in *The Century Dictionary* (London, 1900–1).

PETRUS HISPANUS (*c.* 1215–77)

1. *Summulae Logicales*, edited by I. M. Bochenski (Marietti, Turin, 1947). See Boehner.

PRIOR, ARTHUR NORMAN (1914–)

1. 'Berkeley in Logical Form', *Theoria*, xxi (1955), pp. 117–22.
2. 'Curry's Paradox and 3-valued Logic', *AJP*, Dec. 1955, pp. 177–82.
3. 'Modality and Quantification in S5', *JSL*, xxi (1956), pp. 60–62.
4. 'A Note on the Logic of Obligation', *RPL*, Feb. 1960, pp. 86–87.
5. 'Definitions, Rules and Axioms', *PAS*, 1955–6, pp. 199–206 and Correction.

6. 'Logicians at Play; or Syll, Simp and Hilbert', *AJP*, Dec. 1956, pp. 182–92.
7. *Time and Modality* (Oxford, 1957).
8. Critical notice of Tarski 2, *Mind*, July 1957, pp. 401–10.
9. 'Peirce's Axioms for Propositional Calculus', *JSL*, xxiii (1958), pp. 135–6. System 3.11.
10. 'Epimenides the Cretan', ibid., pp. 261–6.
11. 'Escapism: The Logical Basis of Ethics', in *Essays in Moral Philosophy* (ed. A. I. Melden, University of Washington Press, Seattle, 1958).
12. 'Notes on a New Group of Modal Systems', *Logique et Analyse*, 6–7 (April 1959), pp. 122–5.
13. 'Axiom-Pairs for Material and Strict Implication', *ZML*. Systems 2. 14(*c*), 11.61.
14. Reviews of Kalinowski, *JSL*, xxi (1956), p. 191; Carroll, xxii (1957), pp. 309–10; Anderson, xxiv (1959), pp. 177–8; Suppes and Blyth, *AJP*, Aug. 1958, pp. 146–50; Burleigh, *New Scholasticism* (Jan. 1958); Halldén 2, *Philosophy*, October 1960.

PRIOR, MARY LAURA (1922–), and PRIOR, A. N.

1. 'Erotetic Logic', *Philosophical Review*, 1955, pp. 43–59.

QUINE, WILLARD VAN ORMAN (1908–)

1. 'A Note on Nicod's Postulate', *Mind*, 1932, pp. 345–50.
1. *A System of Logistic* (Harvard University Press, 1934).
3. 'Completeness of the Propositional Calculus', *JSL*, iii (1938), pp. 37–40.
4. *From a Logical Point of View* (Harvard University Press, 1953).

ROSE, ALAN (1927–)

1. 'An Axiom System for 3-valued Logic', *Methodos*, iii (1951), pp. 233–9. Contains a proof, by Meredith and the author, of system 6.11 (less (4)) from 6.12(*d*).
2. 'A Single Axiom for a Partial System of the Propositional Calculus', *ZML*, i (1955), pp. 196–7. System 8.4.
3. 'Sur les éléments universels de décision', *Comptes rendus des séances de l'Académie des Sciences* (Paris), ccxlix (1957), pp. 2343–5. Generalization of Sobociński 4.

RUSSELL, BERTRAND ARTHUR WILLIAM (1872–)

1. *The Principles of Mathematics* (Cambridge, 1903; 2nd ed., Allen & Unwin, 1937).
2. 'The Theory of Implication', *American Journal of Mathematics*, xxviii (1906), pp. 159–202. Systems 1.2 and 5.2.
3. *Introduction to Mathematical Philosophy* (Allen & Unwin, London, 1919).
4. *Logic and Knowledge* (Allen & Unwin, 1956). Ten essays, including 'On Denoting' from *Mind*, 1905, his 1908 paper on 'Mathematical Logic as Based on the Theory of Types' (in which system 6.11 first appeared), and his most rewarding essay in philosophical logic (deeply influenced by the pre-*Tractatus* Wittgenstein), the 1918 lectures on 'The Philosophy of Logical Atomism'.

SHEPHERDSON, JOHN CEDRIC (1926–)

1. 'On the Interpretation of Aristotelian Syllogistic', *JSL*, xxi (1956), pp. 137–47. Systems 10.11, 21, 22, 4, 5, 6.

SIDGWICK, ALFRED (1850–1943)

1. 'A Logical Paradox', *Mind*, 1894, p. 582. Answer to Carroll 2.
2. 'Hypotheticals in a Context', ibid. 1895, p. 143. Answer to Johnson 2. See Johnson 3; Carroll 3.

SŁUPECKI, JERZY (1904–)

1. 'St. Leśniewski's Protothetics', *SL*, i (1954), pp. 44–110.
2. 'St. Leśniewski's Calculus of Names', *SL*, iii (1955), pp. 7–71.

SMILEY, TIMOTHY JOHN (1930–)

1. 'Entailment and Deducibility', *PAS*, 1958–9, pp. 233–54. As near a definitive treatment of this topic as we are likely to get.
2. 'Sense without Denotation', *Analysis*, June 1960, pp. 125–35.
3. 'Syllogism and Quantification', *JSL*.

SOBOCIŃSKI, BOLESŁAW (1906–)

1. 'O kolejnych uproszczeniach aksjomatyki "Ontologji" prof. St. Leśniewskiego' (On the Successive Abbreviations of the Axiomatic of Leśniewski's 'Ontology'), in *Fragmenty Filozoficzne* (Warsaw, 1934). Systems 9.21.
2. *An Investigation of Protothetic*, Éditions de l'Institut d'Études Polonaises en Belgique (Brussels, 1949). See Parry 2.
3. 'L'Analyse de l'antinomie Russellienne par Leśniewski', *Methodos*, i (1949), pp. 94–107, 220–8, 308–16; ii (1950), pp. 237–57.
4. 'On a Universal Decision Element', *JCS*, vol. i, No. 2, Jan. 1953, pp. 71–80. Contains (note 4) tabulated definitions of truth-functions in terms of S (i.e. our X) and D; and in the text an account of a tetradic operator Q such that all monadic and dyadic truth-functions are obtainable by substitutions of p, q, 1 or 0 in $Qpqrs$. (A by-product, perhaps, of the work detailed in the main text of 1.) See Rose 3.
5. 'Note on a Modal System of Feys–von Wright', *JCS*, vol. i, No. 3, July 1953, pp. 171–8. Systems 11.21, 11.22.
6. 'Axiomatization of a Conjunctive-Negative Calculus of Propositions', *JCS*, vol. i, No. 4, Dec. 1954, pp. 229–42. Systems 6.3(*a*), 1.3(*d*).
7. 'Studies in Leśniewski's Mereology', *PSASA*, 1954–5, pp. 34–43, introducing Lejewski 2.
8. 'Note on a Problem of Paul Bernays', *JSL*, xx (1955), pp. 109–14. System 1.3(*e*).
9. 'On Well-constructed Axiom Systems', *PSASA*, 1955–6, pp. 54–65.
10. '*In Memoriam* Jan Łukasiewicz (1878–1956)', *Philosophical Studies* (Maynooth, Ireland), vi (1956), pp. 3–49.
11. 'On the Single Axioms of Protothetic. I', *NDJFL*, i (1960), pp. 52–73.

STRAWSON, PETER FREDERICK (1919–)

1. 'On Referring', *Mind*, 1950, pp. 320–44.

SUPPES, PATRICK (1922–)

1. *Introduction to Logic* (Van Nostrand, 1957). Heavily indebted to Tarski, McKinsey, and Quine. Strong on 'natural deduction' proofs and on the formalizing of scientific theories; many valuable examples taken from this field. See Lemmon 3; Prior 14.

TARSKI, ALFRED (1902–)

1. *Introduction to Logic and to the Methodology of the Deductive Sciences* (Oxford University Press, revised edition 1946).
2. *Logic, Semantics, Metamathematics* (Clarendon Press, 1955). Sixteen papers of from 1923 to 1935, translated by J. H. Woodger. Polished, penetratting, fundamental. Paper I is on the definition of *K* in terms of *E* in protothetic, and on the features which distinguish truth-functions from other propositional functions of propositions, if any; III sets out such properties of the relation of logical consequence as those underlying systems like Jaśkowski's in Appendix II, § 3; IV is a joint account with Łukasiewicz of Warsaw work on propositional calculus; VIII a monumental essay on truth in formalized languages, with much of value thrown out on the way. See Prior 8.

   See also McKinsey and Tarski.

THOMAS, IVO (1912–)

1. 'CS(n): An Extension of CS', *DS*, ii (1949), pp. 145–60. System 10.21.
2. 'Farrago Logica', *DS*, iv (1951), pp. 69–79.
3. 'Recent Contributions to Logic', ibid., pp. 205–6. (Review of Łukasiewicz 4; Boehner 1; and others.)
4. 'A New Decision Procedure for Aristotle's Syllogistic', *Mind*, Oct. 1952, pp. 504–6.
5. 'Kilwardby on Conversion', *DS*, vi (1953), pp. 56–76.
6. 'Note on a Modal System of Łukasiewicz', ibid., pp. 167–70.
7. 'Maxims in Kilwardby', *DS*, vii (1954), pp. 129–46.
8. 'Eulerian Syllogistic', *JSL*, xxii (1957), pp. 15–16. Systems 10.12.
9. 'A 12th Century Paradox of the Infinite', *JSL*, xxiii (1958), pp. 133–4.
10. 'Independence of Faris-rejection-axioms', *NDJFL*, i (1960), pp. 48–51.
11. 'Independence of Tarski's Law in Henkin's Propositional Fragments', *NDJFL*, i (1960), pp. 74–8.
12. 'Functional Completeness of Henkin's Propositional Fragments', *NDJFL*, i (1960), pp. 107–10.

THOMAS, IVO, and ORTH, DONALD LAWRENCE (1939–)

1. 'Axioms for the 'Gergonne'-relations', *JSL*, xxiv (1959), p. 305.

VON WRIGHT, GEORG HENDRIK (1916–)

1. *An Essay in Modal Logic* (North-Holland Publishing Co., Amsterdam, 1951). See Sobociński 5.
2. *Logical Studies* (Kegan Paul, London, 1957).

WHATELY, RICHARD (1787–1863)

1. *Elements of Logic* (1st ed. 1856; last edition the 9th). Mill's views on singular and general terms foreshadowed in 1.6. See Prior, M. L.

WHITEHEAD, ALFRED NORTH (1861–1947), and RUSSELL, BERTRAND ARTHUR WILLIAM

1. *Principia Mathematica* (Cambridge University Press; 1st ed., vol. i, 1910; vol. ii, 1912; vol. iii, 1913; 2nd ed., vol. i, 1925; vols. ii and iii, 1927).

Index